Ex Libris
Alun J. Brookfield

EVANGELICALS ETCETERA

In this well structured survey among Anglican clergy, Dr Randall clearly demonstrates that churchmanship is so much more than an historical curiosity. Churchmanship defines both key theological differences and major psychological differences in today's church.

Professor Leslie J. Francis
University of Wales, Bangor

The ordination of a gay bishop in the USA revealed sharp differences in the Anglican Church world wide. The Church of England is seen as torn apart by divisions. Evangelical churches and clergy threaten separation. Behind the conflicts lies 'churchmanship'. 'Anglo-catholic', 'Evangelical', 'Liberal', 'Charismatic' and similar labels are in regular use; those who stand for particular churchmanships use labels both as battle-cries and as accusations.

Evangelicals Etcetera is a comprehensive and authoritative guide to clergy churchmanship. Four major questions are asked and answered in this book. What is churchmanship? Can it be measured? Are particular kinds of people drawn to particular forms of churchmanship? What difference does churchmanship make to the way Anglican clergy believe and behave?

Explorations in Practical, Pastoral and Empirical Theology

Series Editors: Leslie J. Francis, University of Wales, Bangor, UK
and Jeff Astley, University of Durham and Director of the North of England Institute for Christian Education, UK

Theological reflection on the church's practice is now recognised as a significant element in theological studies in the academy and seminary. Ashgate's new series in practical, pastoral and empirical theology seeks to foster this resurgence of interest and encourage new developments in practical and applied aspects of theology worldwide. This timely series draws together a wide range of disciplinary approaches and empirical studies to embrace contemporary developments including: the expansion of research in empirical theology, psychological theology, ministry studies, public theology, Christian education and faith development; key issues of contemporary society such as health, ethics and the environment; and more traditional areas of concern such as pastoral care and counselling.

Other titles in the series include:

A Reader on Preaching
Making Connections
Edited by David Day, Jeff Astley and Leslie J Francis
0 7546 5003 0 (Hbk); 0 7546 5009 X (Pbk)

Congregational Studies in the UK
Christianity in a Post-Christian Context
Edited by Mathew Guest, Karin Tusting and Linda Woodhead
0 7546 3288 1 (Hbk); 0 7546 3289 X (Pbk)

Divine Revelation and Human Learning
A Christian Theory of Knowledge
David Heywood
0 7546 0850 6 (Hbk)

Engaging with Contemporary Culture
Christianity, Theology and the Concrete Church
Martyn Percy
0 7546 3259 8 (Hbk)

Evangelicals Etcetera
Conflict and Conviction in the Church of England's Parties

KELVIN RANDALL
National Centre for Religious Education
University of Wales, Bangor, UK

ASHGATE

© Kelvin Randall 2005

All rights reserved. No part of this publication may be reproduced, stored in a retrieval system or transmitted in any form or by any means, electronic, mechanical, photocopying, recording or otherwise without the prior permission of the publisher.

The author has asserted his moral right under the Copyright, Designs and Patents Act, 1988, to be identified as the author of this work.

Published by
Ashgate Publishing Limited
Gower House
Croft Road
Aldershot
Hampshire GU11 3HR
England

Ashgate Publishing Company
Suite 420
101 Cherry Street
Burlington, VT 05401-4405
USA

Ashgate website: http://www.ashgate.com

British Library Cataloguing in Publication Data
Randall, Kelvin
 Evangelicals etcetera : conflict and conviction in the Church of England's parties. –
 (Explorations in practical, pastoral and empirical theology)
 1. Church of England – Parties and movemenrs 2. Church of England – Clergy –
 Attitudes 3. Anglican Communion – Great Britain
 I. Title
 283.4'2

Library of Congress Cataloging-in-Publication Data
Randall, Kelvin, 1949-
 Evangelicals etcetera : conflict and conviction in the Church of England's parties / Kelvin Randall.
   p. cm. – (Explorations in practical, pastoral, and empirical theology)
 Includes bibliographical references and index.
 ISBN 0-7546-5215-7 (hardcover : alk. paper)
 1. Church of England – Clergy – Religious life. 2. Church of England – Clergy
Psychology. I. Title. II. Series.

 BX5175.R26 2005
 283'.42—dc22

2004029549

ISBN 0 7546 5215 7

Printed and bound in Great Britain by MPG Books Ltd, Bodmin, Cornwall

*For Jan
without whom ...*

Contents

List of Figures		*viii*
List of Tables		*ix*
Preface		*xi*
Acknowledgements		*xiii*
1	The origins of churchmanship differences	1
2	Measuring churchmanship differences	44
3	Seeking clergy and their churchmanship differences	64
4	Which churchmanship choices are the most popular?	71
5	Extravert or introvert?	78
6	Stable or neurotic?	88
7	Tough-minded or tender-minded?	94
8	More or less likely to burn out?	101
9	Happy or unhappy?	118
10	Masculine or feminine?	133
11	What priorities for ministry?	154
12	What training and support?	167
13	What patterns of belief and behaviour?	174
14	Evangelicals and the rest	183
15	Conclusion	215
Bibliography		*217*
Index of authors		*242*
Index of themes		*249*

List of Figures

2.1	Churchmanship and sources of authority: a framework for plotting churchmanship according to subjective legitimation of beliefs (Daniels, 1967)	48
2.2	The Randall churchmanship measure	61
2.3	Three alternative methods of grouping responses on the Catholic/Evangelical axis	62

List of Tables

4.1	Proportion of clergy in each churchmanship group	73
4.2	Correlation coefficients between churchmanship of curate and churchmanship of incumbent and congregation	74
4.3	Relative position of churchmanship groups on Francis and Thomas' subscales	76
5.1	Extraversion scores for clergy compared to population norms	82
5.2	EPQ and EPQR-S mean scores for Extraversion by sex	83
5.3	Mean Extraversion scores for curates compared to serving clergy	83
5.4	Mean Extraversion scores for curates compared to population norms	84
5.5	Extraversion scores by Catholic/Evangelical churchmanship	85
5.6	Extraversion scores by Liberal/Conservative churchmanship	86
5.7	Extraversion scores by Charismatic churchmanship	86
6.1	Neuroticism scores for clergy compared to population norms	90
6.2	EPQ and EPQR-S mean scores for Neuroticism by sex	91
6.3	Mean Neuroticism scores for curates compared to serving clergy	91
6.4	Mean Neuroticism scores for curates compared to population norms	91
6.5	Neuroticism scores by Catholic/Evangelical churchmanship	92
6.6	Neuroticism scores by Liberal/Conservative churchmanship	93
6.7	Neuroticism scores by Charismatic churchmanship	93
7.1	Psychoticism scores for clergy compared to population norms	96
7.2	EPQ and EPQR-S mean scores for Psychoticism by sex	97
7.3	Mean Psychoticism scores for curates compared to serving clergy	98
7.4	Mean Psychoticism scores for curates compared to population norms	98
7.5	Psychoticism scores by Catholic/Evangelical churchmanship	98
7.6	Psychoticism scores by Liberal/Conservative churchmanship	99
7.7	Psychoticism scores by Charismatic churchmanship	99
8.1	Mean Burnout scores by sex	110
8.2	Correlations between the MBI factors and E, N and P for male clergy	111
8.3	Comparison of MBI mean scores for curates and serving clergy	112
8.4	MBI mean scores by Catholic/Evangelical churchmanship	114
8.5	MBI mean scores by Liberal/Conservative churchmanship	115
8.6	MBI mean scores by Charismatic churchmanship	115
9.1	OHI mean scores by Catholic/Evangelical churchmanship	129

9.1	OHI mean scores by Catholic/Evangelical churchmanship	129
9.2	OHI mean scores by Liberal/Conservative churchmanship	129
9.3	OHI mean scores by Charismatic churchmanship	130
9.4	Multiple regression significance tests for OHI happiness	131
10.1	Correlation matrix between sex role and churchmanship	149
10.2	BSRI mean scores for all clergy by Catholic/Evangelical churchmanship	150
10.3	BSRI mean scores for all clergy by Liberal/Conservative churchmanship	150
10.4	BSRI mean scores for all clergy by Charismatic churchmanship	150
10.5	BSRI mean scores for clergy by Catholic/Evangelical churchmanship	151
10.6	BSRI mean scores for clergy by Liberal/Conservative churchmanship	151
10.7	BSRI mean scores for clergy by Charismatic churchmanship	152
12.1	Levels of support in years 1, 2 and 3 according to Catholic/Evangelical churchmanship, by percentage	171
12.2	Levels of support in years 1, 2 and 3 according to Liberal/Conservative churchmanship, by percentage	172
12.3	Levels of support in years 1, 2 and 3 according to Charismatic churchmanship, by percentage	173
13.1	Differences in belief and practice (Catholic/Evangelical)	175
13.2	Differences in training and conviction (Catholic/Evangelical)	176
13.3	Differences in patterns of behaviour (Catholic/Evangelical)	176
13.4	Differences in belief and practice (Liberal/Conservative)	178
13.5	Differences in training and conviction (Liberal/Conservative)	179
13.6	Differences in patterns of behaviour (Liberal/Conservative)	180
13.7	Differences in belief and practice (Charismatic)	181
13.8	Differences in training and conviction (Charismatic)	181
13.9	Differences in patterns of behaviour (Charismatic)	182

Preface

It seems to me that the continuing public interest in the appointment of the Liberal Catholic Rowan Williams to succeed the Conservative Evangelical Pro-Charismatic George Carey as Archbishop of Canterbury and the debate within the whole Anglican Communion about the ordination of Gene Robinson as bishop have brought the whole issue of churchmanship within the Anglican Church to the attention of the general reader. Issues such as women bishops, the ordination of a gay bishop, same-sex marriages, and laypeople presiding at Holy Communion are often analysed in the national press, let alone the church press, with the use of churchmanship labels. The Church of England has been pictured as torn apart by divisions, and the possibility of a number of Evangelical churches and clergy or whole Provinces separating from the Anglican Church has been threatened. Behind many of these divisions lie sharp differences between Anglicans which are collected together under the shorthand term 'churchmanship'. 'Anglo-catholic', 'Evangelical', 'Liberal', 'Charismatic' and similar labels are now regularly used in newspapers. Those who stand for, or claim to stand for, particular churchmanship positions use those same labels both as battle-cries and as accusations.

In this book churchmanship is the lens through which the contemporary Anglican Church and its professional clergy are examined. The conviction of those who are proud to call themselves 'Anglo-Catholic' or 'Evangelical' is shown sympathetically, but at the same time the historically inevitable conflict with those who differ is revealed. Many churchmanship terms, for example 'Latitudinarians', are seen to have disappeared from usage, so the need for the lens of churchmanship to be accurately focused on the contemporary Church is vital. In order to do this and to encompass the conflicts over the Bible, the Church, the place of reason and the place of the Holy Spirit which mark out churchmanship divisions, the methods of empirical theology are indispensable. As Louden and Francis (2003, p. vii) have said: 'Empirical theology has the capability of stripping bare the illusions and façade which the Church may wish to see and revealing the human reality within.'

This book is a comprehensive and authoritative guide to clergy churchmanship. Using the methods of empirical theology, four major questions are asked and answered: What is churchmanship? Can it be measured? Are particular kinds of people drawn to particular forms of churchmanship? What difference does churchmanship make to what Anglican clergy believe or how they behave?

In order to understand what churchmanship is, there is an examination of the growth and development of different churchmanship designations through the history of the Anglican Church in England and Wales. We see what fascinates sociologists and researchers as they attempt to measure the variety of churchmanship positions empirically. A direct and powerful three-item measure of churchmanship is devised and tested. Then using this measure as a lens we are able to focus in on today's clergy. How many call themselves Evangelical? Are their numbers on the increase? Questions are then explored about the personality differences of Evangelicals and Catholics. Are the churchmanship differences an expression of different kinds of people disagreeing? Are Evangelicals more prone to stress and burnout? Are they happier? Are they able to express both their masculine and their feminine sides? Each time the lens of churchmanship enables us to see a different facet of the personalities who make up the various churchmanship traditions. Perhaps the differences between them are only matters of style not substance.

The rest of the book shows just how far-reaching these differences of style are. The flexibility of the clergy role means that there is a great deal of freedom for clergy to pursue their own priorities in ministry. The lens of churchmanship shows us that Evangelicals have quite different priorities from Catholics, and that the very training they receive is different. This dissimilarity comes into sharpest focus when we look at belief and behaviour, where churchmanship makes a clear difference in areas of belief (for example, 'Is it essential to believe in the Virgin birth?'), practice (for example, 'Should I visit parishioners in hospital?'), vocation (for example, 'Should I leave the ministry?') and behaviour (for example, 'Should I wear robes for church services?').

By means of this lens of churchmanship it is possible to map nine different churchmanship positions within the Anglican Church. Each of these positions is held confidently and with conviction by its adherents, even if conflict is caused with other groups. As a result, churchmanship is shown to be not a peripheral issue in church life, but an essential tool for appreciating today's clergy and for understanding the tensions and conflicts in the Anglican Church.

Acknowledgements

I am above all grateful to those 340 ordained in 1994 to stipendiary ministry in the Church of England and the Church in Wales who so willingly took part in this longitudinal project, and, I hope, will continue to do so in the future; they continue to be a precious resource for the Church.

I thank Lynda Barley and the Archbishops' Council's Research and Statistics unit, alongside Anthony Crockett (now Bishop of Bangor) and the Council for Mission and Ministry, for their invaluable help in establishing the database for this project.

I gratefully acknowledge financial support from Wayne and Margaret Scholer, and Smith's Charity.

I express my indebtedness to Professor Leslie Francis for his stimulus to begin this research and his continuing encouragement and friendship throughout it. My thanks also go to Dr Mandy Robbins and all the staff of the Welsh National Centre for Religious Education.

Dr Christopher Rutledge has been an invaluable mentor and companion throughout. Many have given substantial help along the way but mention must be made of Dr Chris Lewis for help with SPSS, Professor Jeff Astley for the jokes, Professor Gareth Lloyd-Jones, Dr William Kay, Dr Jim Francis and Professor Andrew Walker. Martin Smith's contribution towards the end was incalculable.

Many thanks to the congregation at St Denys' Southampton for being such an honest, human, holy, generous and supportive team.

And to Katherine, Gareth and Matthew for being 'gifts of diversity'.

Chapter 1

The origins of churchmanship differences

Introduction

The account of churchmanship traditions within the Anglican Church is built into the very story of the English Church. From the outset the tension between opposed systems which has marked much of the churchmanship controversy has been present. There were probably five different strands in the Christianity represented in these islands: Roman, British, Anglo-Saxon, Celtic and Petrine. From many places in Roman Britain archaeologists have found items marked with Christian symbols, especially the *Chi Rho*. There are indications of a villa chapel at Lullingstone in Kent, of a mosaic of Christ from Hinton St Mary in Somerset, and of a church at Silchester in Hampshire. Bishops from this country attended the Council of Arles in 314 and the Council of Nicaea in 325. The Roman soldier Alban, killed at the beginning of the third century, is still considered the first British martyr. The evidence for British Christianity after the departure of the Romans in the fifth century is poor but there to be seen in the archaeological record. In particular it held firm in the west of the country where Britons were driven by the invading Anglo-Saxons: the Welsh in particular (the English word *wealas* meant 'foreigners') produced great saints like Illtyd. Across the country there are indications of Anglo-Saxon Christianity with its stone crosses and timber churches. David Edwards (1982, p.15) states that there were once more than four hundred Anglo-Saxon churches in Kent alone. Celtic Christianity was a faith guarded and promulgated by monks as, in monasteries ministering to local Celtic tribes, the Bible was read, copied, illuminated and taught. In 597 Augustine arrived in Kent as the emissary of Pope Gregory. Did he come to convert a country untouched by the gospel? No, for he was met by the Christian Queen Bertha, wife of King Ethelbert, and her chaplain, and introduced to their worship in the little church of St Martin in Canterbury. Did he come to impose orthodox Petrine Christianity on these lands? No, for Gregory had sent him with clear instructions to value the diverse Christian traditions and liturgical forms (churchmanships?) of these lands. Bede recalls Gregory's instructions to Augustine:

> You are familiar with the usage of the Roman Church in which you were brought up. But if you have found customs, whether in the Church of Rome or of Gaul or of any other that may be more acceptable to God, I wish you to make a careful selection of them and teach the Church of the English whatever you have been able to learn with profit from the various Churches ... For things should not be loved for the sake of places, but places for the sake of good things. Choose

> therefore from every Church those things that are pious, religious and upright, and when you have as it were made them up into one body, let the minds of the English be accustomed thereunto.

So though it is always tempting to start at the Reformation when compiling a history of developments within the Anglican Church, it is clear that there existed a pattern of tension and churchmanship before then. Uniformity and variety, centralization and independence come and go in the story of the Church in these islands. Before the Reformation the clergy were often in favour of uniformity, which in those times meant closer dependence on the see of Rome, whereas the monarchs usually solidly supported national independence.

From the Reformation to the Elizabethan Settlement

There is a common error, similar to the 'great man' approach to history, which imagines that religion in this country is at the beck and call of the clergy or the monarchs. So it is important to remember throughout this study that popular religion has always been more diverse than official religion. We have hinted at that before the Reformation. Knight (1995) made this point strongly for nineteenth-century religion, and Harris (1995) did the same for the period from the Reformation to the Elizabethan Settlement.

It is not necessary to chart here the progress of the Reformation: simply to say that the seeds of the Reformation were already in place as part of the many and divisive forces at work in sixteenth-century Europe. The results of the Reformation were complex and ambiguous. In some respects Protestantism was eventually successfully established as the religion of this land, yet the profound changes of the Reformation stirred up, rather than annihilated, existing patterns of popular belief and observance. In Wales, as in many other countries, the translation of the scriptures into the language of the people proved to be the key to the success of the Reformation. An Act of Parliament of 1563 laid down that the Bible and prayer book should be translated into Welsh by 1567 and after that used in public worship in all those parishes where Welsh was the normal language of the inhabitants. Protestantism and the scriptures were wedded together.

Within the broad framework of imposed uniformity there existed, as there usually does, a variety of possibilities for oppositions, evasions and alternative understandings.

> Even in normal circumstances the Church was never a monolithic institution capable of speaking with a single voice, and the variety of official viewpoints – sometimes competing, sometimes merely diverse, and articulated at various levels in the ecclesiastical hierarchy – inevitably fed into the vagaries of popular religious behaviour. Thus to explore popular religion in this period is a complex undertaking. It is first of all vital to recognize the immensely powerful field of force exerted by the official Church, strong enough to keep in check (though not necessarily to eradicate) beliefs and practices of which it disapproved. But within that gravitational field there existed a range of overlapping and interacting

> religious cultures, not related in any clear-cut way to the divisions of the social hierarchy, and in complex interaction with official doctrines and precepts which were themselves by no means unitary or unchanging.
> (Harris, 1995, p.100)

After the stormy oscillations in the reigns of Henry VIII, Edward VI and Mary Tudor, the Elizabethan Settlement emerged either by grace, by accident or by expediency. The Elizabethan Church was no harmonious and agreeable whole, but included disparate groups each wanting to move the Church in their own direction. The Puritans, though not well defined as a group, mainly represented those who saw the Reformation in England as incomplete, and who wished to purify the Church further as they moved it in a Protestant direction (Collinson, 1967, 1982).

> In a few areas they gave their children idiosyncratic names redolent of their hopes, fears and ideals – Fear-God, Flee-sin, Safe-on-high, and so forth. More characteristic was addiction to sermons, lectures, Bible-reading, meetings for 'repetitions' of sermons, the self-examination of the personal diary and spiritual account-book. These features, grounded in a strong conviction of the sovereignty of God, the sinfulness of mankind, the assurance of election and the sanctity of the sabbath, were some of the more obvious manifestations of an intense religiosity which at its best linked a strenuous personal spiritual regime with a powerful sense of fellowship in Christ.
> (Harris, 1995, p.102)

Yet there were also those who challenged the Puritan demand for further reformation, opposed the Puritans' Calvinism and championed some of the features of the pre-Reformation Church (Avis, 1989, Hylson-Smith, 1993).

Russell (1990, p.84) is right to remind us that the complex of ideas described by the word 'Anglican' did not exist in the Elizabethan Church, any more than the word did. Nevertheless the strength of the Elizabethan settlement was the creation of the Anglican ideal, a *via media*, a middle way in which the tension between popery and puritanism was held together and not ignored. Richard Hooker, in his principal work *The Laws of Ecclesiastical Polity*, provided the theology and apologia for this settlement. As a 'contemplative pragmatist' (Williams, 2003, p.116), he was able to find a place in his doctrine of creation for reason and experience within his tripartite model and method of doing theology: scripture as the basis for theology but with a place for the traditions and teachings of a human Church, and a place for human reason, clouded by human sinfulness but not worthless because of that. He strongly valued the place of variety in what he called the outward fashions of church practice. 'Wilful singularity must be avoided, but so must rigid uniformity amongst Churches.'

The Stuart era

The Puritans expected much of King James I because he came from Scotland the land of Presbyterianism. Their murmurings began though as they saw him swing more towards Rome.

> The older view that James alienated Catholics and Puritans alike, and contributed to growing unrest within the Church, has been replaced by a picture of a king dedicated to religious unity who pursued an ecumenical policy which tolerated diverse opinions within a broad national Church. This policy hinged on a fundamental distinction between moderates and radicals: James successfully wooed both moderate Catholics and moderate Puritans, while expelling or repressing radicals of any hue. As a result, although he disappointed small minorities of extremists, he generally pleased the moderate majority, and his conciliatory policies proved remarkably adept at defusing religious conflict. They were in fact just what the Church needed.
> (Smith, 1998, pp.36-37. See also Coward, 1980, and Patterson, 1997)

Puritan murmuring increased in the reign of Charles I and William Laud, his Archbishop of Canterbury.

> Laud's policy tied him, and the Laudianism of which he was the prime author and executive, to a particular political system, partly by accident and partly by design. Laudianism was in fact 'Arminianism as part of the new Caroline synthesis of religion and politics' (Trevor-Roper 1987, p.114), and it alarmed the political classes to such an extent that it drove them, ultimately, to revolt.
> (Hylson-Smith, 1993, p.38)

Charles I was unpredictable and, though he generally supported Laud's emphasis on catholicity and episcopacy with a deep concern for reverence in worship, such support was not dependable and on occasions he gave only lukewarm endorsement to Laud's policies.

The spectrum of English religious life at this time was well summarized by Neill (1958, pp.140-142). On the right stood the recusants, those who still remained faithful to the Church of Rome. Next came 'those who in a later age have been called high churchmen, but were then more generally known as Arminians'. Next came the episcopalian Calvinists, those who were content with the episcopal nature of the Church of the Elizabethan settlement. Next came the Calvinists who still looked for their model of a reformed Church to the European models of presbyterian and congregational churches. Still further to the left came the sectaries, separatists or independents: 'whereas the upper-middle-class man tended to adopt an Erastian form of presbyterianism, the lower-middle-class man often became a separatist' (Davies, 1937, p.193). Finally came 'the lunatic fringe – the Fifth Monarchy men, the Seekers, the Levellers, and so forth'. These groups joined together vivid apocalyptic with revolutionary social and political views in a mix that most governments would have found hard to rein in. It was unfortunate that

Charles I was the one unable to draw all these groups together (Tyacke, 1990, Trevor-Roper, 1987).

> In all the ambiguities of which the Elizabethan Settlement was full, Charles saw one side of the argument, and never fully understood that there was another ... He classified what had been half the leadership of the Church under his father, and the dominant half at that, as 'Puritan', and therefore subversive and to be excluded.
> (Russell, 1996, p.288)

Under Cromwell and the Commonwealth, England engaged in a Puritan experiment: episcopacy was abolished, the use of the Book of Common Prayer forbidden, and a presbyterian form of church government adopted.

Yet for all the image popularly held of the 'godly experiment', Cromwell forged a remarkably serviceable compromise for the majority of the members of the Church of England: an established national Church, retaining its parochial structure, its trained ministry and its tithes, open to a diversity of worship (John Evelyn could find at least one church in London where the Prayer Book liturgy was in regular use), but without bishops and their diocesan control. It was not dissimilar to the settlement made permanent after 1689. There was a group of intransigent Anglicans, some of whom fled into exile, but most of whom remained in England deliberately aloof from the Commonwealth: they are usually called 'Laudians', though they would not have used that term of themselves. Central to their belief was the growing conviction that episcopacy was not just a good thing for the Church, but absolutely essential. In Wales especially the clash between Puritans and Laudians was significant for the future of the churches there (Richards, 1920). During the time of the Commonwealth a new group developed from amongst those who managed to avoid becoming absorbed in the religious contentions of the times and devoted themselves quietly to study and a deeper understanding of their faith. They were the Cambridge Platonists. Their inclination was towards a mysticism of a Neo-platonic type. Like Hooker they believed that human reason is the point at which God made contact with human beings – their favourite text was 'The spirit of man is the candle of the Lord'. They stood against both superstition and 'enthusiasm', by which they meant the growing emphasis on the importance of individuals being guided by an inner light. They were known by their opponents as 'Latitudinarians' (Cragg, 1950, pp.37-86) and their style and tradition continue into the present-day Church.

So far as the ecclesiastical settlement was concerned Charles II came back to England without much in the way of conditions.

> Probably no effective conditions could have been laid down; perhaps it was better that none should have been attempted. But with the King's return came a change of incalculable importance. The balance of power within the Church in England altered, almost overnight. For the life of the Church had to go on, and this necessitated a thousand decisions, almost all of them now settled in accordance with the wishes of the Anglican sympathizers who came back as the royal advisers.
> (Whiteman, 1962, p.52)

At the Restoration the Laudian party emerged as the dominant religious force. Most of the Laudian party were not personal disciples of Laud, nor did they constitute a church party. 'They were High Churchmen who shared the religious viewpoint of Laud, and who were in wholehearted agreement in their method of defending the Church's interests both before and after the Restoration' (Bosher, 1951, p.xv).

The word 'High' began to be used in this context shortly before the Revolution of 1688. It originally meant strict according to Chadwick (1960, p.14); a man who was 'stiff for the Church of England'; rigid, careful and precise in observing the rules of the Church about prayer and fasting, even perhaps when those rules had begun to seem archaic; a man who stood for the privileges of the Church against Dissenters; a strong defender of the Establishment.

Some have seen the Act of Uniformity and the reassertion of the Book of Common Prayer as the Elizabethan Settlement's gift of equilibrium to the Church of England. Most writers though recognized that the same events caused the decisive break between the Established Church and Nonconformity. The Act demanded of ministers three commitments which snagged Puritan and Presbyterian consciences: re-ordination of those who had not been episcopally ordained (implying that their previous ministries counted for nothing); renunciation of the Covenant of 1643 (which thousands had solemnly sworn); and acceptance of every part of the new Prayer Book and its rubrics, including the wearing of 'popish' surplices and 'idolatrous' kneeling to receive Holy Communion. Between 1660 and St Bartholomew's Day 1662 some two thousand clergy left their parishes and colleges. The Five Mile Act excluded ministers from their old parishes and neighbourhoods; the Conventicle Act banned any private meeting for worship of five or more persons; and the Recusancy Acts, used against Catholics in the time of Elizabeth, could be used against anybody who failed to attend parish services. 'Any hope of reconstructing a genuinely national Church had vanished, although nearly thirty years would pass before the fact of religious pluralism was officially recognized' (Smith, 1998, p.210). With Charles II's Declaration of Indulgence in 1672 licences for meetings were granted and the building of chapels began. Circumstances pushed them inexorably towards denominationalism.

The expulsion of Dissenters did not create a uniformity within the Church of England. There was a fund of sympathy for them within Anglicanism and schemes of 'comprehension' to readmit the ejected ministers were proposed (Thomas, 1962). The Latitudinarians who supported such schemes came to be called 'Low Churchmen'. By the 1680s the term 'High Church' had become the regular description for the hard-liners who rejected such a compromise.

Historians now generally hold that James II was not the villain described by Macaulay and later Whig historians (Miller, 1973, Jones, 1972). His aim was not to constitute Catholicism as the sole religion of the country, nor to eradicate Protestantism by force. He simply wanted to establish the rights of English Catholics to worship without persecution and to take a full part in the political life of the country. However because he misunderstood the strength of the attachment of most of his contemporaries to anti-Catholicism, he demonstrably failed to persuade the majority of Anglicans in the first phase of his reign (1685-86) and

Protestant dissenters in the second (1687-88) to accept even limited toleration for Catholics.

> The advent of William of Orange seemed a providential deliverance [to the Protestants], but it did not deliver harmony among English Protestants. Some High-Churchmen were unable in conscience to accept the forcible overthrow of the legitimate monarch, Catholic though he was. They were especially outraged when the new regime sacked several bishops for failing to take the new oath of allegiance to William and Mary. A third of the bishops and some four hundred clergy left the Established Church, forming the Non-juror schism which lasted several decades. This High-Church separatism was to be echoed by the Oxford Movement in Victorian times, and by opponents of the ordination of women in the 1990s.
> (Goldie, 1996, p.309)

With the withdrawal of the Non-jurors William III filled many vacant sees with Latitudinarians; the Lower House of Convocation had a High Church majority. This is the first moment at which the term 'High Church' can be correctly used since it was at about this time that it came into common parlance (Every, 1956). Soon the High Churchmen were using 'Low Churchman' as a term of abuse for the Latitudinarians.

Most commentators viewed the fate of the Established Church in Wales between the Restoration and the Methodist Revival from a sombre and pessimistic viewpoint. They regarded the ties to the English Establishment as too constricting, and this was not helped by the practice of the Hanoverian kings in appointing alien, absentee, Latitudinarian bishops to the Welsh sees (Jenkins, 1987).

With the Toleration Act of 1689 giving legal recognition to the rights of Nonconformists for separate worship, it was publicly recognized that there could be peaceful coexistence of several denominations within a single country. The tensions within the national Church and across the denominations had produced a stormy and sometimes uncomfortable setting for church life.

> As so often happens, Christians were wearing one another out and squandering the spiritual resources of the Church in controversy at a moment at which it was urgently necessary that all good men should stand together.
> (Neill, 1958, p.181)

The long eighteenth century and the Evangelical movement

Historians have adopted the terminology of the 'long eighteenth century' to discuss the period lasting from the Toleration Act of 1689 until the 1830s (see especially Walsh, Haydon and Taylor, 1993). By the end of that time the deist controversy had produced a great challenge to the Churches. The spread and development of the new experimental science had led some people to question traditional Christian beliefs. The vogue for rationalism in religion was part of a new rational approach to all problems. Within the Church of England, one of its manifestations was a concern with the gathering of statistical data within dioceses as the dioceses began to discover their identity (Burns, 1999, pp.109f). Certainties founded on faith or on the writings of the ancients were called into question. Many Christians were strongly opposed to enthusiasm in religious matters in any shape or form.

It was within this climate of belief that John Wesley appeared. As an Anglican clergyman he underwent a personal renewal and conversion of the heart which left him unable to be tamed or restrained by, as he saw it, the cautious and latitudinarian Anglicanism of his day.

> At some time in 1739 Bishop Butler accorded at Bristol an interview to the Reverend John Wesley, Fellow of Lincoln College, Oxford, in the course of which he remarked (according to Wesley's account of the discussion): 'I once thought you and Mr Whitfield well-meaning men; but I cannot think so now ... Sir, the pretending to extraordinary revelations and gifts of the Holy Ghost is a horrid thing, a very horrid thing.'
> (Neill, 1958, p.187)

Wesley's challenge to the Church of England was to find a place for that movement of the Spirit, with its 'extraordinary revelations and gifts' that he represented and had experienced. However such a movement was perceived by the Established Church as too narrow-minded and intense. Thus Methodism and all that it could have meant for renewal within Anglicanism was mislaid.

Wesley was part of a developing Evangelical revival and, though Methodism was lost to the Anglicans for too long, it is important to acknowledge that part of it which did remain within the Church of England. Certainly John Wesley was one of the heroes of some of the Evangelicals in the Church of England. It would however be wrong to regard Anglican Evangelicals as a comparatively small group of Methodists who remained within the Established Church in England or Wales (Jenkins, 1987); they represented a distinct movement with its own characteristics. On the whole they rejected Wesley's concept of a travelling ministry, regarding the parish as the place where the Lord's work was primarily to be carried on. In addition Anglican Evangelicals were generally Calvinists, whereas Methodists were generally Arminians.

Some have believed that the strength of Evangelicals within the Anglican Church, as well as their weakness, was that they were obstinate individualists. In a way this could be supported by the fact that many Evangelicals came to their new faith through some purely individual experience. Charles Simeon of Cambridge (Hopkins, 1977), for example, said of Easter Day 1779: 'I awoke early with these words upon my heart and lips, "Jesus Christ is risen today! Hallelujah! Hallelujah!" From that hour peace flowed in rich abundance into my soul.'

What then were the special beliefs held by these Evangelicals? Their particular concern and the focus of much of their teaching was holiness. Even when narrow in their theology and illiberal in their ideas they always kept their eyes and the eyes of their audience firmly fixed on the ideal of the child of God unsoiled by the world and at the service of God. Religion was not about feelings but about enthusiastic action, directed to the saving of souls.

> An orthodox clergyman [is] one who held in dull and barren formality the very same doctrines which the Evangelical clergyman held in cordial and prolific vitality; or by saying that they differed from each others as solemn triflers differ from the profoundly serious.
> (Neill, 1958, p.183 citing Sir James Stephen's essay in ecclesiastical biography)

Coneybeare, writing in the mid-nineteenth century, saw the Evangelical revival as the end of an age of stagnation, a period of challenge to Latitudinarians when 'truths embodied in every formulary of the Church, enforced in her homilies, and stereotyped in her liturgy, were assailed as heretical novelties by her ministers' (Coneybeare, 1853, p.275). Evangelicals were profoundly serious about the sinfulness of humanity, one's inability to save oneself, and the need for a personal Saviour.

Chadwick (1966), writing about the nineteenth century Church, said that the Evangelicals were never triumphant:

> But there was an epoch when they were powerful; the epoch after 1855, while the memory of papal aggression still rankled, while Sumner was still Archbishop of Canterbury, while Lord Palmerston presided over the cabinet, and while Shaftesbury the noble head of Evangelical laymen was stepson-in-law to the prime minister.
> (Chadwick, 1966, p.440)

In 1846 the Evangelical Alliance was founded. Hylson-Smith (1989) and Bebbington (1989) both saw a high point for Evangelicals at about that time, with Wilberforce and the Clapham Sect pre-eminent. By then though the focus of ecclesiastical attention had moved to Oxford.

The Oxford Movement

> Within the wider political, social, economic and constitutional history of England, the Oxford Movement may be seen both as a product of the age in which it arose, and as a determined effort to turn back the tide of history. The process of industrialization, urbanization, massive and accelerating population growth, erosion of traditional social norms and undermining of social structures had reached a peak by the second quarter of the nineteenth century. It produced a radicalism which was expressed in working class Corresponding Societies and early attempts at trade unionism; in such demonstrations and fierce repressive responses as the Peterloo Massacre of 1819; in Luddite revolts; in the establishment of the 'godless college of Gower Street' as the embryo of the University of London; in Tom Paine's Rights of Man; in Jeremy Bentham's Utilitarian ethics; in the establishment of Mechanics' Institutes as organs of popular education; in the dissemination of handbooks of popular science through the Society for the Diffusion of Useful Knowledge; in the emancipation of slavery movement; in the abolition of the Test and Corporation Acts in 1828, and in the granting of Catholic Emancipation in 1829; and in the Reform Act of 1832.
> (Hylson-Smith, 1993, pp.123-124)

The Church of England had become accustomed to a great deal of harmony between itself and the State, and at times regarded Parliament as a kind of lay synod. The sequence of Acts just mentioned (in 1828, 1829 and 1832) banished Hooker's church ideal for ever. Parliament was no longer an exclusively Anglican body. The Church of England was no longer in quite the same way the Church of the nation. Non-Anglicans were now given access to political power and to leadership in the universities.

At Oxford a group of Anglican academics and clergymen was increasingly unhappy with the lack of seriousness with which the Establishment regarded its religious duties, with its failure to appreciate the Catholic heritage of the Church, in particular its historical and theological insights which predated the Reformation, and with its Erastianism – the willingness to subordinate the legitimate claims and prerogatives of the Church to the requirements of state policy. Their best-known leaders were John Henry Newman, John Keble and Edward Pusey. From the start they were seen as a party with a headquarters, Oxford: thus 'the Oxford Movement' (Chadwick, 1990). Their preferred method was a series of publications which they began in 1833 called 'tracts' and hence they were known as the Tractarians. These argumentative pieces attacked what the writers regarded as the prevailing weaknesses of the Church, and in particular the assault by the liberalism they saw in the Church and in society. By this they meant both the doctrinal laxity and inattention to many aspects of the Church's rich heritage, and the political trends which were threatening the Church of England's status as a national institution with the increasing agitation for disestablishment. Fuller (1986, p.53) usefully differentiated between High Churchmen and Tractarians: High Churchmen took as their standard of catholicity the Anglican formularies supported by scripture and antiquity; Tractarians used the appeal to antiquity to correct and supplement the Anglican formularies.

Although Nockles (1994) has pointed out that the first historians of the Oxford Movement were its detractors rather than its hagiographers, nevertheless much of the history of the Anglican Church in the nineteenth century was written or influenced by High Church historians in the Tractarian mould. That might explain why it was common in the literature to regard the Tractarians as antithetical to the Evangelicals. Some of this could be put down to a confusion of the Evangelicals with Low Churchmen. Clegg reminds us that it was not always so:

> In the early part of the nineteenth century, some Evangelical clergy were high-Churchmen and some even so proclaimed themselves. The terms 'Evangelical' and 'high-Church' were not mutually exclusive, as were 'Evangelical' and 'low-Church'.
> (Clegg, 1966a, p.128)

The Evangelicals originally were opposed to the Low Churchmen, who tended to be latitudinarian and antinomian, prone to the doctrinal and moral laxity that Evangelicals denounced. So at first the Evangelicals appeared as natural allies of the Tractarian movement (see Clegg, 1966a, 1996b, 1967 and Jay, 1983). Both the Tractarians and the Evangelicals had a preoccupation not with the externals, as their accusers often charged, but with the inner religion of the heart. Keble's particular contribution of devotional poetry had an extraordinary impact on people of all parties. That kind of inner fervour, rather than any nostalgia for medieval forms, was what motivated the Tractarians. If the Evangelicals were preoccupied with justification, the Tractarians were similarly preoccupied with sanctification, the striving for inner holiness and zeal (Reardon, 1971). But this was a matter of emphasis and neither side initially denied the other's doctrine, whatever differences may have remained in the way they conceived them. In the early Tractarian days it was possible to make common cause with the Evangelicals, as when they combined to thwart the appointment of a non-orthodox Regius Professor of Divinity at Oxford.

However the alliance could not last. It foundered largely because Evangelicals and others suspected that the Tractarians were, despite their protestations, stalking horses for Roman Catholicism. That suspicion became a near certainty with the publication in 1840 of Newman's Tract 90, which argued that the Thirty Nine Articles rightly understood were compatible with the Roman Catholic Church. When Newman converted to Roman Catholicism in 1845 the strength and power of the Tractarian movement went as well. Given the traditional English antipathy to Popery (in spite of the Catholic Emancipation Act of 1828), Newman's conversion undercut the Oxford movement by suggesting that Tractarianism inevitably led one to Rome.

There was however a continuing Tractarian movement after Newman's departure. The Church Union was founded in 1859: Pusey, Keble and others rallied the Tractarians together. Having survived such difficult years the Movement developed in the direction of increased ceremonial usage in the 1860s. This gave great concern to the Evangelicals (Scotland, 1997). Some scholars drew a contrast between the Tractarian and Ritualist Anglicans of this time – the Anglo-Catholics – and the theology and presuppositions of Gore, the Holy Club and Liberal Catholicism.

> Ritualistic practices became more widespread and adventurous, and new, 'liberal', theological thinking became more prominent among High Churchmen. The more extreme ritualists in a number of ways profoundly shifted the emphasis of the Oxford Movement, and the Liberal Catholics adopted views which were anathema to some of the surviving Tractarians of the 1833 to 1845 period. As the pioneer Tractarians differed from the older High Churchmen of their day and the preceding half century, in seeing themselves and being seen as more progressive and radical, so the Anglican Catholic ritualists and liberals, whilst they had much in common with the earlier Tractarians, perceived themselves and were seen as differing from them in tone and method as well as in belief and practice.
> (Hylson-Smith, 1993, pp.172-173)

The Ecclesiological Society, later the Camden Society, with its list of approved architects including Gilbert Scott, Butterfield and Pugin, wanted more ritual and religious decoration in churches. It was closely associated with the Gothic Revival and so saw itself as looking back to the Middle Ages as a time when the Church met the needs of its parishioners both religiously and aesthetically. However Neill said that 'as liturgical science was at that time almost non-existent in the Church of England, much of what they introduced was direct imitation of the liturgically least defensible mediaeval practices of the Roman Catholic Church' (Neill, 1958, p.267).

The concern with vestments laid the Anglican Catholics open to accusations of femininity, and critics of the movement described it as essentially un-English and unmanly (Hilliard, 1982, Best, 1967). In an important study of Welsh clergy to determine whether there were any links between a more feminine personality profile and Anglo-Catholicism, Francis and Thomas (1996a) cited some of these critics:

> Punch (1865) characterized Anglo Catholic clergy as 'parsons in petticoats' who 'are very fond of dressing like ladies. They are much addicted to wearing vestments ... variously trimmed and embroidered.' Kingsley (1881) wrote of 'an element of foppery even in dress and manner: a fastidious, maundering, die-away effeminacy.' Rigg (1895) in a classic study of the leaders of the Anglo Catholic movement made much of the 'characteristically feminine' mind and temperament of Newman and the lack of virility of most of his disciples.
> (Francis and Thomas, 1996a, p.16)

In assessing the place of the Oxford Movement it can be seen that it added a conservative option to the lively atmosphere of Victorian religious debate. The Victorians disliked the atheism of the Utilitarians and the agnosticism of the scientists, were put off by the enthusiasm of the Evangelicals, found the Broad Church too latitudinarian to have any meaning left to its doctrine, and yet could not stomach going over to Rome, and so found the High Church Anglicans a perfect conservative solution. However, in terms of the impact of the Anglican Church upon the nation, the Oxford Movement contributed greatly to the widening gulf between the Established Church and both the Nonconformist Churches and the Roman Catholic Church. It 'precipitated a new bitterness in inter-church polemic, in which all the Churches expanded on the basis of a fierce hatred for one another' (Sykes and Gilley, 1986, p.135).

The nineteenth century

One of the antecedents of Tractarianism had been Parliament's Irish Church Measure of 1833 which reduced the number of Irish dioceses. This had been the factor which prompted Keble's Assize Sermon. In 1865 Gladstone moved a more sweeping measure for the disestablishment of the Irish Church and this against the almost unanimous hostility of the Church of Ireland. With the disestablishment of the Irish Church the agitation for Welsh disestablishment became strong in about 1885. The Act of Parliament separating the then four Welsh dioceses from the state was passed in 1914, and the disestablished Church in Wales came into operation in 1920 (Bell, 1969, Walker, 1976).

At about this time Gore (Ramsey, 1960) appeared as the chief apologist for what he called 'Liberal Catholicism'. He identified Liberal Catholicism with Anglicanism: the Church of England was Catholicism reformed and preserved in accordance with the teaching of scripture. He did not see Liberal Catholicism as a separate party or dogma, and was hostile to any type of liberalism which tampered with the Catholic creeds. As such he was a strong and prominent opponent to modernism, and especially any undermining of the essential historicity of the events on which Christianity is founded: he believed that express assent should be required at least from the clergy to the literal truth of Christ's virgin birth and bodily resurrection. The publication of *Lux Mundi* (1889) focused the approach and concerns of Liberal Catholicism.

Unlike the Evangelicals and the Tractarians who opposed them, the comparatively tiny Broad Church party never formed an organized, much less essentially homogeneous, group. They were a loosely associated group of intellectuals in the Church of England who in many ways represented what was to become liberal twentieth-century Protestantism. Working under the direct or indirect influence of German liberal thought, members of the Broad Church party emphasized that the Bible, though in some sense divinely inspired, was not, as Evangelicals and Tractarians believed, literally true in every detail, and that therefore the scriptures should be read metaphorically, or even mythologically. These beliefs appeared in the controversial *Essays and Reviews* (1860). Some Broad Churchmen, like Thomas Arnold, the headmaster of Rugby, and F.D. Maurice, the Christian Socialist Professor of Theology at King's College London, also emphasized a social gospel: that one could worship Christ best by working for social justice. In this too the early Tractarians opposed them: in his *Apologia pro Vita Sua* (1864), Newman said repeatedly that the great enemy he was fighting was liberalism, and made it clear that Arnold was a prime example of that ideology he detested.

Knight (1995) analysed that historiographical approach to this period which focuses on changes in the structure and self-understanding of the clergy as a way of understanding the nineteenth-century Church, by summarizing studies by Russell (1970, 1980), Heeney (1976) and Haig (1984). She noted the influence of the rise of party sympathies. She also drew attention to the emergence of new careers taking over what had been traditionally clerical functions, forcing the clergy to retreat into a more specifically ecclesiastical role where differences of churchmanship or style were more discernible (Gibson, W., 1994, pp.171f.). Finally she registered the large number of young men entering the clerical profession so that it remained the largest profession in Victorian England, dominated by the young. (Haig suggested that by the middle of the century over half the clergy were under 45 years old.) The most important focus of Knight's study however arose from 'the conviction that labels of churchmanship do not always offer much assistance in the quest to uncover the concerns of lay members of the Church of England' (Knight, 1995, p.19, see also Knight, 1996): she felt that churchmanship was often the sole preserve of the clergy, and especially the higher clergy.

Another element in understanding churchmanship in the nineteenth-century Church is the establishment of theological colleges for training new clergy. It is important throughout to remember that the history of the founding and development of the colleges for clergy training is a history of private initiative and private funding. There was no policy of co-ordinated central planning, unlike, for example the Methodist Church, whose colleges have always been directly under the control of Conference. Because the Anglican colleges began as private bodies, they have continued to value their independence and have never taken kindly to central control. The nineteenth century begins with Bishop Law of Chester founding a college at St Bees in 1816 'to supply a good and economical education for candidates for Holy Orders'. It was a college to train literates, that is, those without a university degree. Soon after, in 1822, Bishop Burgess of St Davids founded St David's, Lampeter in Wales.

Whilst, in general terms, the establishment of the theological colleges arose from the desire of the Church to train its clergy in a way which approximated more closely to the training of other professional men and to provide training for the increasing number of ordinands who had not been at Oxford or Cambridge, the actual establishment of the colleges owed more to the urgent needs of the cathedrals to defend their wealth from the Ecclesiastical Commission. For this reason most of the early colleges were established in cathedral closes, and cathedrals came to fulfil again an ancient function. So the cathedral colleges advocated by Pusey in 1833, were founded: Chichester, and Wells (1839), Lichfield (1857), Canterbury (1860), Salisbury, and Exeter (1861), Gloucester (1868), Ely (1876), and Truro (1877). The colleges provided the professional component of clergy training for graduates and a general, as well as a professional, education for literates. Haig (1984, p.74) says that 'the plan for theological colleges was thus early associated with the High Church, and indeed all the graduate, and most mixed (graduate and non-graduate) diocesan colleges were to be High Church foundations for at least thirty years'. Wycliffe Hall at Oxford in 1872 and Ridley Hall at Cambridge in 1881 were the first colleges established within the Evangelical model of churchmanship. Apart from these, and Lichfield and Gloucester, all the colleges were High Church foundations. Indeed until the Leeds Clergy School, set up by John Gott, the Vicar of Leeds, all the colleges were the foundations of particular bishops or cathedrals.

Just as diocesan reform was pursued in order to facilitate episcopal control over the parochial clergy, diocesan-based clerical education was designed to allow bishops to supervise and improve the spiritual and moral discipline of prospective clergymen. A significant date is 1854 when Bishop Samuel Wilberforce founded Cuddesdon: by creating a residential institution based in a Catholic seminary tradition he influenced the nature and constitution of theological colleges throughout the rest of the century. This change was accelerated when the Universities Test Act (1871) undermined the exclusively Anglican character of education at Oxford and Cambridge and led to the growth of denominational post-graduate colleges.

The founding of the Society of the Sacred Mission (SSM) by Herbert Kelly in 1891 introduces a factor that has not been mentioned before. All this education, whether at university or cathedral college, had to be paid for, sometimes by the Clerical Education Societies. The poor ordinand was still excluded. So the SSM was explicitly founded to offer free training for ordinands. The Community of the Resurrection followed suit within a few years. By the end of the nineteenth century there were 26 colleges in existence: all providing exclusively male training, for, with few exceptions, younger men embarking on their main profession.

Talk of clergy training is a reminder that this account emphasizes the positions of the clergy since it is the clergy who are the subjects of the empirical research at the heart of this study. It must be remembered too that centuries of custom and canon law had given lay people a very minor role in the affairs of the Church. This too was one of the dissimilarities between the Anglican Church and the Free Churches. As early as 1857 a petition was submitted to the Lower House of Canterbury Convocation asking that faithful laymen be admitted. It was not until 1886 that Archbishop Benson allowed a Canterbury House of Laymen (Thompson, 1970, pp.119f).

Up to the First World War

Vidler, speaking of the Victorian crisis of faith, said, 'Never has any age in history produced such a detailed literature of lost faith or of so many great men and women of religious temperament standing outside organized religion' (Vidler, 1974, p.112). When Randall Davidson went to be Archbishop of Canterbury in 1903 the Daily News published a census of churchgoing in London. It was a careful study, taken Sunday by Sunday for a year, including people at all services in all the denominations.

> Attendances at Anglican services (including missions) had actually fallen from 535,715 to 396,196 [since 1886].
> As Mudie Smith [the census compiler] obtained figures showing how many persons attended more than one service, he was able to give the net number of persons worshipping. They were only 832,051 in a resident population (outside institutions) of 4,470,304, or a little over two in eleven.
> (Ensor, 1936, p.308)

The parish clergy in the larger cities of England knew of this slow but steady decline in church attendance, and appealed to their Church leaders to become aware that the most urgent area for missionary activity was in this country.

> While church people were wasting their strength in fighting the most violent battles against each other, their great enemies, rationalism and indifference, were winning one engagement after another.
> (Lloyd, 1966, p.72)

This was not an easy time for the Evangelicals. The latter part of the nineteenth century can justifiably be viewed as a period of decline.

> By the time Edward VII ascended the throne they were quite seriously dispirited, uncertain of their role within the Church and in society, and without that cohesion, purposefulness and energy which had characterized them in the halcyon days of the past.
> (Hylson-Smith, 1989, p.227)

> The dynamics of the Anglican scene were already telling Evangelicals that any changes in law or liturgy or doctrine were bound to be changes for the worse – and this conviction drew them more and more into a defensive huddle.
> (Buchanan, 1984, p.8)

During this pre-war period Anglo-Catholics continued to live austere and disciplined lives, with a love for human souls and a commitment to slum parishes built upon the strength and richness of their interior devotional lives and their dedication to worship. They were reviving religious orders: the Community of the Resurrection, founded at Radley and established at Mirfield by Gore; the Society of the Sacred Mission at Kelham; and the Cowley Fathers at Oxford. In 1906 *The English Hymnal* was published: it continues to be used in parishes today.

Ecclesiastical attention though was not dominated by the Evangelicals nor the Anglo-Catholics, but rather by the Modernists and their desire to interpret Christianity to the 'cultivated modern man' (Worrall, 1988, pp.115-133). Rashdall (1908) in *Anglican Liberalism* set out five principal justifications for this modernist approach. First, latitude in the interpretation of ecclesiastical formularies had a long and respectable tradition. Second, no one who took an oath of allegiance meant by it what would have been meant in Tudor days. Third, any radical Member of Parliament had to take an oath of allegiance to the Crown, but could still be an honest and consistent republican. Fourth, no one who was ordained could honestly and literally mean just what the ordination oath said when it pledged unfeigned belief in all the canonical scriptures. Fifth, everybody liberalized the creeds, and particularly the Athanasian Creed, whether consciously or not.

During this same period the English translation of Schweitzer's *The Quest of the Historical Jesus* was published (1910). The publication of *Foundations* under B.H. Streeter's (1912) editorship gave additional momentum to modernism (Stephenson, 1984).

In these pre-war years, though, two movements began which, though not linked at all in terms of leaders and motivators, may have both been a response to what was lacking in the Church of that time. The first of these was Pentecostalism (Quebedeaux, 1975, Kay, 2000). While the history of this movement could be traced from the early Christian centuries, through the Wesleyan revival of the eighteenth century and the Irvingites (Strachan, 1975, Roxborough, 1979) and holiness movements of the nineteenth centuries, classical Pentecostalism, or the 'First Wave' (Springer, 1987), made its advent in the wake of the Azusa Street revival in Los Angeles in 1906. The pastor of First Baptist Church Los Angeles, Joseph Smale, had returned from Wales where he had seen the revival under Evan Roberts, and longed for the same in his own church. At the same time William

Seymour, the son of former slaves, who had taught himself to read and write well enough to study at a Bible School in Kansas, began to teach and preach in a Holiness church in Azusa Street using negro spirituals in the worship. Soon there were reports of speaking in tongues and miraculous healings (Bartlemann, 1980). What was distinctive about the meetings was the notion of the baptism of the Spirit as a baptism of power rather than of holiness, and the joining of this experience with the gift of speaking in tongues. Tongues came to be seen as the initial evidence of this baptism of the Spirit and this remains a distinctive doctrine of Pentecostalism to this day. People came to Azusa Street from all over the world to experience this baptism and to take back the message to their own countries.

Pentecostalism, which began as a movement rather than a denomination, spread rapidly, leading to the forming of new churches, like the Assemblies of God, the Elim Church and the Apostolic Church, and the influencing of the Anglican and Free Churches. In Britain the arrival of Pentecostalism coincided with the aftermath of the Welsh revival and gathered strength from it. A Norwegian Methodist, Thomas Ball Barratt, brought the story of Azusa Street to England and Alexander Boddy (1854-1930), vicar of All Saints Sunderland, heard him. His church and vicarage became a centre for those who sought the baptism of the Spirit, including Smith Wigglesworth, the plumber from Bradford (Whittaker, 1983). However it would be necessary to wait until the 1960s for this wave of the Spirit to gain a firm foothold in the Anglican Church in England.

The second movement to find its origin, or, better, its rehabilitation, in the pre-war years was the mystical approach to God. This had never been forgotten but its re-awakening was fostered by W.R. Inge, Baron von Hügel, and Evelyn Underhill. The subject of Dean Inge's 1899 Bampton Lectures was Christian Mysticism. 'Using the historical method and introducing English readers to then little known religious figures, such as Julian of Norwich, he replied to current criticisms of the institutional churches and of the authority of the Bible by basing faith on experience'(Webster, 1983, p.213).

Inge saw himself as a successor to the Cambridge Platonists and was a leader of the Modern Churchman's Union. Von Hügel, though a Roman Catholic, had a large influence on the Anglican Church particularly with his publication in 1908 of *The Mystical Element in Religion*. He was Underhill's spiritual director and laid strong emphasis on the need to recognize three elements in religion, the Institutional, the Intellectual, and the Mystical.

> For in Anglicanism, the most characteristic of its parties, the High Church school, represents predominantly the Historical, Institutional principle. The Latitudinarian school fights for the Rational, Critical and Speculative element. The Evangelical school ... represents the Experimental, Mystical element.
> (Thorold, 1928, p.24)

Underhill made herself an authority on Western mysticism. Her work *Mysticism: study in the nature and development of man's spiritual consciousness* (1911) showed her concern with the growth and healing of the spiritual consciousness. As a result of the work of Inge, von Hügel, Underhill and others, the idea and experience of the transcendent alongside the immanent as the starting-point of thought about the divine and devotion to God became commonplace. It became part of the spirituality of liberals and conservatives, catholics and, in time, evangelicals.

The inter-war years

Hastings (1986, p.298) describes the years between the First and Second World Wars as the beginning of the high summer of Anglo-Catholic theology. There was a vitality and openness about Anglo-Catholicism with names like Ramsey, Thornton, Hebert, Dix, Farrer, Maurice and Forsyth leading the way. The Thomist strain in their theology became more obvious. 'The Anglo-Catholics were beginning to find themselves at the centre of Anglican theology and life, providing both bishops and university professors, and this greater responsibility produced on the whole greater tolerance' (Hylson-Smith, 1993, p.269).

After the First World War the theme of social concern was high on the list of priorities for the Anglo-Catholic Congresses, the first of which was held in 1920 in London (Rowell, 1983, p.241). Lang was Archbishop of York and Canterbury successively from 1909 to 1942, and he is seen as the one who more than anyone else 'catholicized' the Church of England.

> By 1908 he was publicly committed to advocating the legalization of the 'Six Points' – eucharistic vestments, the lighting of candles upon the altar, the use of wafers in the place of common bread for Holy Communion, the eastward position of the celebrant, the ceremonial mixing of water with wine in the chalice, and the use of incense. And these were the main outward symbols which, in the view of both Anglican Catholics and Evangelicals, distinguished the mass of the one from the communion of the other. Lang was the first archbishop since the Reformation to wear a mitre and to make the cope the normal liturgical dress for bishop and archbishop.
> (Hylson-Smith, 1993, p.273)

In order to illustrate the poverty of the Anglican Evangelicals in the inter-war years it is only necessary to turn to a well-known and respected study of the period from 1889 to 1939, Ramsey's (1960) book *From Gore to Temple*.

> The great theological names of this period, such as Gore, Henson, Bicknell, Quick, Temple, and Ramsey himself are mostly 'liberal catholic' in their stance, and none is evangelical. There was no evangelical Anglican to write serious commentaries or useful works of doctrine, and have them published by recognized religious publishers.
> (Buchanan, 1984, pp.8-9)

In fact when the important issue of Prayer Book revision arose, there was no single identifiable Evangelical common mind on it.

What did emerge at that time was Liberal Evangelicalism (Hylson-Smith, 1989, pp.241-255, Bebbington, 1989, pp.181-228, Cocksworth, 1993, p.91). Hickin (1968) charted the extent of that movement from 'The Liverpool Six' to the last annual conference of the Anglican Evangelical Group Movement in 1967. The publication of *Liberal Evangelicalism, an Interpretation* in 1923 called upon Evangelicals to see literary criticism, natural science and philosophy as their allies not their enemies. Through the conventions held at Cromer, which started in 1928, Liberal Evangelicals began to make an impact.

> [They] happily combined what was best in the experimental individualism of the older Evangelical school, with what was best in the corporate sacramentalism of the High Churchman, in a synthesis with what was truest in the scientific liberalism of the Modernist.
> (Hickin, 1968, p.51)

However the serious disagreements between liberal and conservative Evangelicals could be clearly seen when a group of those who had been supporters of the Church Missionary Society broke off and formed the Bible Churchmen's Missionary Society in 1922, a more conservative body than its parent.

In 1898 the Churchmen's Union for the Advancement of Liberal Religious Thought was founded. In 1928 it was renamed the Modern Churchmen's Union and became extremely active in promoting a more identifiable modernism.

> Modernism was especially influential in the 1920s and 1930s when a significant proportion of leading Christian thinkers belonged to this Union, and a plethora of articulate defences of Christianity were published which were proud to include the word 'Modernist' within their titles. The movement is generally held to have reached the peak of its influence with the publication of the report of the Archbishops' Commission on Doctrine in the Church of England in 1938 which either endorsed or recognized as permissible certain liberal re-interpretations of Christian beliefs.
> (Badham, 1998, p.1)

Major, the Principal of Ripon Hall, defined the core of English Modernism as fidelity to 'the operation in human history of the Spirit that was in Jesus Christ, and the aim of the English Modernist is to set free that Spirit from those archaic dogmatic shackles and ecclesiastical burdens, great and grievous to be borne, which are hindering it from exerting its full and proper influence in the modern world' (Major, 1927, pp.6-7). Lloyd cited a letter from Major to *The Times* in 1945.

> As editor of the *Modern Churchman* for thirty years I have no knowledge of Modern Churchmen who do not believe in 'the incarnation, the atonement, everlasting life, divine judgement', but I do know a great number of Modern Churchmen who do not believe in the virgin birth, in the resurrection of the physical body of Jesus Christ, in the descent of Jesus Christ into Hades between his death and resurrection, in his return at the end of the world to judge the quick and the dead at a great assize ... These beliefs are all affirmed in the Apostles'

> Creed and have been held by orthodox Christians until recent times ... If asked why Modern Churchmen do not believe these things, the reply is that modern biblical, historical, and scientific studies have made them incredible.
> (Lloyd, 1966, p.261)

The arrival on the scene of the Modernists prompted a variety of responses. Hoskyns' essay 'The Christ of the Synoptic Gospels' in *Essays Catholic and Critical* (1927) was seen as one of the most significant. Niebuhr's famous criticism of their teaching was another: 'a God without wrath brought men without sin into a kingdom without judgement through the ministration of a Christ without a cross.' (Niebuhr, 1959, p.191)

Another important development in the inter-war years was the Parish Communion movement.

> The seeds ... were sown by W.H. Frere as curate-in-charge of St Faith's Stepney between 1890 and 1892 when he suggested the unknown hour of 9.30 to give the family a chance of worshipping together and going home to prepare the Sunday lunch. In 1904 C.G. Lang, then Bishop of Stepney, advocated 'one great parish communion every Sunday ... of the Household of God at 9.00, 9.15 or 9.30' and in 1931 William Temple in his Primary Visitation as Archbishop of York stated, 'In many places admirable results have followed the custom of holding a parochial Communion at 9.00 or 9.30' and discouraged, as a normal practice, attendance at two Communions on one morning.
> (Melinsky, 1992, p.106)

The rationale for such a practice was the book of essays, edited by Hebert (1937), *The Parish Communion*. Though the Book of Common Prayer had envisaged a celebration of Holy Communion every Sunday and on major feasts, much of the emphasis in the period since then had regarded the eucharist as a personal and private devotion. The Parish Communion movement's stress on a corporate spirituality, and 'the Lord's people at the Lord's table on the Lord's day' found much favour in the Anglican Church.

In the country at large the Church of England did not fare well in the events leading up to the Second World War or during the war itself. There was expressed disquiet at the ease with which the bishops leapt to support Chamberlain's search for 'peace for our time ... peace with honour' at the Munich agreement of 1938. 'Munich proved a moral minefield for the Church. Perhaps above all it raised questions about the character and inclination of the established Church' (Chandler, 1994, p.97). Though many of the war-time troops felt well served by their chaplains, the gap between what was said and what was done caused misgivings among ordinary working people (Wilkinson, 1986, Reeves, 1999). Questions about the rightness of establishment kept recurring.

The 1950s

Perhaps in line with the prediction that liberalism flourishes in prosperous times, the Modernists had a hard time after the Second World War. Stephenson cited the opinion of the anonymous writer of the preface to *Crockford's Clerical Directory* of 1956 about the decline of the Modernist group:

> Although the annual conference of the Modern Churchmen's Union continues to be favoured above all others by *The Times*, it cannot be said that this group counts for much in the life of the Church of England today. That they do not is largely their own fault for allowing themselves to convey the impression that they are a body of bitter ancients whose Modernism is that of the day before yesterday.
> (Stephenson, 1984, p.181)

Page also said that 'English Modernism prepared the way for radicalism but declined in influence as increasingly it came to be seen as a recognizable body of theological conclusions' (Page, 1965, p.138).

The 'renaissance of Evangelicalism after World War II', as described by Hylson-Smith (1989, pp.287f), though was a more observable phenomenon. Buchanan (1984, p.9) saw the seeds of a post-war revival in two pre-war initiatives. The first initiative was the VPS camps ('Bash' camps) founded by E.J.H. Nash (Eddison, 1983), which were summer camps where schoolboys from boarding schools were prepared for Christian leadership.

> It was possible when the movement was at its zenith for a boy to go from public school to Cambridge, to ordination, to a curacy and to a parish of his own without having encountered the kind of life lived outside those particular circles.
> (King, 1969, p.56)

Indeed Goodhew (2003, p.70) in his paper on the Cambridge Inter-Collegiate Christian Union, said that 'between 1935 and 1939 all CICCU's presidents were "Bash campers" and the union was marked by his methods: a very simple Evangelical gospel; meticulous preparation; a wariness of emotions or intellect; and assiduous "personal work" before and after conversion'.

The second initiative was the formation in 1938 of the Biblical Research Committee, which sponsored an Evangelical centre for biblical and theological study and research called Tyndale House at Cambridge in 1945. The growth in Evangelical scholarship after the war came straight from Tyndale House and from the Inter Varsity Press, particularly *The New Bible Commentary* (1951) and *The New Bible Dictionary* (1962). In 1945 the Church of England Commission on Evangelism produced the report *Towards the Conversion of England* which, probably because of the Commission's chairman, the Evangelical Bishop Chavasse, read like an Evangelical treatise. In 1950 John Stott began his long stay at All Souls' Langham Place, London, and in 1955 he refounded the 'Eclectic Society' for Evangelical Anglican clergy under the age of 40, which helped to give younger Evangelicals a sense of corporate importance, strength and purpose.

At the same time there was a growth in the number of Evangelical Anglican ordinands, many of whom came from a public school and VPS background. In 1954 the American evangelist Billy Graham conducted a three-month long crusade in Harringay arena (Tidball, 1994).

> Overnight it gave a national focus not only to Billy Graham, but to evangelism, and to the Evangelicals who sponsored and mainly supported the venture. Thousands were influenced, and many future candidates for the Church of England ministry attributed their conversions to the crusade.
> (Hylson-Smith, 1989, p.288)

It was probably Graham's stance on the Bible which led to a public debate on 'fundamentalism' (Hebert, 1957, Packer, 1959) in which it became clear that the terms 'Evangelical' and 'fundamentalist' did not need to be synonymous. Buchanan (1984, p.10), looking back on the growth of Evangelicalism during this period, identified what he called a 'neo-puritan' movement in Evangelicalism encompassing Jim Packer, Alec Motyer, Martyn Lloyd-Jones and the Banner of Truth Trust.

The post-war years for Anglo-Catholics began positively with the publication in 1947 of the report *Catholicity*, prepared for the Archbishop of Canterbury by a group of Catholic theologians 'to examine the causes of the deadlock which occurs in discussion between Catholics and Protestants, and to consider whether any synthesis between Catholicism and Protestantism is possible'. The report gave an exposition of the function of Catholicism within Anglicanism, but the only ground on which it saw a possibility of Catholics and Protestants standing together was in opposition to liberalism. The formation of the Church of South India in 1947 gave Catholics an opportunity for 'continued, concerted and large-scale opposition ... [and] SPG ... for a time withdrew official financial support for the new united Church' (Wilkinson, 1978b, p.41).

Absalom (1971) however noted several difficulties in the role of Anglo-Catholic priests which were to cause serious problems over the next decades. One of these difficulties was that 'the movement was fragmented in various respects at an early stage; its ideology was diffuse and unified action was possible only to a limited extent' (Absalom, 1971, p.53). This increased priestly isolation (Gunstone, 1968, pp.191-192, Hughes, 1961, chapter 4). Another difficulty noted by Absalom was the problem of coping with the advance of secularization:

> In the post-war period, while the Catholic movement as a whole gained support, individual parishes began to decline. Thus the increased support derived from an increase in the number of Catholic parishes, but seldom from growth within parishes ... A number of established parishes experienced declines which they only partly understood and could not arrest. Moreover, the younger clergy, entering parochial work often after an early period of intense Catholic socialization, found themselves in a situation where triumphalism was brought up against the cold reality of indifference.
> (Absalom, 1971, pp.54-55)

The problems of an increasing national population (the baby boom) and a decreasing number of clergy meant that this was a time for experimentation in strategies for providing for the pastoral needs of a growing population. Many examples could be quoted, from the City of London Guild Churches (1952), through the Pastoral Reorganization Measure (1949), the Parish and People movement (Jagger, 1978), to the South Ormsby experiment in group ministry (1949). New translations of the Bible appeared: *The Revised Standard Version* in 1946, J.B. Phillips' *The New Testament in Modern English* in 1958, and *The New English Bible* in 1961. Still, though, the only authorized Church of England liturgy was the Prayer Book of 1662.

In 1952 Newbigin published his influential work *The Household of God* in which he treated the Pentecostal Churches as serious and respectable. He saw them as the third great movement in the Church of God alongside Catholicism and Protestantism. Most observers at the time however did not so regard the Pentecostal movement: Neill, for example, looking at the state of Anglican churchmanship in 1958, could still only see seven colours in the spectrum:

> At the two extremes is to be found the 'lunatic fringe', the 'Catholics' who seem so much at home with Roman ideas that it is hard to say what keeps them within the Anglican fold, and the 'extreme Evangelicals', who are so much 'Nonconformists in surplices' that one sometimes looks in vain for their point of attachment to the English Church. Moving inwards we meet on one side the convinced Anglo-Catholics and the convinced Evangelicals; then those who must be classed as 'high' rather than 'low', and those who are 'low' rather than 'high'. And finally we have to take account of those who would call themselves liberals or modern churchmen.
> (Neill, 1958, p.399)

The 1960s

'The Bewilderment of the Sixties' is Welsby's (1984) chapter title for the next decade. In this decade, marked in popular culture by the Beatles, hippies, the Maharishi, the space race, Vietnam and the Berlin Wall, the Church of England brought out *Series II*, its first official alternative to the Prayer Book liturgy. The Roman Catholic Church began the decade by convening the Second Vatican Council in 1962, and over the next few years Vatican II promulgated radical reforms with the aim of modernizing the Church.

> Its effect was dramatic and global. It created a great sense of freedom and openness and introduced measures and ideals which were seemingly copied from traditional Protestant Churches. It caused confusion among Anglican Catholics, and little short of panic and despair among Anglo-Papalists.
> (Hylson-Smith, 1993, pp.329-330)

The liturgical changes of Vatican II were particularly overwhelming for those who had seen the Roman Catholic Church as the bastion of traditionalism, conservatism and orthodoxy. The formal structure of the Tridentine mass, secretly and not so secretly copied by Anglican Catholics, was now replaced by a variable pattern in the vernacular with new musical settings. Pickering (1989, p.203) called the new service 'a simple and direct, homely and even folksy gathering'. For Anglo-Catholics the discarding of what had seemed immovable fixed liturgical points served to create uncertainty and confusion, and aggravated a growing identity crisis (Wilkinson, 1978b). Where were they to look to find the stable and unchanging authority that they were seeking?

In the first year of Vatican II *Soundings* (Vidler, 1962) was published, followed in the succeeding year by *Honest to God* (Robinson, 1963). In the introduction to his book Vidler said that *Soundings* was about 'ploughing, not reaping', about 'candidly confessing where our perplexities lie', and about the need to face questions 'which are not yet being faced with the necessary seriousness and determination' (Vidler, 1962, p.ix). *Soundings* was mainly read by people within the Church; *Honest to God* sold almost a million copies within three years. No theological book in recent years had caused such controversy and public debate. Within six months a second book was published (Edwards, 1963) in order to give an account of the highlights of the dispute which Robinson the Bishop of Woolwich's book had engendered.

> *Honest to God* was a book which had tremendous power and vitality. It drew it in part from the resolute honesty of its author, who, convinced Christian though he was, was determined to take nothing whatever for granted, and refused to exempt any sacrosanct symbol, even any divine person, from the agnostic scrutinies of modern secular man – a title he accepted for himself ... [He] began by believing that most religious language is meaningless, that the supernatural scheme of things within which Christianity has been expounded is no longer credible, that religion, having in the past done more harm than good, has now become utterly uninfluential upon the courses of the world.
> (Lloyd, 1966, p.604)

As with the earlier Modernists, Robinson saw his book as part of the search to present old truths in more relevant and more contemporarily compulsive ways: the radical restatement of doctrine would reconcile modern men and women to a God they often did not care to know. In general Evangelicals were suspicious or hostile but the reaction amongst many Anglo-Catholics was quite different.

> *Honest to God* might get a cold reception among the students at the London College of Divinity; it was warmly welcomed by most at Mirfield. While in the stress of the times Evangelicals tended to go more Evangelical, young Anglo-Catholics went less Anglo-Catholic and more 'radical'. Anglo-Catholicism as a consequence lost much of its old cohesiveness as a party, split between an obstinate conservative, rather elderly rump clinging to old ways, and a radical but somewhat leaderless younger group, profoundly influenced by Vatican II as by Bishop Robinson and much else, but not seeing at all clearly where now to go.
> (Hastings, 1986, p.555)

Perhaps surprisingly, the Modernists of the Modern Churchmen's Union were somewhat critical of *Honest to God* (see Stephenson, 1984, p.190f), though some regarded this as a sign of the weakness of the Modern Churchmen's Union compared with its heyday in the 1920s and 1930s (Lithgow, 1983).

1962 also saw a third major development relevant to this study. In that year Michael Harper, John Stott's curate at All Souls' Langham Place, was at a conference in Farnham where he was 'filled with all the fulness of God and had to ask God to stop giving more – I couldn't take it' (Harper, 1965, p.86). By 1963 the name 'Charismatic movement' was in use to signify the recognition and use of some significant parts of Pentecostalism within the traditional Churches. Charismatics often used the term 'second wave' (Springer, 1987) to designate the advent of charismatic renewal. In 1964 the Fountain Trust, an interdenominational organization which aimed to encourage local churches to experience renewal in the Holy Spirit, was established with Harper in its vanguard (Gunstone, 1982, Hocken, 1986), and in the same year he left his curacy to devote his time to that work. 'In the first years there was some influence by Pentecostal preachers, but this declined after the mid-1960s as the two movements settled for largely friendly coexistence rather than close cooperation' (Burgess and McGee, 1989, p.145).

The influence of the charismatic movement in the Church of England was first felt among Evangelicals. The early proponents had a hard time with fellow Evangelicals who were deeply suspicious of any experiential test of conversion. From about 1967 Roman Catholics became significantly influenced by charismatic renewal with their first conference at Roehampton in 1972 (Williams, 1981, pp.103-110). In Europe the support of the Belgian Cardinal Suenens was central (Chadwick, 1992, p.136), and perhaps because of this Roman Catholic involvement, the renewal made inroads among Anglo-Catholics as well with the first Anglican Catholic Charismatic Convention at Walsingham in 1973. Wilkinson saw this as a further contribution to Anglo-Catholicism's problems:

> Anglican Catholicism has always been attractive to those tempted to spiritual legalism, and to those who have felt a temperamental affinity with the Tractarian doctrine of 'reserve' in spiritual matters. To some of these the charismatic movement came as a liberation ... For some Anglican Catholics the charismatic movement has also been legitimized by widespread Roman Catholic participation. Because the charismatic movement has emphasized unity through experience rather than through doctrine and structures, it has been another factor in the erosion of the distinctive coherence of Anglican Catholicism.
> (Wilkinson, 1978b, p.43)

Among Evangelicals the decade started with the founding of the Church of England Evangelical Council in 1960. This was an indication that Evangelical Anglicans were convinced members of the Church of England, something about which people both within and without the Evangelical movement had not been certain. This new conviction found its clearest expression in the National Evangelical Anglican Congress at Keele in 1967 where Evangelicals broke emphatically with the more negative note of their twentieth century past. In answer to the question 'What is the Church?', Keele decided that it was 'a historic, continuing body, from which it was wrong to sever oneself unless it had become so apostate as to be intolerable' (King, 1969, p.121). Hastings (1986, p.553) cited Stott's preparatory address: 'Evangelicals have a very poor image in the Church as a whole. We have acquired a reputation for narrow partisanship and obstructionism. We have to acknowledge this, and for the most part we have no one but ourselves to blame.' The potentially pietist nature of charismatic renewal was not the focus – in fact the charismatic movement had no mention in Keele '67 – but rather an engagement with the world.

> They began to work at the meaning of mission in terms of the reform of society as well as the conversion of the individual. They took the structures of church life seriously. They recognized that ethics should be on the Evangelical agenda. And the more reflective of them began to unearth a science previously undreamed of among them – hermeneutics.
> (Buchanan, 1984, p.11)

The Keele statement about Holy Communion was, from an Evangelical standpoint, revolutionary in stating the intention to work towards the practice of a weekly celebration of Holy Communion as the central corporate service of the Church.

> Evangelicals were here at last re-entering, instead of battling against, the central worshipping development of the century – embracing the principal positive contribution of Anglo-Catholicism, the liturgical movement, Parish and People.
> (Hastings, 1986, p.554)

For many Christian people the 1960s also represented a time of ecumenical advance and ecumenical retreat. The ecumenical advance might best be expressed by the visits of two Archbishops of Canterbury, Fisher and Ramsey, to the Pope at the Vatican. The setting up of the Anglican-Roman Catholic International Commission (ARCIC) gave hope to many that the two sister Churches could draw closer together. ARCIC 1 produced statements on the Eucharist in 1971, the ministry in 1973, authority in 1977, and a Final Report in 1981. The ecumenical retreat would for many be epitomized by the failure of the plans for Anglican-Methodist reunion. In 1963 *Conversations between the Church of England and the Methodist Church* was published as the basis for reconciliation. Lloyd wrote with the cautious optimism of many at that time:

> On the Anglican side the plan was laid before the ruridecanal and diocesan conferences, which, without exception, accepted it, usually by large majorities. The Convocations accepted it in May 1965, as enabling further negotiations to clear up the 'points of concern' which had come to light. On the Methodist side Conference approved the plan in principle on July 5 1965 but also asked for further joint study. The position at this moment therefore is that both the Church of England and the Methodists have endorsed the proposals of the joint committee, that full organic union between the two Churches is both possible and desirable, and that it must be prepared for by a period of full communion. We have now therefore to wait and see what happens next, but it will be surprising if

in the end these proposals, endorsed in principle by large majorities on both sides, come to nothing.
(Lloyd, 1966, p.590)

Melinsky's terse comments are probably sufficient epitaph:

In 1969 prospects for Anglican-Methodist reunion were wrecked by a vote in the General Synod ... The vote was lost by a strange alliance of some Evangelicals who claimed that the Service of Reconciliation was in fact an ordination and some Anglo-Catholics who claimed that it was not.
(Melinsky, 1992, p.192)

The 1970s

Manwaring's (1985) title for his book about Evangelicals in the Church of England was *From Controversy to Co-existence*, and the 1970s seem to have been that period of co-existence. Coggan, the former Principal of an Anglican Evangelical theological college, became Archbishop of Canterbury after Ramsey, and, as Hastings described him:

He was a little too liberal to retain the full confidence of Evangelicals but too Evangelical to be quite on the wavelength of either liberals or Anglo-Catholics. Yet he did in point of fact represent quite well the outlook of the common churchman within the Established Church.
(Hastings, 1986, p.556)

Increasing numbers of Evangelicals and charismatic Evangelicals were training at theological colleges. A rapprochement developed between Evangelicals and charismatics cemented by the joint document *Gospel and Spirit* in 1977. Charismatics played a full part in the preparations for the National Evangelical Anglican Congress at Nottingham in 1977, and with rising numbers and rising confidence all seemed set fair for them. Harper was involved in planning the Anglican Charismatic Conference at Canterbury in 1978 to coincide with that year's Lambeth Conference: three hundred Anglican leaders including thirty bishops attended the charismatic conference. There were signs of Evangelical dissent though and discussions about an 'Anglican Evangelical identity problem' (Packer, 1978, Wright, 1980, Hopkinson, 1983). Wright's five models of the inter-relationship between being Evangelical and being Anglican which was at the heart of the identity problem have been well summarized by Curry (1997, pp.321-323).

The spontaneity, including spontaneity in worship, that the charismatic movement represented was part of the background to a debate within the whole Church about the balance between formality and informality. In 1975 the Prayer Book Society was founded to uphold the worship and doctrine of the Church of England as enshrined in the *Book of Common Prayer*. On the other hand Perham (1978), for example, in an Alcuin manual for revising the presentation of the eucharist, offered release from a single Anglican liturgical tradition that could be called Catholic to new and varied traditions that were no less Catholic. Again, from the Anglo-Catholic tradition, Ramsey, Terwilliger and Allchin testified to the value of the charismatic movement:

> The most powerful force within the Church at this moment is the 'charismatic movement'. It is a great surge of awareness of the Holy Spirit, sometimes pentecostal in form, always an intense revival of vital prayer and the awareness of God's working ... It is possible to sense that in all of this we are in the grip of a divine action to which we must respond, alive and alert to its meaning. Christ is being made known to us by the Spirit; the Charismatic Christ is being revealed in the mind and heart of the Church. This is theology in its deepest sense; this is the knowledge of God. Come, Holy Spirit!
> (Ramsey, Terwilliger and Allchin, 1974, pp.68 & 71)

It was in the 1970s that the 'house church movement' began to establish itself in England.

> Groups of Christians who had been 'baptized in the Spirit' became increasingly disenchanted with the rigid formalism and the lack of warm fellowship within the denominational churches. They started initially to meet together in each other's homes and then, as numbers grew, they began to hire schools, community halls and even cinemas. The house church movement is a loose umbrella title covering a variety of independent charismatic groups which are not linked with any historic denomination.
> (Scotland, 1995, p.10)

Many of the house church leaders would accept the label 'Restorationist' or 'member of the Restoration movement' (Walker, 1985, Wright, 1986) because of their commitment to restore biblical church patterns.

> The restoration movement does not speak with one voice but it does speak the same language. It is the language of thorough obedience. In its perception the work of renewal, although good, is not of itself enough. Where it leaves unbiblical practices unchanged it is considered to be incomplete. New wine requires new wineskins and renewal must be accompanied by the restoration of the New Testament principles of church life.
> (Wright, 1986, p.75)

This call for institutional change found echoes with those Anglican Evangelicals who regarded the Keele '67 statements as too Arminian for their taste. Both clergy and laity from the Church of England joined house churches, though there were no accurate figures for the size of the defection.

What of liberal theology in the 1970s after all the excitements of the previous decade? Like many movements before, it found that in achieving many of its aims it became taken for granted.

> Those who are identified with the theological position which in Anglicanism has been called 'broad' or 'modernist' or 'liberal' ... have lost their sense of mission.

> The liberal point of view is not actively propagated by its adherents; rather, like the lowest level in a pin-ball machine, it is the point at which one arrives when one has passed through all the hazards and barriers that lie above. The parishes which are particularly hospitable to persons of a liberal persuasion seldom reach out to their constituencies with a message of hope and challenge; they function as small and comfortable sects for those who, on their own initiative, drift in.
> (Gibson, 1979, p.164)

Percy (1998, p.216) spoke of the Student Christian Movement which 'declared itself open and removed its boundaries but the life of the body flowed out, rather than the people coming in'. Because the conservative position was often marked by a body of answers to the riddles that people faced, by an authentic corpus of beliefs enshrined in scripture and/or tradition, it had the ability to translate those conclusions reached in the past into valid elucidations for today. Liberal theology tended to stress form rather than content – some would say, over and above content. As a result for the liberal 'the task is to enter into the conversation, to bring one's life and one's society beneath the searching glare of the insights of the past and to offer one's own insights from the unique but familiar experiences of the present' (Gibson, 1979, p.165). Yet there were significant attempts by the liberal constituency to show the world what a worked-out liberal faith and life would look like (for example, Hick, 1977).

Writing in the 1970s Wilkinson could say, not entirely frivolously, that 'Anglican Catholicism understood as an organized movement with a coherent system of doctrine and ethics no longer exists. A few continue to speak of the Catholic movement, but how can there be a movement when there are no longer any agreed goals?' (1978b, p.41). Yet he recognized that 'a Catholic ethos, a Catholic temperament, a set of Catholic attitudes still survive in the Church of England'. There were, however, still more testing times ahead for the Anglo-Catholics as they moved into the 1980s.

The 1980s

For English Anglicans the decade of the 1980s began with the publication of *The Alternative Service Book* (ASB). It offered choices in worship following the tenets of its Preface that 'Christians have become readier to accept that, even within a single Church, unity need no longer be seen to entail strict uniformity of practice', and that 'the gospel of the living Christ is too rich in content, and the spiritual needs of his people are too diverse, for a single form of worship to suffice' (p.9). Parish churches and other places of worship bought copies of the ASB in large quantities. Though it claimed to be within the spirit of Anglican comprehensiveness, it was loved and hated by some from nearly every form of Anglican churchmanship.

> [Some Anglican Catholics saw the changes in liturgy] as in keeping with the decrees of Vatican II, and they delighted in the extent to which Catholic ideas and practices had been incorporated into the new service book. Other more cautious

and conservative Anglican Catholics preferred the 1662 Prayer Book and shunned what they regarded as changes in the ASB which were too Protestant in tone. (Hylson-Smith, 1993, p.331)

Others saw it as part of a wider liberal agenda to change the nature of the Church of England.

> Just as the Book of Common Prayer marked the full emergence of the Church of England, so the ASB will mark its disappearance. The feebleness and lack of urgency of expression, the facile and evasive optimism of its theology, the bewildering multiplicity of its practices, will encourage the proliferation of churches that are minor sects of local quietist groups, constituency parties run by enthusiasts. They will be populist in intended appeal, tiny in actual membership, autocratic in practice, hostile to the traditional virtues, hospitable to passing fashions and with about as much significance for the majority of English people as any other local group.
> (Brewer, in Martin and Mullen, 1981, p.242)

Liberals however had their own doubts about the ASB:

> The point is that worship in all the Christian Churches is thoroughly realist and, under the influence of the ecumenical and liturgical movements, is becoming more and more uniform, focusing on the eucharist and therein rehearsing a constant succession of propositional claims about God and his saving activity in the life and work of Christ. Liberal Christians often find their worshipping marred by the pre-critical way these claims are presented, but by a process of internal reinterpretation they are enabled to continue in their participation.
> (Badham, 1998, p.56)

The 1980s was the decade when the Church of England officially took note of, and in some senses positively welcomed, the presence of the charismatic movement in its midst. (Ironically it was in 1980 that the Fountain Trust closed down, because it felt its object of drawing the Church's attention to the charismatic movement had been achieved.) The General Synod commissioned a report *The Charismatic Movement in the Church of England* (Craston, 1981). After the ensuing Synod debates the Board for Mission and Unity asked Josephine Bax to map the wider field of spiritual renewal (Bax, 1986). Then in 1991 the Doctrine Commission's report *We Believe in the Holy Spirit* was published (Central Board of Finance, 1991). Together this set of official reports treated the charismatic movement as 'the most prominent demonstration of the work of the Holy Spirit in the Church of England's life in the 1980s, and then addresses it with corresponding seriousness' (Buchanan, 1994, p.104).

In the reports mapping the nature of the charismatic movement, the following characteristics of churches under its influence were noted: awareness of the Holy Spirit at work, small group structures, increased lay participation, deeper spiritual life, new forms of corporate worship and liturgy, emphasis on the experiential, extra-parochial communities, and commitment to community living. Scotland (1995, p.230f) added another, that of church-planting (see Hopkins,

1992). In a similar analysis Goldingay (1996) drew attention to the following six characteristics. There is a clear beginning of the Christian life which commonly takes the form of a tumultuous experience of being filled with the Spirit. The ongoing Christian life contains an awareness of the sense of the presence and power of God, a joy in God, and an enthusiasm about God. God is seen as involved and intervening in the world, changing and healing. The Christian community is open to God who acts, guides and speaks to and through the Church. Charism-based ministry has priority over office-based ministry. There is a strong awareness of the devil and the demonic.

The charismatic movement in Britain was also affected by the arrival in the early 1980s of a Californian pastor, John Wimber, whose church had experienced a Pentecostal revival in 1981 which had led him to found a network of 'Vineyard' churches across the USA.

> The Wimber approach is that the words of Jesus must be validated by the works of Jesus. What the Holy Spirit does when he comes is to confirm the message by signs and wonders. In the Wimber jargon this is 'power evangelism'. It is seen as part of the great commission of Matthew 28, where Jesus commands the disciples not only to preach the gospel to all nations but to do 'all that I have commanded you'. This includes all manner of signs and wonders including healing the sick and casting out demons. John Wimber and the Vineyard aim to release this ministry not just to a few but all the people of God.
> (Scotland, 1995, pp.16-17)

This was the so-called 'third wave' (Springer, 1987, p. 44f): 'a new moving of the Holy Spirit among Evangelicals who, for one reason or another, have chosen not to identify with either Pentecostals or the Charismatics' (Hummel, 1993, p.201). Some Anglicans, including clergy, left Church of England churches to join some of the Vineyard churches that were springing up in the UK. Percy, in his doctoral study, interpreted Wimber as a fundamentalist holding rigorously to the doctrine of scriptural inerrancy, engaged primarily 'in his own particular holy war with weak, powerless or dead churches' (Percy, 1993, p.42). Whether fundamentalism and the charismatic movement were essential companions was a question which was not much addressed at this time.

For Anglican Evangelicals the establishment of the Anglican Evangelical Assembly in 1983 provided an important forum for discussion and debate across the different strands of Evangelicalism. Many opportunities were taken in the decade to reach out evangelistically to the people of this country. The Nationwide Initiative in Evangelism (1980) helped local churches across the denominations to look at the needs of their areas, and introduced the idea of a 'mission audit' which the *Faith in the City* report (1986) encouraged all local churches to employ. In 1983 Luis Palau led a Mission to London. In 1984 Billy Graham led Mission England. Graham returned to England for another Mission in 1989. A survey of those who went forward at Mission England found that eighteen months later over half were regularly attending a place of worship (Back, 1989). The Lambeth Conference of 1988 called for a 'Decade of Evangelism', and put pressure on dioceses to make plans for it. As a response to these efforts in evangelism the English Church Census was carried out in October 1989 (Brierley, 1991).

> None of these was a wholly or partisanly 'Evangelical' thrust but, as the Church of England swung (creakingly, of course) towards the objective of evangelism, Evangelicals not only found the official agenda pushing them in the right direction ... but also found themselves up in the vanguard helping to set the route and round up the followers.
> (Buchanan, 1994, pp.105-106)

This growing confidence among Evangelicals enabled them to engage in dialogue with the liberals (Edwards and Stott, 1988), who had themselves come under scrutiny after the appointment of David Jenkins as Bishop of Durham in 1984. The Evangelicals' confidence led them also to joint essays with Anglo-Catholics in preparation for Lambeth 1988 (Baxter, 1987). Baxter in her preface cited Sykes' comment that no-one's loyalty to Anglicanism should 'be more than strictly penultimate' (Baxter, 1987, p.xii).

> So we cannot accept as either fair or accurate other Anglicans' view of us as 'parties' within Anglicanism. Anglicanism at its best is not the pursuit of moderation for its own sake; it is rather the fruitful and positive interaction of our two traditions, and its dynamic is the hope of their final and total reconciliation.
> (Baxter, 1987, p.xiii)

Williams (1981, p.115) though pointed out a continuing antagonistic attitude between the Evangelical Movement in Wales and the charismatic renewal which later surfaced in England as well.

'The Sea of Faith' began in the 1860s as a phrase from Matthew Arnold's picture of the decline of religion as the retreat of the tide on Dover beach. In 1984 the phrase became the title used for a BBC television series and a related book (Cupitt, 1984). The ideas behind Cupitt's approach formed a focus for some liberals and 'Sea of Faith' became the name for a network of radical Christians. For many liberals though Cupitt's move from radical liberalism to non-realism was a step too far (Ward, 1997). Cupitt with Maurice Wiles, Denis Nineham and Leslie Houlden had been involved in the symposium entitled *The Myth of God Incarnate* (1977). Hannaford (2000) saw the liberal scepticism epitomized in works like these continuing to colour the public perception of Anglican theology into the 21st century. He believed that non-believers were confirmed in their doubts, and the faithful were perplexed by figures who appeared to speak on behalf of the Church of England:

> [The authors] are convinced that modern historical scholarship makes it impossible to regard the traditional doctrine of the incarnation as anything more than a mythological or poetic way of expressing Christ's significance for us. Furthermore they regard this as a question of truth and not merely of interpretation. The doctrine of the incarnation is rejected not because of the

evidence, or rather the lack of it, but because no such event could ever have taken place.
(Hannaford, 2000, p.91)

As part of the background to the 1988 Lambeth Conference three books were commissioned in order to review the positions of three emphases within the Church of England: *Catholics in Crisis* (Penhale, 1986), *Evangelicals on the Move* (Saward, 1987), *Rediscovering the Middle Way* (Walker, 1988). Penhale (also Wilkinson, 1978b and Pickering, 1991) saw the post-war years for Anglo-Catholics as 'the age of uncertainty' when they lost their self-confidence, while Saward described the same period as one of growth and movement for the Evangelicals. With that penchant for alliteration that marked a certain kind of Evangelical Saward observed four kinds of Evangelicals: the Pietists, the Parochials, the Puritans, and the Protestants. In their empirical study Francis and Lankshear could say: 'Although numerically more parishes claim allegiance to the Catholic party than to the Evangelical party, it is the Evangelical churches which show most signs of vitality and growth in urban, suburban and rural areas. The Catholic churches, by way of contrast, show most signs of decay in all three areas. Indeed, the Evangelicals are on the move and the Catholics are in crisis' (Francis and Lankshear, 1996, p.19).

Part of the crisis for Anglican Catholics was highlighted by Pickering (1989) as he spelt out the confusion of terms that Catholics had in describing Catholics:

> In Anglo-Catholic terminology it is common to refer to one member of the Church of England as 'Catholic' and another as 'just Anglican'. Indeed, to this very day it is not unknown for someone to say, 'I'm not Anglican; I'm Anglo-Catholic'. It is clear from such statements that not all members can be called Catholic in the sense in which Anglo-Catholics use the word. Those who are called Catholic are so by self-designation. The dilemma is this. The Church of England must be Catholic, since it adheres to the scriptures, the creeds and the ecclesiastical orders of bishops, priests and deacons created by apostolic succession. Hence the Church is Catholic and all members must therefore be Catholic. Yet not all are Catholic! Numerically most are just 'ordinary C of E people!' What kind of Catholicism is it when in the one Church some are held to be Catholic and some are not? ... To make matters more complicated, there are held to be degrees of Catholicism amongst Anglo-Catholics. Thus, one person is 'fairly Catholic' and another is 'very Catholic'. Anglo-Catholics actually disagree amongst themselves as to who among them is 'truly' Catholic and who is not.
> (Pickering, 1989, p.143)

Carey (1988, p.267) stated that 'the Catholic party has run out of steam because it has succeeded in its aims and, consequently, has failed to discover a fresh vision for its existence as a party within the Church'. According to Pickering there was a sense that the halcyon days for Anglo-Catholics were in the past. In the following passage he discussed the Keble conference in 1983 on the Oxford Movement and Rowell's (1986) collection of papers from it: 'The fortunes of the Catholic Revival were such that they were now on the dissecting table of professional analysts, who looked back on the past, glanced at the present, and had nothing to say about the future'(Pickering, 1989, p.251). It seemed that many observers had different theories to account for the problems and struggles within Anglo-Catholicism:

> Many of the aims of the [Catholic] movement had been realised leading to transformations throughout the wider Church of England (Carey, 1988). Changes brought about in the Roman Catholic Church by the second Vatican Council undermined the authority for Anglo-Catholic thinking (Wilkinson, 1978). Structural changes and pastoral reorganization in the Church of England have made it difficult to preserve the strength of traditional Catholic parishes (Penhale, 1986). Changes both in society and in the clerical profession have undermined the Anglo-Catholic view of priesthood (Absalom, 1971, Davies, 1983). The rise of secularism has exacerbated the incomprehensibility of the Anglo-Catholic subculture (Carey, 1988). Misogynism and homosexuality have sharpened the sectarian character of Anglo-Catholic enclaves (Pickering, 1991). The Catholic movement has therefore lacked able and charismatic leaders (Pickering, 1991).
> (Francis and Lankshear, 1996, p.7)

Strains were beginning to show within Evangelicalism as well. In 1983 the Church Society replaced the whole editorial board of *Churchman* after disquiet about an article by Dunn (1982). The former editor of *Churchman* became the first editor of *Anvil*:

> The principle at stake in this case is whether the editor, guided by the editorial board, shall be at liberty to provide a journal that services the range and depth of contemporary Evangelicalism; or whether he must be ever looking over his shoulder ... to satisfy the perceptions of the council members of one society as to what Evangelicalism is, or ought to be.
> (Williams, 1984, p.1)

In 1986 the Proclamation Trust was founded, a society devoted to the traditional Evangelical priority of preaching the word. Members of the trust were seen by other Evangelicals as 'taking themselves very seriously as the last upholders of true Evangelicalism' (Buchanan, 1994, p.108).

Because for many years there had been a feeling that the 'Middle Way', as Walker (1988) designated it, had been the Anglican way, with Catholics and Evangelicals merely as colourful appendages or wings to a Broad Church, there had been little written about it as a specific form of churchmanship. The fact that in preparation for Lambeth 1988 there was a need to 'rediscover the Middle Way' showed how the tide of perception was turning. Some had felt that the Parish and People movement, which had begun in 1949 and influenced the eucharistic life of the Church so much, represented the Middle Way (Jagger, 1978) but when Eric James moved from being its director the movement stuttered and folded. Mayfield (1965) saw the Anglican of the centre in historical terms:

> Historically he is descended from the Broad Churchman who was concerned so to restate the terms of theological teaching that inconsistencies between Christian doctrine and scientific theory were removed ... The Central Churchman cannot

achieve the impossible feat of being exactly central. Indeed precise centrality has never been his goal though appearances have been deceptive. Rather his first objective has been to avoid the acerbity and bitterness of controversy. He makes a protest at the failures of the other traditions. But he is certainly not to be thought of as the uncommitted or uncertain Anglican.
(Mayfield, 1965, pp.175-177)

For most of his book Walker chose to focus not on the doctrines or practices of the Middle Way but on a person who stood as an example of the Middle Way, Bishop Bell of Chichester. Walker regarded 'the seriousness with which the world, in its spiritual needs, is taken as the context in which the Church must order its life and work' (Walker, 1988, p.100) as a mark of the Middle Way. As a result of thus taking the world as the context for the Church he felt that the ordination of women would be right:

> The vital engagement, in continuity with the tradition of the English Church ... , is surely not for us to be seeking a middle way between old party allegiances or approaches, or evangelical and catholic wings, or liberal and traditional positions, but rather that we should be looking for the heart of the matter to which we are to see ourselves as being continually recalled.
> (Walker, 1988, p.133)

Moses (1995) saw the picture of a comprehensive Church as a function of the Middle Way:

> The English tradition of comprehension and liberality have attempted to take account of wider influences; liberal protestantism, modernism, biblical orthodoxy, social reality, existentialism, liberal scepticism, liberation theology, and – in more recent times – a resurgence of theological conservatism alongside a continuing tradition of theological radicalism.
> (Moses, 1995, p.102)

Moses also saw the value of this comprehensive Church having a continuing part in the Establishment, a view that Evangelicals like Buchanan (1998) did not share.

Writing about parties in the Church of England in 1988 as Bishop of Bath and Wells Carey could say of the charismatic movement that 'it is not a party in the accepted sense of the word and for that reason has been ignored in this article' (Carey, 1988, p.271). In hindsight that seems surprising but part of the reason for his view might be that it could be said, and was said by those within and without the charismatic renewal, that the movement was only 'an experience looking for a theology' (Smail, Wright and Walker, 1993).

> The charismatics in Britain, as against, say, France and other countries, have been at best a-theological, indifferent to the theological issues the renewal raises, and at worst anti-theological, suspicious of the questions and questioners that would complicate the experiential simplicities in which they are rejoicing.
> (Smail, 1983, p.1)

The late 1980s and the early 1990s looked like a time when the charismatic movement began to find its theology. Stibbe (1993) advocated Stronstad's (1984) openly charismatic biblical study of St Luke's gospel as the beginning of that process. The advent of the *Journal of Pentecostal Theology* also contributed.

> It is now possible to be filled with the Spirit, to enjoy the specific Pentecostal charismata and Pentecostal spirituality, to believe in Pentecostal mission, and at the same time to use one's critical faculties, to develop them and to use them – as any other charism – for the kingdom of God.
> (Hollenweger, 1992, p.17)

As a result of this Pentecostal and charismatic use of the critical faculties, it became possible to talk about liberal charismatics as well as conservative charismatics. At the beginning of 1994, the first year of collection of data for the empirical research at the heart of this study, the charismatic movement was having to come to terms with the 'Toronto Blessing' which had as its focus the Airport Vineyard Church in Toronto, Canada. The range of manifestations and phenomena associated with the coming of the Holy Spirit in churches affected by the Toronto blessing were still being debated at that time (Scotland, 1995, p.202f, Roberts, 1994, Dixon, 1994, Richards, 1997).

From 1990 to 1994

When the Church of England House of Bishops published its report *Issues in Human Sexuality* in 1991, it constituted an attempt to face up to the issues of homosexuality and sexual morality. It was perceived by many as setting a double standard – one law for the clergy and another for laypeople. Perhaps inevitably a side effect was that much of the ensuing debate focused on male homosexuality (Killick and Peirce, 1997, Schmidt, 1995, Vasey, 1995). Nevertheless that debate for and against changing the Church's traditional teaching on sexuality was drawn from all shades of churchmanship within the Anglican Church.

Many writers have traced the details of progress towards the removal of all barriers to the ordination of women to the priesthood in England, culminating in the General Synod vote on 11 November 1992 (for example, Furlong, 1984 and 1991, Field-Bibb, 1991, Dowell and Williams, 1994). It was at the Lambeth Conference of 1978 that the Anglican bishops had pronounced on the legal autonomy of each province to decide on the admission of women to Holy Orders. The Church in Wales was ahead of the Church of England in ordaining women as deacons in 1980. The years between 1978 and 1992 involved much debate, proposals and counter-proposals, and the failure and success of different Measures. For example, the General Synod debate in 1986 on the Women Ordained Abroad Measure came to be seen as a vote on the specific principle of women priests rather than a Measure which would offer the same rights to visiting priests of both sexes. The Measure failed. As a step on the way to ordaining women as priests the first women deacons were ordained in the Church of England in 1987.

Just as the combination of scripture, tradition and reason had been seen as the distinctive spirit which Anglicanism holds out to the worldwide Church, so the debate about women priests could be divided into three main areas: scripture, tradition and reason.

The argument from scripture against the ordination of women could be put very simply. It stressed that Christ was male and that he chose only male apostles (so Mascall in Moore, 1978, p.23: 'Because the ordained priest is not exercising a priesthood of his own but is the agent and instrument through which Christ is exercising his priesthood, he too must be male'). This argument noted passages in the epistles which taught that women should be quiet and submissive in church, and that they should not teach or have authority (headship) over men. It identified a motif in scripture whereby woman's role from creation onwards was to be man's helper and to submit to his authority as head. Opponents to this argument (for example, Witherington, 1989) claimed that it proved too much: Christ chose only Jewish apostles; the injunction of silence would exclude women from reading the Bible or leading prayers in church; the teaching about authority would exclude the Queen as Supreme Governor of the Church of England.

The argument from tradition could be grossly simplified by saying that since the Church had never had women priests, it never could. The Church of England could not act independently of the worldwide Church. 'Multilateralist opponents of women's ordination argue that the kind of disunity introduced into the Church's ministry by allowing women to minister in one part of the Church and not others is theologically unacceptable' (Dowell and Williams, 1994, p.95). Some opponents to this argument sought evidence that there had been women priests in the past (Torgessen, 1993, Morris, 1991, Otranto, 1991). Others focused on the question of whether there was a single 'tradition' in the Church, and at what points it was right and necessary to depart from it; for example, in the creation of the Church of England itself, or over questions like slavery or clergy marriage.

The argument from reason focused on whether or not the Church of England had been pushed into the idea of ordaining women as a result of feminism and the secular movement for equality between the sexes. 'Some of these people see the ordination of women as the last straw in a growing pile of liberal straws' (Dowell and Williams, 1994, p.94). Opponents to this argument felt that, rather than being guided by secular society, the Church, because of the example of Jesus and the teaching of the New Testament, should be leading the women's movement and standing up for equality. Robbins (1996, p.64) cited Field: 'Sexism and Christianity is as much a contradiction as slavery and Christianity.'

With the passing of the motion in 1984 to prepare the legislation for the ordination of women to the priesthood the campaigns for and against began to pick up momentum. Three organizations in particular were formed to campaign actively against the legislation: the Association for the Apostolic Ministry, Women Against the Ordination of Women, and Cost of Conscience. Such groups brought together Anglo-Catholics and Evangelicals in a common cause. At about the same time Affirming Catholicism came into existence.

> It is fair to say that a major impetus behind the start of Affirming Catholicism was a reaction against the assumption, still made in some quarters, that to be a Catholic Anglican means to be opposed to the ordination of women to the priesthood.
> (John, 1995, p.12, see also Sedgwick, 1993)

At the Synod in November 1992 the motion to allow the ordination of women to the priesthood was passed by 39 votes to 13 in the House of Bishops, 176 to 74 in the House of Clergy and 169 to 82 in the House of Laity, thus achieving the two-thirds majority necessary in each House. Though there were demonstrations outside Church House and a variety of attempts in assorted courts of law to have the decision declared *ultra vires*, the voting itself was conducted in what the Archbishop of Canterbury called 'a spirit of sensitivity and understanding of one another'.

> There always seemed to be present the vague idea that when the vote went through everything would quieten down and people would 'get on with the job'; that those who could not accept the decision and decide to leave the Church would be few and once they had gone people would pull together. However, this was not to be, 'the decision did not bring peace' (Armstrong, 1993). There was a brief period of celebration which was rapidly followed by both the Church and media focusing on those who could not in conscience accept the decision.
> (Robbins, 1996, p.51)

Those opposed to the decision coalesced into two groups mainly according to churchmanship. The first group, Forward in Faith, which was primarily comprised of Anglo-Catholics, made their major stratagem the recommendation of a Church within a Church, a move which the appointment of Provincial Episcopal Visitors (flying bishops) and the language of 'two integrities' seemed to encourage:

> As part of the recognition of those in conscience opposed, three bishops ... have been consecrated to look after the interests of those parishes, priests and people who wish to preserve the faith and order in which they believe. Many of these regard themselves as Catholics within the Church of England, but many others are firmly Evangelical in theology and practice. It is the so-called liberal establishment of the Church which has brought about this change and altered the self-understanding of our Church.
> (Forward in Faith publicity material)

The second group opposed to the decision to ordain women as priests was Reform, substantially comprised of conservative Evangelicals – though the conservative Evangelical John Stott had concerns about the group (Dudley-Smith, 2001, p.414). One of the actions of their members was the withholding of part of their Church's annual financial quota from dioceses. Reform felt that it represented mainstream Evangelicals:

> These clergy would have been described as 'mainstream Evangelicals'. The 1989 English Church Census by MARC Europe distinguished 'broad', 'mainstream' and 'charismatic' Evangelicals. While there is some overlap in these categories,

the survey shows that the only consistently growing segment of the Church of England is made up of mainstream Evangelicals. This group, therefore, felt the responsibility for asking the question, 'how can we help the nation and the Church?' They saw three options.

The first is to 'opt-out', to ignore the wider Church, and simply to engage in a caring, intelligent, and thorough local parochial ministry. This was a strategy employed by Anglican Evangelicals earlier this century. The long-term result, however, was an unchallenged liberal-Catholic leadership and the present situation.

The second option is to work for 'evolution' and to follow the strategy adopted since the Evangelical Congress at Keele in 1967. Evangelicals then decided to 'enter' the structures of the Church at every level and participate fully so as to 'capture the Church of England' for an Evangelical gospel. It is now clear, however, that this strategy has resulted in many Evangelicals being captured by the Church of England and themselves appearing ineffective for Jesus Christ. The third option is to work for 'reform' – not through the centre but through the parishes and congregations of our land – the grass roots – committed together and helping each other. This is a policy of deliberate and, where necessary, revolutionary change from the 'bottom'. The parochial clergy that met on 20/21 January [1993] were convinced that the only hope for the Church of England was in such reform.
(Holloway, 1993)

Other Evangelicals more in favour of the ordination of women as priests felt that Reform was a single-issue organization:

Although its initial statements did not make it clear that the movement stood against such ordinations as its prime task, yet its being occasioned by that decision was symptomatic of its stance. The Synod decision may have been more of a last straw than a sole test of apostatizing, but the relationship of the decision and the formation of Reform looks fairly close.
(Buchanan, 1994, p.108)

The late Cardinal Basil Hume seemed almost impatient after the vote in favour of the ordination of women to seize the time and said that 'this could be a moment of grace, it could be the conversion of England, for which we have prayed all these years' (Petre, 1994).

The first women priests were ordained in Bristol Cathedral by the Bishop on Saturday March 12th 1994 with ordinations in other dioceses following during the course of the year. As a result, in April the former Bishop of London, Graham Leonard, left the Church of England and was re-ordained as a priest of the Roman Catholic Church. By November it became apparent that the number of clergy who had resigned over the ordination of women was far lower than expected. Two Provincial Episcopal Visitors, or 'flying bishops', were appointed to give oversight to those opposed to the ordination of women. They were chosen because, according to the Archbishop of Canterbury, 'they have both opposed ordination of women to the priesthood but believe the arrangements provided by Synod enable them, and others also opposed, to remain with dignity and integrity within the Church of England'.

It had been expected that the Church in Wales would vote to ordain women as priests before the Church of England because there had been women deacons in its ministry since 1980, but the Governing Body did not reach the level of approval necessary to take the same step as their English colleagues. At that time out of nearly seven hundred stipendiary clergy in the Church in Wales 62 were women deacons with another 30 in training (Francis and Robbins, 1996a).

The surveys on which the empirical study reported later in this book was based began with all those ordained as stipendiary deacons in the Church of England and the Church in Wales in 1994. The year is seen to be particularly significant because women training alongside men knew for the first time that they too would be ordained to the priesthood after a year as a deacon.

What was 1994 like?

In the prologue to *The Go-Between* L.P. Hartley wrote: 'The past is a foreign country: they do things differently there.' Though this study will be looking at those who were first ordained in the recent past, 1994, it is all too easy to forget what was in the forefront of people's minds and attentions at that time. It is important to remember some aspects of the immediate ecclesiastical, social and political context for this was the atmosphere that these new clergy were breathing. The decrees, publications and practices of the Church of England and the Church in Wales coalesced with these contemporary influences in the minds of the newly ordained clergy.

Within the Church of England declining numbers of ordinands led to the closure at the end of the summer term of Chichester theological college and Salisbury and Wells theological college as the proposals of the Hereford report were put into practice.

In October the new Bishop of Salisbury, David Stancliffe, after spending three months touring all 452 parishes in his new diocese announced a plan to deal with the serious shortage of clergy in Salisbury diocese. Stancliffe had nearly 600 churches spread across his two thousand square mile diocese with only 270 full-time stipendiary clergy to care for them so he decided that the only solution to the clergy shortage was to ordain up to two hundred more. He asked each parish without a vicar to nominate a man or woman to be ordained. The chosen lay leader, already likely to have an active role in the church, would then become a non-stipendiary part-time member of the clergy. If the local vicarage had not been sold they could move into it. A diocesan spokesman said in *The Times* of October 18th, 'This is answering the cry of "Give us back our vicar", in the same way as villages cried "give us back our bobbies". Villagers didn't realise until they lost him what a vital, unifying figure the vicar was.'

Anthony Freeman, the Bishop of Chichester's chaplain and Director of Ordinands, was dismissed by his Bishop in July for 'taking leave of God'. His views were seen as too liberal for the Church of England. In his final sermon Freeman compared himself with Jeremiah. The fact that he was able to be dismissed because he was serving as a diocesan officer on a contract rather than having a parson's freehold, raised questions about the job security of the clergy. Concern too was expressed about low clergy pay which left numbers of clergy on the breadline. It was not entirely coincidental that the Manufacturing, Science and Finance trade union established a clergy section to defend clergy working rights. It and its predecessor, the Association of Managerial, Scientific and Technical Staff, had had clergy members for nearly twenty years, but now the clergy were to have their own section.

The General Synod meeting in York in July agreed to the Liturgical Commission undertaking a survey of the way in which inclusive language was used in church worship. The synod was told that the commission would not seek to introduce liturgies that addressed God using feminine forms, but that new writing would be sensitive to the use of gender-specific pronouns. Traditionalists saw this as reinforcing their fear that the ordination of women priests had set in motion a whole feminist agenda.

The severe decline in the value of the assets of the Church Commissioners as a result of poor investment policy reported in February led to the setting-up of a commission under the Bishop of Durham to look at the overhaul of the decision-making structures of the Church of England. The Church Commissioners, in their annual review of spending, gave consideration to selling some of their historic bishop's palaces in order to fund stipends. Out of 43 see houses only 14 were secure: the fate of the others was not clarified.

In January the Duchess of Kent's decision to join the Roman Catholic Church raised questions about the repeal of the Act of Settlement. Fuel was added to this discussion in July when Prince Charles spoke on television both of his adultery, and of his being a 'defender of faith', rather than Defender of the Faith. Questions were raised about his position as Supreme Governor of the Church of England when and if he became King. There was much discussion about disestablishment. In July the Prince of Wales confessed in a television documentary to adultery. Soon afterwards the Prime Minister gave his backing to the Prince of Wales' statement that divorce would not prevent his succession to the throne. In October the Prince and Princess of Wales denied that they were planning to divorce. In December the General Synod debated a private member's motion allowing divorcees to remarry in church.

In November the Bishop of Durham called for a wider exploration within the Church of England of the issues surrounding homosexuality. At the end of the month the homosexual protest group OutRage publicly named ten Anglican bishops as homosexuals in a demonstration outside Church House, Westminster.

At the beginning of the year the religious phenomenon known as the 'Toronto Blessing' was first reported in Britain. It reached national attention in June when Holy Trinity Brompton carried a report in its parish newsletter under the headline 'Holy Spirit fever hits London'. According to a report in the *Church of England Newspaper* of June 18th, a service at Holy Trinity the previous weekend ended in chaos as dozens of people burst into spontaneous laughter or tears, trembled and shook or fell to the floor. The phenomena were seen by some as signalling a new revival in the Church.

In national politics the death of the Labour party leader, John Smith, on Thursday May 12th led to the election of Tony Blair as the leader of the party.

Some indication of the varieties within churchmanship labels

In understanding the influence of churchmanship on who the clergy are and on what they do, this historical setting and particularly the debate over the ordination of women, contributed enormously. The range of churchmanship positions was vast, and within what previous generations had seen as united and like-minded parties there were significant and subtle differences.

This could be seen amongst those who belonged to the Middle Way as they saw their centrist position invaded by those who were calling the Church and its churchmanships to rediscover and reconstruct the Middle Way (McGrath, 1993, pp.99-133). Was there still to be a place for the Broad Church (Badham, 1998)?

Amongst Anglican Catholics there could clearly be seen charismatics, liberals and conservatives, but could they ever again have a common mind?

> Affirming Catholicism ... well captures the essence and flavour of that wing of Anglo-Catholicism in the last decade of the twentieth century which saw itself as a true inheritor of the Anglican Catholic tradition, and its role as a true and faithful interpretor [sic] of that tradition. It also demonstrates the profound divisions within late twentieth century Anglican Catholicism. For on the one hand the liberal Anglican Catholics were highly critical of the conservative Anglican Catholics, while on the other hand some of the conservatives were even of the opinion that certain of the liberals had discarded so much basic Christian doctrinal and moral teaching that it brought into question their right to be called Christian, let alone Catholic.
> (Hylson-Smith, 1993, p.366)

There was a range of opinions within Anglican Evangelicalism. 'Evangelicalism, once a coalition of Arminians and Calvinists, baptists and paedo-baptists, is now so stretched and varied that those at opposite ends of the spectrum are scarcely able to recognize one another' (Wright, 1986, p.48). Cocksworth (1993, p.3) commented: 'the breadth of contemporary Evangelicalism ... spans Reformed rigorists on the one side and charismatic innovators on the other – with a good deal in between'. Kings, writing about Conservative Evangelicals, said:

> Currently there is a firm belief that liturgical revision is moving the Church away from Reformation doctrine and that many Evangelicals who hold positions of responsibility in the Church are no longer authentically Evangelical. Is this feeling of marginalization essential to Conservative Evangelicalism, so that it is difficult to recognize the position of strength Evangelicals generally have in the Church of England?
> (Kings, 2003, p.174)

Within the charismatic movement too it was recognized that a wide range of churchmanship was represented. Some thought that this was part of the movement's strength, that it was found among people of all theological persuasions; catholic, liberal, conservative and fundamentalist (Scotland, 1995, p.17). Others, like Cuthbert (1994), regarded this as a sign of crisis for the charismatic movement.

> There seems a growing tendency to encapsulate the earlier vigorous charisma in intellectual bookish spiritualities. Ignatian and Celtic spiritualities seem to be favoured by Anglicans in particular. The danger here is that the whole charismatic experience will become routinized in a sedate and sophisticated cultural ethos based on bookish middle-class disciplines. All of this looks like becoming a classic illustration of Richard Niebuhr's theory that vital charisma experiences degenerate into church-type experiences in one generation.
> (Scotland, 1995, p.250)

Postscript

This chapter has shown that there is colossal diversity in Anglican practice. The following extract, cited by Davie (1994) from a bishop's diocesan news-sheet in 1992, describing – from the point of view of a visiting bishop – the liturgical unpredictability characteristic of much Anglicanism at that time, may serve as an appropriate postscript to that diversity.

> We come across every rite authorized for use in the Church of England, and occasionally liturgies which seem to have been borrowed from other sources or simply originated in the mind of the incumbent; we move from places wreathed in incense to those in which the unwary production of a stole causes a sharp intake of breath; we lead services in which the congregational response barely amounts to a background murmur, and those in which there are so many participants it is difficult to find something to do; we change musical key from decorous Anglican chant to deafening, enthusiastic chorus; we bellow to a handful of 20 scattered throughout a mini-cathedral, and we whisper through technological devices concealed in our garments to sardine-packed hundreds; we find ourselves in totally impracticable medieval buildings of great beauty, and in modern liturgically-efficient warehouses; we sing from more hymn books and hear the bible read from more translations than Wesley or Wycliffe ever dreamed of; at the Peace we may give the congregation the most imperceptible half-smile before moving swiftly to the safety of the sanctuary, or we may be expected to greet every member of the congregation like a long-lost relative.
> (Davie, 1994, p.54)

Chapter 2

Measuring churchmanship differences

Introduction

The first chapter has shown what a significant part churchmanship and churchmanship groups have played in the history of the Anglican Church in England and Wales. The range of groups encountered is large: Latitudinarians, Modernists, High Church and so on. Researchers have recognized the need to take account of churchmanship, if only at the level of wanting to know the strength of the parties. In this chapter therefore an overview of the use of churchmanship in empirical research will be set out. Though the account is mainly chronological it will follow two different paths. In the first part the focus will be on those quantitative studies which used a labelling approach with the respondent either choosing a churchmanship self-designation from a list provided, or offering their own designation. In the second part the focus will be on the use of bipolar scales along which the respondents mark their churchmanship position.

Early research

The history of Anglican churchmanship in the nineteenth century outlined in the previous chapter led, perhaps inevitably, to a focusing on one dimension only, that of Tractarians and Evangelicals. However when Coneybeare (1853), one of the earliest researchers in the area of churchmanship, looked at this matter, he recognized that there were not two, nor even three, but nine parties in sight:

> They are commonly called the Low Church, the High Church, and the Broad Church parties; but such an enumeration is the result of an incomplete analysis. On a closer inspection, it is seen that each of these is again triply subdivided into sections which exemplify respectively the exaggeration, the stagnation, and the normal development of the principles which they severally claim to represent. And these subdivisions, though popularly confounded with each other, differ amongst themselves, as much as the delirium of fever or the torpor of old age differs from the calm circulation of health.
> (Coneybeare, 1853, p.273)

Coneybeare subsequently collated two of the Broad Church sections in order to make a choice of eight churchmanship patterns. His statistical enquiry however was not particularly rigorous: 'we have gone through the Clergy List, marking the names of all the clergymen whose opinions we knew, to the number of about 500.

The result of this examination has been that supposing those unknown to us to be in the same proportions with those known, we should be led to classify the 18 000 clergy of the Church of England as follows' (p.338). He also excluded '1000 peasant clergy in the mountain districts who must be classed apart'. He identified 41 per cent of the clergy as 'High Church': this comprised 3500 'Anglican', 2500 'High and Dry' and 1000 'Tractarian'. He identified 38 per cent as 'Low Church': this comprised 3300 'Evangelical', 2500 'Recordite' (those who read *The Record* newspaper) and 700 'Low and Slow'. Finally he identified 21 per cent as 'Broad Church': this comprised 2500 'Anti-theoretical' and 1000 'Theoretical' clergy. Of the 28 bishops and archbishops, Coneybeare designated 13 as belonging to various shades of High Church, 5 to the Evangelical parties, and 10 to the Broad Church. The under-representation of Low Churchmen among the bishops was accounted for partly by reference to the social background of the Low Church tradition which, according to him, tended to be lower class. For Coneybeare such variety was a cause for rejoicing:

> Whatever may be the relative strength of these subdivisions, it is evident that the triple cord in which they interlace could not easily be untwisted; nor could either of its strands be cut, without a risk of severing the rest. The object of every wise churchman should be to keep each of the main schools of opinion from extravagance on the one hand, and from stagnation on the other; and the existence of counteracting parties is a check providentially operating for this end. Nor should we forget that the differences which divide each from each are much exaggerated by party-spirit. Most of them can be resolved into mere disputes about terms, which might be ended by stricter definition. Those which lie deeper result from a difference of mental constitution, and belong to the domain of metaphysics rather than of religion.
> (Coneybeare, 1853, p.339)

Despite Coneybeare's awareness that High Church, for example, was not the definition of one group but of several parties grouped together, most researchers in the first half of the twentieth century preferred the simplicity of 'Catholic' or 'Evangelical' or 'Broad church' as the only categories they used when studying churchmanship.

Research by Towler and Coxon

The assumption that churchmanship was only related to the Catholic/Evangelical spectrum began to change with Towler and Coxon. Though their major study of clergy and their churchmanship was not published until 1979 it drew most of its data from two studies in the 1960s: the first by Coxon in 1962 was of 30 per cent of all ordinands in training at English theological colleges; the second by Towler in 1966 was of that year's intake of ordinands at five theological colleges. An important focus in their study was the two types of ordinand whom they called 'puritan' and 'antipuritan'. The puritan tended to live in a wholly religious world, appeared to be a philistine in cultural and artistic matters, and really enjoyed services, prayer meetings and private devotions. The antipuritan treated church activities as something of a chore, was very committed to particular secular interests, and was almost completely detached from worship and prayer, regarding them as matters of observance and obligation.

Towler and Coxon (1979) offered six churchmanship labels to their respondents (Anglo-catholic, Prayer Book catholic, central churchman, modernist, liberal evangelical, and conservative evangelical) which they then collapsed into three groups: catholics, modernists and evangelicals. The following passage shows their awareness of the complexity of the task that such labelling presented:

> We recognise that these labels imply generalizations which, like all generalizations, are no more than approximations. Many complexities and variations of belief are gathered under each of these umbrellas. But none the less the labels are a useful shorthand description of different types of churchmanship. 'Modernist' is the most unsatisfactory of the three labels, since it was so specific to one historical period, but we shall employ it while bearing this in mind, not least because our analysis will tend to undermine the tripartite division from which we start.
> In the 1960s there were many clergymen and ordinands who felt less than comfortable with these labels, but there can be little doubt that they were worn. The modernists were out of sympathy with both the catholic and evangelical parties, seeing certain other considerations as more important than the things which divided those two groups.
> Others were out of sympathy with the two major parties without wishing to think of themselves as modernists; they were in some ways the latitudinarians of the 1960s, and sometimes they called themselves 'Central Churchmen', but we classed them with the modernists because they shared the objections to the 'two-party system'. A great many Anglicans, however, and most ordinands, were ready to describe themselves as catholics or evangelicals, even if with strong reservations. Catholics who were definite and extreme in their identification designated themselves as Anglo catholics, leaving their more cautious brethren to refer to themselves as Prayer Book catholics, meaning that their sympathies would not permit them to stray far outside the usages permitted by the Book of Common Prayer interpreted in a catholic sense. Anglo-catholics, by contrast, made free use of the Roman Missal and looked to Rome for guidance. The evangelicals were subdivided into conservative and liberal evangelicals. The former group were strongly committed to belief in the supreme authority of scripture and in the importance of a Christian's having a personal experience of conversion. The latter group placed rather less emphasis on these beliefs but shared with the conservative evangelicals a dislike of strong church authority, preferring individual commitment, and thus feeling themselves generally at one with other non-extreme Protestants and opposed to the spirit of the Church of Rome.
> (Towler and Coxon, 1979, pp.106-107)

Towler and Coxon found that 47 per cent of the ordinands described themselves as catholics, 23 per cent as modernists, and 30 per cent as evangelicals. 'Almost all the puritans are evangelical, and the antipuritans are either catholic or modernist; conversely, evangelicals are puritans, modernists are antipuritans, and catholics are a mixture' (Towler and Coxon, 1979, p.108). Towler and Coxon observed some changes occurring to these ordinands' definitions of their churchmanship while they were at theological college. Most of the men at St Chad's Durham began as Prayer Book catholic and there was little change after two years; Mirfield men were either Anglo-catholic or Prayer Book catholic and again there was little change over two years; those going to Westcott House identified themselves predominantly as central churchmen, with some Prayer Book catholics and some Anglo-catholics – after two years more of them had identified themselves as central. At Oak Hill by the end of two years only two men persisted in calling themselves 'liberal evangelicals', all the rest chose to be known as 'conservative evangelicals'. If there was a pattern in these results it was that the catholics were becoming less dogmatic, and the evangelicals (though admittedly Towler and Coxon studied only one evangelical college, Oak Hill) more dogmatic.

Research by Daniel

Daniel (1967) was the first to see the need for, and make use of, a second dimension as well as the standard Catholic/Evangelical axis. His was a sociological study arising from interviews with 96 clergymen serving in the Greater London Council area and ordained in 1955, 1960 or 1965. He was concerned to discover whether or not the new currents of theological thought in the 1960s, outlined in chapter 1 of this book, were changing the clergy's self-image. His conclusion was that churchmanship was the main criterion for determining the clergy's reaction to new ideas. 'The factor determining which alternative a clergyman will choose is the particular religious ideology which he already holds – that nexus of beliefs and interpretations which in the Church of England is called churchmanship' (Daniel, 1968, p.117).

Daniel made an attempt to infer churchmanship from the theological college which a member of the clergy had attended, but it proved impossible. So in order to formulate a question with which to ask the clergy about their churchmanship, Daniel explored the concept of churchmanship as an ideological position. He plotted churchmanship positions on two axes representing sources of authority. 'In practice, churchmanship positions usually appeal to authority of the Bible (evangelical), or of the Church (catholic), in the first place, and after that to tradition (conservative), or to human reason (liberal).' (Daniel, 1967, p.45)

He therefore constructed a chart of the empirical churchmanship position of individuals (figure 2.1). 'Thus an Anglo-Catholic might have conservative or liberal leanings. Billy Graham would probably occupy a position in the bottom left hand corner of the diagram, and the Bishop of Woolwich in the top right hand corner' (Daniel, 1967, p.46). (The Bishop of Woolwich at that time was Bishop John Robinson, the author of *Honest to God.*)

In the light of this elegant and objective approach to an area of subjective self-identification, it is rather extraordinary that the question that Daniel actually asked of his interviewees was, 'Would you be willing to be described as High Church, Low Church, Anglo-Catholic, Evangelical, Central, Modernist, Liberal, Radical, or what other description would you accept?' (p.52). Since that is the question he asked, it is not therefore surprising that he received 66 different answers from his 96 interviewees, including 'Anglo-Papist', 'Don't know any more, used to be Anglo-Catholic, perhaps liberal High Church', and 'Kinky. Any of them. High middle' (pp.129-130).

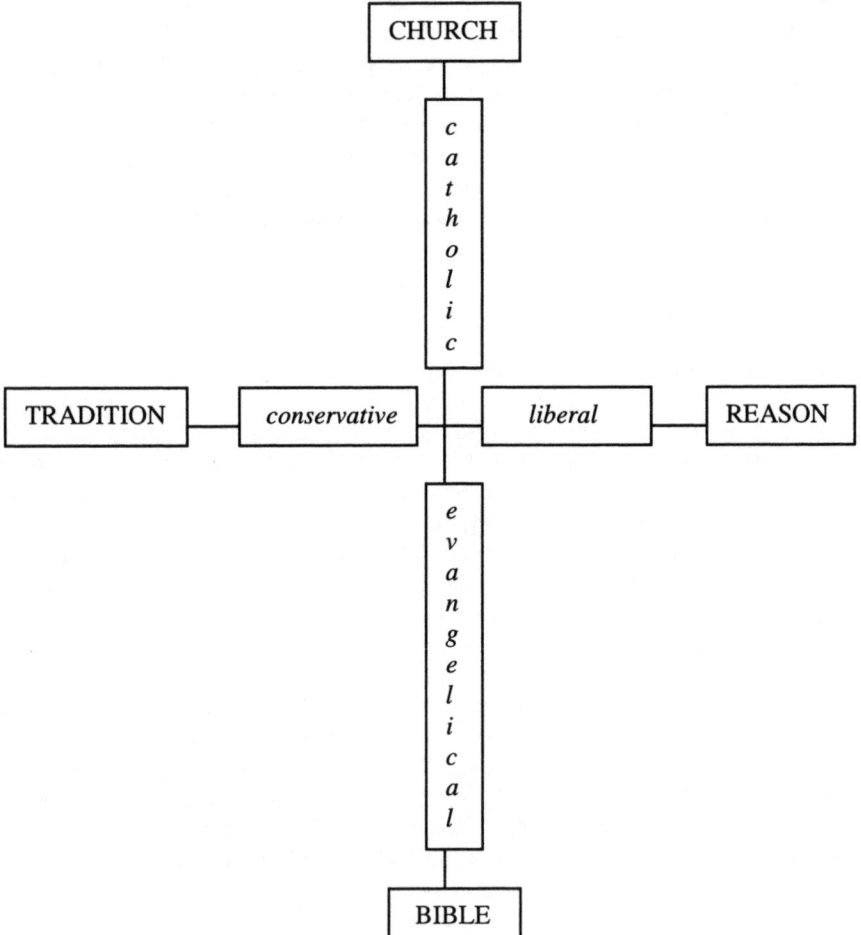

Figure 2.1 Churchmanship and sources of authority: a framework for plotting churchmanship according to subjective legitimation of beliefs (Daniel, 1967)

As a result it was rather difficult for him to draw empirical conclusions from his data. However he gained a number of 'impressions':

> Most of the evangelicals seem to have kept their theological principles intact while changing their modes of practical parish work to some extent. The catholic clergy, on the other hand, tend to have vastly changed not only their practical approach to people but also their theology, both in a liberal direction. Distinctions once clear

tend to have become blurred. There is a tendency among them to undertake more social work outside the church for the sake of its own importance, instead of for its potential as a field for religious influence, and they seem less certain about their theology than the evangelicals.
(Daniel, 1967, p.153)

On his other dimension, Conservative/Liberal, Daniel's impressions were that 'nearly half the clergy thought that they were, theologically speaking, conservatives, while almost a third thought that they were theologically liberals. Nevertheless, more than half said that they had become more liberal than they were a few years ago, and only less than a fifth said they had moved the other way' (Daniel, 1968, p.120).

The Runcie Report

In 1970 the Church of England published the Runcie Report on the reorganization of theological colleges. It set the typology for colleges that Daniel had been seeking by allocating each of them to one of three groups, Evangelical, Tractarian, and Other. At the time of the report there was a great deal of debate about the propriety of putting certain colleges in certain groups but the overall classification was accepted by the House of Bishops. This classification has continued in use in official Church of England documents about theological training and as a means of assessing the balance of churchmanship of ordinands. At the time of the Runcie Report 34 per cent of ordinands attended Evangelical colleges, 27 per cent Tractarian colleges, and 40 per cent Other colleges.

Research by Ranson, Bryman and Hinings

Bryman, Ranson and Hinings described churchmanship as 'that theological stance, or framework of religious belief, which defines a person's relation to God in specific forms of devotional and ritualistic activities, and defines for that person how to interpret his or her faith in the secular world' (Bryman, Ranson and Hinings, 1974, p.469). For them the basic polarity of churchmanship within Anglican theology was the Catholic/Evangelical axis. On that axis they found a Catholic pole, an Evangelical pole, and between them a 'Central' or 'Broad Church' position. However they recognized that this was inadequate as a complete methodology, and so they identified a further category of churchmanship, represented by Modernism.

Their survey group was 310 lay members of Anglican deanery synods. Their respondents defined themselves as: 21 per cent Catholic, 55 per cent Central or Broad Church, 12 per cent Evangelical, 8 per cent Modernist, and 3 per cent Other. When the respondents were asked to rate seven ministerial roles (administrator, celebrant, leader, preacher, official, pastor, and counsellor) in order of priority, first or second priority was given to the role of celebrant by 78 per cent of Catholics, by 54 per cent of Centralists, by 39 per cent of Modernists and by 20 per cent of Evangelicals. Similarly, the preacher role was rated first or second in priority by 68 per cent of Evangelicals, by 33 per cent of Catholics, by 31 per cent of Centralists, and by 28 per cent of Modernists.

In 1977 Ranson, Bryman and Hinings published a study of Anglican clergy, Methodist ministers and Roman Catholic priests. By that time they had increased the range of choice of churchmanships, or 'theological cosmologies' as they sometimes preferred to call them, from the five in their 1974 study to eight. They offered two catholic choices (Anglo-Catholic, and Prayer Book Catholic), two modernist choices (Modernist, and New Theology), and two evangelical choices (Liberal Evangelical, and Conservative Evangelical), alongside Central/Broad Church, and Other. Again they recognized that not all forms of churchmanship can be located on the Catholic-Evangelical axis. 'Anglo-Catholic' and 'Prayer Book Catholic' comprised 40 per cent of the Anglican clergy, 'Central' and 'Broad Church' 25 per cent, 'Liberal Evangelical' and 'Conservative Evangelical' 19 per cent, 'Other' 9 per cent and 'Modernist' and 'New Theology' 7 per cent. In noting how these figures compared with those found by Coneybeare (1853) they drew attention to the stability of the numbers for High Churchmen and those of a Broad Church persuasion. However they also noted that younger clergy were more likely to class themselves as Modernists or Evangelicals, whereas older clergy were more likely to be Catholic or Broad Church. 'Whereas in Coneybeare's day more than a third of clergymen supported an Evangelical theological cosmology, this brand of churchmanship is now followed by less than 20 per cent of clergy. Evangelicalism within the Anglican faith has been somewhat eroded by the incipient development of a more radical theological persuasion' (Ranson, Bryman and Hinings, 1977, p.147).

However this was one of several of their conclusions about which Bryman (1989) raised questions after his partial re-study in 1985 in which he found that the Evangelicals were increasing in number and then comprised about a quarter of his respondents. He also made an important point about future development of churchmanship categories:

> The churchmanship categories with which Anglican respondents were presented in 1971 were reasonable for that time; but in 1985 if the researcher wanted to reflect contemporary theological issues, the response categories would be different, probably reflecting the influence of the charismatic movement.
> (Bryman 1989, p.49)

This is the first recognition by an empirical researcher of the importance of including the charismatic in a definition of churchmanship.

Surveys of theological training

Hodge (1988) was commissioned by the Church of England to produce a report on patterns of ministerial training. He used the Runcie (1970) classification of theological colleges in order to report on the balance of churchmanship amongst those training for stipendiary ministry. In 1985 the figures were: 49 per cent at Evangelical colleges, 25 per cent at Tractarian colleges, and 26 per cent at Other colleges (Hodge, 1988, p.11). These results showed a gradual rise in the number at Evangelical colleges, a stable number at Catholic colleges, and a steady decline in the number training at colleges in the Other category. This was leading to a difficulty for Evangelicals in finding parishes in which to serve their curacy. Hodge reported 'a larger proportion (59.4%) of men trained at Evangelical colleges were ordained in dioceses other than their sponsoring diocese than was the case among those trained at Catholic (36.0%) and Central (33.9%) colleges' (Hodge, 1988, p.16).

Bunting (1990) reported a survey of all the Christian theological colleges and courses in the United Kingdom. In analysing the results for Anglican colleges and courses he also made use of the Runcie classification (though calling the groups 'High', 'Middle', and 'Low'). Across the colleges and courses he found that overall the trainers gave the highest priority to developing in the clergy under training the role of practical theologian. However trainers at High and Middle colleges, as in Towler and Coxon's (1979) study, continued to give the highest priority to the role of priest and the lowest to the role of evangelist, and trainers at the Low colleges gave the highest priority to the role of preacher and the lowest to the role of priest.

Research by Brierley

On Sunday October 15th 1989 tens of thousands of English churches took part in a Church Census. It was one of the most thorough and comprehensive surveys of churchgoing ever undertaken in this country and was reported by Brierley (1991). Almost 27 000 forms were returned by churches giving a response rate of 70 per cent. One of the questions related to the churchmanship of each church. Of those who responded 89 per cent answered the question, 'Which of these terms or which combination of them would best describe your congregation?' The choices offered were: Anglo-Catholic, Liberal, Catholic, Evangelical, Broad, Charismatic, Low Church, Orthodox, Radical, and Other (which mostly seemed to cover members of the Quakers and the Salvation Army). Respondents could choose up to three responses. Because 54 per cent chose one, 31 per cent two, and 15 per cent three, the total number of replies came to 169 per cent of the responses. The categories were therefore grouped for analysis. The results for Anglican churchgoers were as follows: Broad Evangelical (13 per cent), Mainstream Evangelical (4 per cent), Charismatic Evangelical (9 per cent), Low Church (10 per cent), Broad (18 per cent), Liberal (20 per cent), Anglo-Catholic (12 per cent), Catholic (13 per cent), and 1 per cent for all other choices. Brierley commented on these Anglican results: 'Truly something for everyone, and perhaps a correct feature for the State Church' (1991, p.162).

The Rural Church Project

Between 1988 and 1990 research was conducted for the Rural Church Project, a study comprising both quantitative and qualitative research methods: a postal survey of 572 Anglican clergy in five dioceses and face-to-face interviews with 101 clergy and 489 of their parishioners. It overlapped with the 1990 *Faith in the Countryside* report of the Archbishops' Commission on Rural Areas (ACORA).

Davies and colleagues saw the prime dimension of churchmanship as being Catholic/Evangelical. They therefore offered the clergy respondents to the questionnaire the opportunity to identify themselves in terms of one of five categories: Conservative Evangelical, Open Evangelical, Traditional Catholic, Modern Catholic or Central Churchmanship. Their rationale for these five was that 'these categories are widely recognized in the contemporary Church of England as descriptions of degrees of commitment to forms of doctrine and liturgical practice. They are, for example, regularly used in *The Church Times* newspaper in advertisements for parish priests' (Davies, 1993, p.8). However they also recognized that 'churchmanship in its traditional form is no longer the only major influence on the clergy because of more recent intellectual and emotional trends in theology' (Davies, 1993, p.7). So, in addition to the five categories of churchmanship offered, the questionnaire also gave respondents the opportunity to tick a box to indicate whether or not they also saw in themselves what the authors called a 'spiritual style', namely Charismatic, Liberal, or Radical. By 'spiritual style' they meant 'the stress, emphasis, and ethos brought to a priest's interpretation of the faith and to his ministry'.

> It was assumed that although many individuals define themselves in terms of churchmanship for some aspects of their identity, there were additional factors that would be ignored unless some such notion as spiritual style was used to discover them. Many clergy remain within the broad tradition of churchmanship in which they were brought up whilst subsequently undergoing a change of theological perspective. This change could be assessed through these qualifying descriptions but would be ignored if the study had only used the traditional categories of churchmanship.
> (Davies, 1993, p.13)

Open Evangelical was the choice of 13 per cent of the clergy, Conservative Evangelical 7 per cent, Traditional Catholic 12 per cent, Modern Catholic 27 per cent and Central Churchmanship 38 per cent. Fifty four per cent chose to use a spiritual style modifier as well as the churchmanship category, but 46 per cent felt that the churchmanship category was sufficient. It was the Evangelical and Central groups who proved more likely to use a spiritual style modifier.

The Rural Church Project showed that churchmanship was also strongly affected by age, with open evangelicals and modern catholics firmly represented in the 'under forty year old' age group, and central churchmen and traditional catholics accounting for a sizeable majority of clergy over the age of sixty. When the Rural Church Project looked at the number of staff, lay and ordained, paid and unpaid, working in a parish, it found that churchmanship was a significant variable, with the general rule being the more evangelical the clergyman, the greater the number of staff he is likely to have around him. This relationship was especially clear in the case of lay staff, where the average number of staff in conservative evangelical benefices was nearly three times as high as that in traditional catholic benefices.

In 1999 the Clergy Appointments Adviser, who helps Church of England clergy to find ministerial posts, was using a modified version of the Rural Church Project's list of labels. His questionnaire offered five churchmanship traditions: Conservative Evangelical, Open Evangelical, Central, Modern Catholic or Traditional Catholic. In addition respondents were offered the choice of one of two modifiers: 'Charismatic' or 'Influenced by Renewal'.

All the empirical studies reported so far in this chapter have relied on a label-choosing method for ascertaining churchmanship: a set of labels is laid out for the respondents to tick a box or boxes for the ones which they would apply to themselves. What limits the respondent is the range of labels which the researcher provides. Coneybeare (1853) had eight labels; Towler and Coxon (1979) six; Daniel (1967) offered eight but was given 66 different answers; Ranson and colleagues offered five (1974) or eight (1977); Brierley (1991) offered nine but allowed up to three choices; Davies and colleagues (1990) offered five, but each of those could be modified in one of three ways, giving potentially 15 choices.

Research by Francis and colleagues

There has been a different strand of quantitative research on churchmanship focused on Professor Leslie Francis' work with fellow researchers formerly at the Centre for Theology and Education at Trinity College Carmarthen, and latterly at the Welsh National Centre for Religious Education at the University of Wales, Bangor. It is to this different strand of research that we now turn.

In place of the labelling approach, this strategy concentrates on using two bipolar 7-point scales for the respondent to assess his or her churchmanship. The first continuum measures the Catholic/Evangelical axis, the second the Liberal/Conservative axis. The rationale for this two dimensional model of churchmanship is the same as Daniel's (1967), with each axis representing sources of authority or legitimation, whether it be Bible, Church, tradition or reason. The combination of the two scales gives a theoretical range of 49 churchmanship positions. For many practical purposes each scale is collapsed to form three groups and thus the combination of the two scales produces nine churchmanship positions.

As part of the preparation for a major Church of England report on the place of children in the Church, Francis and Lankshear conducted a detailed survey between 1986 and 1988 throughout 24 dioceses and one additional archdeaconry. Their questionnaire was developed from one previously used by Francis (1985). The response rate of 72 per cent produced information on 7159 churches. Preliminary analysis was published in chapter seven of *Children in the Way* (Board of Education, 1988). This report continues to have a significant impact on Church of England policy-making. Overall profiles of the Church of England were constructed from the data (Francis and Lankshear, 1991a). Later more sophisticated analyses of the data were undertaken to assess a range of issues from the impact of church schools on local church life in rural areas (Francis and Lankshear, 1990) to the difficulties faced by small congregations in making contact with the young (Francis and Lankshear, 1991c).

Francis and Lankshear (1995b) found that Catholic churches were more actively involved in infant baptisms, in presenting young people for confirmation, and in youth clubs than the Church of England as a whole. They also found (1995c) that Evangelical churches were less actively involved in infant baptisms, but more involved in the baptism and confirmation of older teenagers and adults and more actively involved in Sunday schools and youth work than the Church of England as a whole.

Looking at the data from these two studies, Francis and Lankshear (1996) recognized the need to undertake a more sophisticated analysis by focusing on two particular areas. First, they acknowledged the difference that environment made to the nature of churches by selecting three distinct subsets of churches – urban, suburban, and rural. Second, they used the statistical methods of multiple regression and path analysis on each subset to control for differences in size of population and electoral roll before examining the influence of churchmanship. Thus they were able to show how geographical environment influenced churchmanship: the urban churches were more likely to identify with either Evangelical or Catholic churchmanship (35 per cent as Catholic, 24 per cent as Evangelical); the rural churches were least likely to do so (17 per cent as Catholic, 13 per cent as Evangelical). So it was necessary to examine the implications of churchmanship separately in different environments. Amongst urban and suburban churches Francis and Lankshear (1996) found that the conclusions of their earlier studies (1995b and 1995c) about Catholic and Evangelical churchmanship reported above were confirmed. However the picture was more complicated in rural churches where, for example, churchmanship made no significant difference to the number of Easter communicants (Francis and Lankshear, 1996, p.17). Noting that throughout urban, suburban and rural parishes Evangelical churches are involving more adults in house groups than Catholic or Middle way churches, Francis and Lankshear came to this conclusion:

> Although numerically more parishes claim allegiance to the Catholic party than to the Evangelical party, it is the Evangelical churches which show most signs of vitality and growth in urban, suburban and rural areas. The Catholic churches, by way of contrast, show most signs of decay in all three areas. Indeed, the Evangelicals are on the move and the Catholics are in crisis.
> (Francis and Lankshear, 1996, p.19)

The charismatic element in churchmanship

Reference has been made already to the use of 'charismatic' as a contributory factor to measures of churchmanship, recognizing the impact of the Pentecostal and Charismatic movements on all the main-line churches in the twentieth century. Francis, Lankshear and Jones (2000) used the same three subsets of churches, urban, suburban and rural, as Francis and Lankshear (1996) to explore the comparative performances of churches influenced by the charismatic movement. Those completing the questionnaires were asked to assess whether each church or worship centre had been influenced by the charismatic movement. They found that the charismatic movement had touched a higher proportion of urban churches than suburban and rural ones. They showed first that in all three geographical environments churches influenced by the charismatic movement had a higher number of adults attending house groups, a higher number of 18-21 year olds and adults attending Sunday services, and a higher number of 10-13 year olds involved in young people's activities. Second, urban and suburban churches influenced by the charismatic movement had a higher number of under two year olds at Sunday services and activities, a higher number of 6-9 and 14-17 year olds involved in children's work or youth work, and a higher number of over 17 year olds seeking confirmation. Third, urban churches influenced by the charismatic movement had a higher number of 2-5 year olds at Sunday services and activities, as well as involved in children's work. Fourth, suburban churches influenced by the charismatic movement had a higher number of 14-17 year olds involved in Sunday services and activities. Fifth, urban and suburban churches influenced by the charismatic movement had fewer 10-13 year olds in church choirs and fewer 14-21 year old servers. Sixth, urban churches influenced by the charismatic movement had fewer infant baptisms, fewer Christmas communicants, and fewer 14-21 year olds and adults in church choirs.

This survey clearly suggests that the charismatic element needs to be included in any whole-hearted assessment of churchmanship.

Measuring the refinements of churchmanship

Francis, Lankshear and Jones (1998) recognized that Francis and Lankshear's original 1996 database provided sufficient refinement that differences within Evangelicalism could be acknowledged and empirically analysed. First, the positive influence of the charismatic movement could be highlighted. Second, the degree of Evangelical adherence could be displayed by distinguishing between those churches which were rated 1 or 2 or 3 on the Evangelical end of the 7-point scale. Third, by drawing on the 7-point Liberal/Conservative scale Liberal Evangelicals could be identified as different from Conservative Evangelicals. As a result they discovered that the degree of Evangelical adherence changed with the environment of the parish, with urban churches promoting the strongest and clearest identification with Evangelicalism, and rural and suburban Evangelical churches being far less intense. Urban environments were more likely to be the places where Evangelical churches were positively influenced by the charismatic movement. Cities and large towns were also the environment where the more conservative form of Evangelicalism was to be found.

Francis, Lankshear and Jones (1998) went on to run a series of regression equations with their data. The mathematical model used was powerful enough to pick up differences in the strength of Evangelical identity: strongly Evangelical churches were less likely to encourage young people to join the church choir, and in urban and suburban areas less likely to present candidates for confirmation under the age of 14. The strength of Conservative or Liberal positions made no statistical difference to the effectiveness of Evangelical churches. What did make a difference was the positive influence of the charismatic movement, leading the researchers to say: 'charismatic Evangelical churches are promoting a more effective ministry among young people in suburban, urban and rural environments than non-charismatic Evangelical churches, at least in terms of the number of young people in contact with the local churches' (1988, p.266).

Studying clergy and churchmanship

These studies by Francis and colleagues have all been analyses of the churchmanship of churches or places of worship as perceived by that church's minister. What of the minister's own churchmanship?

Rutledge (1993) used the two Francis scales of churchmanship (Catholic/Evangelical and Liberal/Conservative) with a random sample of five per cent of all serving stipendiary male clergy in England. The clergy were invited to describe their churchmanship by marking a point on two 7-point scales. Given the nature of Rutledge's sample his results are the best estimate available of the overall churchmanship of serving male Anglican clergy in England. His results are as follows: 'Strongly Catholic' 13 per cent, 'Catholic' 20 per cent, 'Mildly Catholic' 19 per cent, 'Central' 15 per cent, 'Mildly Evangelical' 8 per cent, 'Evangelical' 14 per cent and 'Strongly Evangelical' 12 per cent.

Robbins (1996) surveyed all the Anglican women deacons, deaconesses and priests in stipendiary or non-stipendiary ministry in England, Wales, Scotland and Ireland. Given the high response rate and the nature of the population studied her results are the best estimate available of the overall churchmanship of female Anglican clergy. Her results are as follows: 'Strongly Catholic' 4 per cent, 'Catholic' 12 per cent, 'Mildly Catholic' 20 per cent, 'Central' 21 per cent, 'Mildly Evangelical' 13 per cent, 'Evangelical' 18 per cent and 'Strongly Evangelical' 11 per cent. Compared to Rutledge's figures for male clergy Robbins' figures show a higher proportion of female clergy describe themselves as Evangelical compared with those describing themselves as Catholic.

Comparing the two approaches to measuring churchmanship

We have now seen that over the years there has been a substantial amount of empirical research on churchmanship following these two different approaches, the labelling approach, and the bipolar scale approach. Each have had their value and have produced much useful data for research. However both have their deficiencies. The deficiency of the labelling approach is the lack of refinement it offers for the range and subtlety of churchmanship self-designations. The deficiency of the bipolar approach is the lack of a measure that includes the charismatic. A new and fuller measure is needed which should be simple and self-explanatory, which should encompass the wide range of churchmanship positions, and which should include the charismatic.

As the history of the Anglican Church has revealed, churchmanship is an emotive and emotional concept. In attempting to measure churchmanship by applying a quantitative index to it, the researcher is likely to encounter ecclesiological, philosophical and methodological issues. The ecclesiological issues for some will concern the rightness or the possibility of measuring something which they regard as personal. However, as the first chapter revealed, language about churchmanship is widespread in the Anglican Church, both in clergy conversation about other clergy and parishes, and in the Church's official documents: the Runcie report on the reorganization of theological colleges enshrined churchmanship language and the need for a balance between churchmanship groups in Church of England policy.

What, then, are we trying to measure? The language of intrinsic and extrinsic religious orientation is useful here (Gorsuch, 1988, Kirkpatrick and Hood, 1990, Maltby and Lewis, 1996). In studying churchmanship, especially among the clergy, there is already an extrinsic dimension to the religious orientation of the respondents, marked not just by their membership of a religious body, the Anglican Church, but by their paid employment by and for that body. Is it to be extrinsic churchmanship then that is measured, marked by membership of groups like, for example, Reform or Forward in Faith? No, since the reasons for joining or not joining organizations such as those are many and not necessarily related to strength of feeling about particular churchmanship positions: there are, for example, many Conservative Evangelicals who are not members of Reform. Rather, it is an intrinsic orientation which may be deeply personal to the individual that we are concerned with. Such an intrinsic orientation is marked by accepting and using designations such as 'Liberal' of oneself and then of others. It is affective meaning we wish to measure – the emotional reactions attached to particular words or descriptions of churchmanship.

The pioneering work in the field of measuring meaning, especially affective meaning, was by Osgood, Suci and Tannenbaum (1957). Their work, drawing on Osgood (1952), subjected a word to a test that they called a 'semantic differential' – the name reflecting the view that it was possible to analyse meaning into a range of dimensions which were capable of being differentiated and measured.

> We begin by postulating a semantic space, a region of some unknown dimensionality and Euclidean in character. Each semantic scale, defined by a pair of polar (opposite-in-meaning) adjectives, is assumed to represent a straight line function that passes through the origin of this space, and a sample of such scales then represents a multidimensional space ... To define the semantic space with maximum efficiency, we would need to determine that minimum number of

orthogonal dimensions or axes (again, assuming the space to be Euclidean) which exhausts the dimensionality of the space – in practice, we shall be satisfied with as many such independent dimensions as we can identify and measure reliably.
(Osgood, Suci and Tannenbaum, 1957, p.25 and chapter 3)

Heise (1970) reviewed the field of research into attitude in which the semantic differential had been used as a research instrument and found that evaluative scores from the use of the semantic differential correlated highly with scores produced by other attitude scaling techniques such as Breckler, 1984 and Fishbein and Azjen, 1974.

So what are the 'minimum number of orthogonal dimensions or axes' which exhaust the dimensionality of the semantic space of 'churchmanship'? One of the most prolonged and systematic attempts to explore attitudes among churchgoers and clergy in the United Kingdom has been that of Francis and his colleagues. Earlier in this chapter it has been seen how they developed and used two 7-point scales for churchmanship research. The empirical clarity, as well as the reliability and validity, of the two Catholic/Evangelical and Liberal/Conservative scales, first used by Francis, commended them for further use in quantitative research. The high response rates to these scales suggest that respondents have little difficulty in using them. In addition Daniel's (1967) understanding of the two dimensions drawing on different sources of authority is reflected in the scales. In practice though, even amongst researchers using both the Liberal/Conservative and the Catholic/Evangelical scales, most published research has focused on the Catholic/Evangelical scale. Francis, Lankshear and Jones (1998) provide a rare exception.

Bearing in mind Osgood, Suci and Tannenbaum's dictum about the minimum number of dimensions needed to define a semantic space, should there only be one dimension, that of Catholic/Evangelical, to measure 'churchmanship'? Certainly, as we have seen, the early researchers in this field preferred this. It was not long though before researchers, particularly those using the labelling method of defining churchmanship, found that such an approach did not encompass the richness of the concept. Davies (1993, p.15), for example, found that each of his churchmanship groups, with the exception of 'Conservative Evangelical' accepted 'Liberal' as a designation appropriate to their spiritual style. Modernists, Liberals, Radicals, New Theologians and Sea of Faith supporters have all felt the need to modify their churchmanship self-designation. The Liberal/Conservative dimension is needed as well.

Are there other dimensions to churchmanship, or is two all that we need? Will Catholic/Evangelical and Liberal/Conservative suffice? In the Rural Church Project Davies (1993, pp.13-14) found that the proportion of clergy choosing the designation 'charismatic' was more or less equal to that of the Liberals. Twenty two per cent of the clergy in his sample acknowledged this label as part of their spiritual style, including, for example, 19 per cent of the Modern Catholics. He found that the designation 'charismatic' was used by some clergy in each of his five Catholic/Evangelical churchmanship categories. Nevertheless, as with the

Liberal/Conservative dimension, the charismatic dimension to churchmanship has been relatively under-researched.

One of the few empirical studies making use of this dimension was that of Francis, Lankshear and Jones (1998), reported earlier in this chapter. They found that charismatic Evangelical churches were promoting a more effective ministry among young people than non-charismatic Evangelical churches. So it seemed that 'Evangelical' was not by itself a sufficient designation: the charismatic dimension was also a significant contributor and needed to be included in a comprehensive empirical definition of churchmanship.

In the light of this need to encompass the charismatic, how best to measure it? Would it be possible to include it within the semantic differential grid, or would a different approach be needed? The superficially simple question, 'Are you a charismatic?' was rejected because it would not be subtle enough for empirical purposes: potentially all clergy could claim that they were what they were by the grace (*charis*) of God. 'Have you been baptized in the Spirit?' is open equally to all to say 'yes' to since, according to 1 Corinthians 12:13, 'we were all baptized by one Spirit'.

What about the direct question, 'Do you speak, or have you spoken, in tongues?' This question was used by Francis (2000) in the Evangelical Alliance study of church leaders but it presents problems to the researcher because, as the first chapter showed, one of the differences between the first wave of the Pentecostal movement and the second wave of the Charismatic movement was over this very question of the necessity of speaking in tongues as the sure sign of the baptism of the Spirit. Not all who would accept for themselves the title of charismatic would speak in tongues, or would believe that they needed to.

In looking at the growth and development of things charismatic in the Anglican Church it is not just charismatic experience but rather the influence of the charismatic movement itself that is important. It is the charismatic movement in the Church of England (Craston, 1981) that has had such noticeable effects on some parishes. It could be expected therefore that it would be the charismatic movement that would have both positive and negative effects on individual clergy.

Francis, Lankshear and Jones (1998) used a yes/no question to ask whether each church or worship centre had been influenced by the charismatic movement. That is a simple and attractive route. However, though the word 'influence' is meant to mean 'positive influence', a 'yes' answer could mean either positive influence or negative influence. Equally a 'no' answer could include both those uninfluenced by the charismatic movement and those negatively influenced by the charismatic movement, for whom Martin and Mullen (1984) would claim to speak.

If the charismatic was to be treated, in Osgood's word, as an 'orthogonal' dimension of churchmanship it would need to be comparable to the Catholic/Evangelical and Liberal/Conservative dimensions. (In using Osgood's terminology of 'orthogonal' here it is not being presumed that the scales are orthogonal in the sense that psychometricians usually use the term, that is, uncorrelated with regard to factor structure. In fact there is evidence to suggest that Liberal may have links with Catholic, and Conservative may have links with

Evangelical.) The poles of a charismatic axis were established therefore as 'positively influenced by the charismatic movement' ('Pro-charismatic' for brevity of reporting) and 'negatively influenced by the charismatic movement' ('Anti-charismatic'). The use of seven points on that axis, in line with Osgood's practice, would give a range of positions from which to measure the degree of influence of the charismatic movement.

Osgood called for the semantic differential grid to be mapped by the minimum number of orthogonal dimensions which would exhaust the dimensionality of the space. A semantic differential grid therefore with three quantifiable dimensions (Catholic/Evangelical, Liberal/Conservative, Positively/Negatively influenced by the charismatic movement), each with an axis of seven points, seemed best suited to the task in hand. It would allow for the precision and subtlety that are often needed in assessing one's own and, more particularly, other people's churchmanship. Using seven points on three dimensions would allow, if needed, a semantic space for the concept 'churchmanship' with 343 different positions, more than enough even for the Anglican Church. When necessary each of the three dimensions could be analysed on its own, and at those times the use of a 7-point axis would allow comparability with research previously done by Francis and colleagues using their two 7-point scales.

Osgood used a 7-point grid for his studies using the semantic differential grid. Why seven points? Symonds (1924) was the first to suggest that seven categories gives the most reliable results, and Ghiselli's (1955) review of research bore that out. Miller (1956) argued that the human mind has a span of absolute judgement that can distinguish about seven distinct categories, and a span of immediate memory for about seven items, which suggested that any increase in response categories above seven might be futile. The use of seven points also allows for the middle point on each axis to be used as a neutral point, both in the sense of not being able to choose between two alternatives, and also in the sense of holding the two extremes together in tension (Sykes, 1982, p.127, Vidler, 1957, p.166). Osgood, Suci and Tannenbaum (1957, p.29) in the same way describe the mid-point between the polar terms, scale position 4 on a scale of seven points, as 'neither X nor Y; equally X and Y'. Thus the shorthand term for the mid-point on the Positively/Negatively influenced by the charismatic movement axis – 'Non-charismatic' – includes those uninfluenced by the charismatic movement and those for whom the positive and negative influences of the charismatic movement balance out.

The study reported in this book would use therefore a semantic differential grid (figure 2.2) with three quantifiable dimensions each with an axis of seven points. In reporting results from these axes the modifier 'strongly' is used for points 1 and 7 (for example, 'strongly Catholic'), and the modifier 'mildly' for points 3 and 5 (for example, 'mildly Conservative'), with no modifier for points 2 and 6 (for example, 'Pro-charismatic').

> Please judge how Catholic/Evangelical and how Liberal/Conservative you are by drawing a circle round one number on each of these lines
>
> Catholic   1   2   3   4   3   2   1 Evangelical
>
> Liberal   1   2   3   4   3   2   1 Conservative
>
> Have you been influenced by the Charismatic movement?
>
> positively 1   2   3   4   3   2   1 negatively
>
> **Figure 2.2 The Randall churchmanship measure**

When the seven points need to be collapsed to form three groups, easily understood designations would be needed. For the Catholic/Evangelical and Liberal/Conservative dimensions these are at hand, with both 'Central' and 'Middle-of-the-road' in common parlance in clergy circles. It would have been good to use Walker's (1988) 'Middle Way', however it was not clear from reading Walker whether he saw the Middle Way as between Catholic and Evangelical, or between Liberal and Conservative, or neither. The charismatic scale would form three groups: Pro-charismatic, Non-charismatic and Anti-charismatic.

Using seven points on each of three dimensions would allow, if needed, a semantic space for the concept of churchmanship with 343 different positions. In practice, though, for the empirical researcher it would be imperative to order the results in a smaller number of overall categories. By collapsing, when necessary, each of the scales to three headline categories, 27 distinct churchmanship positions within the semantic space could be explored. How then to collapse a 7-point grid to form three groups? Figure 2.3 shows the three methods by which this can be done using the Catholic/Evangelical axis as an example. The choice is as much a psychological, theological and ecclesiological one as a mathematical one. There are no reported studies where method #1 has been used. Such a method would imply ecclesiologically that Catholics and Evangelicals are extremists, on the fringes of the Anglican Church, and certainly at various times in church history that would have been a reasonable assumption. However the first chapter has shown that Anglo-Catholics and Evangelicals were major influences on the church scene of the early 1990s when the clergy considered here were ordained.

Francis and Lankshear (1995b, 1995c and 1996) used method #2. 'In this analysis the Middle Way churches provide the central core against which both Evangelical and Catholic churches are assessed' (Francis and Lankshear, 1996, p.11). Certainly their analysis produced discrete and significant results. However, it relied on seeing the 'Middle Way' as the heart of the Church with Evangelicals and Catholics as anomalies:

The data demonstrate that the notion of churchmanship remains alive and well among Church of England parishes. Overall 37% of Anglican places of worship continue to claim clear identity with one of the party wings of the Church of England. As demonstrated in the recent debate concerning the ordination of women to the priesthood, party wings of this magnitude can exert considerable pressure over the liberalizing and progressive tendencies of the centre.
(Francis and Lankshear, 1996, p.16)

Method #1
              catholic | central | evangelical
                   1 | 2 3 4 3 2 | 1

Method #2
              catholic | central | evangelical
                  1 2 | 3 4 3 | 2 1

Method #3
              catholic | central | evangelical
                 1 2 3 | 4 | 3 2 1

Figure 2.3 Three alternative methods of grouping responses on the Catholic/Evangelical axis

---

Such statements show that method #2 leads the researcher to see Catholics and Evangelicals as 'party wings of the Church of England', with each party a separate and unified group able to act together in a common cause. Though that may have been the case at some times in the twentieth century, in the early 1990s there were many internal differences among Evangelical churches: Tidball (1994) draws attention to the ways in which such diversity has always been characteristic of Evangelicalism.

Francis, Lankshear and Jones (1998) used method #3 in their study of Evangelical Anglican churches because of their awareness of this very diversity among Evangelicals. One of the refinements that method #3 offered to their analysis was a successful way of measuring the degree to which individual churches aligned themselves with the Evangelicals. They concluded that 'the mathematical model is powerful enough to pick up the consequences of theological emphases associated with different strengths of commitment to Evangelical identity' (Francis, Lankshear and Jones, 1998, p.265). Method #3 enabled measurement of 'Evangelical identity' (and Catholic identity too), rather than solely allegiance to a party.

The methodology chosen here therefore is that of method #3, enabling the study of identity and style on each of the dimensions first and foremost, but with the opportunity to see the influence of different strengths of commitment to an identity, or to a party, where necessary. In some ways this methodology has parallels with the Myers-Briggs Type Indicator (Myers and McCaulley, 1985), where types are seen as a way of describing a preference between two ways of perceiving events.

> Under this theory, people create their 'type' through exercise of their individual preferences regarding perception and judgement. The interests, values, needs, and habits of mind that naturally result from any set of preferences tend to produce a recognisable set of traits and potentialities.
> (Myers, 1980, p.10)

We need the Evangelicals in the Anglican Church, but we need all the other churchmanship strengths as well. The methodology chosen for this study provides an opportunity to see all churchmanship positions and identities as, in the words of Myers, 'gifts of diversity' to the Church.

Chapter 3

Seeking clergy and their churchmanship differences

Introduction

The last two chapters have looked at the history of churchmanship within the Anglican Church in England and Wales, and at the way previous empirical research has made use of churchmanship as a way of understanding what kinds of differences there are among clergy and laypeople. It is obvious that measuring churchmanship has produced some interesting and clear results. The fuller three-dimensional churchmanship measure explained in the previous chapter has some benefits for the researcher. How best to test and use it with Anglican clergy?

First, we need to find out if this newly-developed churchmanship measure works. Second, having seen the development of churchmanship groups in Chapter 1, it would be good to find out whether or not particular types of personality are drawn to particular forms of churchmanship. Third, the pressures on clergy are demanding: are there certain churchmanship groups which are more or less likely to burn out under the pressures of the work? Fourth, certain churchmanship groups are referred to as 'happy-clappy': are there groups which are more or less happy? Fifth, the Victorian era – when churchmanship was a sharp issue – was also the time when 'muscular Christianity' made its appearance (see Graham, 2001, Putney, 2001, Ladd and Mathisen, 2002). (The phrase appeared first in an 1857 review of a book by Charles Kingsley and was later used by Thomas Hughes in his sequel to *Tom Brown's Schooldays*.) Are there certain churchmanship groups which are more masculine or more feminine? Sixth, does churchmanship foster different patterns of belief or behaviour amongst Anglican clergy?

Empirical theology

Churchmanship has played such a significant part in the life of the Anglican Church, yet there has been almost no substantial quantitative study of its role. There is a significant amount of work that looks at churchmanship in the Anglican Church from a historical, anecdotal or sociological viewpoint, but nothing that asks the clergy directly about their understanding of their own churchmanship and the difference that it makes to their lives.

These questions fall within the sphere of practical, pastoral and empirical theology. Within the comparatively short history of empirical theology there have been two main approaches to the task. Professor Johannes van der Ven at the Catholic University of Nijmegen is seen as pioneering that approach to theology which takes seriously the contribution of the techniques of the social sciences when addressing the issues raised by theology. A linked but different approach can be seen in the work within the University of Wales led by Professor Leslie J. Francis and his colleagues.

Van der Ven's work (1993, 1998) is directed by the principle that the tools of the social sciences such as sociology, anthropology and psychology are appropriate and legitimate tools for the empirical theologian to use. In addition he intends that those tools should be integrated within empirical theology itself. A helpful introduction to this field is Cartledge (1999). He called van der Ven's an intra-disciplinary approach: the tools of the social scientist become the tools of the empirical theologian. However this can mean that the language and assumptions of empirical theology become impenetrable to social scientists.

In contrast (according to Cartledge) Francis prefers an inter-disciplinary approach alongside the intra-disciplinary: he wishes to see empirical theology engage equally with debates in social sciences and in theology. Francis is a practical, pastoral and empirical theologian who is competent in the field of the social sciences. This inter-disciplinary approach is favoured for two reasons.

First, Francis argues that if empirical theology is serious about employing and indeed developing the tools of social sciences, then work undertaken by empirical theologians needs to be accessible to and publicly tested by social scientists themselves. It is for this reason that the United Kingdom tradition of empirical theology insists on being published widely through the peer review journals in the social sciences (and psychology in particular). Second, Francis argues that when problems are set up in empirical theology which resemble problems set up in other aspects of the social sciences, the practical theologian can properly learn from the relevant theoretical and methodological debates which are being pursued in the social sciences themselves (Francis, 2002, p.40).

Within the discipline of empirical theology as guided by Francis then, this study uniquely addresses the question of personality and churchmanship in a major study of ordained ministry. It is based on facts and empirical data rather than on opinions. It uses the tools of the social sciences to answer questions about the Anglican clergy. 'This is no alien social scientific enterprise peering in at the Church from without' (Louden and Francis, 2003, p.vii). Rather, this is an empirical theologian looking at his brother and sister clergy from within the Church and holding up a mirror to what is there.

How to answer the questions raised about churchmanship?

The choice of an identifiable cohort of clergy with which to work was important. It would have been entirely possible to create a representative and random sample of clergy with which to work, a route chosen by Rutledge (1993, 1999). He established a ten per cent sample of Anglican clergy from *Crockford's* for his studies on burnout. However by researching the opinions of the newly ordained and by comparing them with other research, including Rutledge, on established clergy it should be possible to observe the kind of men and women choosing and being chosen for the ordained ministry at the end of the twentieth century. It should then be possible to discover the churchmanship of the clergy who will be leading the Anglican church in the new millennium. Furthermore by studying the newly-ordained in a longitudinal study rather than in a single snapshot it should be possible to discover developments of belief, thought and practice as the clergy mature in ministry. In addition by studying all those ordained to stipendiary ministry as deacons in the Anglican Church in England and Wales in 1994, the year that the Church of England first ordained women as priests, it becomes possible to discover whether this new generation of clergy are more at ease with masculinity and femininity and whether gender makes a difference to churchmanship.

It goes without saying that a longitudinal study takes time. Questionnaires covering the first, second, third and seventh years in ordained ministry need to be prepared, sent out, returned and analysed. In order to derive full quantitative information a specially constructed questionnaire for each year of the study is necessary. Wherever possible all the questions would be pre-coded. This has advantages for the respondent as well as for the researcher: the respondent is able to complete the questionnaire more quickly and is therefore more likely to complete the task; the quantitative researcher is able to make more precise comparisons between answers if they are numerically coded. If a convention existed in previous research for coding categories, for example with the five year banding of age groups, then that was followed in order to assist in comparison with other empirical research.

The administration of the questionnaires

The questionnaire 'Curates, Courses and Colleges: the first year' was sent out in 1994. It consisted of 314 questions divided between five parts. Questions were asked about age and gender; about educational achievement, first in any discipline, and then in theology; about employment before ordination; about selection for training, age when recommended, sponsoring diocese; about the theological college or course attended and about whether or not the ordinand was married. The new churchmanship measure asked how each curate assessed his or her own churchmanship at the beginning of ordination training. Questions were asked about the role priorities of the curates and about how much help was given by the theological training institution towards developing that role. There were questions about the curate's first parish and the curate was asked to judge the churchmanship of the congregation using the churchmanship measure. Questions were asked about the training incumbent, including his churchmanship (all of the curates ordained in 1994 to stipendiary ministry served with male training incumbents). In addition questions were asked about the curate's support systems, marital status and whether or not the curate's partner was ordained. Three personality measures were included: the Eysenck Personality Questionnaire (Eysenck and Eysenck, 1975), the

Maslach Burnout Inventory (Maslach and Jackson, 1981) as adapted by Rutledge and Francis (2004), and the Oxford Happiness Inventory (Argyle, Martin and Crossland, 1989).

The questionnaire 'Curates, Priests and Deacons: the second year' was sent out in 1995. As in the first year there was a variety of questions of a socio-biographical nature. The churchmanship measure was used to discover the curate's present understanding of his or her churchmanship. There were questions about diocesan post-ordination training, about Bible versions used by the curate, and about whether the curate had been ordained priest yet, and, if so, what meaning priesthood had for him or her. There were questions about the curate's attitude to, and experience of, parish ministry, specifically related to finances, housing, continuing training, time-management and spirituality. The adapted Maslach Burnout Inventory (MBI) and the Oxford Happiness Inventory (OHI) were again used.

The questionnaire 'Curates Moving On: the third year' was sent out in 1996. As in the previous years there was a variety of questions of a socio-biographical nature. The churchmanship measure was again used to discover the curate's present understanding of his or her churchmanship. Questions were asked to determine whether the curate was still with their original training incumbent and training parish, whether the curacy had overall been happy and effective, and also about the curate's support systems and future plans. Fuller questions were asked about religious experience and about items related to the varieties of different beliefs and practices associated with different Anglican churchmanship positions. The Bem Sex Role Inventory (Bem, 1981a), the adapted MBI and the OHI were also included.

The questionnaire 'Developing Clergy Today' was sent out in 2001. The clergy had now been ordained for seven years. As in previous years there was a variety of questions of a socio-biographical nature and again the churchmanship measure was used to discover the curate's present understanding of his or her churchmanship. There were questions about role priorities, about the particular workload of baptisms, weddings and funerals, about the number of clergy posts held and about how rewarding those posts had been. The shorter Revised Eysenck Personality Questionnaire (Eysenck, Eysenck and Barrett, 1985), the OHI, the Scale of Emotional Exhaustion in Ministry (Francis, Kaldor, Shevlin and Lewis, 2004) and the Francis Psychological Type Scales (Francis, 2004) were also included.

The Church Commissioners' Computer Department provided addresses and labels for all those ordained as stipendiary deacons at Petertide and Michaelmas in England in 1994; the Board of Ministry provided the same service for those ordained in the Church in Wales. Without the help, support and encouragement of these two institutions and their staff this research would not have been possible. The total number of newly-ordained Anglican stipendiary clergy for England and Wales in 1994 was 340. Within the total list curates came from each of the residential theological colleges in England and Wales, and from each of the non-residential theological courses with the one exception of the St Alban's Diocese Ministerial Training Scheme.

Copies of the 1994 survey were sent to all 340 curates in November 1994. Accompanying the questionnaire was a letter explaining the purpose of the survey and its longitudinal nature and requesting their cooperation. In order to increase the response rate a stamped addressed envelope was included with the questionnaire. In order to assure anonymity regarding the content of the replies, but also to allow the tracking of those who had not responded, two separate databases were established. The first listed the curates' names, addresses and telephone numbers alongside a four-digit identification number, and the second held the coded replies identified only by the four-digit number. After six weeks telephone-call reminders were made to 128 non-respondents which led to the sending of 34 replacement questionnaires. Where it proved difficult to make telephone contact, a reminder letter was sent by post to a further 34 non-respondents, enclosing a copy of the original questionnaire. Two months later a second and final reminder with another copy of the original questionnaire was sent to the remaining 92 non-respondents. A total of 275 replies were received: 80.8 per cent of the total. This is an extremely high response rate for a postal questionnaire study and indicates the generally favourable attitude of the curates to the longitudinal project.

A similar process followed the sending of the second and third year questionnaires. A response rate of 72.6 per cent was achieved in the second year. In the third year there was a surprising number of changes to the original list: changes of name where female clergy had married; changes of address; changes of parish; and for some of the curates, posts of responsibility as incumbents or team vicars. Eight curates had asked not to receive any more questionnaires. Another 46 curates were not sent a copy of the third questionnaire because they had not responded to either of the first two. Six curates had left stipendiary ministry. As a result 272 copies of the third (1996) survey were sent out. The response rate was 82 per cent of questionnaires sent out and 66.7 per cent of the original stipendiary group ordained in 1994.

In sending out the questionnaire in 2001, the seventh year in ordained ministry for the group, the Research and Statistics Unit of the Archbishops' Council were helpful in providing data for the English clergy and the Board of Ministry for the Welsh clergy. Of the original 340 clergy ordained in 1994 ten no longer held any appointment, eleven had retired or had a permission to officiate, one had died, one had gone missing and four were listed as 'addresses unknown'. That left 313 clergy. The response rate was 74.7 per cent of this group or 69 per cent of the original population.

A total of 57 per cent of the original population responded to each of the four questionnaires, and thus provided the core data for the longitudinal research in this study. A total of 78 per cent of the original population responded to two or three of the questionnaires. A total of 84 per cent of the original population responded to at least one of the four questionnaires, and thus, since the opportunity to evaluate one's own churchmanship was offered in each questionnaire, provided the data for many of the correlations between churchmanship and the other instruments in this study.

One of the great advantages in studying the Anglican clergy empirically is that it is possible to find out certain details about them all from *Crockford's*

Clerical Directory. Such details include age, gender, theological college or course attended, and the diocese in which they are serving. In preparation for a report on whether clergy response rates to surveys are a function of age, Randall and Francis (1996) analysed the data provided by respondents and the data available from *Crockford's* for non-respondents by means of the SPSS^X statistical package (SPSS, Inc., 1988). It was discovered that more female curates than male curates responded, but not significantly so; that the mean age for respondents was higher than that for non-respondents, but not significantly so; and that there was no significant difference in response between the three provinces of Canterbury, York and Wales. There was also no significant difference between individual theological colleges or courses; no significant difference between responses from those who attended theological colleges as distinct from theological courses; and finally (most importantly for this study), when the colleges were grouped according to the Runcie classification of Evangelical, Tractarian and Other, there was no significant difference in response rates. As a result it is clear that the respondents are fully representative of the population of curates being studied.

Describing the curates

Before beginning in the next chapter to see the effects of churchmanship we need to get some idea of who is being ordained to stipendiary ministry in the Anglican Church these days. This information has not been previously available. This study gives us the first opportunity to map out the characteristics of these men and women.

In 1994, the first year of our study, 77 per cent of those ordained to stipendiary ministry were men and 23 per cent were women. Since then as a result of the opening up of the priesthood to women, the proportion of women being ordained has increased. The average age of an English curate was 36 and of a Welsh curate was 34. Twenty one per cent of the clergy at ordination were under 30, 46 per cent in their thirties, 27 per cent in their forties, five per cent in their fifties and one per cent in their sixties.

Before ordination training 72 per cent of the curates were graduates. Such a high figure needs to be set against the background of comparable professional and semi-professional groups which saw their entry level requirements rise during this period. Nevertheless for nearly three-quarters of the new entrants to a profession to begin their theological training as graduates is remarkable. Twenty nine per cent of the graduates were graduates in theology before ordination training. On the other hand 49 per cent of those entering theological training did not even have a CSE in Religious Education, and 69 per cent had no more than a GCSE in Religious Education. This gives an insight into the daunting task faced by theological colleges and courses in training men and women for ministry.

Eighty per cent of those entering theological training had previously been engaged in formal secular employment classed as either full-time or part-time. The school-university-theological college path to ordination was followed by only 11 per cent. Using the Standard Occupational Classification (SOC) 45 per cent of those new clergy surveyed had previously had professional jobs, 17 per cent managerial, 17 per cent associate professional and nine per cent clerical. The range of jobs was vast (covering 75 different SOC groups) but the teaching profession formed by far the largest occupation, representing over a quarter. Of those teachers, 49 per cent had been in secondary education, 16 per cent in higher and further education, 16 per cent in primary education and 11 per cent in university teaching.

Using the Runcie (1970) classification 56 per cent of those who attended English theological colleges went to Evangelical colleges, 22 per cent to Tractarian colleges and 22 per cent to Other colleges. Across the whole cohort 47 per cent went to Evangelical colleges, 18 per cent to Tractarian colleges, 18 per cent to Other colleges, four per cent to the Welsh college at Llandaff and 13 per cent to the non-residential theological courses. Eighty six per cent trained on full-time courses: of those, 61 per cent were fully resident in college, six per cent were resident on weekdays but away with their families at weekends, while 19 per cent were living at home and commuting to college.

At the beginning of training a third were single, 63 per cent married, two per cent widowed and three per cent divorced. By the end of training a quarter were single and 70 per cent married. By the seventh year of ministry single clergy represented just 14 per cent of the total: 75 per cent were married, one per cent were separated, four per cent were divorced, two per cent were divorced and remarried, two per cent were widowed and one per cent (three clergy) were living in a same-sex relationship.

Chapter 4

Which churchmanship choices are the most popular?

Introduction

In this and the following chapters the results of the empirical study are presented. The aim of the study was to examine a set of six specific questions about churchmanship and the three-dimensional churchmanship measure. In this chapter we shall see whether the measure is effective in measuring churchmanship.

Proportions of clergy in each churchmanship group

Six per cent of the 1994 curates were Strongly Catholic, 15 per cent Catholic, 14 per cent Mildly Catholic, 16 per cent of Central churchmanship, 13 per cent Mildly Evangelical, 24 per cent Evangelical and 13 per cent Strongly Evangelical. When these results are collapsed into three groups they represent 35 per cent Catholic, 16 per cent Central and 50 per cent Evangelical. This is the highest proportion of Evangelicals in a sample of Anglican clergy reported in any of the studies detailed in Chapter 2.

Rutledge (1993) obtained a five per cent random sample of all serving Anglican clergy in England and used a similar Catholic/Evangelical scale as his measure of churchmanship. Collapsing that 7-point scale into three groups gives these results: 52 per cent Catholic, 15 per cent Central and 33 per cent Evangelical: amongst serving clergy Rutledge finds about a half were Catholic and about a third were Evangelical. Amongst the 1994 newly-ordained this study reveals that about half are Evangelical and about a third are Catholic. Those entering the ministry are clearly different to those already in the ministry. Rutledge's study is a guide to the churchmanship of established clergy serving in the ordained ministry in the 1990s, and this study is a guide to the churchmanship of those whose ministry began after the vote to accept the ordination of women to the priesthood. Half of these call themselves Evangelical. We shall see later in this chapter whether or not this means that large numbers of curates served their curacy with a training incumbent from a significantly different churchmanship group.

On the Liberal/Conservative dimension the 1994 curates are seen to be eight per cent Strongly Liberal, 12 per cent Liberal, 14 per cent Mildly Liberal, 15 per cent Middle-of-the-road, 21 per cent Mildly Conservative, 22 per cent Conservative and nine per cent Strongly Conservative. When these results are collapsed into three groups they represent 33 per cent Liberal, 15 per cent Middle-of-the-road and 52 per cent Conservative. Here too the lack of useable comparative data means that it is not possible to tell if these results are different from those of serving clergy. Certainly Badham (1998) regarded Liberals as being the dominant group from this dimension within the Anglican Church. However this study shows that, even if that were the case at some stage or for the Church at large, it is not now the case among those joining the ordained ministry as stipendiary clergy after the vote for the ordination of women.

On the Charismatic dimension the 1994 curates are seen to be 17 per cent Strongly Pro-charismatic, 18 per cent Pro-charismatic, 22 per cent Mildly Pro-charismatic, 22 per cent Non-charismatic, five per cent Mildly Anti-charismatic, five per cent Anti-charismatic and 11 per cent Strongly Anti-charismatic. When these results are collapsed into three groups they represent 57 per cent positively influenced by the charismatic movement, 22 per cent uninfluenced by the charismatic movement and 21 per cent negatively influenced by the charismatic movement. That result in itself shows the importance of including the charismatic dimension within a working definition of churchmanship: it is important to clergy self-understanding of churchmanship. It is a factor which should be acknowledged in all studies of clergy churchmanship from now on.

As with the Liberal/Conservative dimension there are no equivalent empirical studies with which to compare these results for clergy. Bax (1986, pp.218-219), reporting the results of the Renewal Questionnaire that she sent to Anglican diocesan missioners, said that an average of 20 per cent of the parishes in the dioceses surveyed were 'undergoing renewal', with between one and thirty three per cent 'undergoing charismatic renewal'. The situation at theological colleges was different: 'From the two Evangelical theological colleges I visited, the staff at one of them estimated that 80 per cent of the ordinands had been affected by the charismatic movement, while at the other the staff said that most of them had been affected by it' (Bax, 1986, p.143). Here again we see how the present study is providing information which had not previously been available.

Correlation between the churchmanship dimensions

This observation from Bax illustrates the need to discover whether the three axes used in the churchmanship measure are inter-correlated, whether Evangelicals are more likely to be positively influenced by the charismatic movement. Though Osgood, Suci and Tannenbaum (1957) speak of 'orthogonal dimensions' in constructing a semantic differential grid, the term 'orthogonal' is usually reserved by those in the field of psychometrics for items which are unrelated. In this study the three dimensions of churchmanship are inter-correlated. Each dimension correlates at an extremely high level of significance with the other two. So the Evangelical is significantly more likely to be Pro-charismatic and Conservative, the Catholic is significantly more likely to be Liberal, and the Liberal is significantly more likely to be Anti-charismatic.

Which churchmanship choices are the most popular?

This correlation between the three dimensions is not surprising when one considers the historical development of the churchmanship groups. Evangelicals, for example, were the group who were most concerned to uphold the primacy of scripture and a conservative interpretation of it against the Modernists. In Europe as well as in the United States there has long been a fundamentalist conservative element among the Evangelical constituency. Again, one of the starting points for the charismatic movement's influence within the Anglican Church in the United Kingdom was a curate at the Conservative and Evangelical church of All Souls' Langham Place. Francis (2000), in his study of church leaders of churches affiliated to the Evangelical Alliance, found that 95 per cent of the Evangelicals would say that they were 'baptized in the Spirit'. However it must also be said that, though there is a correlation between the three dimensions, the dimensions themselves are not homogeneous: there are Pro-charismatic Liberal Catholics and Anti-charismatic Liberal Evangelicals amongst the clergy (see table 4.1).

Table 4.1 Proportion of clergy in each churchmanship group

	%		%		%
Catholic	34.4	Liberal	21.9	Pro-charismatic	6.7
				Non-charismatic	6.3
				Anti-charismatic	8.7
		Central	5.6	Pro-charismatic	>1.0
				Non-charismatic	1.2
				Anti-charismatic	3.6
		Conservative	6.3	Pro-charismatic	2.0
				Non-charismatic	1.6
				Anti-charismatic	2.8
Middle	15.8	Liberal	4.7	Pro-charismatic	2.0
				Non-charismatic	>1.0
				Anti-charismatic	2.0
		Central	5.9	Pro-charismatic	2.0
				Non-charismatic	2.8
				Anti-charismatic	1.2
		Conservative	5.1	Pro-charismatic	3.9
				Non-charismatic	>1.0
				Anti-charismatic	>1.0
Evangelical	49.8	Liberal	6.4	Pro-charismatic	5.5
				Non-charismatic	>1.0
				Anti-charismatic	>1.0
		Central	4.3	Pro-charismatic	3.9
				Non-charismatic	>1.0
				Anti-charismatic	>1.0
		Conservative	40.1	Pro-charismatic	30.3
				Non-charismatic	7.1
				Anti-charismatic	2.4

In fact there exist in a group of 340 new clergy almost all of the possible combinations of churchmanship positions. A simple labelling approach would not be able to provide the subtleties of self-designation that this table charts. Nevertheless, among this population there is a substantial number of Pro-charismatic Conservative Evangelicals, 30 per cent of the total – the largest of the three-dimensional groupings. On the other hand their polar opposites, the Anti-charismatic Liberal Catholics, comprise nine per cent of the total.

The key relationship in training new curates for lifelong ordained ministry in the Anglican Church is that between the curate and his or her training incumbent. The 1994 curates were asked not just to assess their own churchmanship but also that of their training incumbent and that of the congregation in their training parish. Given Rutledge's figures earlier about the proportions of Catholic, Central and Evangelical clergy in the Anglican Church as a whole, it might be predicted that there would be a churchmanship mismatch between curates and their training incumbents and parishes. Table 4.2 shows this not to be the case. In fact every relationship but one ('NS' in the table) shows a significant correlation.

Table 4.2 Correlation coefficients between churchmanship of curate and churchmanship of incumbent and congregation

		curate			congregation			vicar	
		C/E	L/C	P/A	C/E	L/C	P/A	C/E	L/C
curate	Lib/Con	+0.6							
	Pro/Anti-char	- 0.5	- 0.3						
cong	Cath/Evan	+0.5	+0.4	- 0.3					
	Lib/Con	+0.2	+0.4	- 0.1	+0.4				
	Pro/Anti-char	- 0.3	- 0.2	+0.5	- 0.4	NS			
vicar	Cath/Evan	+0.6	+0.4	- 0.4	+0.8	+0.4	- 0.4		
	Lib/Con	+0.4	+0.5	- 0.2	+0.5	+0.6	- 0.2	+0.6	
	Pro/Anti-char	- 0.3	- 0.3	+0.4	- 0.3	- 0.2	+0.6	- 0.4	- 0.3

The correlation coefficients in table 4.2 have been rounded up to one decimal point. A plus sign (+) shows that the significant relationship is between the first named of each dimension: so in the top left cell +0.6 means there is a significant relationship between the curate being Liberal and being Catholic, whereas the negative sign (-) in the bottom right cell means that there is a significant relationship between the vicar being Pro-charismatic and being Conservative.

Despite the difference between Rutledge's serving clergy and these new curates, most curates are serving their titles with training incumbents and alongside congregations which they perceive as sharing their churchmanship. Given the shifting number and nature of training posts available this is a remarkable achievement by the English and Welsh dioceses, their bishops and directors of ordinands. Also this correspondence continues on all three dimensions: thus, the Catholic congregation is significantly more likely to have a Liberal curate, the Liberal incumbent is significantly more likely to be training an Anti-charismatic curate, and so on.

The content validity of the three dimensional churchmanship measure

Part of the testing of the three dimensional churchmanship measure used in this study was to compare its results with other measures of churchmanship and religious experience. Francis and Thomas (1996a, 1996b, 1997) in a series of studies of male Welsh Anglican clergy considered the relationship between religious experience and the Eysenck personality measures. In order to do this they compiled a fifty-four item instrument to measure religious experience. It comprised six nine-item subscales measuring Catholic, Traditional, Born Again, Evangelical, Mystical and Charismatic orientations. Respondents rated the importance of each item on a five-point scale, ranging from 5, 'a great deal', to 1, 'not at all'. In the reports published so far using three of the subscales (Francis and Thomas, 1996a, 1996b, 1997) satisfactory alpha coefficients (Cronbach, 1951) were reported of 0.91 for the Catholic subscale, 0.82 for the Mystical subscale, and 0.90 for the Charismatic subscale. Coefficient alpha (Cronbach, 1951, Cortina, 1993) is a widely used statistical measure of scale reliability.

Francis and Thomas' instrument was used in this longitudinal study. The Catholic subscale achieved the satisfactory alpha reliability coefficient of 0.94. The Mystical subscale achieved the satisfactory alpha of 0.79. The Charismatic subscale achieved the satisfactory alpha of 0.91. The Born Again subscale achieved the satisfactory alpha of 0.83. The Traditional subscale achieved the lowest, but still satisfactory, alpha of 0.76. Finally the Evangelical subscale achieved the satisfactory alpha of 0.87. No standardized scores have yet been published for the Francis/Thomas instrument.

Table 4.3 shows the relative position of each of the nine churchmanship groups on each of the six scales with the highest scoring group at the top and the lowest scoring group at the bottom. On the three scales which match the name of churchmanship groups adopted for this study it can be seen that the comparison between the Francis/Thomas instrument and this dimensional model shows a clear pattern. Catholics top the Catholic subscale with their polar opposite, Evangelicals, at the bottom. Pro-charismatics top the Charismatic subscale with their polar opposite, Anti-charismatics, at the bottom. Evangelicals top the Evangelical subscale with their polar opposite, Catholics, in the penultimate position. (The

Non-charismatics come bottom of this subscale as they do on two other subscales. They never come higher than third from the bottom on any of the measures of religious experience operationalized by Francis/Thomas. In the future there may be value in research into whether Non-charismatics generally have lower levels of religious experience than other groups.) These results suggest that we are right to see the Randall three-dimensional churchmanship measure as measuring what it claims to measure – it has content validity.

Table 4.3 Relative positions of churchmanship groups on Francis and Thomas' subscales

Catholic	Traditional	Born Again	Evangelical	Mystical	Charismatic
Catholic	Catholic	Conservative	Evangelical	Liberal	Pro-charis.
Middle.	Middle.	Evangelical	Pro-charis.	Central	Evangelical
Anti-charis.	Anti-charis.	Pro-charis.	Conservative	Pro-charis.	Central
Liberal	Liberal	Middle.	Central	Middle.	Conservative
Central	Central	Central	Middle.	Catholic	Middle.
Pro-charis.	Pro-charis.	Anti-charis.	Liberal	Anti-charis.	Liberal
Non-charis.	Evangelical	Liberal	Anti-charis.	Non-charis.	Catholic
Conservative	Conservative	Catholic	Catholic	Evangelical	Non-charis.
Evangelical	Non-charis.	Non-charis.	Non-charis.	Conservative	Anti-charis.

The three other subscales, Traditional, Born Again, and Mystical, raise separate and interesting questions about what is being measured by the Francis and Thomas instrument. The near match between the ordering on the Catholic subscale and the ordering on the Traditional subscale suggests that they are both tapping into the same orientation. In the absence of other published studies, and given the weak alpha reliability score it achieved, this subscale calls for further research to see whether or not it is a necessary part of the Francis/Thomas scale of religious experience.

Similarly there is an affinity between the ordering of the Born Again subscale and the ordering of the Evangelical subscale. Again in the absence of published studies further research would be needed to discover whether these subscales discriminate between two separate orientations.

In constructing the Mystical subscale, Francis and Thomas (1996b) undertook research built on Happold's (1963) definition of mysticism. Happold spoke of three interconnected aspects of mysticism: the mysticism of knowledge and understanding, the mysticism of love and union, and the mysticism of action. These were formulated into six main characteristics of the mystical orientation: ineffability, noesis, transiency, passivity, consciousness of the oneness of everything, and a sense of timelessness. These characteristics were operationalized within the Mystical subscale of Francis and Thomas' measure. It was Dean Inge's 1899 Bampton Lectures on Christian Mysticism which provided part of the impetus for the increased interest in the mystical in English religion. Inge saw himself as a successor to the Cambridge Platonists and was also a leader of the Modern Churchman's Union. That historical link between Liberal churchmanship and mystical orientation seems to be borne out by the results for the Mystical subscale shown in this table: Liberals top the subscale with their polar opposite, Conservatives, at the bottom. Here too further research is required with other groups to see if this connection between the Liberal and the Mystical can be replicated. The links too between the Pro-charismatics and the Mystical require further research (cf. Hocken, 1975).

The satisfactory links between these subscales and the three-dimensional churchmanship measure are a strong indication that the measure is satisfactorily mapping the content as well as the labels of churchmanship. In this chapter we have begun to answer two of the questions at the heart of this study, 'What is churchmanship?' and 'Can it be empirically measured?' Taking the second question first, we have seen that the new churchmanship measure based on a three dimensional semantic differential grid works: it produces discriminate results. The first question about the need for a wider range of churchmanship categories than a two dimensional measure would give is answered in two ways: first, the large number who opted for the Pro-charismatic position; second, the fact that with this group of curates – numbering 340 in all – many of the twenty-seven potential categories of churchmanship are chosen. In addition comparison with at least three of the subscales of the Francis/Thomas scale of religious experience has shown that the three dimensional churchmanship measure is tapping in to the same religious experiences which accompany particular churchmanship self-definitions. The churchmanship measure therefore fulfils the stated intention to use the minimum number of orthogonal axes which Osgood, Suci and Tannenbaum (1957) required. It allows for clarity, precision and subtlety in assessing one's own churchmanship, and it is simple to use and to analyse. As such it commends itself for future use in other empirical research.

Chapter 5

Extravert or introvert?

Introduction to personality research

We have seen in the last chapter that the three dimensional churchmanship measure works effectively and shows quite different patterns of religious experience between different churchmanship groups. In this and the next five chapters we shall answer the question, 'Are the distinctions between different churchmanship groups rooted in differences of personality so that the traits of a Catholic, for example, are fundamentally different to the traits of an Evangelical?' In other words, are people of particular churchmanships drawn from distinct personality types?

In the first half of the twentieth century large scale theories of personality were developed by innovators such as Sigmund Freud. Early personality theorists like Freud usually worked as therapists treating psychologically disturbed and distressed individuals and used their cases as the basis for generalizing broadly about the nature of personality as they assessed it. In the second half of the twentieth century researchers working both with normal and disturbed populations developed and applied increasingly sophisticated scientific methods to address the issues of personality psychology. There are five main theoretical approaches to personality and individual differences: a psycho-dynamic approach; a trait and biological approach; a phenomenological approach; a behavioural approach; and a cognitive social approach. The personality trait model is the one being followed in this study. It is adequately summarized by Mischel:

> People readily characterize each other in terms of personality traits: friendly, assertive, submissive, conscientious, and so on. Enduring personal qualities are the essence of trait concepts, and it is assumed that people are consistent and stable with regard to at least some important traits. A major goal is to discover the set of traits that apply to most people and on which they are relatively consistent.
> (Mischel, 1993, p.12)

Hans Eysenck

Eysenck (1953) defined personality as 'the more or less stable and enduring organization of a person's character, temperament, intellect and physique which determines his unique adjustment to the environment'. In order to understand personality he chose an objective and inferential approach whereby, after scientific analysis, behavioural tendencies are classified as traits or personality factors. By means of factor analysis such traits can be grouped around various personality dimensions. His theories seek to explain personality in terms of differences in individual nervous systems (Eysenck, 1967). Descriptive classifications or taxonomies of individual differences have been a tradition in personality theories since the ancient Greeks. Most taxonomic systems of cognitive and non-cognitive attributes are hierarchical, that is, clustering similar behaviours into narrow traits, then clustering these into higher order traits, and eventually into a limited number of dimensional types. The problem for taxonomists is to determine the optimal number of factors to describe these structures after factor or principal component analysis.

There is strong agreement among personality researchers that the dimensions of extraversion/introversion and neuroticism/emotional stability are fundamental parts of any personality taxonomy. Eysenck (1991) also suggested that agreeableness and conscientiousness are both parts of a higher order factor of psychoticism. There has been a substantial amount of research on the stability of the traits measured by Eysenck's personality measures so that Matthews and Deary were able to say 'large-scale reviews and large single studies, therefore, offer overwhelming evidence for the stability of personality traits over many years' (Matthews and Deary, 1998, p.54).

Eysenck (1947) gave seven hundred patients at Mill Hill Psychiatric Hospital a 39-item questionnaire. By the use of factor analysis he identified two dimensions: extraversion-introversion and neuroticism, or 'emotionality'. From the main neurotic factors he produced a 40-item questionnaire (Eysenck, 1952) to measure neuroticism entitled the Maudsley Medical Questionnaire (MMQ). Though this questionnaire was able to distinguish between normal and neurotic subjects its main use was with psychiatric populations. After further work to measure more carefully the dimension of extraversion-introversion, the Maudsley Personality Inventory (MPI) was produced (Eysenck, 1959). This inventory included a lie scale (L) to discover whether respondents were 'faking good'. The EPI, Eysenck Personality Inventory (Eysenck & Eysenck, 1964), was produced and considered to contain more independent and more reliable measures of neuroticism (N) and extraversion (E) than the MMQ. The Eysenck Personality Questionnaire (EPQ) went on to refine the extraversion and lie scales and added the further dimension of psychoticism (Eysenck & Eysenck, 1975).

Several writers, for example Block (1977) and Bishop (1977), criticized the psychometric properties of the psychoticism scale (P). Three major faults were recognized particularly when the questionnaire was used for individual diagnosis rather than group comparisons: the first was the low reliability of the scale; the second was the low range of scoring; and the third was the skewed distribution of the scores. The fact that, despite these admitted faults, the scale still behaved consistently and predictably suggested that the validity of the scale would need only modification to work acceptably. So the Revised Eysenck Personality Questionnaire (EPQR) was devised in order to improve the measurement of psychoticism (Eysenck, Eysenck & Barrett, 1985). At the same time, and in the same study, a shortened version (EPQR-S) was constructed comprising twelve questions for each of the four scales of E, N, P and L.

Extraversion and introversion: the E scale

'Extraversion' and 'introversion' derive from Latin roots meaning 'turned outwards' and 'turned inwards'. The Swiss psychiatrist Carl Jung had originally grouped people as introverts and extraverts in terms of personality types. Eysenck however investigated introversion-extraversion as a dimensional trait. The definition of the idealized extreme extravert and extreme introvert are as follows:

> The typical extravert is sociable, likes parties, has many friends, needs to have people to talk to, and does not like reading or studying by himself. He craves excitement, takes chances, often sticks his neck out, acts on the spur of the moment, and is generally an impulsive individual. He is fond of practical jokes, always has a ready answer, and generally likes change; he is carefree, easygoing, optimistic, and 'likes to laugh and be merry'. He prefers to keep moving and doing things, tends to be aggressive and loses his temper quickly; altogether his feelings are not kept under tight control, and he is not always a reliable person.
>
> The typical introvert is a quiet, retiring sort of person, introspective, fond of books rather than people; he is reserved and distant except to intimate friends. He tends to plan ahead, 'looks before he leaps', and mistrusts the impulse of the moment. He does not like excitement, takes matters of everyday life with proper seriousness, and likes a well-ordered mode of life. He keeps his feelings under close control, seldom behaves in an aggressive manner, and does not lose his temper easily. He is reliable, somewhat pessimistic and places great value on ethical standards.
>
> (Eysenck and Eysenck, 1975)

Eysenck and his colleagues recognized that these descriptions may sound like caricatures because they portray 'perfect' extraverts and introverts whereas in fact most people are found along the line between extraversion and introversion.

The E scale and religiosity

Eysenck (1954) postulated a relationship between personality and social attitudes in terms of a theory of socialization. He argued that aggressive and sexual impulses are socialized by means of conditioning. Since there is empirical evidence that introverts condition more easily than extraverts (Eysenck, 1967), it follows that introverts should be more thoroughly socialized than extraverts. Socialization will be reflected in tender-minded attitudes (Eysenck, 1961): tough-minded attitudes will be concerned with immediate satisfaction of aggressive or sexual impulses, while tender-minded attitudes will be concerned with ethical and religious ideas which act as barriers to such satisfaction. Tender-minded attitudes, introversion and religiosity would go together.

However attempts to test this hypothesis with empirical data have shown no significant correlation between attitude to religion and introversion (Francis and Pearson, 1985a, Watson, Morris, Foster and Hood, 1986, Caird, 1987, Francis and

Pearson, 1988, Francis, Lankshear and Pearson, 1989, Gillings and Joseph, 1996, and Maltby, 1997). Francis and Astley (1996) and Francis and Daniel (1997) also found no correlation between extraversion and the personal practice of prayer of adult churchgoers. Francis, Jones and Martineau (1996) found an appreciation of fun and humour in worship was correlated positively with extraversion amongst 923 adult churchgoers. 'Extraverts may be inclined to go to church seeking fun and humour in the service, while introverts may be more inclined to reject such styles of worship as irrelevant or irreverent' (Francis, Jones and Martineau, 1996, p.73).

The E scale and the clergy

There has been a sequence of studies identifying the personality characteristics of professionally religious people, the clergy, using the Eysenck personality scales. Towler and Coxon (1979) were the first to administer the EPI to 76 male ordinands at four theological colleges in the 1960s. They reported E scores almost identical to the population norms reported in the test manual. Francis and Pearson (1990) administered the EPQ to 40 clergy attending mid-career development consultations. They too found E scores matching the population norms. Since there is seen to be no correlation between E and religiosity, if ordinands and clergy are typical of religious people in general, they should be no more nor less extraverted than the population as a whole.

Francis (1991a) however using the EPQ with 252 male and female ordinands in theological training had quite different results. He found that the male ordinands in his sample had lower E scores than the general male population, and the female ordinands had higher E scores than the general female population: the female ordinands emerge as slightly more extraverted than men in general, while the male ordinands emerge as slightly more introverted than women in general. Jones and Francis (1992) produced a similar result with 39 male Methodist clergy. However Francis (1992a), with 112 male and female clergy attending residential summer schools, and Francis and Thomas (1992), with 40 male clergy attending a residential training conference, found E scores which were not significantly different from the population norms. As a result of this disagreement questions were asked about the samples on which these studies had been based, and whether the results obtained could be generalized to the whole clergy population.

In order to address this issue of generalizability, Robbins, Francis and Rutledge (1997) based their study on two questionnaires, one sent to a randomized sample of five per cent of all male stipendiary Anglican clergy in England, and one sent to all Anglican women clergy in England, Ireland, Scotland and Wales. Using the EPQR-S they produced the following table of results for E. Table 5.1 shows that there is no significant difference between male clergy and men in general, and between female clergy and women in general. Though in the general population men tend to record higher extraversion scores than women, there are no significant (NS) differences between the extraversion scores of male and female clergy (t = 1.365, NS) compared to the general population.

Table 5.1 Extraversion scores for clergy compared to population norms

	Clergy sample		General norms			
	Mean	SD	Mean	SD	t	P<
Male	6.88	3.44	6.36	3.80	+2.01	NS
Female	7.19	3.47	7.60	3.27	-1.99	NS

Source: Robbins, M., Francis, L.J. and Rutledge, C. (1997)

Rutledge (1999, p.175), in his study of male parochial clergy, confirmed Eysenck and Eysenck's (1975) finding that men become more introverted with advancing age. With the exception of the 50-59 age group of clergy who score higher on extraversion than the matching group from the general population, there is no significant difference between the clergy scores and the norms across the age groups.

There is a small group of studies concerned with churchmanship or denomination and personality. Jones and Francis' (1992) study mentioned above had a sample of only 39 male Methodist clergy: it found that these male clergy produced lower E scores than the population norms. Francis and Kay (1995) found in their study of 364 Pentecostal ministry candidates, both male and female, that they resembled Anglican clergy in not differing from the population norms for E. Francis and Thomas (1996a, 1996b, 1997), in a series of three studies using the EPQR-S with a group of male Welsh Anglican clergy, found no correlation between Anglo-Catholic orientation and extraversion. They did find a significant positive correlation between mystical orientation and extraversion, and between charismatic experience and extraversion. Equally Francis and Jones (1997), using the EPQR-S with a sample of committed adult Christians, found a positive correlation between charismatic experience and Eysenckian extraversion. They suggested that since an important element of Eysenck's operationalization of extraversion is sociability and many charismatic churches appear to emphasize the social dimensions of Christian fellowship, it would not be surprising if such churches tended to recruit more extraverts. Robbins, Hair and Francis (1999) found that E was positively correlated with their Index of Charismatic Experience among male Anglican clergy.

Eysenck made a huge contribution to the psychometric study of personality with over a thousand publications to his credit. His personality scales are seen as reliable and consistent. Their use is widespread with the journal *Personality and Individual Differences* regularly recording significant studies making use of them.

> All these lines of evidence – the replicable clarity of the factor structure, the correlations with external variables, the high heritability indices and the clear implication of physiological structures – firmly support the validity and psychological importance of these factors.
> (Kline, 1993, p.62)

The use of Eysenck's scales with measures of religiosity seems to generate secure results. There is no significant correlation between E and religiosity. There is no significant difference for scores on the extraversion scale between male or female clergy and the general population. In general there are no distinct results for Catholic/Evangelical or Liberal/Conservative churchmanship but there is evidence to suggest that mystics, charismatics and Pentecostals are more likely to be extraverts.

The results of this study

Does churchmanship contribute to significant personality profile variations? In order to answer this question it is necessary, first of all, to consider the personality profile of the whole cohort of clergy studied and after that to consider differences between churchmanship groups.

Table 5.2 EPQ and EPQR-S mean scores for Extraversion by sex

	male		female			
	mean	SD	mean	SD	t	P<
EPQ E	13.49	4.50	11.62	4.93	+2.77	.01
EPQR-S E	7.78	3.27	6.82	3.43	+1.97	.05

Table 5.2 presents the mean scores for the male (N = 202) and female (N = 60) curates on the EPQ and the EPQR-S scales for Extraversion. The male clergy produced significantly higher Extraversion scores on both instruments than the female clergy. This result differs from Robbins, Francis and Rutledge's (1997) study which found no difference between the E scores of male and female clergy. It appears that the male clergy entering the ordained ministry of the Anglican Church at the end of the twentieth century are more extraverted than the female clergy.

Table 5.3 Mean Extraversion scores for curates compared to serving clergy

	curates		clergy			
	mean	SD	mean	SD	t	P<
male	7.78	3.27	6.88	3.44	+3.04	.001
female	6.82	3.43	7.19	3.37	- 0.81	NS

Source: Robbins, M., Francis, L.J. and Rutledge, C. (1997)

Table 5.3 presents the mean scores for the male and female curates of the EPQR-S scores for E alongside those of Robbins, Francis and Rutledge (1997) for male and female clergy in general. Male curates recorded significantly higher

Extraversion scores than male clergy. Female curates do not differ significantly from female clergy on Extraversion.

Table 5.4 Mean Extraversion scores for curates compared to population norms

	curates		general norms			
	mean	SD	mean	SD	t	P<
male	7.78	3.27	6.36	3.80	+4.54	.001
female	6.82	3.43	7.60	3.27	- 1.74	.05

Table 5.4 presents the mean scores for the male and female curates of the scores for EPQR-S Extraversion alongside the population norms. The statistics show that male curates record significantly higher scores on the Extraversion scale than men in general. The female curates recorded significantly lower Extraversion scores than women in general.

There are a number of observations to be made about these results. First, Francis' (1991a, 1992c) finding that the established gender differences are reversed among clergy is not fully supported. While Francis had found that female clergy scored higher scores on the Extraversion scale than male clergy, the opposite is found in this study: not only do the male clergy record higher Extraversion scores than the female clergy, they also record higher Extraversion scores than men in general. In fact, apart from the 50-59 age group of clergy in Rutledge's (1999, p.176) study, they are the first male clergy sample to be reported as more extraverted than the general population. Given the links between Extraversion and leadership skills it may be that today's curates are well prepared by their personality to take on leadership roles in the churches of the twenty first century.

Second, comparison of the curates with the established clergy, as measured by Robbins, Francis and Rutledge (1997), shows the personality profile of the women curates identical to that of the women clergy. It may well be that the profile thus depicted represents the norm for Anglican clergywomen.

Third, clergywomen differ on Extraversion from women in general. Those women who entered the ordained ministry of the Anglican Church after the successful vote to ordain women as priests are different in personality to the women to whom they will minister: they are more introverted than women in general. Higher Extraversion scores would have predisposed women clergy to show a sense of ease in company and in social situations. They would be able to inspire others to follow their lead. They would feel at home in public meetings and in leadership situations. They would welcome opportunities for engaging others in conversation. On the other hand these more introverted female clergy may find it easier to appreciate and value the contribution to be made to church life by its more introverted members.

Four, comparison of the curates with the established clergy, as measured by Robbins, Francis and Rutledge (1997), shows the male curates scoring higher on the E scale than serving clergy. Does the higher E score match the traditional perception of curates as bright, young things, full of energy and new ideas compared to their training incumbents? Unfortunately the only empirical study of ordinands before the 1990s which might have fleshed out that traditional perception was Towler and Coxon's (1979) use of the EPI in the 1960s: it found not that the ordinands had higher E scores but that their E scores were almost identical to the population norms. In addition today's curates may be bright but they are not all that young: their average age at ordination is in the mid-thirties. So a different explanation is needed than the traditional perception of curates.

Two studies that looked for correlations with E scores among Christian subjects might point us in the right direction. Francis and Jones (1997) found a positive correlation between charismatic experience and Extraversion amongst adult Christians. Certainly 57 per cent of the curates define themselves as positively affected by the charismatic movement. However that figure represents 56 per cent of the male curates and 60 per cent of the female curates so it would be expected that the female curates would also have higher E scores.

Francis, Jones and Martineau (1996) found an appreciation of fun and humour in worship was correlated positively with Extraversion among adult churchgoers. It is tempting to find here the reason for fun-loving male curates having higher E scores than their more established male colleagues. However such a conclusion does not explain why female curates should be different to male curates; clearly more research is needed in this area.

Five, since the male curates differ significantly from men in general in being more extraverted, there must be concerns about their ability to get alongside their parishioners. Will they be too hearty for their quieter members?

As we turn to the churchmanship differences between different groups of clergy in our study it is worth remembering that there are so few empirical studies where churchmanship has been used as a variable. The findings in this study therefore provide us with the main snapshot of the newest clergy in the Anglican Church.

Table 5.5 Extraversion scores by Catholic/Evangelical churchmanship

Catholic		Central		Evangelical			
mean	SD	mean	SD	mean	SD	F	P<
12.44	4.79	12.78	4.75	13.62	4.53	1.78	NS

Table 5.5 shows the results from this study on the Catholic/Evangelical dimension. One-way analysis of variance (ANOVA) is used to analyse for any significant difference between the mean scores of the churchmanship groups. Though the Evangelicals had the highest scores for Extraversion, analysis of variance reveals no significant difference on E. A post hoc t-test between the Catholic and Evangelical groups alone showed the Evangelicals to be significantly more extraverted than the Catholics ($t = 1.97$, $p < 0.05$). However, when analysis of variance was computed with E as the dependent variable and sex and Catholic/Evangelical churchmanship as independent variables, sex was seen to be

significantly related to extraversion (F = 7.72, p < 0.01) and churchmanship unrelated. (Men are more extraverted than women, and the different proportions of men and women in the Catholic and Evangelical groups was skewing the previous result.) The ANOVA finding in this table differs from Nauss (1973) who concluded that Protestants are more extraverted than Catholics, but concurs with Rutledge (1999) and with Francis and Thomas (1996a) where Anglo-Catholics did not differ from other clergy on Extraversion. There is a popular perception that Evangelicals are more energetic and enthusiastic than Catholic and Central clergy: this is not borne out by these results.

Table 5.6 Extraversion scores by Liberal/Conservative churchmanship

Liberal		Middle-of-the-road		Conservative			
mean	SD	mean	SD	mean	SD	F	P<
13.10	4.73	12.79	4.77	13.14	4.66	0.08	NS

Table 5.6 shows the results when the churchmanship groups are compared on the Liberal/Conservative dimension. The Conservative curates are the most extraverted and the Middle-of-the-road curates the least extraverted, but not to a significant level.

Table 5.7 Extraversion scores by Charismatic churchmanship

Pro-charismatic		Non-charismatic		Anti-charismatic			
mean	SD	mean	SD	mean	SD	F	P<
13.31	4.56	12.45	4.78	12.89	4.87	0.73	NS

Table 5.7 shows the results when the churchmanship groups are compared on the Charismatic dimension. The Pro-charismatic curates are the most extraverted and the Non-charismatics the least extraverted, but not to a significant level. This differs from the results of Francis and Thomas (1997):

> The Anglican clergy who respond to the charismatic experience differ from clergy who do not respond to the charismatic experience on the two dimensions of Neuroticism and Extraversion. They score higher on the Extraversion scale and lower on the Neuroticism scale.
> (Francis and Thomas, 1997, p.67)

In the present study Pro-charismatic clergy scored highest on E and lowest on N, but not at a significant level. The differences may lie in the nature of the groups studied and also in the measures used. Francis and Thomas' sample were male, Welsh, serving clergy. Their scale of charismatic experience was just that, a measure of experience. It included, for example, an item about speaking or praying in tongues, whereas the measure used in this study is one of influence from the charismatic movement. It may be that within the group of clergy positively influenced by the charismatic movement, those with greater degrees of charismatic experience are more extraverted.

In order to test whether the differing proportions of male and female curates within the churchmanship groups were influencing the results, a partial correlation coefficient was computed between each of the churchmanship dimensions and Extraversion while holding sex as a constant. On none of the three churchmanship dimensions did the relationships achieve adequate levels of significance. None of the nine churchmanship groups are significantly more extraverted than any of the others. Contrary to some expectations Evangelicals are not brash extraverts.

Chapter 6

Stable or neurotic?

Stability and neuroticism: the N scale

The term 'neuroticism' has its etymology in the Greek word for nerves and means 'weakness of the nerves'. Eysenck's neuroticism scales measure weakness of the nerves in the sense of emotional lability and over-reactivity. The opposite of neuroticism is emotional stability. Eysenck and Eysenck (1975) defined the typical neurotic person as follows:

> an anxious, worrying individual, moody and frequently depressed; he is likely to sleep badly and to suffer from various psychosomatic disorders. He is overly emotional, reacting too strongly to all sorts of stimuli, and finds it difficult to get back on an even keel after each emotionally arousing experience.

They suggested that if the high scorer on the N scale had to be described in one word, it would be 'worrier': the main characteristic is a constant preoccupation with things that might go wrong. At the opposite end of the N scale is the typical stable person:

> tends to respond emotionally only slowly and generally weakly, and to return to baseline quickly after emotional arousal; he is usually calm, even tempered, controlled and unworried.
> (Eysenck and Eysenck, 1975)

The characteristics of neuroticism are generally seen as socially undesirable. For example, it was found that when respondents were asked to present an ideal self they suppress their N scores (Cowles, Darling and Skanes, 1992), and when respondents are warned that 'faking good' can be detected they record higher N scores (Lodhi and Thomas, 1991). Francis (1993b) draws together much of the literature that records the empirical correlates of neuroticism: its negative correlation with measures of self-concept and job-satisfaction, with measures of loneliness and mental and physical ill-health, but also with greater empathetic and creative skills.

The N scale and religiosity

The problem of locating social attitudes, and therefore religiosity, within Eysenck's personality model revolves around the idea of conditionability and socialization. It was seen that introverts condition more easily than extraverts (Eysenck, 1967), though that did not seem to suggest that religious people are more introverted. In the same way neuroticism was seen to play a part in the conditioning process (Eysenck, 1977). Some theories in the psychology of religion suggested that religion fosters or is an expression of instability (Vine, 1978). However Francis, Pearson and Kay (1982) raised serious doubts about the link between neuroticism and religiosity by underlining the importance of taking into account sex differences when investigating this supposed link. 'The problem arises because both religiosity scores and personality scores are correlated with sex. Women tend to be more religious (Argyle and Beit-Hallahmi, 1975, Francis, 1979), and more neurotic than men (Saklofske and Eysenck,1978).' That being the case, the consensus of research has shown that religiosity is not related to neuroticism (Francis, Pearson, Carter and Kay, 1981, Francis, Pearson and Kay, 1983b, Caird, 1987, Francis, Lankshear and Pearson, 1989, Robinson, 1990, Francis, 1993a).

Such a consensus measures religiosity in terms of attitudes to religion. However Heaven (1990), in a study of religious values amongst Australian adolescents, found a correlation for male students only between N and religious values. Francis (1991b), in a study of committed regular adult churchgoers in England, found, after controlling for sex differences, a significant negative correlation between N and attitude to Christianity. He suggested that aspects of personality theory and measurement relating personality with religious attitudes may function differently in a relatively committed sample. Amongst student churchgoers however he found no correlation between N and religious behaviour (Francis, 1993a), and, amongst adult churchgoers, no correlation between N and the practice of personal prayer (Francis and Astley, 1996, Francis and Daniel, 1997). Dunne, Martin, Pangan and Heath (1997) in a longitudinal study of Australian churchgoers found that those who maintained a stable pattern of church attendance over their eight year period of study had lower N scores, suggesting that high N scorers are less likely to maintain stable long-term patterns in many behaviours, including that of religious practice.

The N scale and the clergy

Towler and Coxon (1979) found their ordinands' N scores approximated closely to those of the general population. Francis and Pearson (1990) found their clergy on mid-career development consultations scored higher than the population norm for N. Francis's (1991a) study showed male ordinands' N scores not significantly different from the general population, but female ordinands scoring significantly lower than women in general, and comparable to men in general. Jones and Francis' (1992) Methodist clergymen, and Francis and Thomas' (1992) conference-going clergymen were not significantly different from the test norms. However Francis (1992a) with a group of male and female clergy attending residential summer schools found a negative correlation between N and attitude to Christianity. He stated that among non-religious samples there was generally no relationship between levels of Neuroticism and attitude toward Christianity, but that among religiously committed samples the more stable members of church congregations and of the clerical profession report more intensely favourable attitudes toward Christianity.

Table 6.1 Neuroticism scores for clergy compared to population norms

	Clergy sample		General norms			
	Mean	SD	Mean	SD	t	P<
Male	4.46	3.14	4.95	3.44	-2.08	NS
Female	4.54	2.98	5.90	3.14	-7.21	.001

Source: Robbins, M., Francis, L.J. and Rutledge, C. (1997)

Table 6.1 shows Robbins, Francis and Rutledge's (1997) results. They demonstrated that male and female clergy did not differ significantly from each other on scores for N; that male clergy did not differ from the population norms; and that female clergy recorded significantly lower scores than women in general, and thus are closer to the N scores for men in the general population.

In looking at links between Neuroticism and churchmanship or denomination, Francis and Kay found both male and female Pentecostal ministry candidates scored significantly lower N scores than the general population, and thus found support for the view that 'glossolalia promotes positive aspects of psychological health' (Francis and Kay, 1995, p.589). Francis and Thomas (1997) found the same to be true of charismatic Anglican clergymen, as did Francis and Jones (1997) with charismatic adult Christians; Robbins, Hair and Francis (1999), however, found their male charismatic Anglican clergy had similar N scores to the general population.

To summarize we can say that research shows a significant negative correlation between N and religiosity among regular churchgoers. There is no significant difference for scores on the Neuroticism scale between male clergy and the general population; female clergy record lower Neuroticism scores than women in general. There is evidence that charismatics or Pentecostals record lower N scores than the general population.

The results of this study

Table 6.2 presents the mean scores for the 1994 male ($N = 202$) and female ($N = 60$) curates on the EPQ and EPQR-S scales for Neuroticism. There are no significant differences between male and female clergy. This concurs with Robbins, Francis and Rutledge's (1997) study.

Table 6.2 EPQ and EPQR-S mean scores for Neuroticism by sex

	male		female			
	mean	SD	mean	SD	t	P<
EPQ N	9.13	5.29	10.05	4.94	-1.19	NS
EPQR-S N	4.46	3.20	4.77	3.02	-0.65	NS

Table 6.3 presents the mean scores of EPQR-S Neuroticism for the male and female curates alongside those of Robbins, Francis and Rutledge (1997) for male and female clergy in general. The statistics demonstrate that male curates do not differ from male clergy and nor do female curates differ from female clergy on the Neuroticism scale.

Table 6.3 Mean Neuroticism scores for curates compared to serving clergy

	curates		clergy			
	mean	SD	mean	SD	t	P<
male	4.46	3.20	4.46	3.14	0.00	NS
female	4.77	3.02	4.54	2.98	+0.57	NS

Source: Robbins, M., Francis, L.J. and Rutledge, C. (1997)

Table 6.4 presents the mean Neuroticism scores for the male and female curates alongside the population norms established for the EPQR-S. The statistics show that male curates differ significantly from men in general, and female curates from women in general by recording lower Neuroticism scores.

Table 6.4 Mean Neuroticism scores for curates compared to population norms

	curates		general norms			
	mean	SD	mean	SD	t	P<
male	4.46	3.20	4.95	3.44	-1.69	.05
female	4.77	3.02	5.90	3.14	-2.64	.01

There are a number of observations to be made about these results. First, since comparison of the curates with the established clergy, as measured by Robbins, Francis and Rutledge (1997), shows the personality profile of the 1994 curates identical to that of serving clergy, it may well be that the profile thus depicted represents the norm for Anglican clergy, both male and female.

Second, since women curates are more stable than women in general and male curates than men in general, it seems that those who enter the ordained ministry of the Anglican Church are different in personality from the men and women to whom they will minister. This bears out the research of Francis (1991b, 1992a) and Orchard and Francis (1998) that amongst religiously committed groups there is a significant negative relationship between Neuroticism and attitude toward Christianity. Those who are more religiously committed are more stable.

As we turn to the churchmanship differences between different groups of clergy in our study it is worth remembering again that there are so few empirical studies where churchmanship has been used as a variable. The findings of this study provide us with the best gauge of the newest clergy in the Anglican Church.

Table 6.5 Neuroticism scores by Catholic/Evangelical churchmanship

Catholic		Central		Evangelical			
mean	SD	mean	SD	mean	SD	F	P<
9.62	5.05	10.83	5.19	8.59	5.28	3.13	0.05

Table 6.5 shows the results from this study on the Catholic/Evangelical dimension. One way analysis of variance (ANOVA) is used to analyse for any significant difference between the mean scores of the churchmanship groups. This table shows that there is a significant difference in Neuroticism. When Rutledge studied serving clergy (1999, p.181) he found that the Catholic clergy scored significantly higher on N than the Evangelical clergy. This differed from Francis and Thomas (1996a) who found no differences between Anglo-Catholics and other clergy on this scale.

> Whilst it is possible that the Catholic clergy may demonstrate less stability than their Evangelical colleagues, suffering greater degrees of anxiety, it is also possible that they may exhibit more feminine characteristics of emotional care with a greater degree of empathy for their parishioners.
> (Rutledge, 1999, p.182)

In this study, though, when all three of the groups on this dimension are compared and not just Catholics versus Evangelicals, we find a significant difference: the Central curates score highest on Neuroticism and the Evangelicals score lowest. Evangelicals are the most stable and those of a Central churchmanship are the most neurotic. So the present study supports Francis and Thomas' conclusion that Anglo-Catholic clergy are not more neurotic. It is worth remembering Rutledge's words that the high N scores for Central clergy may indicate 'more feminine characteristics of emotional care with a greater degree of empathy for their parishioners'.

Table 6.6 shows the results when the churchmanship groups are compared on the Liberal/Conservative dimension. The Middle-of-the-road curates score highest on Neuroticism and the Conservatives lowest but not to a significant level. However when a post hoc t-test was run between the Middle-of-the-road and Conservative groups alone, it showed the Middle-of-the-road to be significantly more neurotic than the Conservatives ($t = 1.96$, $p < 0.05$).

Table 6.6 Neuroticism scores by Liberal/Conservative churchmanship

Liberal		Middle-of-the-road		Conservative			
mean	SD	mean	SD	mean	SD	F	P<
9.80	4.92	10.38	5.21	8.63	5.41	2.29	NS

Table 6.7 shows the results when the churchmanship groups are compared on the Charismatic dimension. The Anti-charismatic curates score highest on Neuroticism and the Pro-charismatics lowest, but not to a significant level.

Table 6.7 Neuroticism scores by Charismatic churchmanship

Pro-charismatic		Non-charismatic		Anti-charismatic			
mean	SD	mean	SD	mean	SD	F	P<
8.95	4.82	9.72	5.97	9.81	5.48	0.79	NS

In order to test whether the differing proportions of male and female curates within the churchmanship groups were influencing the results, a partial correlation coefficient was computed between each of the churchmanship dimensions and Neuroticism while holding sex as a constant. Only one of the relationships achieved adequate levels of significance, that which shows a correlation between low scores on the Neuroticism scale and Evangelical churchmanship. This was significant at $p < 0.05$. This means that, after allowing for the differences between male and female clergy, Evangelicals are significantly more stable than the other churchmanship groups on the Catholic/Evangelical dimension. Lower Neuroticism scores should predispose Evangelical clergy to maintain a degree of emotional detachment from the tensions and frustrations that are part of Anglican parish life. They should be equipped to deal with pastoral matters with objectivity. However they may find it harder to show real empathy and sympathy in pastoral situations: they may prefer other roles to that of pastor and counsellor as they play to their strengths in parish ministry.

Chapter 7

Tough-minded or tender-minded?

Tough-minded or tender-minded: the P scale

'Psychosis' comes from a Greek word meaning 'coldness'. In his earlier works Eysenck (1953, 1961) had looked at the element of 'tough-mindedness', which he had seen as a projection of the extraverted personality, with 'tender-mindedness' as the projection of the introverted personality. In *Psychoticism as a Dimension of Personality* (1976) Eysenck and Eysenck presupposed that all functional psychoses (schizophrenia, manic-depressive illness, schizo-affective disorders and monopolar depression) are related and do not form independent categories. They also presupposed that psychoses as such are continuous with a whole spectrum of abnormal states (schizoid disorders, psychopathy, alcoholism and criminality) which occur significantly more frequently in relatives of psychotics, and shade into perfectly normal forms of behaviour. With these assumptions they created a test to measure the hypothesized continuum of psychoticism (P) and produced a scale to measure P as an independent personality factor, orthogonal to extraversion.

The test of whether the scale actually measures psychoticism would be that 'markers which clearly divide psychotics from normals should also divide high P and low P scorers in the normal (and perhaps also the psychotic) population ... The evidence strongly favours such a view' (Eysenck, 1992). So P in the EPQ measures that dimension of personality identified as psychoticism, including some of the primary factors on which psychoticism is based such as impulsivity, sensation-seeking, Machiavellianism, and lack of agreeableness and lack of conscientiousness.

There have been, and continue to be, criticisms of the psychometric properties of the P scale. Block (1977) for example found that, even using Eysenck and Eysenck's (1975) figures, one out of every four 'normal' males gained a P score higher than the mean P score of the diagnosed psychotic. So Eysenck, Eysenck and Barrett (1985) declared their intention to try and improve the psychometric weaknesses in the P scale of the EPQ. They designed new items for the scale based on the development of the original concept. They tested the relevance of those items by factor analysis and constructed improved questionnaires in the hope of improving upon the original version of the P scale. Thus the revised Eysenck Personality Questionnaire (EPQR) was created.

One of the criticisms of the EPQ psychoticism scale had been its low reliability: the new scale produced improved reliabilities of 0.78 for male and 0.76 for females which contrasted with 0.74 for males and 0.68 for females for the EPQ (Eysenck and Eysenck, 1975). Although this is still not as high as the reliabilities achieved for E and N, it must be remembered that the P scale taps several different facets (hostility, cruelty, lack of empathy, non-conformism etc) which may hold reliabilities lower than would be true of a scale like E (Eysenck, Eysenck and Barrett, 1985, pp.25-26).

At the same time Eysenck, Eysenck and Barrett (1985) chose twelve items from each of the four scales of E, P, N and L for a short scale (EPQR-S) that could be used when time was limited.

The typical high scorer on the P scale is described as:

> being solitary, not caring for people; he is often troublesome, not fitting in anywhere. He may be cruel and inhumane, lacking in feeling and empathy, and altogether intensive. He is hostile to others, even to his own kith and kin, and aggressive, even to loved ones. He has a liking for odd and unusual things, and a disregard for danger; he likes to make fools of other people, and to upset them.

It is therefore results from the EPQR-S that are reported here because of the increased reliability of the EPQR-S over the EPQ in measuring psychoticism.

The P scale and religiosity

Given the kind of personality represented by high P scores, it is no surprise to find the prediction that a favourable attitude to religion should be associated with the reverse of these psychotic tendencies. Francis (1976), in constructing his scale to measure affective attitude to religion and specifically the explicit and central aspects of Christianity (the Francis Scale of Attitude towards Christianity, or FSAC), certainly expected this. However, because of the tendency for attitude to religion scores to decline with age (Francis, 1979) and for psychoticism scores to increase with age (Eysenck and Eysenck, 1975), any correlation must take age into account. Kay (1981), in a study of 1431 secondary schoolchildren using the FSAC and the junior EPQ, found P to be negatively correlated with attitude to religion for boys, but not for girls. Francis and Pearson (1985b) by administering both the EPQ and the junior EPQ to 132 fifteen year-olds discovered that there is a significant negative correlation between P and religiosity for both boys and girls using the EPQ, but not with the junior EPQ. In his Australian study amongst students, Heaven (1990) found that P did not correlate with religious values for females, but was significantly related to traditional religiosity among males.

Francis (1991b) was the first to study the relationship between the FSAC and religiosity with adult churchgoers: he found a negative correlation between P and religiosity. In a further study using the EPQ and the junior EPQ with 1347 teenagers Francis (1992b) produced further evidence that psychoticism is the dimension of personality fundamental to religious behaviour and attitude. This result was repeated amongst college students (Francis, 1993a).

However in Francis and Pearson's (1993) study of student churchgoers, male student churchgoers record significantly lower P scores than students in general, but female student churchgoers do not differ significantly from female student norms. This seemed to suggest that for women a lower P score is related to religious attitudes but not to religious behaviour. Francis and Wilcox (1993), in a study of 230 teenage girls, found significant relationships between low P scores and both personal prayer and public attendance at church. Maltby (1995, 1997) found a correlation between low P and frequency of personal prayer. However Francis and Daniel (1997) were unable to corroborate this link among churchgoing Methodists. White, Joseph and Neil (1995) confirmed the relationship between religious attitudes and low P in a study of 183 adults, as did Gillings and Joseph (1996) with 106 adults. This was supported by Lewis and Maltby (1995), Maltby, Tally, Cooper and Leslie (1995), Carter, Kay and Francis (1996) and Maltby (1997). Dunne, Martin, Pangan and Heath (1997) studied 7616 Australian twins and found a significant correlation between P and frequency of church attendance, as did Lewis and Maltby (1996) in the USA, Maltby (1997) in the Republic of Ireland, and Francis and Katz (1992) in Israel. Francis and Bolger (1997) found the same inverse relationship between P and religiosity with retired people. To sum up, research indicates that the more religious the person, the more tender-minded they will be.

The P scale and the clergy

Francis and Pearson (1990) found that the P scores of their mid-career male Anglican clergy matched the population norms, as did the male ordinands of Francis (1991a), but the female ordinands scored higher than the female norms. Francis' (1992c) study of clergy on residential summer schools indicated a negative relationship between attitude toward Christianity and P. Francis and Robbins (1996b) found that non-stipendiary women clergy record significantly lower P scores than stipendiary women clergy. Since this implies that the non-stipendiaries are more tender-minded and less tough-minded than the stipendiaries, they suggested that 'the selection procedures seem to be looking for less exacting standards of leadership, management and decision-making potential among its female non-stipendiary candidates'. Robbins, Francis and Rutledge's (1997) results (shown in table 7.1) show that both male and female clergy record significantly lower P scores than the general population.

Table 7.1 Psychoticism scores for clergy compared to population norms

	Clergy sample		General norms			
	Mean	SD	Mean	SD	t	P<
Male	2.03	1.62	3.08	2.20	- 8.15	0.001
Female	2.00	1.50	2.35	1.88	- 3.72	0.001

Source: Robbins, M., Francis, L.J. and Rutledge, C. (1997)

Francis and Rodger (1994) found a significant negative correlation between P scores and the priority given to the role of administrator. The role of administrator is not one which is central to most ordinands' image of ministry, but it has to be recognized as a frequent and inevitable demand of ministry. They said that tough-minded clergy are more likely to 'resist accommodating their earlier established preferences to the demands made upon them by other individuals or by the institutional church.' (Francis and Rodger, 1994, p.951) Also the amount of influence attributed to the hierarchy of bishop and archdeacon is negatively related to P scores which suggests that tough-minded clergy are least likely to take notice of the hierarchy.

In their study of Pentecostal ministry candidates, Francis and Kay (1995) found the male candidates had significantly lower P scores than men in general, but the female candidates were no more nor less tough-minded than women in general. Francis and Thomas (1996a, 1996b, 1997) found no correlation between P scores and Anglo-Catholic orientation, mystical orientation or charismatic experience. Robbins, Hair and Francis (1999) found no correlation between P scores and charismatic experience.

The results of this study

Table 7.2 presents the mean scores for the 1994 male (N = 202) and female (N = 60) curates on the EPQ and EPQR-S scales for Psychoticism. There are no significant differences between male and female clergy.

Table 7.2 EPQ and EPQR-S mean scores for Psychoticism by sex

	male		female			
	mean	SD	mean	SD	t	P<
EPQ P	2.50	2.14	2.25	1.89	+0.81	NS
EPQR-S P	2.06	1.80	1.85	1.30	+0.86	NS

Table 7.3 presents the mean scores of EPQR-S Psychoticism for the male and female curates alongside those of Robbins, Francis and Rutledge (1997) for male and female clergy in general. The statistics demonstrate that male curates do not differ from male clergy and female curates do not differ from female clergy in terms of scores recorded on the Psychoticism scales. It may well be that the profile thus depicted represents the norm for Anglican clergy, both men and women.

Table 7.3 Mean Psychoticism scores for curates compared to serving clergy

	curates		clergy			
	mean	SD	mean	SD	t	P<
male	2.06	1.80	2.03	1.62	+0.20	NS
female	1.85	1.30	2.00	1.50	-0.75	NS

Source: Robbins, M., Francis, L.J. and Rutledge, C. (1997)

Table 7.4 Mean Psychoticism scores for curates compared to population norms

	curates		general norms			
	mean	SD	mean	SD	t	P<
male	2.06	1.80	3.08	2.20	-6.01	.001
female	1.85	1.30	2.35	1.88	-2.03	.05

Table 7.4 presents the mean Psychoticism scores for the male and female curates alongside the population norms established for the EPQR-S. The statistics show that male curates differ from men in general, scoring significantly lower scores on Psychoticism. The female curates recorded significantly lower Psychoticism scores than women in general. Male and female clergy are more tender-minded than men and women in general. In fact they differ so much from the general population in personality on all three Eysenckian scales of personality that there must be concerns about their ability to get alongside their parishioners.

Table 7.5 Psychoticism scores by Catholic/Evangelical churchmanship

Catholic		Central		Evangelical			
mean	SD	mean	SD	mean	SD	F	P<
2.76	2.44	2.24	1.79	2.25	1.64	1.83	NS

Table 7.5 shows the results from this study on the Catholic/Evangelical dimension. One way ANOVA is used to analyse for any significant difference between the mean scores of the churchmanship groups. Francis and Thomas' study (1996a) is again supported by the results on the Psychoticism scale where the Catholic curates score highest and the Central curates the lowest, but not to a significant level.

Table 7.6 Psychoticism scores by Liberal/Conservative churchmanship

Liberal		Middle-of-the-road		Conservative			
mean	SD	mean	SD	mean	SD	F	P<
2.68	2.54	1.85	1.48	2.41	1.86	2.17	NS

Table 7.6 shows the results when the churchmanship groups are compared on the Liberal/Conservative dimension. The Liberal curates score highest on the Psychoticism scale and the Middle-of-the-road curates the lowest, but not to a significant level.

Table 7.7 Psychoticism scores by Charismatic churchmanship

Pro-charismatic		Non-charismatic		Anti-charismatic			
mean	SD	mean	SD	mean	SD	F	P<
2.35	1.74	2.57	2.08	2.48	2.77	0.26	NS

Table 7.7 shows the results when the churchmanship groups are compared on the Charismatic dimension. The Non-charismatic curates score highest on the Psychoticism scale and the Pro-charismatics the lowest, but not to a significant level.

Personality and churchmanship

In this and the previous two chapters we have provided an answer to the question, 'Are personality and churchmanship linked?' First let us summarize the findings for the whole cohort of clergy ordained to stipendiary ministry in England and Wales in 1994. The male curates are more extraverted than the female curates. The male curates are more extraverted than male clergy in general. The male curates are more extraverted, more stable and more tender-minded than men in general. The female curates are less extraverted, more stable and more tender-minded than women in general. The men and women being called into the ordained ministry in these times are quite different from the men and women among whom they are working.

So are personality and churchmanship linked? Hardly at all. Apart from the highly stable Evangelicals, the stable Conservatives, the neurotic Middle-of-the-roads, and the more neurotic Centrals.

This lack of correlation between churchmanship and personality might seem surprising but it is consistent with other research. As we have previously remarked, Francis and Thomas (1996a) found no difference on E, N and P between Catholics and Evangelicals. Likewise Rutledge (1999) found no difference between Catholics and Evangelicals on E and P, and also found Evangelicals scored much lower on the Neuroticism scale than Catholics.

Whenever clergy hear the results of this study, that churchmanship and personality are hardly inter-linked, they breathe a sigh of relief. Some of that relief is related to an overly deterministic understanding of personality psychology. They seem to be saying that if membership of Reform or Affirming Catholicism were linked to personality type there might seem to be less room for dialogue. Mostly though the relief is associated with an intuitive feeling that churchmanship is a choice, a preference rather than a development of who they are essentially as people.

Luther's words in his speech at the Diet of Worms in 1521 ('Here I stand. I can do no other.') have an honourable Protestant pedigree. Our research is beginning to suggest that such words may be too lofty for a personal preference such as churchmanship. Goldsmith (1994) said, 'Much contemporary debate and division in theology is, to my mind, not so much about theology as about personality.' This research suggests that Goldsmith's statement is not true. Personality is important, but the debates and divisions between churchmanship groups recounted in the first chapter of this book are about theology.

Chapter 8

More or less likely to burn out?

Introduction

The last three chapters have looked at the lack of substantial links between churchmanship and the personality of clergy as operationalized by Eysenck. So what about the work that the clergy do? Though at its best wonderfully fulfilling, parish ministry can also be tough and demanding. Perhaps different churchmanship groups are more prone to burn out when the pressure begins to mount?

What do we mean by 'clergy burnout'? When studying Roman Catholic priests in the USA Fichter expressed the view that clergy burnout was a myth and pointed out that 'all through history and in all cultures – and long before the art of psychiatry was discovered – people have had old-fashioned nervous breakdowns, have cracked up and burned out' (Fichter, 1984, p.374). Selye similarly put stress and burnout in an historical context: 'The existence of physical and mental strain, the manifold interactions between somatic and psychic reactions, as well as the importance of defensive-adaptive responses, had all been more or less clearly recognized since time immemorial' (Selye, 1956, p.263). Nevertheless in the last forty years there has been a great deal of attention to burnout, and not just within the academic community. An early example in popular culture of the use of the term was Graham Greene's novel, *A Burnt-Out Case* (Penguin, 1961).

The origins of burnout research were in the sphere of psychological stress. In the 1970s a great deal of exploratory work was undertaken, based mainly on personal experience, observations and interviews, in order to understand workplace stress and to find ways of measuring it quantitatively. From a sociological point of view much of the discussion focused on role conflict and role ambiguity (Rizzo, House and Lirtzman, 1970), though later there grew a recognition that sources of stress, or stressors, are themselves subject to variation as a result of changes in society (Glowinkowski and Cooper, 1985).

Freudenberger (1974, 1975) was one of the earliest to popularize the term 'burnout' and report on what burnout felt like. He believed that it was a discrete factor, signified by physical and emotional indicators and linked with a predisposition to fail, to wear out, or to become exhausted by making excessive demands on energy, strength or resources.

Christina Maslach

Christina Maslach's early research was concerned with the phenomenon of 'detached concern' that she noticed in health service professionals (1973). She began to separate out the notion of 'depersonalization' as a factor in burnout (1976, 1978a). As a result of her research she published, with Sandra Jackson, the Maslach Burnout Inventory (MBI) (1981, 1986) that has been widely used since in the empirical study of burnout.

Maslach and Jackson saw burnout as a syndrome of emotional exhaustion and cynicism that occurs frequently among those who work in people-related areas of work. They recognized three elements to burnout. First, there are increased feelings of emotional exhaustion: as their emotional resources are depleted, workers feel no longer able to give of themselves on a psychological level. Many subsequent researchers have seen emotional exhaustion as the central facet of burnout (Cordes and Dougherty, 1993). Second, there is the development of depersonalization, of negative, cynical attitudes and feelings about clients: workers can develop a callous or even dehumanized attitude towards their clients, seeing them as somehow deserving of their troubles. Third, there is a reduced sense of personal accomplishment marked by the tendency to evaluate oneself negatively, particularly with regard to one's work with clients: workers feel unhappy about themselves and dissatisfied with their work accomplishments.

Maslach and Jackson recognized that the consequences of burnout are potentially very serious for both staff and clients, leading to a deterioration in the quality of care or service being provided, and also to an increase in staff stress.

> The staff person who burns out is unable to deal successfully with the chronic emotional stress of the job, and this failure to cope can be manifested in a number of ways, including low morale, impaired performance, absenteeism and high turnover. A common response to burnout is to get out, by changing jobs, moving into administrative work, or even leaving the profession entirely.
> (Maslach, 1978a, p.56)

The construction and testing of the MBI

Having hypothesized three aspects of burnout (emotional exhaustion, depersonalization and reduced personal accomplishment) Maslach and Jackson devised the MBI (1981) to measure each of these aspects. They drew upon their earlier interview and questionnaire research into the attitudes and feelings which characterize a worker who is suffering burnout. Forty-seven items were written in the form of statements about personal feelings or attitudes, for example, 'Working with people all day is really a strain for me'. Each statement was to be rated by the respondent on two dimensions, frequency (a 6-point scale ranging from 1 'a few times a year' to 6 'every day') and intensity (a 7-point scale ranging from 1 'very mild, barely noticeable' to 7 'major, very strong'). A place was provided for the respondent to mark 'never' if the feeling or attitude described was never experienced.

This preliminary scale was administered to 605 people from a variety of health and service occupations. After factor analysis, four factors were found and the number of items reduced to the 25 which had a loading greater than 0.40 on a single factor. This 25-item scale was then administered to 420 people in a similar range of occupations as the first set of respondents. The same four factors emerged. They were similar for both samples, and featured on both the frequency and intensity ratings.

The first three factors had eigenvalues greater than unity and are considered as subscales of the MBI. The nine items on the Emotional Exhaustion subscale describe feelings of being emotionally over-extended and exhausted by one's work. The five items on the Depersonalization subscale describe an unfeeling and impersonal response towards recipients of one's care or service. Higher mean scores on these two subscales indicate higher degrees of experienced burnout. The moderate correlation between these two scales would suggest that they are separate, but related, aspects of burnout. The eight items on the Personal Accomplishment subscale describe feelings of competence and successful achievement in one's work with people. Unlike the previous two subscales, lower mean scores on this subscale correspond to higher levels of experienced burnout. (A fourth factor appeared during factor analysis comprising three items. It appeared to reflect a dimension of involvement with other people. Because it had a lower eigenvalue than the first three factors Maslach and Jackson did not include it as a subscale of the MBI.)

The test-retest reliability reported for the MBI after 2 to 4 weeks was satisfactory. Content validity was checked by co-workers and by spouses of the respondents. An alpha coefficient of 0.83 (frequency) and 0.84 (intensity) showed a good level of internal consistency for the whole scale.

One of the first published independent critiques of the MBI came from Iwanicki and Schwab in 1981. They examined the reliability and validity of the inventory within a single profession when they administered the MBI to 469 teachers. They omitted the three questions of the Involvement subscale, and thus used a 22-item scale. Using the same form of factor analysis as Maslach and Jackson, Iwanicki and Schwab found the same factors of Emotional Exhaustion and Personal Accomplishment. However they found that Depersonalization broke down into two factors, one affected by the job, and the other affected by the clients. They raised questions too about the need for the two ratings for frequency and intensity:

> Because of the high relationship between subscale scores on the frequency and intensity dimensions, serious consideration should be given to whether the two dimensional format is necessary when using the MBI with teachers. Administration time could be reduced by asking teachers to respond to the MBI in terms of either the frequency or intensity with which feelings of burnout are experienced.
> (Iwanicki and Schwab, 1981, p.1172)

Belcastro and Gold (1983) also omitted the Involvement subscale when studying the relationship between burnout and ill-health among 359 teachers in Illinois. They found that the MBI was indicative of the presence of physical complaints amongst teachers. Further support for the validity of the MBI came from Gold (1984, 1985), Meier (1984), Powers and Gose (1986), Rafferty, Lemkau, Purdy and Rudisill (1986) and van Horn, Schaufeli and Enzmann (1999).

The revision of the MBI

In 1986 Maslach and Jackson produced the second edition of the MBI. The Involvement subscale was removed. The intensity dimension was also removed, leaving frequency as the measure of the attitudes and feelings of burnout. The authors also made clear the concept of burnout that the MBI is measuring. 'Burnout is conceptualized as a continuous variable, ranging from low to moderate to high degrees of experienced feeling. It is not viewed as a dichotomous variable, which is either present or absent' (Maslach and Jackson, 1986, p.2). The scores on each subscale therefore indicate 'a high degree of burnout', or 'an average degree of burnout' or 'a low degree of burnout'.

After the second edition of the MBI, Green and Walkey (1988) subjected Iwanicki and Schwab's data to factor analysis again. As a result they concluded that the MBI is a brief, readily interpretable questionnaire with a consistently replicable three-factor structure that measures the three corresponding aspects of burnout. Pierce and Molloy (1989) and Lee and Ashforth (1990) found the same level of construct validity. Green, Walkey and Taylor (1991) also produced a multicultural and multinational confirmatory study of the three-factor structure.

The nature of burnout

To sum up, the MBI in its revised form has become an accepted, standardized and psychometrically sound instrument for measuring burnout. Burnout is comprised of three factors. Emotional Exhaustion is characterized by a lack of energy and a feeling that one's emotional resources are used up. This 'compassion fatigue' may be accompanied by feelings of frustration and tension as workers realise that they cannot continue to give of themselves or be as responsible for clients as they have been in the past. The second factor Depersonalization is marked by the treatment of clients as objects rather than people. Workers can exhibit a detached and unemotional callousness, and they may be cynical towards co-workers, clients and the organization. Some symptoms of this are the use of derogatory or abstract language, the use of jargon, strict compartmentalization of professional lives, and withdrawal through longer breaks or extended conversations with co-workers (Maslach and Pines, 1977). The final component of burnout, diminished Personal Accomplishment, is characterized by a tendency to evaluate oneself negatively. Individuals experience a decline in feelings of job competence and successful achievement in their work or their interactions with people. Frequently there is the perception of a lack of progress or even of losing ground.

In considering the relationship between age and burnout, Maslach (1976) found that burnout is likely to occur in the first few years of a person's career. McCarthy's (1985) study of nurses found that those nurses scoring highest on the burnout scale were in the younger 21 to 29 year old age group rather than the older 29 to 59 year old one. van der Ploeg, van Leeuwen and Kwee (1990) found that age was negatively related to burnout in all three aspects, and Byrne (1991) found that younger teachers experienced more Emotional Exhaustion and lower levels of Personal Accomplishment than their older colleagues. Various reasons have been adduced for this inverse relationship between burnout and age. It is suggested that with increased age people become more stable and mature, developing a more realistic perspective on life and changed behavioural patterns which reduce the likelihood of burnout. Stevens and O'Neill (1983) suggested that older workers would develop new expectations grounded not on their clients but on themselves, with their satisfaction coming from their own sense of competence. Two studies suggested that burnout is progressive in nature (Golembiewski, Munzenrider and Carter, 1983, Gryskiewicz and Buttner, 1992). They indicated that burnout begins with depersonalization which increases, leading to a feeling of greatly reduced personal accomplishment, and subsequently to emotional exhaustion.

Personality and burnout

There have been few longitudinal studies on the MBI but those that have been reported (eg Capel, 1991, Piedmont, 1993) have found that a respondent's position on the burnout continuum is stable over time. This leads to a consideration of just what it is that the MBI is measuring. It could be argued that the stability of burnout scores reflects the long-term stress of the workplace environment: Costa and colleagues (Costa, McCrae and Zonderman, 1987, McCrae and Costa, 1988) have shown that certain individuals are able to adapt quite well to stressful conditions and are able to return quickly to their original levels of well-being; others who have a lower intrinsic capacity for coping are not so resilient and remain distressed. Because these experiences of life satisfaction and coping ability are linked to enduring qualities of individuals, the stability of the burnout scores may be due to stable dispositions as well as stable environments. Maslach (1978b) felt that the prevalence of the burnout phenomenon and the range of different staff who were affected indicated that the cause of burnout was primarily situational and that research should therefore be focused on uncovering the characteristics of the bad situation. Burke and Greenglass argued that 'research findings accumulated over the past 10 years have shown few significant and consistent personality correlates of burnout but many significant and consistent job, work setting, and organizational correlates of burnout' (Burke and Greenglass, 1989b, p.272).

Yet there are research reports which suggest the presence and influence of personality factors on burnout. In a study of commercial airline pilots using

Eysenck's personality measures, Evans (1986) found indications that it was personality factors rather than environmental factors which played a causal role in generating a stress reaction within individuals. Using the same personality measure Kirkcaldy, Thorne and Thomas (1989) studied job satisfaction among psychosocial workers:

> Neuroticism was positively correlated with job pressure and dissatisfaction. Extraverts were inclined to be more dissatisfied with their work and yielded higher career motivation scores compared to introverts. There was some indication that the combinative effects of trait Psychoticism and Neuroticism may relate to a composite 'fusing' general job dissatisfaction and job pressure.
> (Kirkcaldy, Thorne and Thomas, 1989, p.194)

Piedmont (1993), in an exploratory longitudinal study with occupational therapists, found personality factors accounting for a significant portion of the variance in burnout scores. Other researchers too have found that personality as a variable should be included into research on burnout (Matthews, 1990, Greenglass, Burke and Ondrack, 1990, Eastburg, Williamson, Gorsuch and Ridley, 1994). Rutledge's (1993) study of the clergy, which is reported later in this chapter – see 'MBI and the clergy' – found a significant correlation between each of the three MBI burnout subscales and each of the four Eysenck personality dimensions for male clergy, though fewer correlations for female clergy.

Such research on the links between personality and burnout shows that burnout is a stable phenomenon clearly associated with enduring qualities in the individual. Personality seems to play a large role in influencing perceptions, reactions and interpretations of situational events in the work environment. This is not to deny that a situation can become so overwhelming that even the hardiest and most stable of individuals would succumb to emotional and physical exhaustion. Generally however individuals will vary in the degree to which they perceive and experience an event as stressful, with a moderate stressor having a more disorientating effect on someone with a high Neuroticism score than someone with a lower N score.

The MBI and religiosity

There has been a great deal of research into the correlation between religiosity and measures of stress, but very little research into the correlation between religiosity and burnout as measured by the MBI. Generally intrinsic religiosity is seen as acting as a buffer against stress (Williams, Larson and Buckler, 1991, Maton, 1989). A study of American students found that those high in intrinsic religiosity and those who had the support of religion to cope with problems became less depressed and anxious when experiencing stressful life events which were beyond their control (Park, Cohen and Herb, 1990). In addition most religious people find that their religious beliefs help them to find meaning in very stressful events, for example, the death of a child (McIntosh, Silver and Westman, 1993) or their own impending death (Swenson, 1961).

The handful of reported studies examining religiosity and burnout find no link. No significant relationship was found by Liller and McDermott (1990) in their sample of health educators, nor by Belcastro, Gold and Grant (1982) in their study of correctional teachers.

Given that the MBI is mainly used to measure burnout in the workplace (and particularly among human service workers) it is not surprising that much of the work concerned with burnout and religiosity is directed at religious professionals, the clergy.

The MBI and the clergy

The Jesuit priest Alfred Kammer asked, 'Why is it that brevity seems to be the one common characteristic of a wide variety of forms of social ministry in direct contact with the poor and the problems of the poor?' The answer he gives is 'burnout' which he defines as a physical, emotional, psychological and spiritual phenomenon (Kammer, 1978). Brockman (1978) noted how the many changes in the Roman Catholic Church had led to increasing instances of burnout among church leaders. As long ago as 1980 Gill was asking what steps church leaders could take to prevent unnecessary and costly burnout:

> First, they can ensure that candidates for high-intensity, people-contact jobs are carefully evaluated before being assigned. Adequate educational preparation for their work is needed, as well as the development of personality, qualities and habits that will enable them to cope effectively with the stresses their occupation generates.
> (Gill, 1980, p.70)

There is much agreement in the literature that prime causes of stress in the ministry are role conflict and role ambiguity (Winton and Cameron, 1986, Gross, 1989, Coate, 1989, Malony and Hunt, 1991). However, as Fimian (1984) observed in his study of those caring for mentally retarded adults, whilst there is every reason to believe that role problems are a small predictor of stress, they are not indicators of burnout.

Daniel and Rogers, in their review of research into ministers and burnout before the MBI was published, noted that the traditional personality pattern of clergy 'corresponds to the personality description in the burn-out phenomenon' (Daniel and Rogers, 1981, p.246). Yet Rayburn, Richmond and Rogers (1982, 1986) did not find any evidence in their small sample that clergy suffered high stress. Brierley, Myers and Marshall found in their sample of clergy from many denominations that 55 per cent said 'I am overworked, but not seriously', 30 per cent said 'My workload is just about right', 14 per cent said 'I am seriously overworked', and one per cent said 'I am under-employed, but not seriously' (Brierley, Myers and Marshall, 1991, p.23). Francis' study of Evangelical ministers said 'the fact that 38 per cent of pastors feel overwhelmed by pastoral care demands indicate a high level of stress and possible burnout' (Francis, 2000, p.10).

Though Fichter's article is called *The myth of clergy burnout*, he asked no questions in his survey about burnout nor used the MBI or any other psychometric measure of burnout. Rather 'we did probe for signs of emotional stress and psychological disorders, and found a very small proportion (3.8 per cent) of all respondents who report that they are troubled with mental illness, mainly in the form of depression' (Fichter, 1984, p.375). Again he says 'following the lead of the bishops we speculated that if there are any prospective, or actual, burnout victims among our clergy respondents, they ought to be found among the stressful hard-workers', and discovers that 'the dynamic, dedicated, up-to-date priest thrives in this situation' (Fichter, 1984, p.376). In this context Gill (1980) made a distinction between workaholics and candidates for burnout:

> It is not uncommon to hear someone say to a hardworking person who spends unusually long hours on the job every day, 'Don't work so hard; you'll burn yourself out'. The usual, but hardly original, response 'I'd rather burn out than rust out', reveals both the high level of commitment and the sense of immunity experienced by the person voluntarily enslaved by work. Workaholics like that are not generally the type to burn out. Their compulsive work habits, management psychologist Marilyn Machlowitz has found, flow from a genuine love for what they are doing. In her recent book *Workaholics*, Machlowitz (1980) describes them as 'those whose desire to work long and hard is intrinsic and whose work habits always exceed the prescriptions of the job and the expectations of the people for whom they work'. ... They are not capable of relating to others in a deeply personal or intimate way, but they can and usually do succeed in going through their entire lifetimes without burning out. Perhaps their ability to utilize compulsive work as a defence mechanism protects them from getting emotionally close to people and experiencing the anxieties, frustrations, and stress felt by the more vulnerable individuals who do burn out.
> (Gill, 1980, p.69)

Certainly Fichter was right to emphasize the generally high level of health of the clergy. As regards physical health the clergy have historically enjoyed longevity. King and Bailar (1969) noted that with few exceptions demographic studies carried out on clergy in Europe and America have shown that their life expectancy is longer than that for comparable males in the general population. Holme, Helgeland, Hjerman, Leren and Lund-Larsen (1977) studied a variety of symptom-free people in their 40s in Oslo for coronary risk factors and found that those in religious work had by far the lowest coronary risk score. Argyle (1987, p.47) reported on stress levels for various occupations: clergy came in the 10 per cent with the lowest stress levels, with only librarians, museum workers, nursery nurses and astronomers less stressed. Fletcher (1990) reported the Standardized Mortality Ratios showing the mortality risks for clergy for the major causes of death:

> The table shows that clergy have low mortality rates for most causes, which would support the view that their job is not particularly stressful. They do, however, show particular elevations for cancer of the colon, cancer of the brain, cancer of

the lymph and haematopoietic tissue, and chronic liver disease and cirrhosis. Whether this may be due to some other aspect of the lifestyle of the clergy is another matter.
(Fletcher, 1990, p.19)

In the ongoing Bath University *Work Centrality, Work Careers, and Household* project for the ESRC Future of Work research programme, Rose (1999), using data from the British Household Panel Survey, suggests that clergy show the second highest level of satisfaction with their jobs, with only medical secretaries scoring higher.

> Although the clergy OUG's [occupational unit group] median score for quality aspects is also one of the very highest of all OUGs, it still falls substantially below that of the clergy's satisfaction with the material rewards and conditions of its work. This finding, in itself interesting, provides evidence that is valuable in two quite different ways. Firstly it suggests that normative factors may be of considerable importance within certain occupations in setting benchmarks for satisfaction. For the clergy, low material wants and expectations as it were 'go with the job', and entrance to the clergy, of whatever denomination, is conditional upon accepting them. Moreover, those members of the clergy who may be less satisfied with their material rewards may feel morally constrained to understate their dissatisfaction. Secondly, the results for the clergy provide evidence of a 'known groups' type that the two composite job satisfaction measures produce findings that are, in all likelihood, broadly valid. The material rewards of the clergy are indeed very low in absolute terms for a professional group, yet expressed satisfaction with them is abnormally high.
> (Rose, 1999, p.9. See also Penn, Rose and Rubery, 1994)

When it comes to empirical measures of burnout, and specifically the MBI, there is less research focused on the clergy. Warner and Carter (1984), in a study of 33 pastors and 28 pastors' wives using the MBI, found that it was the pastors' wives who scored highest on the Emotional Exhaustion subscale, whereas the pastors did not score significantly higher than the non-pastors. They believed that this was influenced by the age of their sample of pastors. 'Pastors who have been in the ministry longer will have developed coping techniques to prevent or reduce emotional exhaustion. Those who have not developed adequate coping techniques would be expected to have left the ministry many years prior' (Warner and Carter, 1984, p.130).

The most widespread study of the MBI and clergy was undertaken by Rutledge (1993, 1999) and his results are reported below. He used an adapted form of the MBI. Professor Leslie Francis had obtained permission from the Consulting Psychologists Press in California to adapt the MBI for use, under licence and at a cost, with clergy in the UK. The original adaptation was undertaken in consultation with Rutledge and in preparation for his study. This adaptation modified the original inventory in five ways. First, the American original was Anglicized. Second, the items were shaped to reflect the experience and language of pastoral ministry. For example, Maslach and Jackson's 'I deal very effectively with the problems of my recipients' was changed to 'I deal very effectively with the problems of my parishioners'. Third, additional items were developed to bring each of the three subscales to the same length of ten items each. Fourth, the response scale was changed from a 7-point measure of frequency to a 5-point Likert (1932) scale of attitudinal intensity, ranging from 'agree strongly', through 'agree', 'not certain', and 'disagree' to 'disagree strongly'. Fifth, the thirty statements were randomized. Because of the possibility of drawing comparisons with Rutledge and others' studies of Anglican clergy it is this adaptation of the MBI that has been used here. This Revised MBI produced the following satisfactory alpha coefficients: 0.89 for Emotional Exhaustion; 0.81 for Depersonalization; and 0.78 for Personal Accomplishment.

Rutledge's studies with the MBI and the clergy

Rutledge's 1993 investigation is a major study of Anglican stipendiary parochial clergy in England covering a five per cent sample of all male clergy and a 25 per cent sample of female clergy (at the time of study, women deacons). The response rate at 78 per cent was high. For his 1999 study he added another random sample of five per cent of the male serving clergy so that his total database now represents a tenth of all male Anglican clergy.

It is not possible to compare his burnout results with Maslach and Jackson's demographic norms because of the adaptations made to the MBI but until this adapted scale is used enough to generate clergy norms Rutledge's results (shown in table 8.1) provide the best baseline for understanding clergy burnout.

Table 8.1 Mean Burnout scores by sex

	male clergy		female clergy			
	mean	SD	mean	SD	t	P<
Emotional Exhaustion	21.50	7.34	20.96	5.88	+0.66	NS
Depersonalization	19.17	5.49	17.31	4.31	+3.02	.005
Personal Accomplishment	24.84	4.81	24.11	3.92	+1.35	NS

Source: Rutledge, C. (1993)

Contrary to predictions that women would score more highly than men on the Emotional Exhaustion and the Personal Accomplishment subscales (Maslach and Jackson, 1985), Rutledge's data suggest that there is no significant difference. Male clergy do score significantly higher than female clergy on the Depersonalization subscale in line with the theoretical prediction (Maslach and Jackson, 1985).

Age is seen to have a link with burnout. When the under 30 year old age group was compared with the 60-64 year old age group the younger group scored significantly higher on Emotional Exhaustion and on Depersonalization. However the age picture was not as simple as this. The highest scores on Emotional

Exhaustion came from the 45 to 49 year olds and the 30 to 34 year olds, on Depersonalization from the under 30s and the 45 to 49 year olds, and on Personal Accomplishment from the 30 to 34 year olds and the 50 to 54 year olds. Randall and Francis (1996) pointed out that in questionnaire surveys amongst clergy number of years in the ministry may be a more significant variable than chronological age. There would be value in controlling for the variable of number of years in the ministry when studying the relationship between age and clergy burnout.

By means of factor analysis Rutledge isolated two critical groups of clergy whom he named 'traditional parish clergy' and 'new professional clergy':

> [The traditional parish clergy] would use traditional forms of service, fulfil traditional Sunday expectations of service taking, and perform rites of passage for all in their parish irrespective of church attendance. They felt they ought to be available at all times to those in their community, chair committees, be involved in the local school, and take an active part in fetes, fairs and other fund raising activities ... [The new professional clergy] enjoy contemporary and non structured services involving lay leadership; teaching within the context of house groups and preparation groups for baptisms and marriage. They do not possess a desire to serve the whole community nor do they feel they ought to be involved in fund raising activities. They see value in in-service training, a need to have structured time away from the parish and recognise the need to keep abreast of contemporary theological thinking.
> (Rutledge, 1999, pp.65-66)

He found that the new professionals had generally spent less time in the ministry. For both male and female new professional clergy there was a significant positive relationship between scores on the Personal Accomplishment scale and tasks relating to the new professional role.

Table 8.2 Correlations between the MBI factors and E, N and P for male clergy

	Extraversion		Neuroticism		Psychoticism	
		P<		P<		P<
Emotional Exhaustion	- 0.18	.001	+0.54	.001	+0.24	.001
Depersonalization	- 0.13	.01	+0.40	.001	+0.34	.001
Personal Accomplishment	+0.41	.001	- 0.34	.001	- 0.13	.01

Source: Rutledge, C. (1993)

A major research finding in Rutledge's 1993 study was the significant relationship between personality and burnout. In every case for the male clergy (as table 8.2 shows) there is a significant correlation between the three burnout subscales and three of the Eysenck personality dimensions. This high degree of correlation 'is exciting, warrants further exploration and development, and ... could produce an extremely useful instrument in the care of the male parochial clergy' (Rutledge, 1993, p.275). There is not the same degree of correlation for the female clergy between personality and burnout, but there are significant relationships. There is a significant positive relationship between Neuroticism and both Depersonalization and Emotional Exhaustion. There is also a positive relationship between Extraversion and Personal Accomplishment.

The results of this study: year 1 data

In the previous chapter it was seen that, except for the link between Neuroticism and the Catholic/Evangelical dimension, churchmanship is not significantly correlated with personality as measured by the Eysenck personality measures. In continuing to explore whether and in what way churchmanship interacts with the inmost experience of the clergy, the Maslach Burnout Inventory as modified by Rutledge and Francis was used with this cohort of clergy.

Table 8.3 Comparison of MBI mean scores for curates and serving clergy

	curates		clergy			
	mean	SD	mean	SD	t	P<
EXH	21.27	5.81	22.30	7.36	- 1.41	NS
DEP	19.98	4.94	19.87	5.36	+ 0.57	NS
ACC	23.19	3.60	24.62	4.68	- 2.12	.01

Source: Rutledge, C. (1999)

Table 8.3 shows the comparison between the mean scores of Rutledge's 1999 respondents and the curates in this study. The serving clergy have a significantly higher level of expressed burnout on the Personal Accomplishment (ACC) subscale suggesting that the new clergy who completed this Inventory during their first year in stipendiary ministry have a greater sense of achieving something in their ministry than those who are well established. The fact that there are no significant differences between curates and serving clergy on the other two subscales might suggest that these mean scores are approaching normative levels for Anglican clergy. Further research to establish such norms would be desirable.

When items on the Personal Accomplishment subscale are examined – the subscale on which the curates showed less signs of burnout than the serving clergy – the vast majority of the curates (93 per cent) gain a lot of personal satisfaction from working with people, with 60 per cent feeling exhilarated after working closely with their parishioners. Sixty nine per cent feel that they are having a positive influence on the lives of others and about three in five (58 per cent) feel that they have accomplished many worthwhile things in their parish ministry. Seventy eight per cent can easily create a relaxed atmosphere with parishioners and

68 per cent deal with emotional problems very calmly. However the fact that only 23 per cent feel that they deal effectively with other people's problems may be as much a function of their newness in ministry as of their potential for burnout. Rutledge (1999, p.216) found that only 18 per cent of his clergy felt that they dealt effectively with the problems of others so this may be a common feeling for those in ordained ministry. Only 35 per cent of the curates feel very energetic but that is still a greater proportion than Rutledge's 24 per cent of serving clergy. Given that these curates are only in their first year of stipendiary ministry it is perhaps not too surprising that if they were to have their time over again 87 per cent would still go into parish ministry. Yet some would regard it as strange that in their first year in ordained ministry 13 per cent say that they would not go into parish ministry again. An explanation may lie in the fact that a curacy in parish ministry is regarded as the essential first step after theological training even if the person intends to move out of parish ministry and into sector ministry.

When scores on the Emotional Exhaustion subscale (EXH) are examined, it is clear that the great majority do not find that working with people directly puts too much stress on them (81 per cent), nor that they are at the end of their tether (81 per cent), nor that they are burned out in their ministry (76 per cent). They do not sense that they would feel better if they got out of parish ministry (85 per cent). However the signs of strain are there. A fifth find working with people all day a strain, about the same proportion (21 per cent) feel emotionally drained from their ministry, more than a quarter (27 per cent) feel that they are working too hard, and that they are frustrated (29 per cent) by the ministry. Almost half (44 per cent) feel used up at the end of a day, and 14 per cent feel fatigued when they get up in the morning to face another day in the parish.

In the same way the scores on the Depersonalization subscale (DEP) show a group of people who are in general retaining their humanity in ministry. Nearly all (95 per cent) are concerned to understand how people feel about things, care about what happens to their parishioners (84 per cent), and believe that there is help for most people's problems (87 per cent). They have not become so bothered by people that they want to be left alone (87 per cent), nor have they begun to treat people as impersonal objects (81 per cent) or become callous towards them (84 per cent). About two thirds do not feel that they are in danger of becoming emotionally hardened, of becoming less patient (62 per cent), of not listening to people (63 per cent), or of being blamed for the problems of parishioners (61 per cent). However within the group as a whole 12 per cent are finding it difficult to listen to what people are really saying, 13 per cent are worried about becoming emotionally hardened, 15 per cent are less patient than they used to be, and over a fifth (22 per cent) feel that parishioners blame them as clergy for their own problems.

If the results of the entire group show few signs of burnout compared to serving clergy, should we be expecting to find that particular churchmanship groups are more prone to burnout than others? In his studies of burnout and the clergy Rutledge (1993, 1999) found that the Eysenck personality dimensions of Neuroticism, Psychoticism and Extraversion contributed significantly to burnout, whereas the influence of role prioritization was less important. Since this study has discovered little correlation between Eysenck's personality dimensions and churchmanship, and Rutledge found many correlations between Eysenck's personality dimensions and burnout, it might be expected that few if any of the churchmanship groups would be more prone to burnout than others.

Table 8.4 MBI mean scores by Catholic/Evangelical churchmanship

	Catholic		Central		Evangelical			
	mean	SD	mean	SD	mean	SD	F	P<
EXH	20.68	5.71	22.59	5.79	21.26	5.86	1.51	NS
DEP	18.94	5.36	20.44	4.51	20.54	4.69	2.94	0.05
ACC	23.05	4.25	24.05	2.95	23.01	3.30	1.40	NS

Table 8.4 shows the burnout scores for the churchmanship groups on the Catholic/Evangelical dimension. Of the nine churchmanship groups these three score highest on three of the MBI subscales and lowest on two of the subscales. Of all the churchmanship groups the Central clergy have the highest mean score, and therefore the highest possibility of burnout, on both the Personal Accomplishment subscale and the Emotional Exhaustion subscale. Remember, the Central curates scored highest on EPQ Neuroticism and lowest on EPQ Psychoticism (see tables 6.5 and 7.5). It is to these personality dimensions that one looks for an explanation of the higher burnout scores of this group of clergy.

The Catholics have the lowest and the Evangelicals have the highest scores of all the churchmanship groups on the Depersonalization subscale, and this result is statistically significant. Depersonalization refers to a negative, cynical and dehumanized attitude towards clients which can include compartmentalism, intellectualism and other withdrawal techniques (Maslach and Pines, 1977). Researchers have regularly found higher Depersonalization scores for male respondents than for females (Schwab and Iwanicki, 1982, Maslach and Jackson, 1985, Gold, 1985, Byrne, 1991). However though 81 per cent of the Evangelicals are male as compared with 76 per cent of the Catholics, the difference in scores still remains when sex is held constant. There are suggestions in other studies that younger people are more prone to burnout than older people, but there is less than a year's difference in the mean ages of Catholic curates and Evangelical curates.

A possible reason for the difference in scores on this subscale might lie in the wording of the adapted version of the MBI used in this study. When Rutledge and Francis adapted the MBI for use with Anglican clergy, in place of the word 'clients' they used the word 'parishioners'. The nature of the Anglican parochial system means that all the parishioners – those who live within the geographical area of the parish – are in the care of the vicar. However there is some suggestion in other studies and in results recorded elsewhere in this study that Evangelicals are more prone to an associational rather than parochial model of the local church: they are less concerned for the (non-Christian) members of their geographical area than the (Christian) members who attend church. If so, they are more likely to perceive their 'clients' as being the members of the congregation rather than the parishioners. If that were so, then it is possible that Evangelical curates might have 'a negative, cynical and dehumanized attitude' towards parishioner-clients, but a positive, affirming and human attitude towards congregation-clients. Further research in this area is required. However if these results are indicative of an increasing sense of Depersonalization amongst Evangelical clergy, then care will need to be taken. Research suggests that burnout is progressive in nature (Golembiewski, Munzenrider and Carter, 1983, Gryskiewicz and Buttner, 1992), and that it begins with depersonalization which increasingly leads to a feeling of greatly reduced personal accomplishment, and subsequently to emotional exhaustion. Randall (2004) shows the links between burnout and increasing consideration of leaving the ministry.

Table 8.5 MBI mean scores by Liberal/Conservative churchmanship

	Liberal		Middle		Conservative			
	mean	SD	mean	SD	mean	SD	F	P<
EXH	20.87	5.86	21.41	5.61	21.45	5.93	0.26	NS
DEP	19.40	5.29	19.77	4.40	20.36	4.83	0.97	NS
ACC	23.09	3.85	23.41	3.39	23.30	3.53	0.13	NS

Table 8.5 suggests that though the Liberals have the lowest scores on each of the three subscales statistically they are no more and no less prone to burnout than the other groups on this dimension.

Table 8.6 MBI mean scores by Charismatic churchmanship

	Pro-charis.		Non-charis.		Anti-charis.			
	mean	SD	mean	SD	mean	SD	F	P<
EXH	21.01	5.85	21.45	5.81	21.72	5.79	0.33	NS
DEP	20.14	4.80	20.31	5.40	19.22	4.87	0.83	NS
ACC	23.00	3.37	23.74	3.14	23.30	4.49	0.85	NS

Table 8.6 suggests that the score for the Pro-charismatics on the Personal Accomplishment subscale records the lowest level of potential burnout on this scale for any of the nine churchmanship groups. This would suggest that they feel more than others that they are achieving a great deal in their parochial ministry. Nevertheless none of the scores reaches statistical significance under analysis of variance and therefore none of these groups is more prone to burnout than the

others. However when a post hoc t-test was carried out between the Non-charismatics and the Anti-charismatics on the Depersonalization subscale it showed the Non-charismatics to be significantly more prone to burnout than the Anti-charismatics ($t = 1.99$, $p < 0.05$).

In looking at the development of research into the phenomenon of burnout it was seen that Maslach and Jackson originally saw burnout as a syndrome of emotional exhaustion and cynicism that occurs among those who work in people-related areas of work. As such the consequences of burnout are potentially very serious for both workers and their clients, leading to a deterioration in the quality of care or service being provided, and also to an increase in stress. Later longitudinal studies using the MBI (Capel, 1991, Piedmont, 1993) which found that a respondent's position on the burnout continuum is stable over time raised questions about whether the MBI was measuring a personality trait. Though Burke and Greenglass (1989b) argued that there were few significant and consistent personality correlates of burnout but many significant and consistent job, work setting, and organizational correlates of burnout, there have been a variety of studies (Evans, 1986, Kirkcaldy, Thorne and Thomas, 1989, Garden, 1989, Matthews, 1990, Greenglass, Burke and Ondrack, 1990, Piedmont, 1993, Manlove, 1993, Eastburg, Williamson, Gorsuch and Ridley, 1994) which have found indications that it is personality factors which play a causal role in generating a stress reaction. If the links between personality and burnout show that burnout is a stable phenomenon clearly associated with enduring qualities in the individual's personality, then – with the exception of the link between Evangelicals and Depersonalization – the lack of correlation between churchmanship and personality may be sufficient explanation of the lack of correlation between churchmanship and burnout.

The results of this study: data from years 2 and 3

Support for Capel (1991) and Piedmont (1993) comes from the longitudinal data supplied by this ongoing research. The lack of correlation between churchmanship and burnout continues in both year 2 and year 3 and therefore points towards Capel's and Piedmont's view that the MBI is measuring a personality trait.

The only changes from the pattern of results from year 1 are with two groups, the Evangelicals and the Liberals. The Evangelicals' high scores on Depersonalization cease to be statistically significant in years 2 and 3. This suggests that of all the churchmanship groups Evangelicals may have the most trouble in undertaking the task of developing warm and intimate relationships in pastoral ministry. Their cold and negative attitudes towards clients in the first year may show insecurity rather than burnout.

In both year 2 and year 3 it becomes clear that Liberals suffer from a reduced sense of Personal Accomplishment. While other churchmanship groups show no significant scores on this subscale, there is a correlation between Liberal churchmanship and reduced Personal Accomplishment. This correlation means that the more Liberal, the lower the sense of Personal Accomplishment. At a time when other clergy are reaping one of the rewards of personal pastoral ministry, the Liberals are experiencing a decline in feelings of competence in ministry and in their interactions with people.

Chapter 9

Happy or unhappy?

Introduction

No-one, it seems, uses the phrase 'happy-clappy' of themselves; it is a pejorative term used of a churchmanship – usually Evangelical or Pro-charismatic – and a style of worship of which one disapproves. To ask the question, 'Shouldn't happiness be part of worship?' is to miss the point. And as for clapping! We saw in Chapter 1 how the Victorians were suspicious of the enthusiasm of the Evangelicals, and how, according to Goldingay (1996) a joy in God and an enthusiasm about God were characteristics of the charismatic movement. Is there then a link between Evangelicals or Pro-charismatics and happiness?

Throughout history philosophers have concerned themselves with defining happiness. Such definitions can be grouped into three categories: the first category has to do with happiness being achieved by fulfilling objective criteria; the second category with happiness as a subjective perception of life satisfaction; and the third category with happiness as a personal perception of subjective well-being.

First, happiness has been defined by external criteria such as virtue or holiness. Coan (1977) reviewed conceptions of the ideal life that have been prominent in different cultures and eras. 'In normative definitions happiness is not thought of as a subjective state but rather as possessing some desirable quality. Such definitions are normative because they define what is desirable' (Diener, 1984, p.543). So when Aristotle wrote that *eudaemonia* is gained mainly by leading a virtuous life, he did not mean that virtue leads to feelings of joy, but that virtue is the normative standard by which people's lives are judged. So *eudaemonia* is not 'happiness' in the modern sense of the word, but a desirable state judged from a particular framework of values.

The second group of definitions of happiness has to do with the subjective perception of satisfaction with life, what leads people to evaluate their lives in positive terms. This subjective perception may go back to Marcus Aurelius who wrote that 'no man is happy who does not think himself so'. Shin and Johnson defined this form of happiness as 'a global assessment of a person's quality of life according to his own chosen criteria' (Shin and Johnson, 1978, p.478).

Third, happiness has been defined as denoting a preponderance of positive affect over negative affect (Bradburn, 1969), that is, more positive feelings than negative ones. This definition stresses pleasant emotional experiences or subjective well-being. It is this area of happiness and subjective well-being which has generated much research in psychology to try to understand people's evaluations of their own lives. In this field of study the focus is on the causes and explanations of positive happiness. It is concerned both with the cognitive, reflective emphasis – subjective well-being – and also with the affective, emotional emphasis – happiness. It is interested in both the frequency and the intensity with which people experience pleasant or unpleasant emotions. This is the direction of research that will be followed in the next section, though we shall return to the concept of satisfaction with life later in the chapter.

Research on the dimensions of emotional happiness can be found in Wundt (1897, cited by Argyle and Crossland, 1987, p.127), who suggested a three dimensional structure comprised of the components pleasant-unpleasant, excitation-inhibition, and strain-relaxation. Some of the fundamental research in measuring happiness was conducted by Gurin, Veroff and Feld (1960) who used the simple and straightforward device of asking respondents if they were 'very happy', 'pretty happy' or 'not too happy'. In 1967 Wilson produced a broad review of the research up to that point. He recognized that much of the research had reflected an underlying theoretical assumption that the degree to which people's needs were met by external circumstances and personal resources determined happiness. So on the basis of the limited data then available he concluded that the happy person was a 'young, healthy, well-educated, well-paid, extraverted, optimistic, worry-free, religious, married person with high self-esteem, job morale, modest aspirations, of either sex and of a wide range of intelligence' (Wilson, 1967, p.294). This approach was known as the 'social indicators movement' in happiness and well-being research (Ryff and Keyes, 1995).

For the next thirty years growth in research into subjective well-being developed apace as researchers shifted their emphasis from external factors and demographics to psychological variables that moderated the effects of external variables. As a result it was discovered that resources such as health (Okun and George, 1984), income (Diener, Sandvik, Seidlitz and Diener, 1992), physical attractiveness (Diener, Wolsic and Fujita, 1995), or winning the lottery (Brickman, Coates and Janoff-Bulman, 1978) had little effect on happiness. Andrews and Withey (1976) found that demographic factors such as age, sex, income, race, education and marital status accounted for only eight per cent of the variance in subjective well-being. This counter-intuitive finding, that the influence of socio-demographics explains only a small portion of the individual differences in happiness, has been termed the paradox of well-being (cf. Ryff, 1989). It unleashed an expansion in research into subjective well-being and happiness.

It has been noted that psychologists generally focus on the negative aspects of individual lives: Myers and Diener (1995) found that the number of psychological articles published on negative states exceeded those published on positive states by a ratio of 17 to 1. In 1973 Psychological Abstracts International began listing happiness as an index term because the growth of this research field was so notable. Growth in the field of subjective well-being reflects larger societal trends concerning the value of the individual, the importance of subjective views in evaluating life, and the recognition that well-being necessarily includes positive elements that transcend economic prosperity. The scientific study of subjective well-being developed in part as a reaction to the overwhelming emphasis in psychology on negative states.

The measurement of affect

It was Bradburn and his colleagues who opened up the research into subjective well-being by measuring feelings or affects. Taking the idea that happiness is the sum of pleasures minus pains, he developed a 10-item Affect Balance Scale (Bradburn, 1969, see also Strack, Argyle and Schwarz, 1991). The score was found by subtracting negative affects such as loneliness and boredom experienced during the previous two weeks from positive affects such as pleasure and excitement. He discovered that positive affect was not negatively correlated with negative affect: in practice the two scales were almost entirely independent of each other. Harding (1982) replicated this study with a British sample and since then this two-factor structure has frequently been replicated (Costa and McCrae, 1980, Zevon and Tellegen, 1982, Warr, Barter and Brownbridge, 1983, Diener and Emmons, 1985, Watson, Clark and Tellegen, 1988).

However while the frequencies of positive and negative affect are inversely related, the intensities, that is the strength with which emotions are felt, are positively related. People who feel intense happiness also often experience intense unhappiness (Diener, Sandvik and Larsen, 1985).

> The partial independence of positive and negative affect has also been found in the field of marital satisfaction. Partners can have strong positive feelings (related to frequency of intercourse, for example) as well as negative ones (related to the frequency of rows, for example) (Argyle and Henderson, 1985). It is still possible to combine positive and negative affect in a single measure, and a lot of research has done this.
> (Argyle, 1987, p.4)

Costa and McCrae hypothesized that 'one set of dispositions is responsible for positive affect ... whereas another, independent set of dispositions influences negative affect' (1980, p.670). Using the Eysenck Personality Inventory (EPI) (Eysenck and Eysenck, 1964) alongside Bradburn's scale they established that Extraversion (E) predisposed individuals towards positive affect and Neuroticism (N) predisposed individuals towards negative affect. These results were supported by Emmons and Diener (1985) and Eysenck and Eysenck (1985). In addition, Costa and McCrae gave a second test using the same scales to the same group ten years later which showed the same inter-relationship. Thus they demonstrated that it was personality rather than short-term mood which determined positive and negative affect.

Warr, Barter and Brownbridge created an 18-item scale (1983, p.651) based on Bradburn's scale. It was devised with equal numbers of items to measure positive and negative affect. They also administered Eysenck's EPQ to their respondents. They found as Costa and McCrae had that 'extraversion and neuroticism were significantly correlated with positive and negative affect, respectively, but the crossover associations were nonsignificant' (Warr, Barter and Brownbridge, 1983, p.648). Headey, Glowacki, Holmstrom and Wearing (1985) carried out a repeat panel study of 600 Australians in 1981, 1983 and 1985. They found that extraversion disposed people, especially young people, to have favourable life events, particularly in the areas of friendship and work; these in turn led to a high level of positive affect, and to increases in extraversion. If personality traits influence levels of positive and negative affect, then people should behave in ways that are consistent with our knowledge of traits, for example in terms of stability over time. In a longitudinal study over four years Magnus and Diener (cited by Diener and Lucas, 1998) found that life satisfaction correlated 0.58 with the same measure administered four years later. Positive and negative affect also showed a moderate level of stability over time when assessed over a six year interval (Watson and Walker, 1996).

There have been a number of studies to determine whether individuals judge that they are happy because of the frequency of their positive emotional experiences, or because of the intensity of these experiences.

> Lucas and Diener (1998) reported that judgements of well-being are based primarily on the frequency of pleasant affect, and less so on the intensity of affect. They argued that intense positive emotions are less important to the experience of long-term emotional well-being because such intense emotions are so rare, and also because they are often counterbalanced by costs.
> (Diener and Lucas, 1999, p.406)

Other researchers had found that individuals who experienced pleasant emotions intensely also had a tendency to experience unpleasant emotions intensely as well (Diener, Emmons, Larsen and Griffen, 1985, Larsen and Diener, 1987, Schimmack and Diener, 1997). Diener, Larsen, Levine and Emmons (1985) showed that, in fact, intense pleasant emotions often occur because of the same processes that cause intense unpleasant emotions: life histories of people who had intense 'highs' often revealed that they had intense 'lows' as well (see also Magnus, Diener, Fujita and Pavot, 1993). So researchers seemed to have found that frequency of positive experience contributed more to emotional well-being than intensity of feeling.

Affect and satisfaction with life

Earlier in this chapter the three different categories of definitions of happiness were stated. So far the definition concerned with positive and negative affect has been considered and from that definition empirical researchers have constructed scales to measure affect. In their study Andrews and Withey (1976) found that satisfaction with life could be measured as a separate factor alongside positive and negative affect. Of this component Diener says: 'it is a cognitive judgemental evaluation of one's own life. As such, it may be indirectly influenced by affect but is not itself a direct measure of emotion' (Diener, 1984, p.550). In order to measure this separate cognitive component of life satisfaction Diener, Emmons, Larsen and Griffen (1985) devised a 5-item scale, the Satisfaction with Life Scale. Pavot and Diener (1993) later reviewed the use and working of this scale.

Campbell, Converse and Rodgers (1976) put forward the theory that satisfaction with life is greater when achievements are close to aspirations, lower when they fall short and that aspirations in their turn are based on comparisons with other people and with one's own past experience. Additional support for this was provided by Emmons (1986), Emmons and King (1988), and Carver and Scheier (1990). Brunstein (1993) found in a longitudinal study that perceived progress towards goals caused positive changes in life satisfaction rather than vice versa. McKennell and Andrews (1980) recognized that self-ratings of life satisfaction are more likely to be based on comparisons with others whereas reports of happiness depend more on immediate moods. Argyle (1987) acknowledged that there might be a 'Pollyanna effect' with people looking on the bright side in self-evaluations of satisfaction with life:

> In the surveys that we have reviewed most people claim to be very satisfied or 'happier than most', or tick points 6 and 7 on 7-point scales of satisfaction. Perhaps they are not telling the truth, or perhaps they are not facing up to the truth. Take marital satisfaction for example: 68 per cent said they were very happily married (point 7 on a 7-point scale) and 22 per cent nearly as happy (point 6) (Abrams, 1973). Yet we know that over a third of marriages end in divorce, and that there is physical violence between many couples.
> (Argyle, 1987, p.154)

Andrews and Withey (1976) were the first to suggest that happiness was a three dimensional construct composed of a) positive affect, b) average level of satisfaction over a period, and c) absence of negative affect. Each of these dimensions could be broken into subdivisions. Satisfaction with life could be divided into satisfaction with the various domains of life such as work, marriage, friendship, recreation and so on. Positive affect could be divided into specific emotions such as joy, affection and self-esteem. Finally negative affect could be divided into specific emotions or moods such as shame, guilt, sadness, anger, and anxiety. Lucas, Diener and Suh (1996) used multitrait-multimethod analyses to show that positive affect, negative affect, and life satisfaction were separable constructs. Over two years and across multiple methods of assessment validity coefficients for each of the three constructs were stronger than the inter-correlations among different constructs.

The construction and testing of the Oxford Happiness Inventory

Furnham and Brewin observed: 'Although there are numerous psychometrically sound synonymous measures for unhappiness and negative affect, there are not for happiness. An exception is the Oxford Happiness Inventory devised by Argyle et al' (Furnham and Brewin, 1990, p.1094).

Argyle and Crossland (1987) had begun developing an understanding of the dimensions of positive affect. This led to the development of a concept akin to Andrews and Withey's (1976), that is, that happiness comprised the three components of life satisfaction, positive affect, and absence of negative affect. Argyle, Martin and Crossland (1989) recognized that the Beck Depression Inventory (Beck, Ward, Mendelson, Hock and Erbaugh, 1961) had general acceptance as a measure of depression. Working with Beck, therefore, they reversed the 21 items of his inventory, adding 11 other items to cover aspects of subjective well-being. After a trial run three of these items were removed and the 29-item scale tested for reliability and validity. This 29-item scale was called the Oxford Happiness Inventory (OHI). For each item respondents were asked to pick out the statement from four incremental steps which best described the way they had been feeling over the past week, including that day. For example, 'I get by in life' (i.e. unhappy, mildly depressed), 'life is good' (i.e. a low level of happiness), 'life is very good' (i.e. a high level of happiness), 'I love life' (i.e. manic).

The test–re-test reliability of the Inventory was 0.78 after 7 weeks. A five month follow-up with a different set of respondents had a test–re-test reliability of 0.67. It showed a content validity of 0.43 when subjects' self-ratings were correlated with friends' ratings of happiness. The Oxford Happiness Inventory correlated at between 0.40 and 0.60 with other measures of positive affect, negative affect and satisfaction with life. It presented an alpha coefficient of 0.90 (Cronbach, 1951) for the whole scale used with 347 subjects and between 0.64 and 0.84 for sub-sets of the items showing a good level of internal consistency.

> Researchers who performed factor analyses on the OHI with several groups of participants (young and old, male and female, students and community residents) found a relatively stable structure consisting of seven components of happiness: (a) positive cognition, (b) social commitment, (c) positive affect, (d) sense of control, (e) physical fitness, (f) satisfaction with self, and (f) mental alertness.
> (Lu and Shih, 1997, p.182)

The nature of happiness as measured by the Oxford Happiness Inventory

A series of studies has mapped some of the correlates of the operational definition of happiness underlying the OHI. Argyle and Lu (1990b) found that social competence was a significant predictor of happiness among 63 adults. Argyle (1991) and Lu and Argyle (1991) found that cooperativeness was one of the social skills that was a significant predictor of happiness among 114 adults. Lu and Argyle (1992) found that satisfactory relationships with those people who gave support predicted happiness. Rim (1993a) found a relationship between happiness and coping styles and (1993b) between happiness and the importance of values. Noor (1993) showed the link between happiness and locus of control. Lu and Argyle (1993) found an inverse relationship between happiness and the time spent watching television, though the watchers of soap operas were somewhat happier, perhaps because of their 'imaginary friends'. A positive correlation between happiness and engaging in a serious leisure activity was shown by Lu and Argyle (1994), and Hills and Argyle (1998a) found a positive correlation between membership of a sports club and happiness. Hills and Argyle also found that 'in detail, if not in general, musical and religious experiences are positively associated with happiness' (Hills and Argyle, 1998b, p.99).

The OHI and personality

It has been reported already that Costa and McCrae (1980, 1984), and later Emmons and Diener (1985), using the Eysenck Personality Inventory with Bradburn's Affect Balance Scale established that extraversion predisposed individuals towards positive affect, and neuroticism predisposed individuals towards negative affect, and that it was personality rather than short-term mood which determined happiness or subjective well-being. Both groups continued to find longitudinal research evidence to support such a conclusion (Costa, McCrae and Zonderman, 1987, Diener and Diener, 1996, and cf. Watson and Walker, 1996).

There has been a series of studies designed to discover whether this same relationship held good when the Oxford Happiness Inventory was used with Eysenck's personality measures. Argyle, Martin and Crossland (1989, p.196) found a correlation of 0.48 between happiness measured by the OHI and extraversion measured by the EPQ. They considered various explanations for the correlation between extraversion and happiness: extraverts seek out more positive activities than introverts (Furnham, 1981); extraverts emit more positive non-verbal signals which are reciprocated (Argyle, 1988); extraverts tend to talk about more pleasant things, and joke and laugh more (Thorne, 1987); and while extraverts magnify rewards, introverts tend to emphasize punishments (Gray, 1972). They also recognized that there is a difference in attributional style. Happy people make internal (i.e. due to themselves), global (i.e. will happen in other spheres) and stable (i.e. will continue to occur) attributions for good events, whereas depressives make internal, global and stable attributions for bad events (Martin and Clark, 1985).

Furnham and Brewin (1990) tested the OHI and the EPQ with 101 subjects. Their results showed a positive correlation between happiness and Extraversion ($r = 0.55$, $p < 0.001$) and a negative correlation between happiness and Neuroticism ($r = 0.43$, $p < 0.001$), and no correlation with Psychoticism. This was supported in separate studies by Argyle and Lu (1990a), Lu and Argyle (1991, 1992 and 1993) and Lu (1999). In none of these reports did happiness correlate with age, sex or Eysenck's P or L scales.

> Happy people tend to be extraverted, not neurotic, and high on internal control, and to have certain social skills and cognitive styles. Which of these is the most fundamental? The strongest correlation is with extraversion, at .4 or .5 or more, and this survived multiple regressions. The most likely explanation of this is in

terms of extraverts' greater social skills. However, extraverts have other properties, and their tendency to magnify rewards may be important.
(Argyle, Martin and Lu, 1995, p.185)

Francis (1998a) in a study of 456 students correlated each of the 29 items of the OHI with the EPQ-R (Eysenck, Eysenck and Barrett, 1985). He found that all the items were negatively correlated with Neuroticism, that only three items were not correlated with Extraversion, that eight items were positively correlated and one negatively correlated with Psychoticism, and that seven items were positively correlated with Lie scale scores:

> The significant correlations between the Oxford Happiness Inventory and both extraversion and neuroticism are not an artefact of some items being loaded on extraversion and other items being loaded on neuroticism. Individual differences in responses to the majority of the items are a function of both extraversion and neuroticism.
> (Francis, 1998a, p.10)

In a major study of 1076 students in the UK, USA, Australia and Canada Francis, Brown, Lester and Philipchalk (1998) demonstrated the same correlations. Using Veenhoven's (1994) argument that 'Happiness can be regarded as a trait if it meets three criteria ... temporal stability, cross-situational consistency and inner causation', they concluded that 'these results support the validity of happiness as a trait in Argyle's operationalization of it' (Francis et al., 1998, p.170).

In a meta-analysis of all previously published studies reporting tests for sex differences in well-being Wood, Rhodes and Whelan (1989) found that women reported greater happiness and life satisfaction than men. They explained this difference in terms of men's and women's different social roles where the female role specifies greater emotional responsiveness. Their study did not however include the Oxford Happiness Inventory. No significant sex differences using the OHI were reported by Argyle and Lu (1990a) in their study of 75 male and 56 female students, by Furnham and Brewin (1990) in their study of 72 male and 29 female students, by Lu and Argyle (1991, 1993) in their study of 72 female and 42 male adults, by Lu and Argyle's (1992) study of 65 adults, by Francis (1998a) in his study of 456 students, or by Francis, Brown, Lester and Philipchalk (1998) in their four international samples of students.

Argyle and Lu (1990b) were the first to report a significant difference between the sexes using the Oxford Happiness Inventory in their sample of adults. They found that women had higher scores for happiness – the mean scores for men (N = 32) were 29.63, SD 12.58, and for women (N = 31) 35.55, SD 10.96 (t = 1.99, $p < 0.05$) – and they found that women had higher scores for EPQ extraversion as well. Neither marital nor employment status showed a significant effect on happiness. Rim (1993a) found a similar difference in an Israeli study: in a group of 62 men and 51 women the mean score for men was 37.6 and for women 39.2 ($p < 0.05$).

Francis, Jones and Wilcox (2000) in their large study of three samples of adolescents, young adults and senior citizens found no significant differences between the sexes in mean scores on the OHI during young adulthood or later life. They did find that adolescent males recorded a higher mean score for happiness (41.6, SD 13.6) than adolescent females (39.0, SD 11.4, $F = 9.9$, $p < 0.001$).

The OHI and religiosity

One of the earliest studies of the links between religiosity and subjective well-being was carried out by O'Reilly (1957). He found that 55 per cent of the 'very happy' respondents were church attenders compared with 47 per cent of the 'moderately happy' and 44 per cent of the 'less happy'. Since then there have been a variety of other American studies into the links between subjective well-being and religiosity (Wilson, 1965, Campbell, Converse and Rodgers, 1976, Blazer and Palmore, 1976, Hadaway and Roof, 1978, Peterson and Roy, 1985, Ellison, Gay and Glass, 1989).

In the *Quality of American Life* study Campbell, Converse and Rodgers (1976) found that though 38 per cent regarded having a strong religious faith as extremely important and another 22 per cent saw it as very important the relationship between satisfaction with religion and overall life satisfaction, with other factors held constant, was rather weak. However because the American studies used a diversity of measures of both religiosity and well-being their results are hard to compare. Batson, Schoenrade and Ventis (1993) in a review of the link between religion and mental health found positive correlations between well-being and intrinsic religiosity. These were confirmed by Levin (1994).

Robbins and Francis (1996) were the first researchers to report on the links between happiness measured by the OHI and a tested measure of religiosity. In their study of 360 British undergraduates they found happiness was positively correlated with Extraversion, measured by the EPQ-R, negatively correlated with Neuroticism and uncorrelated with Psychoticism. They also found no significant difference in mean levels of happiness between women (N =262) and men (N =98). They also found a positive correlation between attitude to Christianity measured by the Francis Scale of Attitude Toward Christianity (FSAC) (Francis and Stubbs, 1987) and happiness:

> In order to confirm that the relationship between attitude toward Christianity and happiness was not contaminated by the variables of sex and personality, a multiple regression equation was calculated to take into account the influence of sex, extraversion, neuroticism, psychoticism, and the lie scale scores before examining the influence of religiosity on happiness scores. The results of this equation ... confirm the significant positive relationship between attitude toward Christianity and happiness, and demonstrate that this relationship is independent of individual differences in personality. The beta weights demonstrate that the happiest individuals are religious stable extraverts, while the least happy individuals are irreligious neurotic introverts.
> (Robbins and Francis, 1996, p.212)

However Lewis, Joseph and Noble (1996) in a study using 150 Northern Irish undergraduates found no significant association between scores on the FSAC and scores on the Satisfaction With Life Scale (SWLS) (Diener, Emmons, Larsen and Griffen, 1985). Lewis, Lanigan, Joseph and de Fockert (1997) in two separate studies with a group of 154 Northern Irish undergraduates found no correlation between religion, as measured by the FSAC, and happiness, as measured by three different measures of happiness and subjective well-being, the SWLS, the Purpose in Life test (Crumbaugh, 1968) and the Depression-Happiness Scale (McGreal and Joseph, 1993). They suggested that the association between religiosity and happiness was not robust and might depend on the operational definition of happiness being used. They postulated that since the Depression-Happiness scale measured frequency of positive thoughts and feelings whereas the OHI provided an overall index of the intensity of happiness Robbins and Francis' (1996) results might simply show that religious people had more intense emotional states.

However Lewis (1998) in a study using two samples, one of Northern Irish adults and one of Northern Irish students, found a positive correlation between the FSAC and the SWLS for both men ($r = 0.43$, $p < 0.05$) and women ($r = 0.54$, $p < 0.01$), but no significant correlation for students, either male or female. When Francis, Jones and Wilcox (1997) used the FSAC and Bradburn's (1969) Balance Affect Scale with 242 sixth-form students they found that there was no significant relationship between attitude toward Christianity and any of Bradburn's three measures of psychological well-being: positive affect, negative affect or balanced affect. This study too suggested that the OHI is measuring a different dimension to other well-being scales.

Francis and Lester (1997) used the OHI, the FSAC and the EPQ-R with a group of 212 American undergraduates. They confirmed previous research findings: the positive correlation between OHI happiness and E and the negative correlation between OHI happiness and N; and the significant positive correlation between FSAC religiosity and OHI happiness. Since scores on the FSAC correlated negatively with Psychoticism, and were uncorrelated with both E and N, they pointed out that 'the personality dimensions implicated in happiness are quite distinct from the personality dimension implicated in religiosity' (Francis and Lester, 1997, p.84).

Francis, Jones and Wilcox (2000) used the OHI, the FSAC and the shorter form of the EPQ-R with three different age groups in order to ascertain the stability of the links between these instruments previously reported by Robbins and Francis (1996) and Francis and Lester (1997). Their first sample comprised 994 Year 11 pupils from the north east of England, their second sample comprised 456 first year undergraduates in Wales, and their third sample comprised 496 members of the University of the Third Age, an informal education network for senior citizens. After controlling for differences between the sexes they found a positive correlation between OHI happiness and the FSAC among all three age groups. They found the same result in all three age groups after controlling for personality as well.

Francis and Robbins (2000) used the OHI, the shorter form of the EPQ-R and the FSAC among a sample of 295 participants attending a variety of courses and workshops in the psychology of religion. These participants ranged in age from older teenagers to late seventies. Once again these data confirmed a positive correlation between religiosity and Oxford Happiness Inventory happiness after controlling for personality.

The OHI and the clergy

So far no studies have reported the use of the OHI with the clergy. However, as was reported earlier, there has been a number of studies of the clergy using Eysenckian scales. The most comprehensive is Robbins, Francis and Rutledge's (1997) study of both male and female Anglican stipendiary parochial clergy. It showed that male clergy did not differ from the population norms in terms of E and N scores, and female clergy did not differ from the population norms for E scores, but recorded significantly lower N scores than women in general. If, as seems clear from this chapter, happiness equates to stable extraversion it would be expected that male clergy would be no more and no less happy than the general population, but that female clergy because of their lower N score would be happier than women in general.

The results of this study: year 1

We have already seen that this group of clergy, all those ordained to Anglican stipendiary ministry in England and Wales in 1994, have higher Extraversion scores than the general population and higher than serving clergy as well. In addition they have lower Neuroticism scores than the general population. If happiness equates to stable extraversion it would be expected that both male and female curates would be happier than men and women in general.

The Oxford Happiness Inventory achieved a satisfactory alpha coefficient of 0.8999 in this study. However there are as yet no published norms by which to compare the OHI results with the general population. The male clergy scored more for happiness than the female but not at a statistically significant level. Three other studies report mean scores for men and women separately and none find significant differences between men and women in the adult population (Robbins and Francis, 1996, Francis, Brown, Lester and Philipchalk, 1998, and Francis, Jones and Wilcox, 2000). There seems to be emerging in the research literature a consensus that there is no significant difference between the scores of men and women on the Oxford Happiness Inventory. The results here support Francis' analysis:

> Inspection of the correlations between sex and the individual scale items reveal that, while the majority of items do not discriminate between men and women, among those items which do discriminate between men and women there is an almost even balance between those on which men record higher scores and those on which women record higher scores.
> (Francis, 1998a, p.10)

Table 9.1 OHI mean scores by Catholic/Evangelical churchmanship

	Catholic		Central		Evangelical		F	P<
	mean	SD	mean	SD	mean	SD		
OHI	39.19	10.12	35.44	8.72	37.66	8.66	2.38	NS

Table 9.1 shows the mean scores on the OHI for each of the churchmanship groups on the Catholic/Evangelical dimension using analysis of variance. As in other chapters, it is the Catholic/Evangelical dimension which provides the most marked results: the highest and lowest scores for the Oxford Happiness Inventory amongst all the nine churchmanship groups are on this dimension. The Catholic curates are the happiest of all the clergy and the Central curates are the least happy. In order to explore this finding further, even though analysis of variance yielded no significant difference between the three groups, a post hoc t-test between the Catholic and Central groups alone was carried out. It revealed the Catholics to be significantly happier than the Central curates ($t = 2.41$, $p < 0.01$). The Catholic movement within the Church of England can take a measure of comfort from such a result since, it will be remembered from Chapter 1, it had been seen to be a beleaguered and struggling group in 1994, the year when these clergy were first ordained.

Table 9.2 OHI mean scores by Liberal/Conservative churchmanship

	Liberal		Middle		Conservative		F	P<
	mean	SD	mean	SD	mean	SD		
OHI	38.04	9.41	37.67	10.09	37.41	8.70	0.12	NS

Tables 9.2 and 9.3 (which show the Liberal/Conservative and Charismatic dimensions respectively) reveal scores which do not differ significantly from each other. As before, analysis of variance did not reveal a significant difference on the Charismatic dimension but a post hoc t-test was run between the Pro-charismatic and Non-charismatic groups alone which showed the Pro-charismatics to be significantly more happy than the Non-charismatics ($t = 1.96$, $p < 0.05$).

Table 9.3 OHI mean scores by Charismatic churchmanship

	Pro-charismatic		Non-charismatic		Anti-charismatic			
	mean	SD	mean	SD	mean	SD	F	P<
OHI	38.05	8.90	37.12	8.65	37.39	10.73	0.24	NS

In the light of the non-significant results that analysis of variance reveals, a correlation matrix between the Oxford Happiness Inventory, the three churchmanship dimensions and the three personality dimensions of the Eysenck Personality Questionnaire was run. In line with previous studies (Argyle and Lu, 1990a, Furnham and Brewin, 1990, Lu and Argyle, 1991, Brebner, Donaldson, Kirby and Ward, 1995, Francis, Brown, Lester and Philipchalk, 1998) scores on the OHI correlated strongly and positively with Extraversion, negatively with Neuroticism and were independent of Psychoticism. In this sense happiness is as much a function of personality among the clergy as among people whose lives are not so professionally associated with religiosity. The correlations between the three churchmanship dimensions and the Oxford Happiness Inventory were all non-significant. However comparing the results in the previous tables in this chapter gives rise to an interesting anomaly. The correlation matrix showed that while the Liberal/Conservative and the Charismatic dimensions of churchmanship were unrelated to Eysenck's E, N and P, the Catholic/Evangelical dimension was related: Evangelicals tend to be significantly more extravert and less neurotic than Catholics. Since both happiness and an Evangelical stance are associated with stable Extraversion, it would be expected that Evangelicals would score particularly high on the Oxford Happiness Inventory. However, as tables 9.1, 9.2 and 9.3 show, four other churchmanship groups score more highly.

In order to investigate this further table 9.4 employs multiple regression to examine the relationship between churchmanship and happiness after controlling for individual differences in personality. This table shows that after controlling for sex, Extraversion, Neuroticism, Psychoticism and Lie scale scores, just one of the three churchmanship variables emerges as a significant predictor of happiness. According to this model Evangelicals are not just less happy as a group than Catholics but significantly less happy than Catholics of the same sex and of the same personality disposition.

Table 9.4 Multiple regression significance tests for OHI happiness

Predictor variables	R^2	increase			Beta	t	P<
		R^2	F	P<			
sex	0.0002	0.0002	0.1	NS	+0.0590	+1.1	NS
extraversion	0.1142	0.1140	32.7	.001	+0.3348	+6.0	.001
neuroticism	0.2379	0.1237	39.8	.001	-0.3986	-6.1	.001
psychoticism	0.2478	0.0099	3.2	NS	-0.0815	-1.5	NS
lie scale	0.2808	0.0329	11.1	.001	+0.1961	+3.5	.001
Cath/Evang	0.3401	0.0233	8.1	.01	-0.2602	-3.5	.001
Lib/Cons	0.3091	0.0050	1.8	NS	+0.0805	+1.2	NS
Charismatic	0.3174	0.0082	2.9	NS	-0.1082	-1.7	NS

This finding may seem surprising: after all, the name 'Evangelical' derives from *eu-aggelion*, the Good News of the Christian gospel. If any churchmanship group were going to be happy (let alone clappy!), many people would expect it to be the Evangelicals. In addition two essential parts of Evangelical belief which could be expected to contribute to increased happiness are a personal relationship with Jesus Christ and the assurance and hope of eternal life that such a relationship gives. However Evangelicals are also inclined to stress the doctrines of the Fall and redemption which can lead either to a warm personal devotion to Christ, a joyful quality of worship and a desire to share the good news with others, or to a gloomy piety.

Saward (1987), with that penchant for alliteration that is common to Evangelicals, reviewed the state of Evangelicalism in the post-war years and observed four kinds of Evangelicals: the Pietists, the Parochials, the Puritans, and the Protestants. The humourist H.L. Mencken defined Puritanism as 'the haunting fear that someone, somewhere may be happy'. At times when the Puritans have been to the forefront in the Evangelical movement writers have had to warn their colleagues that their public image and self-presentation can be sombre and serious. King (1969) for example spoke in *The Evangelicals* about the uninteresting nature of Evangelical church interiors brought about by a reaction against images, elaborate vestments and architectural exuberance:

> Evangelicals have not for many years made a noticeable contribution to the arts, either as creators or critics. Why this should be so is a fascinating subject for inquiry; it is doubtless connected with the utilitarian theology, as it were, of the best of the Puritans, with the debased Puritan tradition that failed to appreciate the function of the imagination, with the preponderance of a Plymouth Brother, Schofield Bible, crude mission-hall type of Christianity that was as far removed from the Romantic movement and the Oxford Movement as it was possible to get. (King, 1969, p.83)

Buchanan (1994) expressed concern about the influence of the puritan and protestant Proclamation Trust within Evangelicalism:

> I cannot tell whether they have recreated a theology of monologue preaching at a time when others have been almost desperately looking for other means of communication, but again the impression is of taking themselves very seriously as the last upholders of true evangelicalism when everyone else has gone soft-edged or soft-bellied. I would add that 'taking themselves very seriously' should be questioned at the level of principle, a principle of Christian lifestyle ... I submit that no-one can live at peace in a comprehensive church and both propagate his or her own theological priorities, and live in the interim with other people's, unless that person has a richly developed sense of humour.
> (Buchanan, 1994, pp.107-108)

There is a need for more research to discover whether Protestantism and Puritanism, represented perhaps by other clergy from the Free Churches, produce similar lower scores on the Oxford Happiness Inventory.

Chapter 10

Masculine or feminine?

Introduction

The question of gender differences has arisen several times in previous chapters. The year when this cohort of clergy was ordained, 1994, was the year that the Church of England first ordained women as priests. Has that changed clergy awareness of gender roles? Is this new generation of clergy more at ease with both masculinity and femininity? 'Muscular Christianity' made its appearance in the nineteenth century: the Young Men's Christian Association (YMCA) was founded in London in 1844 and was known as 'Young Muscular Christians'. Thanks to men like the Studd brothers, the pre-eminent cricketers of that era, the link between muscular Christianity and Evangelicalism became established (Graham, 2001, Putney, 2001, Ladd and Mathisen, 2002). At about the same time Tractarians were being mocked as un-English and unmanly (Best, 1967, Hilliard, 1982). In this chapter therefore we shall consider the whole area of gender roles using a fourth and final personality measure, the Bem Sex Role Inventory (BSRI).

The research that led to the development of the BSRI showed that results of personality studies needed to take into account sex role differences rather than just gender differences. The BSRI was chosen as the best instrument with which to measure gender role choices. In this chapter a review of research material focuses particularly on the relationship between sex role, personality and religiosity. In the absence of any published work using the BSRI with clergy consideration is given to other predictive work on the clergy and sex role or gender orientation.

The concept of gender differences in personality typology and the resulting gender-linked behaviour has been the subject of a large volume of research. From the time of Freud psychologists have expressed different theories about the origin of differences between the sexes. These theories may conveniently be divided into six groups: psychoanalytic, biological, social learning, cognitive, cultural, and self-presentation.

Psychoanalytic theories

Freud saw the young child, at the age of 5 or thereabouts, having to resolve questions of sexual identity. The male child did so, he argued, through the Oedipal conflict. The libido was now in the phallic stage, focused on the genitals, and at this time the young boy developed an unconscious longing to possess his mother. The father however was a rival for his mother's love and very much larger and more powerful than the young child. This meant according to Freud that the young boy developed an unconscious castration threat anxiety – worried that his father would deal with competition by these drastic means. Since living with such anxiety was intolerable, the boy had to resolve it in some way. This was achieved by the ego defence mechanism known as 'identification with the aggressor'. Working unconsciously on the assumption that his father would be less likely to be hostile to him if he saw him as being an ally, the boy stressed how similar he was to his father and tried to become as masculine and like his father as possible. In this way he came to adopt his father's gender role, and to identify himself as male.

Young girls on the other hand were supposed to become aware (unconsciously) that they had been born without a penis, and to develop 'penis envy' at a similar age. This according to Freud was eventually resolved by their striving to regain their missing penis by having sexual relations with men and by having children, particularly male children. Later psychoanalytic theorists added the idea of an 'Electra conflict' in which the young girl was supposed to see herself, unconsciously, as having been castrated. She blames her mother for this, which produces a conflict similar to that of the young boy and his father: the mother is bigger and more powerful and therefore a threat. The girl resolves the unconscious anxiety and aggression resulting from this conflict by identifying with her mother and emphasizing her femininity. Furnham comments, 'Needless to say it takes courageous psychoanalysts these days to state belief in these classical Freudian ideas' (Furnham, 1996, p.188).

Biological theories

According to biological theories the perceived differences between women and men are innate. Since this is seen to be true for some physical characteristics and physiological processes, it must be true too for psychological choices. For these theorists biology is destiny. Wilson (1978) for example argued that because women throughout evolutionary history have been responsible for bearing, nursing and caring for children, they have evolved to be more nurturing and communicative. In the same way because men were responsible for hunting and fighting, they have evolved to be more aggressive and with a better visual-spatial ability. Since men and women have different strategies to ensure optimal reproduction – women must guarantee that the relatively few children they produce will survive and flourish, men by producing millions of sperm can father an immense number of offspring – women have evolved to be more sexually coy and keener on committed relationships that provide stability, and men have evolved to be more sexually aggressive and promiscuous. Sometimes these theories are stated in evolutionary terms as here, and sometimes in physiological terms emphasizing hormonal and brain differences between the sexes. There have been numerous writers who have challenged the apparent givenness of such theories (Firestone, 1971, Brownmillar, 1975).

Social learning theories

Social learning theories explain differences between the sexes by means of classical learning theory concepts, such as 'conditioning' by rewards and punishments and 'modelling' by observing and copying the example of others. Classical conditioning shows how negative labels such as 'sissy', 'wimp' or 'drip' acquire strong emotional connotations. Operant conditioning works by rewarding and punishing different behaviours for boys or girls. Observational learning goes on all the time as children see their parents providing different toys for their girls and boys or decorating their bedrooms in different ways.

> Children often learn about 'female' and 'male' behaviours without being directly rewarded or punished, simply by observing their friends, parents, relatives and the portrayal of various characters by the mass media, especially television. Such models (parents) are particularly influential when they have a nurturing relationship with the children, are powerful, and control salient rewards for the children.
> (Eagly, 1987, p.143)

Social learning theory draws a distinction between acquiring and performing appropriate behaviour; people can learn behaviours through observation, but that does not necessarily mean that they behave in accordance with that learning. So the theory would say that men and women are capable of performing the same behaviours: they behave differently because of past conditioning, rewards, punishments, observational learning and all the situations that occur in a society where women and men are treated differently (Eagly and Wood, 1991). For such theorists therefore differences between the sexes are learned and can be unlearned.

Cognitive theories

Cognitive theories suggest that children progress through a number of separate cognitive stages in becoming psychologically male or female, so that their conceptions of gender develop in step with their more general levels of cognitive growth. Cognitive developmental theories argue that the act of self-categorization ('I am a girl' or 'I am a boy') leads the child to develop stereotypically female or male behaviours. Cognitive theory sees the sequence as this: I am a boy, therefore I want to do boy-type things, therefore the opportunity to do boy-type things is rewarding, therefore it is better than being a girl.

Under this same heading come the gender-schema theories which argue that the child constructs cognitive schemata to help them understand and come to terms with the world.

> Basically schema theory suggests that schemas and scripts provide cognitive tools for thinking about the past, present and future. They are essentially networks of associations and general knowledge which aid thinking about and understanding not only the external world but also the internal one. Furthermore they provide a

set of flexible cognitive networks into which new experiences or information can be assimilated ... Sex-typing is a gender schema that varies from culture to culture ... The cultural content of gender schema will undoubtedly be affected, not only by what the society labels as appropriately masculine or feminine behaviour, but also by the extent to which the culture or subculture rewards or punishes adherence to such sex-typing.
(Siann, 1994, pp.73-74)

People who are strongly gender-schematic are more prone to see the world in 'masculine' or 'feminine' terms, and to try to keep their own behaviour consistent with stereotypical standards for their sex.

Cultural theories

According to cultural theories the sex-based division of labour in many cultures leads necessarily to differences in behaviour between the sexes and to the stereotypical perceptions that men and women are different (Sarup, 1996). Different social roles lead to different gender stereotypes. Women, constrained by their social roles to rear children and take care of a home, show more nurturing behaviour, while men, guided by their social roles in the competitive world of work, display more battling and assertive behaviour (Mol, 1985). Ideology and culture influence gender. Steele (1997) for example found that when mathematical tests were defined as being measures on which men generally out-perform women, the performance of mathematically talented women on these tests was lower than the performance of similarly talented men. When the same measures were defined as tests in which sex differences were not normally found, the average performance of talented women and similarly talented men did not differ. For cultural theorists therefore sex roles are a matter of conforming with a prevailing culture and the option of a counter-cultural choice is available.

Self-presentation theories

Self-presentation theories hold that gender is a cultural invention, a social construction, and a 'self-presentation' that people enact in certain settings (Harel and Papert, 1991, Kafai and Resnick, 1996). As such gender is seen within the purview of the epistemological approach called 'constructionism'. Constructionism is derived from the term constructivism used by epistemologists to refer to a theory of knowledge in which knowledge does not reflect an 'objective' ontological reality, but exclusively an ordering and organization of a world constituted by our experience (von Glaserfeld, 1996).

Gender is a social performance that varies depending on gender schemas, on the social setting or on the audience's expectations. Thus the cold, stand-offish boss might be a warm and caring father to his children. These constructionist views suggest that gender and gender-related behaviour is not fixed but switched on and off at certain times.

Empirical measures of gender differences

The problem for the empirical researcher therefore is that the literature on the conceptual theory of gender differences is enormous, the findings often contradictory, the issues frequently value-laden and emotionally volatile yet the conclusions are potentially tremendously valuable for social policy. The same is true in approaching empirical measures of gender differences where there are also a variety of different psychological measures used by researchers. Yet for all the fuzziness of the conceptual framework that researchers have employed, there continues to be an extensive canon of work on gender differences. Some of it reinforces 'common-sense' perceptions, but, as Maccoby and Jacklin (1974, p.335) showed in a major review of the literature, many popular beliefs about the psychological characteristics of the two sexes have proved to have little or no basis in fact. Some of the beliefs they discovered to be unfounded were that girls are more social than boys; that girls are more suggestible than boys; that girls have lower self-esteem; that boys are more analytical; that girls are more affected by heredity and boys by environment; that girls lack motivation to achieve; and that girls are auditory and boys are visual. Yet there are research findings which show significant differences between the sexes.

Sandra Bem

Much of the work on instruments to measure gender differences took its methodology from social psychological research on stereotypes: people were given long lists of adjectives and asked to choose those that applied for example to particular racial and ethnic groups (Katz and Braly, 1933). Similar techniques were used to study gender stereotypes (Komarovsky, 1950, Rosenkrantz, Vogel, Bee, Broverman and Broverman, 1968, Ellis and Bentler, 1973, Williams and Bennett, 1975). It was assumed that these methods reflected the stereotyping process itself – that people made sense of their social world by categorizing other individuals according to easily observable characteristics that signal age, gender or racial background, and by then attributing other adjectives or traits on the basis of group membership. However all the earlier researchers before Bem and her Bem Sex Role Inventory then arranged their adjectives and the stereotypes of Femininity and Masculinity that they represented at either end of a single orthogonal scale. Terman and Miles (1936) are usually credited with the first uni-dimensional bipolar measurement of within-sex gender-related individual differences.

The Bem Sex Role Inventory (BSRI) was created by Sandra Lipsitz Bem. In the early 1970s she discovered that sex-biased wording in job advertisements and sex segregated advertisements discouraged people from applying for jobs traditionally done by the opposite sex. This led to work with the Californian

Highway Patrol into the way in which they recruited women, and to wider work on sex roles. Her theoretical basis for the empirical research which led to the creation of her inventory was Constantinople's (1973) hypothesis that masculinity and femininity are not mutually exclusive nor the two ends of a bipolar continuum but distinct orthogonal constructs. In popular thought it was assumed that to be more feminine was to be less masculine. This 'congruence model' (Whitley, 1984) contended that the healthiest and most socially competent orientation for an individual was the one that was consistent with his/her biological sex: males were supposed to demonstrate the masculine sex role while females were supposed to demonstrate the feminine sex role. Bem (1974) summarized the perception of these roles. 'Both historically and cross-culturally, masculinity and femininity seem to have represented two complementary domains of positive traits and behaviours', with masculinity being associated with an instrumental orientation, 'a cognitive focus on getting the job done', and femininity being associated with an expressive orientation, 'an affective concern for the welfare of others' (Bem, 1974, p.156).

She saw three main beliefs concerning men and women in Western society: 'that they have fundamentally different psychological and sexual natures, that men are inherently the dominant or superior sex, and that both male-female difference and male dominance are natural' (Bem, 1993, p.1).

To regard masculinity and femininity as distinct social constructs, as Bem did, would explain how someone can have a high level of both masculine and feminine outlooks and characteristics (Spence, Helmreich and Stapp, 1975). To be both masculine and feminine is called 'androgynous'. It was this concept of androgyny that Bem (1974) intended to measure. From an androgyny perspective behavioural flexibility, which might be more needed in a modern, complex and fluid society, came from the ability to demonstrate traditionally feminine or masculine behaviours depending on what was appropriate in each situation. Bem (1975) concluded that the most productive and healthy gender orientation was androgyny and that psychological well-being increased for those with an androgynous gender orientation.

The development of the Bem Sex Role Inventory

The masculine and feminine items chosen by Bem for her scale were selected as being those items which were judged to be more desirable in American society for men rather than women and vice versa. In this way the scale would measure the degree to which a person was culturally influenced by gender roles. Gender expression is formed by both biology and culture. Culture is seen as developing stereotypical behaviour models based on averaged observations of gender traits and these traits are in turn affected and altered by cultural expectations. The end result is a feedback loop, with culture arising out of an observed biological basis and then affecting the development of an individual as they grow to express their biology. In that way the Bem Sex Role Inventory (BSRI) could be seen as an indirect measure of gender identity and a direct measure of an individual's internalization of society's sex-typed standards of desirable behaviour for men and women.

A preliminary list of two hundred personality characteristics was compiled which according to Bem and several of her students appeared to be 'positive in value and either masculine or feminine in tone' (Bem, 1974, p.156). This list was the pool from which the final items were chosen. The judges who determined the social desirability for each sex of the items were a group of one hundred undergraduates studying at Stanford University in 1972-73: fifty were male and fifty were female. The judges were asked to use a 7-point scale, ranging from 'not at all desirable' to 'extremely desirable', in order to rate the desirability in American society of each of the items 'for a man' or 'for a woman'. A personality characteristic qualified as feminine if it was independently judged by both male and female judges as significantly more desirable for a woman than a man. Equally a personality characteristic qualified as masculine if it was independently judged by both male and female judges as significantly more desirable for a man than for a woman.

There were 76 personality characteristics which fulfilled these criteria: twenty were selected for the Masculinity scale and twenty for the Femininity scale. An additional twenty 'neutral' characteristics were added to the scale from the original pool of items. These items were intended both to be neutral in the sense that they were no more desirable for one sex than the other and also to function as a measure of whether respondents of both sexes were tending to answer in a socially desirable way. Later Bem (1981a) revised the BSRI using these neutral items only as fillers in the inventory and not as a separate scale.

The differentiation of sex roles into four groups was suggested by Spence, Helmreich and Stapp (1975) and adopted by Bem (1977). The four groups were formed by splitting the Masculinity and Femininity scores at the median. The 'androgynous' group scored above the median on both scales. The 'masculine' group scored above the median on Masculinity and below it on Femininity. The 'feminine' group scored above the median on Femininity and below it on Masculinity. Finally, the 'undifferentiated' group scored below the median on both scales.

Though Bem conducted no further empirical work on item selection she took note of some of the criticisms by producing a shorter form of the BSRI with only 30 items: the feminine and masculine items for this were chosen from the full inventory in order to maximize both the internal consistency of the Masculinity and Femininity scales and the orthogonality between them (Bem, 1981a). This revision was tested and validated by Heerboth and Ramanaiah (1985). At this time too Bem began to expound her gender schema theory (1981b, 1982), and to point out the advantage that the BSRI had over other Masculinity-Femininity scales in measuring the extent to which respondents spontaneously sort information relevant to the respondent into distinct masculine and feminine categories.

Because the BSRI used adjectives rated as masculine to compose the Masculinity scale and those rated feminine to compose the Femininity scale, the question kept arising, rated in comparison to what? Bem had described the ratings as based not on the differential endorsements of males and females but rather on the basis of sex-typed social desirability: the adjectives or traits were rated as masculine or feminine to the degree that the raters thought that social standards dictated. Some researchers saw difficulties with this norming procedure. Since the internalized sex-role standards that result in any given sex-role orientation are learned through socialization, if society's perception of these sex-linked traits changed then the normative data for the scale would become outdated, and the operationalization of Masculinity and Femininity would become inaccurate.

Since Bem's first inventory in 1974 society's perception has changed. Increased egalitarianism between men and women is an ongoing trend in western society: the differences between the societal roles of men and women are steadily diminishing and have been for the last twenty-five years at least. Stake, Zand and Smalley (1996) had suggested therefore that evidence for Bem's androgyny hypothesis could only be found in studies that took into consideration social context variables. They pointed out that meta-analyses indicated that gender differences in social behaviours were affected by the saliency of gender-role expectations within various settings. For example men's and women's leadership behaviours were linked to the contextual social expectations for the individuals who occupied the leadership roles (Eagly and Johnson, 1990). The Bem categorization of individuals as sex-typed or androgynous was based on the broader society's prescriptions of gender-appropriate traits as the raters themselves expressed them. So the more the individuals involved perceive the social cues, the more the smaller-scale social context should influence and affect the expression of gender-appropriate behaviour.

So Ballard-Reisch and Elton (1992) undertook the testing of whether the BSRI items were continuing to represent society's perceptions of masculinity and femininity and whether the items on the scale were perceived as positive characteristics. Their subjects were 265 adults in Nevada. They found alpha reliabilities (Cronbach, 1951) of 0.78 for the Masculinity scale, and 0.86 for the Femininity scale, showing that the original factors were reliable. Yet they did not find that the BSRI masculine and feminine items reflected positive traits. They concluded that 'the BSRI and its modifications are in fact measuring different personality characteristics, but that these characteristics may no longer have anything to do with masculinity and femininity as identified through traditional sex role stereotypes' (Ballard-Reisch and Elton, 1992, p.304).

Since the publication of the professional manual of the BSRI (1981), a large number of studies have been conducted using the BSRI so that in 1994, the year of ordination of the respondents in this study, the Social Sciences Citation Index showed a total of 1484 articles which used the BSRI.

The use of the BSRI in the UK

Though the justification for including items in the BSRI had been their social desirability for an American male or female, there have been many uses of the inventory with British subjects. Archer (1989) had reviewed the range of gender role measures available and was one of the early users of the BSRI in Britain (Archer and Rhodes, 1989). Archer and Rhodes (1989) studying male undergraduates at Lancashire Polytechnic felt that the concept of androgyny involved no emergent properties which were not readily predictable from the separate M and F scores.

Arnold and Bye (1989) found, in a study of English polytechnic students, a significant positive correlation between Masculinity and Femininity which showed the usefulness of treating them as separate dimensions rather than opposite ends of the same continuum (Bem, 1977). They also discovered that it was sex-role rather than sex which had a closer relationship with effective career decision-making. Though they counselled that it would be appropriate to check periodically whether the items on the BSRI were consistently seen as desirable for each sex across countries and across time (Arnold and Bye, 1989, p.205), they believed that the American BSRI worked with their English subjects.

Walker and Baker (1993) however made the same point as Ballard-Reisch and Elton (1992) about what the BSRI is actually measuring when they said that the terms 'feminine' and 'masculine' arising from the BSRI referred to empirically-established stereotypes extant in the American college culture of the mid-1970s. So it would be likely that such terms would have changed in meaning for a British audience. In the same way Wilcox and Francis (1997a) in their replication study of the BSRI items with 236 English female sixth-formers found very few of the items differentially judged to be desirable in men and women, and concluded that the dimensions being assessed had less to do with the assimilation of cultural stereotypes than with basic personality differences between men and women. Argyle came to a similar conclusion:

> These dimensions were found to have little or no relation with self-related masculinity or femininity; they are rather two unrelated dimensions of expressive and instrumental styles of behaviour. Those who score high on both scales, formerly described as 'androgynous', really have two sets of desirable attributes; the male ones are about leadership qualities, the female ones about sympathy and concern ... All that has really been found is that there are two sets of desirable qualities which members of either sex may possess and that it is desirable to have each set of qualities.
> (Argyle, 1994, p.128)

This judgement is gaining ground among researchers. Because the BSRI labels some attributes as either masculine or feminine it tends to make the student give cognitive and linguistic labels to attributes that are essentially human rather than typically sex-typed. Thus a woman who describes herself as highly self-reliant, ambitious and analytical increases her Masculinity score on the BSRI but it might be better to regard her simply as high on these human attributes, rather than as masculine. This finds favour with researchers who follow the cultural, social learning and gender-schematic theories of sex differences including, interestingly, Bem (1993) herself: she noted that the masculine and feminine scales may turn gender-related individual differences into inappropriate concepts and confuse psychologists' formal constructs of M and F with lay conceptions of masculinity and femininity.

If it is true that the dimensions being assessed by the BSRI may have less to do with the assimilation of cultural stereotypes than with basic personality differences between men and women, then it would be valuable to study the BSRI alongside more robust personality measures. Wilcox and Francis (1997b) in a development of a previous study (1997a) found that those women who had high scores on the EPQ Neuroticism scale emphasized greater gender role differentiation between the cultural stereotypes of men and women. This seemed to support the theory that those with greater personal insecurity would seek social compensation through clearer gender role differentiation.

There have, in fact, been only four studies, two British and two American, relating the BSRI to the full range of Eysenck's personality measures (Williams, 1982, Kimlicka, Sheppard, Sheppard and Wakefield, 1988, Nagoshi, Pitts and Nakata, 1993, Francis and Wilcox, 1998a). In all four BSRI Masculinity correlated positively with Extraversion and was unrelated to Psychoticism in both males and females. In three of the studies Masculinity was inversely related to Neuroticism and unrelated to Lie scale scores. There is less clarity about the relationship between BSRI Femininity and personality though the majority of the studies found Femininity negatively associated with Psychoticism.

BSRI and religiosity

In the area of sex differences and religiosity Argyle and Beit-Hallahmi could say quite categorically that 'it is obvious that women are more religious on every criterion' (Argyle and Beit-Hallahmi, 1975, p.71). Such a statement could be supported by studies of church attendance (Field, 1993), Bible reading (Harrison, 1983), prayer (Poloma and Gallup, 1991), as well as by studies of beliefs and attitudes (Greeley, 1992). Francis (1997, pp.89-90) adduced a large amount of additional statistical evidence to support this, but pointed out that 'the real major source of controversy, however, is less concerned with establishing the empirical grounds for the observation that females are more religious than with establishing a satisfactory theoretical basis to provide an adequate account of the reasons for the observed difference' (Francis, 1997, p.81).

Three general groups of explanations for this difference have emerged. The first group contains gender role socialization theories and structural location theories and is comparable to the cultural theory and social learning theory for sex differences explored earlier. According to these theories women are more religious than men because of their different social roles or structural locations in society. Women's religiosity is consistent with their socialization and internalization of the 'proper' female role (Nelsen and Potvin, 1981). Women's greater religious commitment and participation in church activities are congruent with the communal emphasis of the mother/homemaker roles, and incompatible with full-time participation in the workforce and involvement in the provider role (Moberg, 1962, Martin, 1967, Nelsen and Nelsen, 1975, de Vaus and McAllister, 1987).

Glock, Ringer and Babbie (1967), for example, argued that the mother's social role was domestic and the father's economic so that, since the bonds between family and church are stronger than between economy and church, females who are more heavily involved in the family role would be expected to be more church-oriented. Azzi and Ehrenberg (1975) suggested that church attendance was considered a household activity performed by the wife who was more able to allocate the time necessary to it. Similarly Iannaccone (1990) pointed to an implicit division of labour between women and men whereby religion was seen as a household commodity.

As part of these structural location theories to account for the greater religiosity of women, Francis (1997) drew out four strands in the argument from the different place of women in the workplace:

> One strand of this argument is a development of the classic secularization theses, as illustrated by Lenski (1953), Martin (1967) and Luckman (1967). According to this argument, religious involvement declines with participation in the modern secular world. Since women are less likely to be fully a part of the ongoing secular world, at least in terms of outside-the-home employment, they are also likely to be less secularized than men ... A second strand of this argument suggests that women seek social support from religion to alleviate the greater isolation they experience as a consequence of not benefiting from the social contacts of the workplace (Moberg, 1962); that women seek comfort from religion to compensate for not benefiting from the more socially valued role of the wage earner (Yinger, 1970). A third strand of this argument suggests that women are more likely than men to avoid the conflicts between the competitiveness of the workplace and the essence of Christian values which in turn leads to a greater distance from the churches (de Vaus, 1984). A fourth strand of this argument simply suggests that lower commitment to the workplace releases more time for women to devote to the church (Glock, Ringer and Babbie, 1967).
> (Francis, 1997, pp.83-84)

The second group of arguments to explain the greater religiosity of women focuses on depth psychology theories and is comparable to the psychoanalytic theory for sex differences explored earlier. According to Freud (1950) God is in every case modelled after the father and our personal relationship to God is dependent on our relation to our natural father (Batson, Schoenrade and Ventis, 1993). Empirical research however in order to support such a theory yielded either inconsistent or contradictory results. The research by Vergote and colleagues (Vergote, Tamayo, Pasquali, Bonami, Pattyn and Custers, 1969, Vergote and Aubert, 1973, Vergote and Tamayo, 1981) and Gibson, H. (1994) gave some support to the theory whereas Tamayo and Dugas (1977) showed a strong relation between the concept of God and the mother image for both women and men. Nelsen, Cheek and Au (1985) showed that women held a more feminine image of God than the image held by men. Though the empirical support for such a theory is weak, nevertheless it is a theory which still has a hold in popular consciousness.

> The image of God as a man is very deeply entrenched, even in people who have rejected the idea of God: the God we no longer believe in is still envisaged as male. It's hardly surprising, and very convenient for a world ruled by men to see

its creator as a man. Where power is equated with masculinity, the most powerful figure must be masculine.
(Collins, Friedman and Pivot, 1978, p.13)

The third group of arguments to explain the greater religiosity of women focuses on personality theories and gender orientation theories and is comparable to the cognitive theories for sex differences explored earlier. According to these theories women are more religious than men because of their different personality, their different sex-type or their different gender-schema. Researchers using the Eysenckian personality measures in which females record lower Psychoticism scores than males (Eysenck and Eysenck, 1976) have drawn attention to low Psychoticism scores as the personality dimension fundamental to religiosity (Kay, 1981, Francis and Pearson, 1985b, Francis, 1992a, Francis, Lewis, Brown, Philipchalk and Lester, 1995) and thus that would account for gender differences in religiosity in terms of fundamental gender differences in levels of Psychoticism.

However Feltey and Poloma (1991) showed by means of multivariate analysis that gender role ideology is more important than gender in predicting differences in religiosity. This led on to the question that scholars like Bem asked, how much can the sex difference in religiosity be explained by the different proportions of women and men with a feminine world-view? If it can be, then religiosity should be affected more by gender role than by gender. Thompson (1991) in a study of 358 New England undergraduates was the first to test this hypothesis using the BSRI. By means of multivariate analysis Thompson was able to control for the effects of both gender and gender role. He found that possessing a feminine perspective was more significant in explaining religiosity than was gender. In addition the within-gender variations in religiosity were much more predictable among men than among women:

> For men, the effects of both religious affiliation and a feminine perspective on religiosity were consistent and substantial. Two different ex post facto explanations for this pattern warrant further attention. I have argued that the ways in which men in our culture experience the construction of their gendered perspective precedes their religiosity. Thus men who have developed a feminine side to their gender perspective might feel more comfortable 'crossing over' (Giele, 1978) traditional gender boundaries to participate actively in a cross-sex gendered institution, be it religion or family life. These men might adhere to the 'modern' masculinity norms, which have redefined the 'feeling rules' and given a new importance to maintaining close relationships. They might experience the reality of connectedness as a given (Gilligan, 1986). Ironically their 'femininity' can create new problems. Rose's (1987) analysis of the negotiation of gender in a religious community revealed that Evangelical women regarded most religious men as weak and emasculated.
> (Thompson, 1991, p.391)

Francis and Wilcox (1996) aimed to test Thompson's theory in a British context using the Francis Scale of Attitude toward Christianity as the measure of religiosity. In their study of 159 undergraduates in Wales they found results supporting the view that higher levels of religiosity were a function of gender orientation rather than a function of being female. Francis and Wilcox (1998b) used the BSRI and the FSAC with two samples of British teenagers. Multiple regression analysis showed that with the older teenagers gender role explained all the variance in attitude toward Christianity between males and females.

Francis (1997) recognized the criticism that had been levelled at the BSRI but felt it still provided a legitimate research tool:

> If recent attempts to apply gender orientation theory to account for individual differences in religiosity are valid, this approach may help to explain the inadequacy of earlier theories, grounded either in social and contextual factors or in other forms of psychological theory, and the ambiguity of the empirical data shaped to test these theories ... The usefulness of the theory to account for the different levels of religiosity among men and women, seen as two social groups, should provide the springboard for a fruitful line of future research.
> (Francis, 1997, p.89)

BSRI and the clergy

In looking at the relationship between gender role and the clergy as church leaders it is possible to draw on discoveries about leadership and gender role from other careers and professions. The leadership categorization theory, for example, proposed that a person's schematic conception of a leader strongly influenced how that person perceived a leader's effectiveness (Nye and Forsyth, 1991). If the leader possessed a high number of characteristics that matched the observer's schematic conception the leader would be perceived as effective; likewise if the leader possessed few or none of the schematic characteristics he or she would be perceived as ineffective. Traditionally characteristics which are associated with an effective leader have been stereotypically masculine, such as being task-oriented, ambitious and assertive; stereotypically feminine characteristics however such as being people-oriented, compassionate and sensitive tend not to be associated with leader effectiveness (Bem, 1974, Schein, 1973, 1975, Eagly and Johnson, 1990). Thus according to the leadership categorization theory men rather than women will tend to be viewed as effective leaders.

Several studies have found this to be the case (Dobbins, Long, Dedrick and Clemons, 1990, Eagly and Karau, 1991). When females do emerge as leaders, they are in groups that require complex social interaction, a stereotypical female task (Eagly and Karau, 1991). Other studies though found no significant differences in leadership emergence or effectiveness as a function of gender (Goktepe and Schneier, 1988, 1989, Ragins, 1991). The studies conducted by Goktepe and Schneier were ambivalent however on the effects of psychological gender or sex-type upon leadership effectiveness and the emergence of leaders. It was first found that those subjects who were androgynous, or high in both feminine and masculine qualities, received higher ratings measuring leadership effectiveness than did masculine or feminine sex-typed subjects (Goktepe and Schneier, 1988).

In a subsequent study which measured leadership emergence, those subjects who were sex-typed as masculine emerged as leaders significantly more than did feminine or androgynous subjects (Goktepe and Schneier, 1989).

Cann and Siegfried (1990) found that consideration behaviours were perceived as being feminine, while structuring behaviours were perceived as being masculine, and that both of these qualities needed to be present in a leadership style for that style to be effective. Studies also found that when women leaders were perceived as possessing a stereotypically masculine style, such as being authoritarian and potent, they tended to be less positively valued and viewed as more threatening than their male counterparts (Morrison, Greene and Tischler, 1985, Eagly, Makhijani and Klonsky, 1992). Since stereotypical gender characteristics are often associated with leadership effectiveness, it could be inferred that both physical gender and psychological gender could influence perceptions of the leader's abilities. If such stereotypes held true, females would be expected to be perceived as more effective leaders in situations that involved social interaction and required strong interpersonal skills. Males would be perceived as more effective leaders in situations that required strong assertive and disciplinary skills.

Such research is noteworthy for those who study the reactions to the debate about, and the decision in favour of, the ordination of women to the priesthood. It will be remembered that the data at the heart of this research began to be collected in 1994, the year in which women were first ordained as priests in the Church of England. Because of the potency of this issue, there have been several studies on the masculinity or femininity of the clergy and these studies have used a range of psychological instruments.

Rose's (1987) research revealed that Evangelical women regarded most religious men as weak and emasculated. In addition some people have regarded men with personalities that draw on their femininity as more likely to be homosexual. In Chapter 1, for example, it was seen that one facet of the 'unmanly' Victorian homosexual subculture was Anglo-Catholic religion (Hilliard, 1982, Marshall, 1980). Westwood in a pioneering study of male homosexuality in Britain in 1960 stated that 'some of the contacts maintained that the highest proportion of homosexuals who are regular churchgoers favoured the Anglo-Catholic churches' (Westwood, 1960, p.54). Fletcher (1990) in his study of stress amongst homosexual clergy in the Church of England discovered that 'the vast majority of those belonging to the support groups contacted could be described as Liberal-Catholics' (Fletcher, 1990, p.61).

Yet it is not homosexuality but the nature of the ordained ministry which may predispose male clergy towards a more feminine personality profile. Several studies in the USA have drawn attention to the feminine characteristics of male clergy (Nauss, 1973). Ekhardt and Goldsmith (1984) and Goldsmith and Ekhardt (1984) reported a relevant investigation. Their sample was 90 men and 114 women preparing for ordained ministry at eleven American Protestant seminaries. The data for this sample were compared with those for secular students preparing to work in schools. In the first study the seminarians scored feminine personality profiles on the Personality Preference Form (Jackson, 1974). In the second study they used the

BSRI and discovered that it was able to discriminate in 85 per cent of the cases between seminarians and education students. They warned therefore that there appeared to be a powerful set of response biases in religious subjects which affects many of the BSRI items. They found that male and female seminarians did not differ significantly from each other on either the Masculinity or Femininity scales, but that seminary men had more feminine traits and seminary women more masculine traits than do students from the general population. In addition they found that significantly more of the seminarians were androgynous and fewer conformed to the same-sex stereotype than would be found in the general population.

Until this present book there have been no reported British studies using the BSRI with clergy.

Using the EPI (Eysenck and Eysenck, 1964) Towler and Coxon (1979) reported little difference between the personality profile of male clergy and men in general. Using the EPQ Francis (1991a) examined the personality profiles of 252 male and female ordinands at Anglican theological colleges. He was not surprised to find that the female ordinands displayed radically different personality characteristics from the male ordinands 'given the long battle in which women had to engage in order to achieve admission to the ranks of the clergy as deacons' (Francis, 1991a, p.1137). Yet he found that compared with the norms for the general population the gender expectations were reversed, so that the female ordinands recorded a characteristically masculine profile and the male ordinands a characteristically feminine profile. His sample though was limited to two residential theological colleges and two non-residential theological courses. Using the EPQR-S Francis (1992b) examined the personality profiles of 112 male and female clergy attending two residential summer schools. There too he found that 'the personality profile of the current generation of female clergy is neither representative of women in general, nor a female copy of the male personality profile' (Francis, 1992b, p.36) since the female clergy had higher scores on the two dimensions of Extraversion and Psychoticism. He did recognize though that 'the church might well expect a different kind of female clergy to emerge once the acceptance of women priests is well established' (Francis, 1992b, p.36).

In order to test the generalizability of Francis' (1991a, 1992b) findings, Robbins, Francis and Rutledge (1997) carried out full random cross-sectional surveys of male and female parochial clergy. Contrary to the usual differences between the personality profiles of men and women found in general population samples, the female clergy were not significantly different from the male clergy in terms of their scores recorded on the Extraversion, Neuroticism, Psychoticism or Lie scales. It is unscientific, but maybe the old joke that there are three sexes, men, women and clergy, has a measure of truth.

The place of churchmanship within the question of the femininization of male clergy received some interesting evidence when Louden and Francis (1999) using the EPQ found that Roman Catholic secular parish priests in England and Wales have a more feminine personality profile, that is, more introverted and more neurotic than men in general. In order to test the theory that male Anglo Catholic clergy present a more feminine personality than other male Anglican clergy,

Francis and Thomas (1996a) surveyed a random sample of 222 male clergy from the Church in Wales:

> The major conclusion to emerge from this study is that the data provide no support for the theory that male Anglo Catholic priests present a more feminine personality profile than other male Anglican priests. The interpretation of the nineteenth century critics is not supported by late twentieth century empirical data. According to these empirical data there is no evidence to support the view that there is something more feminine about the appeal of the Anglo Catholic orientation and something more masculine about the appeal of the Evangelical orientation. However, before this theory is properly laid to rest, it would be wise to replicate the present study using a more sensitive index of gender orientation like the Bem Sex Role Inventory (Bem, 1981a) alongside the Eysenck Personality Questionnaire employed in the present study. Further research is still required. (Francis and Thomas, 1996a, p.20)

Summary of research so far

Up to now we have considered the variety of theories to account for gender differences in religiosity with a particular focus on gender orientation theories. We have seen how in Bem's conceptualization masculinity and femininity are seen as two separate orthogonal dimensions. We have seen also how Bem, in the light of this understanding, developed and tested the Bem Sex Role Inventory. In considering the links between religiosity and gender or gender role we have noted Thompson's (1991) study which showed that being religious is a function of the feminine gender orientation in both men and women. Though there have been no reported studies of the use of the BSRI with clergy, we have paid attention to those studies using other personality measures which suggest that clergy by the nature of their role may be prone to a more feminine orientation, and to those studies which suggest that Anglo-Catholic clergy are more prone than Evangelical clergy to have a feminine gender. Though Francis and Thomas (1996a) when using the EPQ with male Anglican clergy found this not to be the case, it is important to test the generalizability of such a conclusion with a more sensitive index of gender orientation.

The results of this study

The Masculinity subscale of the BSRI achieved an alpha coefficient of 0.85 and Femininity subscale one of 0.76 revealing satisfactory internal reliability and homogeneity comparable to previous studies (Bem, 1974). Even though the BSRI has been widely used there are no published norms for a British population and it is hard to find mean scores in the literature for British subjects with which to compare these clergy scores. Francis and Wilcox's (1998a) study of Welsh undergraduate students recorded mean scores for men of 71.8 SD 9.5 on Masculinity and 70.3 SD 6.5 on Femininity, and for women of 66.2 SD 9.5 on

Masculinity and 72.6 SD 8.0 on Femininity. In the present study male clergy recorded mean scores of 68.59 SD 7.53 on Masculinity and 69.61 SD 5.65 on Femininity, and female clergy 66.25 SD 6.46 on Masculinity and 72.68 SD 5.95 on Femininity.

Reference was made earlier to those replication studies of the BSRI which found that few of the scale items differentiated between men and women, and raised the question of whether the dimensions being assessed were not so much cultural stereotypes as basic personality differences between men and women, not so much self-related masculinity or femininity as two unrelated dimensions of expressive and instrumental styles of behaviour (Argyle, 1994). Those researchers who follow the cultural, social learning and gender-schematic theories of sex differences, such as Bem (1993) and Lippa (1995), now see the BSRI as having less to do with the assimilation of cultural stereotypes than with basic personality differences between men and women. Seeing the BSRI as a personality measure may change the predictions about the relationship between gender orientation and churchmanship, for in this study so far we have seen little correlation between churchmanship and three other measures of personality.

Table 10.1 Correlation matrix between sex role and churchmanship

	Catholic/Evangelical	Liberal/Conservative	Charismatic
Masculinity	+0.0819	+0.0905	- 0.0134
	NS	NS	NS
Femininity	- 0.1760	- 0.1682	- 0.0189
	0.05	0.05	NS

Table 10.1 shows the correlation matrix between the BSRI and the three churchmanship dimensions. There are two significant correlations: the first shows higher scores on the Femininity scale correlated with Catholic churchmanship; the second shows higher scores on the Femininity scale correlated with Liberal churchmanship.

The results from an analysis of variance are presented in two sections. In the first the results for the whole group of clergy will be presented on each of the three churchmanship dimensions. However, in order to separate out the influence of gender on scores on the BSRI subscales, in the second section the tables for churchmanship groups have been calculated for male and female clergy separately.

Table 10.2 BSRI mean scores for all clergy by Catholic/Evangelical churchmanship

	Catholic		Central		Evangelical			
	mean	SD	mean	SD	mean	SD	F	P<
masc	67.72	7.32	66.12	6.10	68.65	7.77	0.95	NS
fem	70.98	6.29	72.18	6.42	69.43	5.15	2.29	NS

Table 10.2 shows no significant difference between the mean scores of the groups on the Catholic/Evangelical dimension.

Table 10.3 BSRI mean scores for all clergy by Liberal/Conservative churchmanship

	Liberal		Middle		Conservative			
	mean	SD	mean	SD	mean	SD	F	P<
masc	67.79	7.71	65.45	5.64	69.29	7.28	3.10	0.05
fem	71.01	6.23	71.56	5.99	69.21	5.25	2.52	NS

Table 10.3 shows no significant difference between the mean Femininity scores of the groups on the Liberal/Conservative dimension. It shows a statistically significant difference between the mean Masculinity scores, with Middle-of-the-road clergy recording the lowest scores and Conservatives the highest.

Table 10.4 BSRI mean scores for all clergy by Charismatic churchmanship

	Pro-charis.		Non-charis.		Anti-charis.			
	mean	SD	mean	SD	mean	SD	F	P<
masc	68.01	7.52	67.23	7.53	68.31	6.89	0.19	NS
fem	70.17	5.22	72.85	6.06	69.63	6.85	2.81	NS

Table 10.4 shows no significant difference between the mean scores for Masculinity or Femininity of the groups on the Charismatic dimension.

Table 10.5 BSRI mean scores for clergy by Catholic/Evangelical churchmanship

	Catholic		Central		Evangelical			
	mean	SD	mean	SD	mean	SD	F	P<
male								
masc.	68.52	7.31	66.10	7.00	69.03	7.82	0.66	NS
fem.	70.07	5.87	70.90	7.65	68.98	5.10	0.84	NS
female								
masc.	65.96	6.39	66.14	5.08	66.86	7.53	0.09	NS
fem.	73.12	6.85	74.00	3.92	71.33	5.12	0.61	NS

We turn, therefore, to consider the male and female churchmanship groups separately. Table 10.5 shows that when male and female clergy are scored separately none of the groups on the Catholic/Evangelical dimension score significantly differently on Masculinity or Femininity. Though analysis of variance revealed no significant differences the correlation matrix in table 10.1 had shown a correlation on this dimension. So a post hoc t-test between the male Central and Evangelical groups alone showed the Evangelicals scoring significantly higher on Masculinity and significantly lower on Femininity than the Central group. A Student's t-test between the female Central and Evangelical clergy showed the Central clergy scoring significantly higher on Femininity.

Table 10.6 BSRI mean scores for clergy by Liberal/Conservative churchmanship

	Liberal		Middle		Conservative			
	mean	SD	mean	SD	mean	SD	F	P<
male								
masc.	68.33	8.36	66.13	6.09	69.73	7.13	1.99	NS
fem.	70.20	6.21	70.65	5.05	68.72	5.33	1.42	NS
female								
masc.	66.87	6.46	63.50	3.78	66.60	8.02	0.87	NS
fem.	72.46	6.11	73.89	7.79	72.20	3.65	0.23	NS

Table 10.6 shows that when male and female churchmanship groups are considered separately none of the groups of clergy on the Liberal/Conservative dimension score significantly different scores on Masculinity or Femininity. Yet table 10.1 had shown a correlation for this dimension. So Student's t-tests were again used and showed significant results when pairs of groups were compared: the male Conservative clergy scored significantly higher than the Middle-of-the-road clergy on Masculinity and significantly lower on Femininity, whereas the female Liberal clergy scored higher than the Middle-of-the-road clergy on Masculinity.

Table 10.7 BSRI mean scores for clergy by Charismatic churchmanship

	Pro-charis.		Non-charis.		Anti-charis.			
	mean	SD	mean	SD	mean	SD	F	P<
male								
masc.	68.30	7.75	68.82	7.16	69.17	7.32	0.18	NS
fem.	69.32	5.13	72.65	6.85	68.79	5.91	3.01	0.05
female								
masc.	67.00	6.70	64.22	7.68	66.27	5.39	0.59	NS
fem.	73.08	4.49	73.22	4.58	71.64	8.66	0.30	NS

Table 10.7 shows the results for male and female clergy respectively on the Charismatic dimension. There are no significant differences for female clergy across this dimension. However the only significant results using analysis of variance with the BSRI when churchmanship groups are separated out by sex are that Non-charismatic male clergy score significantly higher on the Femininity subscale than the other two groups. When t-tests were run for the female clergy on this dimension, the Non-charismatics scored significantly lower on Masculinity than the Pro-charismatics, and significantly higher on Femininity than the Anti-charismatics.

Conclusion

The research evidence about feminine men and masculine women among the clergy is shown by this research with a dedicated sex role measure to be untrue: male clergy are higher on Masculinity and lower on Femininity than female clergy.

There are differences in gender role amongst the churchmanship groups. In fact we have seen the male Evangelical clergy representing a more masculine orientation than the Central clergy with higher scores on Masculinity and lower scores on Femininity. There would be value in finding out if other groups of male Evangelical clergy share the same gender-role orientation. This result adds support to Francis and Wilcox's (1998a) finding that the image of masculinity promoted by the BSRI is that of extraversion since these male Evangelical clergy scored high on Eysenck's Extraversion. What we can say is that these results accord with Francis and Thomas' (1996a) finding that there is no support for the view that male Anglo-Catholic clergy are more feminine.

Certainly the male Middle-of-the-road clergy represent a more feminine orientation than the Conservative clergy with lower scores on Masculinity and higher scores on Femininity. Again the female Non-charismatic clergy represent a more feminine orientation with lower scores on Masculinity and higher scores on Femininity. Continuing use of the Bem Sex Role Inventory with groups of clergy will provide further data to explore this fascinating area. However, if researchers are right in seeing the BSRI as having less to do with the assimilation of cultural stereotypes and more to do with basic personality differences, then the lack of correlation between churchmanship and personality seen in the previous chapters may be sufficient explanation of the general lack of correlation between churchmanship and gender orientation as measured by the Bem Sex Role Inventory.

In this and the previous five chapters we have seen clearly that the question, 'Is churchmanship a function of personality so that particular types of people are drawn to particular forms of churchmanship?' receives a decisive 'No'. In general different forms of churchmanship do not attract different personality types. Also different forms of churchmanship customarily do not lead to greater or less happiness, greater proneness to burnout or greater adoption of particularly masculine or feminine roles. Churchmanship differences amount to style over substance.

Chapter 11

What priorities for ministry?

Introduction

The focus of this study now turns from personality and the inner life of the clergy to its outward and visible expression. Despite the fact that personality and churchmanship are not substantially correlated, Chapter 1 has reminded us that churchmanship has been and still is a very important component in Anglican self-understanding. Does churchmanship then foster different patterns of belief or behaviour amongst Anglican clergy? Do Evangelicals have different role priorities in their ministry in the parish? In this chapter a new inventory is developed and tested to measure clergy role priorities.

Paul (1964) wrote an influential report on the state of the clergy of the Church of England in the 1960s called *The Deployment and the Payment of the Clergy*. He commented later on the report, drawing attention to the confusion in the minds of clergy about the roles they should play (Paul, 1973, p.226). Certainly there is much agreement in the literature that prime causes for stress in the ministry are role conflict and role ambiguity (see for example Winton and Cameron, 1986, Gross, 1989, Coate, 1989, Malony and Hunt, 1991, Warren, 2002).

> The prime mover behind this uncertainty was deemed to be the continuing secularization of the environing society which engendered doubt about the role of the religious professional. In addition, the growing bureaucratization of the churches was seen as imposing a new set of demands on the clergy for which (in the view of many commentators) they were poorly trained and disinclined to meet. (Bryman, 1989, p.38)

This sense of role uncertainty in the history of the Church since the Second World War and concern for its effects on the life of the clergy led to a variety of studies into role prioritization among clergy.

Role inventories in empirical research with clergy

Blizzard (1955, 1956, 1958a, 1958b) is generally credited with creating the first six-item role inventory for clergy (administrator, organizer, pastor, preacher, teacher, priest). Coates and Kistler (1965) and Jud, Mills and Burch (1970) adopted the same list. Lauer (1973) used an 18-item list: prayer and worship, preaching and teaching, care and comfort, evangelism and mission, organization and administration, stewardship and finance, fellowship and service, publicity and promotion, public relations, personal counselling. Towler and Coxon (1979), influenced by both Blizzard and a list from the Columbia University Seminar on Professions, used a seven-item list: administrator, celebrant, leader of local community, preacher, official, pastor, counsellor. Ranson, Bryman and Hinings (1977) adopted Towler and Coxon's list. Tiller (1983) worked with eight items: leader, pastor, focus of the community, public spokesman, guardian of the tradition, professional minister, enabler of the laity, church builder. Francis and Rodger (1994) devised a list of seven roles: administrator, celebrant of sacraments, community leader, leader of public worship, pastor/counsellor, preacher and teacher. This group of seven has found much favour with others linked to the study of empirical and practical theology in the University of Wales, including Rutledge (1993, 1999). Robbins (1996, see also Robbins and Francis, 2000) used this group of seven with an additional three (evangelist, spiritual director and visitor) for her study. Bunting (1990) following the work of Hough and Cobb (1985) preferred the seven items of priest, master, preacher, builder, manager, therapist, practical theologian in his study of the provision of theological education in Great Britain. He found however that the theological colleges regarded his list as too limited and so wanted to add other models, specifically enabler, evangelist, servant of the Church, social activist, prophet, continual learner, missionary, witness and pioneer.

That bears out the nature of the problem: too short a list will leave out elements of clergy life or role that particular clergy will feel are central to their identity; too long a list will lead to less discrete categories with the possibility of confusion for the respondent. As an example, consider the commitment of a priest to intercede for his congregation. Ramsey (1972) in his book *The Christian Priest Today* regards this as one of the four answers to the question 'why the priest?'

> The priest, in the Church and for the Church, is the man of prayer. Do not all Christians pray? They do indeed, and from many of them we priests can learn to pray and to pray better. Yet 'man of prayer' is in a special way the role of the priest, and because it is so the Church's prayer will be stronger.
> (Ramsey, 1972, p.9)

In Blizzard's list the researcher could assume that the intercessory role is subsumed under 'priest' or 'pastor', in Lauer's under 'prayer and worship', and in Towler and Coxon's presumably under 'celebrant'. It is not that clear however to the respondent.

It can be seen then that the range and diversity of roles which Anglican ordained ministers are expected to fulfil is wide. In fact such is the variety of functions which they have to perform and the uncertainty of the roles which they have to fulfil that the role conflict to which Leslie Paul referred earlier seems inevitable. Clearly with such a wide range of clerical functions and roles classified by previous empirical researchers, the adoption of one set of roles rather than another might well appear to be arbitrary. In their studies the researchers argued for the inclusion of particular roles within their lists, but perhaps by the nature of the role construction exercise did not – at least in print – explain why other roles were excluded.

On the other hand there is the danger of catch-all categories. For example, Blizzard speaks of one of his six roles, the pastor, thus: 'the pastor does the visiting among the parishioners and prospective members, ministers to the sick and distressed, and counsels all who seek for guidance' (Blizzard, 1955, p.387). But are the skills required of the pastor ministering to the sick and distressed the same as those of the visitor or of the counsellor, or should that represent three distinct roles? There are advantages in taking Blizzard's route of six portmanteau categories for role classification but the experience of Anglican parochial ministry is more varied than that.

It seemed therefore both important and necessary to build a new role inventory to recognize the range and subtlety of Anglican ministerial roles. To be adequate and rational such a role inventory would need to draw together strands from each of the previous approaches. Such a task has a theological and not just a managerial rationale (*pace* Boyd, 1995) for it is possible by understanding the priority that clergy give to the range of roles that ministry calls for, to comprehend the theological aims and ends that they wish to pursue in and through these duties. This is particularly important when studying churchmanship since there have traditionally been different weights of emphasis between, for example, the Evangelical and the Catholic.

A new role inventory

In constructing a role inventory Randall (1997) began with the biblical models of apostle, prophet, evangelist, pastor and teacher from Ephesians 4:11. Stambaugh and Balch (1986, pp.138 & 142) showed that not every first-century term for leader was taken into the Christian vocabulary, that most of the terms associated with the synagogue and the pagan religions were avoided, but that these five roles have had a continuing place in the Christian Church's understanding of its ministry from the New Testament era to today. Within this five-item list the one that has caused some uncertainty is that of 'apostle'. Some have felt that the gift of apostle ended with the Twelve. Certainly the original twelve apostles have a unique place in Christian history and in the hereafter but they were not the only New Testament apostles. 1 Corinthians 15:5,7 mention that after the resurrection Jesus appeared to the Twelve and then also to 'all the apostles', indicating that there were apostles other than the Twelve. Several are mentioned by name: Matthias (Acts 1:26), Paul (Romans 1:1), Barnabas (Acts 14:14), Timothy and Silas (1 Thessalonians 2:6), and Andronicus and Junias (Romans 16:7). (It is interesting that when Chrysostom preached on this passage in Romans he had no problem with the suggestion that the second name was the female name Junia.) Some have felt that the gift of apostle ended with the end of the New Testament era. Yet historically the expectation that some form of apostolic ministry would continue in the church has been relatively constant. The concept of apostolic succession, however it is delineated, indicates an historical awareness of an ongoing apostolic ministry. In the last thirty years the churches of the Restoration movement have retrieved the word 'apostle' to describe those within their churches who are translocal leaders with oversight (Walker, 1985, Wright, 1986). In such a climate it was felt that 'apostle' could again be used as an indicator in a list of clergy roles.

To the Ephesians 4 list Randall next added Towler and Coxon's list of administrator, celebrant, leader of local community, preacher, official, pastor, counsellor. On consideration 'celebrant' was seen as unsuitable for a survey directed at curates who because they were in their first year of ministry would not therefore be presiding at a celebration of Holy Communion. The term 'celebrant' therefore became the two items of 'leader of public worship' and 'minister of sacraments'.

Next the role of 'theologian' was added. This was the role most chosen by Anglican theological colleges and courses as top priority in their training of ordinands in Bunting's (1990) study. Then the practical tasks of fund-raiser, manager, and visitor, and the spiritual tasks of spiritual director and man or woman of prayer were attached in the light of Hodge's (1988) strictures about ordinands' desires for more practical, skills-oriented training in theological education.

The Restoration churches have had an influence on those who have been influenced by the charismatic movement. They make much of the minister's role as 'pioneer', and this was one of the additional roles written in by the theological colleges in Bunting's study. It too was added.

In testing out the list with a group of clergy undergoing post-ordination training, 'fellowship-builder' and 'social worker' were suggested as missing roles. In that same process of sample-testing 'official' (which was the one least chosen by Towler and Coxon's respondents) was removed from the list. With the one exception of 'apostle', to which (see above) some curates had objections, the whole list commended itself to two sample groups of curates who tested it.

In Randall's (1997) study of curates the Clergy Role Inventory produced significant and discrete results. The curates perceived that their theological colleges and courses gave highest priority in training to the roles of theologian, leader of public worship and preacher, whereas the curates' own highest priorities were the roles of person of prayer, pastor and preacher. There were two particular emphases in that study; the first was the difference between male and female curates:

> What stands out most of all ... is how little significant difference there is between female and male curates in their awareness of role priorities, and in their estimation of the help they have received for those roles from their theological training. There are differences ... but what is clear is that, in selecting the men and women it does for ordained ministry, the church is choosing a range of people whose role expectations are similar.
> (Randall, 1997, pp.149-150)

The second emphasis was the difference between curates aged under 40 and those aged over 40 at ordination. The older curates gave highest priority to the roles of pastor, person of prayer and preacher, whereas the younger curates gave highest priority to the roles of teacher, person of prayer and pastor:

> The older curates gave a significantly higher role priority to five of these roles as they began training: spiritual director ... , pastor ... , counsellor ... , apostle ... , and prophet ... . For all of the older curates pastor was the role with the highest priority; for 91 per cent of the younger curates it was that of teacher.
> (Randall, 1997, p.170)

This Clergy Role Inventory has since been used in other empirical studies including research into the role of Roman Catholic parish clergy (Louden, 1998), and a major study of all the leaders of churches affiliated to the Evangelical Alliance (Francis, 2000, Francis and Robbins, 2004). In that study it was called a 'well established test of 20 ministry roles employed in other research studies' (Francis, 2000, p.24). It commends itself for use in this study alongside the three dimensional measurement of churchmanship in order to discover whether churchmanship makes a difference to clergy role prioritization.

Results from previous studies of role prioritization

Blizzard (1955) with his rural American Protestant sample of 344 clergy found that preacher and pastor were rated the two most important roles. In their 1962 study Towler and Coxon (1979) found that their ordinands rated pastor, priest and preacher as the most important roles. Daniel (1967) in his study of 96 Anglican clergymen in Greater London found that overall the role of pastor was most important but that Evangelicals were more likely to emphasize the role of preacher and Catholics the roles of pastor and priest.

Bryman, Ranson and Hinings (1974) in their survey asked lay members of Anglican deanery synods to rate seven ministerial roles (administrator, celebrant, leader, preacher, official, pastor, and counsellor) in order of priority: first or second priority was given to the role of celebrant by 78 per cent of Catholics, by 54 per cent of the Centralists, by 39 per cent of the Modernists, and by 20 per cent of Evangelicals. Similarly the preacher role was rated first or second in priority by 68 per cent of Evangelicals, by 33 per cent of Catholics, by 31 per cent of Centralists, and by 28 per cent of Modernists.

Ranson, Bryman and Hinings (1977) in the part of their study that dealt with Anglican clergy found that churchmanship was a potent variable for discriminating how clergy rank their ministerial roles. They showed that the role of pastor is ranked highest by each group with the exception of Catholics for whom celebrant is the most important. For both Modernists and Evangelicals the roles of preacher and counsellor are more important than that of celebrant (see also Bryman, 1989).

Bunting (1990) used the Runcie classification of theological colleges to assess the different perceptions by those institutions of the roles for which they were training ordinands. The High Church colleges trained priests and pastors. The

Middle colleges trained priests and preachers. The Low Church colleges trained preachers and practical theologians. The non-residential training courses trained practical theologians and priests. He drew attention to the higher priority that the colleges gave to preaching and evangelism than the theological training courses with the courses having a more practical concern with facilitating the life of the local church. The very low emphasis given by Low Church colleges to the role of priest put them very clearly alongside the non-Anglican training institutions in his survey.

Francis and Rodger (1994) in a study of all the full-time stipendiary male clergy in one diocese found that 'celebrant of sacraments' and 'pastor/counsellor' were the two roles with the highest priority. Robbins (1996), using Francis and Rodger's (1994) seven-item list, found that the role of pastor/counsellor was rated highest among female stipendiary Anglican clergy, with 'preacher', 'leader of public worship' and 'visitor' close behind.

Robbins went on to analyse her results with greater sophistication (Robbins and Francis, 2000). Amongst clergywomen she found that the roles of pastor/counsellor, preacher, and leader of public worship were the highest priority during initial training; the roles of pastor/counsellor, preacher, and visitor were the highest priority during the curacy; and the roles of leader of public worship, pastor/counsellor, and preacher were the highest priority during the women's current appointment. In measuring the shift of role emphasis between first and current appointments she found that the largest increase in priority had occurred with the role of administrator, and the only decrease was in the role of visitor.

Robbins and Francis (2000) also studied the influence of Catholic/Evangelical churchmanship on role prioritization:

> At the time of initial training, church tradition is a strong predictor of role prioritization in specific areas. Catholics give a higher priority to the sacraments and to spiritual direction. Catholics also give higher priority to being a leader in the local community. Evangelicals give higher priority to the roles of evangelist and teacher. On the other hand, church orientation is irrelevant to the priority ascribed to administration, leadership in public worship, preaching, visiting and to the role of pastor and counsellor.
> (Robbins and Francis, 2000, pp.18-19)

Results from this study

Because of the longitudinal nature of this study covering the first seven years in ordained stipendiary ministry of the respondents it has been possible to take snapshots of their role priorities at five different points: the beginning of ordination training; the beginning of ordained ministry; the beginning of the second year in ministry; the beginning of the third year in ministry; and the beginning of the seventh year in ministry.

The beginning of ordination training

On the Catholic/Evangelical dimension the Catholic clergy gave the highest priority to minister of sacraments and person of prayer. The Central clergy gave the highest priority to person of prayer and pastor. The Evangelical clergy gave highest priority to preacher and person of prayer. All three groups saw being a person of prayer as a high priority for them. This role has often been conspicuously lacking from previous role inventories but has always been an important part of a minister's self-understanding of her or his position.

As in Ranson, Bryman and Hinings' (1977) study and Robbins and Francis' (2000) study the role of minister of sacraments is significantly more important for Catholic curates, being their highest priority, than for Central curates (4th highest) or for Evangelical curates (13th highest).

Compared with the other groups, Catholic clergy gave a higher priority to the roles of minister of sacraments, leader of public worship, visitor, theologian, spiritual director and administrator: the focus of their ministry is corporate and individual spirituality. Compared with the other groups, Central clergy gave a higher priority to the roles of person of prayer, pastor, counsellor, prophet, apostle, leader of the local community and social worker: the focus of their ministry is compassionate care. Compared with the other groups, Evangelical clergy gave a higher priority to the roles of preacher, teacher, fellowship-builder, evangelist, pioneer and manager: the focus of their ministry is church growth through sound doctrine.

On the Liberal/Conservative dimension the Liberal clergy gave the highest priority to person of prayer and pastor. The Middle-of-the-road clergy gave the highest priority to person of prayer and leader of public worship. The Conservative clergy gave the highest priority to preacher and person of prayer. Compared with the other groups, Liberal clergy gave a higher priority to the roles of prayer, pastor, minister of sacraments, theologian, spiritual director, counsellor, manager and leader in the local community. For this group Carr's words seem appropriate: 'my aim therefore is to help working pastors to integrate their pastoral experience and practice with their professed systematic theology and their religious activity in worship, prayer and spirituality' (Carr, 1989, p.14). Compared with the other groups, Middle-of-the-road clergy gave a higher priority to the roles of leader of public worship, visitor, prophet and apostle. For Child (1970) these were key attributes of the Anglican parish priest. In the same way this group appear to share some similarities with the 'traditional parish clergy' grouping that Rutledge (1993, pp.203f) found when he used principal components analysis with his data on clergy. Compared with the other groups, Conservative clergy gave a higher priority to the roles of preacher, teacher, fellowship-builder, evangelist and administrator.

All the churchmanship groups on the Charismatic dimension regarded prayer as the highest priority in ministry for themselves as they began their ordination training. For the Pro-charismatic clergy preacher came second: for the Non-charismatic pastor came second; and for the Anti-charismatic minister of sacraments came second. Compared with the other groups, Pro-charismatic clergy gave a greater priority to the roles of person of prayer, preacher, pastor, fellowship-builder, evangelist, counsellor and pioneer. Compared with the other groups, Non-charismatic clergy gave a greater priority to the role of teacher. Compared to the other groups, Anti-charismatic clergy gave a greater priority to the roles of minister of sacraments, leader of public worship, visitor, spiritual director and apostle.

The beginning of parish ministry

In assessing their different views on the priorities they have in ministry between beginning training and beginning in the parish, Catholic clergy showed only small changes. Prayer was still the first priority with the sacraments still as second only to prayer. There were some changes which are noteworthy. The roles of leader of public worship, visitor and preacher have become more important as the role of pastor has been given a lower priority. These may be the more visible roles in which the training parish and training incumbent expect to see the new curate engaged. Compared to the other groups, Catholics gave a significantly higher priority to the roles of minister of sacraments, visitor, spiritual director and apostle.

Though their highest priority – person of prayer – has not changed the role of preacher was now second highest for the Central clergy. Visiting has become more important, whereas the two roles of counsellor and spiritual director have moved down the list of priorities.

For the Evangelical clergy the roles of person of prayer and preacher remain the highest. Leader of public worship has the third highest priority as the curate begins to spend a large amount of time preparing for leading and participating in worship in the parish. However the role to which they give a significantly more important place than the other groups is that of manager.

When we look at the changes in priorities for the clergy on the Liberal/Conservative dimension we find similar small but significant differences. For both Liberal and Middle-of-the-road clergy the two most important roles are person of prayer and leader of public worship. For the Conservative clergy the role of preacher was still most important.

The role of pastor for Liberal clergy has declined as leading worship and preaching sermons have risen. Three other noticeable rises in priority are for the roles of visitor (which has a significantly high priority for this group), fellowship-builder and administrator. The new importance being given to these roles may well be brought about by the interaction between the curate's priorities and those of the parish and incumbent. Compared to the other groups, Liberals gave a significantly high priority to the role of spiritual director.

For the Middle-of-the-road clergy there were no major changes from their order of priorities at the beginning of training. However they are the group who gave a significantly high priority to the role of minister of sacraments.

The only significant change for the Conservative curates is the rise in importance in their minds for the role of administrator.

When we look at the difference that the Charismatic dimension makes to role prioritization at the beginning of public ministry, there is only one significant change from the priorities at the start of training. The Anti-charismatic clergy give a significantly higher priority to the role of minister of sacraments.

The second year of parish ministry

The second year in ministry is the time when 96 per cent of the curates have added ordination to the priesthood to their ordination to the diaconate. Though as deacons they were able to conduct the sacrament of baptism, now they are able to preside at Holy Communion and so the role of minister of sacraments takes on a greater importance.

For the Catholic clergy, perhaps not unsurprisingly, the sacramental role now takes first place at a significantly higher level than the other groups with leader of public worship second, displacing person of prayer. The visitor role drops in importance as the roles of preacher, pastor and teacher rise. The other noticeable change is the continuing drop for the Catholic clergy in the position of the role of spiritual director.

For the Central clergy the role of minister of sacraments drops in importance as the role of pastor rises, and the two most important roles are now leader of public worship and preacher. In three areas the Central clergy record significantly higher levels of priority; those of counsellor, apostle and spiritual director.

The importance of the sacramental role does increase slightly for the Evangelical clergy but there are seven other roles that have a higher priority. Two notable changes during this year are the decline of the visitor role, and the rise of the role of prophet.

On the Liberal/Conservative dimension there were very few significant changes between the first year and the second year. The person of prayer role dropped for the Liberal clergy as the worship-based roles (minister of sacraments and leader of public worship) rose to the two highest priorities. For the Middle-of-the-road clergy there were no significant changes. The Conservative clergy were the most consistent with no change at all in the top seven priorities in ministerial roles. They continue to give a significantly high priority to the role of evangelist.

On the Charismatic dimension too there were some changes between the first year and the second. Among the Pro-charismatic clergy the highest priorities are preacher and leader of worship. Pro-charismatics gave significantly greater priority to the roles of fellowship-builder, evangelist and manager.

The most notable change for the Non-charismatics is that they now see the role of preacher as the most important priority in ministry with leader of worship close behind. For the Anti-charismatic clergy leading public worship replaces the prayer role as the most important priority. They gave a significantly higher priority than the other groups to the role of minister of sacraments.

The third year of parish ministry

The curates' time in their curacy is drawing to an end in their third year. They are all beginning to look towards new jobs often at incumbent or team vicar level. After the training experience of a curate's post their priorities for their own ministry may well be the ones they carry forward into a ministry in which they have responsibility for their own emphases and allocation of time and energy. A proportion of the group, 16 per cent, are already working in a different parish, either because they have already moved on to a second post, or because of problems working with their original training incumbent. In addition to that group, a further 20 per cent will no longer be working with their original training incumbent, usually because of his move, retirement or death. That means that only 64 per cent of the curates in their third year of ministry are still serving with the vicar who chose them as colleagues.

The pattern of priorities that has been developing for each churchmanship group seems to be becoming settled. The Catholic clergy in their third year have the first seven roles in the same order of priority as in the second year (minister of sacraments, leader of public worship, person of prayer, preacher, pastor, teacher and visitor). Leading public worship remains the highest priority for the Central clergy, and the pastoral role is regaining prominence: it is now the second highest priority. In two roles, counsellor and leader in the local community, the Central clergy show a significantly greater priority over the other two groups on this dimension. For the Evangelical clergy the role of preacher continues to have pre-eminence with leader of public worship in second place. They give a significantly higher priority to the role of fellowship-builder.

At the end of these three years of on the job training it is worth noting that, when compared with the other churchmanship groups, a greater proportion of Catholic clergy gave a high priority to the roles of minister of sacraments, person of prayer, visitor, apostle, prophet, spiritual director and social worker: the focus of their ministry is a challenging personal and sacramental spirituality. Compared with the other groups, a greater proportion of Central clergy gave a high priority to the roles of leader of public worship, pastor, counsellor, leader in the local community, administrator and fund-raiser: the focus of their ministry is celebration, care and organization. Compared with the other groups, a greater proportion of Evangelical clergy gave a high priority to the roles of preacher, teacher, fellowship-builder, evangelist, theologian and manager: the focus of their ministry is proclaiming, building up and planning.

As with the Catholic/Evangelical dimension, so with the Liberal/Conservative dimension we find that the clergy groups have only made small changes in their role prioritization between the second and the third year. It is the Liberal clergy who give a significantly higher priority than the others to the roles of minister of sacraments, prophet, counsellor and spiritual director. The comments made in Chapter 4 about the affinity between Liberals and mystics seem to be borne out by this set of role preferences. Compared with the other groups, a greater proportion of Liberal clergy gave a high priority to the roles of minister of sacraments, pastor, prophet, counsellor, apostle, pioneer, spiritual director and manager: the focus of their ministry is celebration, personal care and challenge. Compared with the other groups, a greater proportion of Middle-of-the-road clergy gave a high priority to the roles of leader of public worship, person of prayer, visitor and leader in the local community: the focus of their ministry comes closest to a traditional Anglican model. Compared with the other groups, a greater proportion of Conservative clergy gave a high priority to the roles of preacher, teacher, fellowship-builder, evangelist and administrator: the focus of their ministry is building and growing a church congregation.

Compared to the other dimensions, the Charismatic shows a larger number of role priority changes amongst the clergy between the second and third year. For the Pro-charismatics the preacher role has dropped as the person of prayer and leader of public worship roles have risen to the top priority. This is the only one of the nine churchmanship groups for whom prayer is the most important of the priorities in this third year of ministry. In two areas the Pro-charismatics continue to give a significantly higher rating; fellowship-builder and evangelist. For the Non-charismatics worship-leading has moved to first position. The most obvious movement though is the decline in the importance of the counsellor role: in the second year 32 per cent of Non-charismatics gave it a high priority, in the third year only 11 per cent do. There are no significant changes for the Anti-charismatics for whom sacramental ministry and leading worship are the most important roles.

Compared with the other groups, a greater proportion of Pro-charismatic clergy gave a high priority to the roles of person of prayer, leader of public worship, fellowship-builder, evangelist and administrator: the focus of their ministry is prayerfully drawing people in to an effective congregation. Compared with the other groups, a greater proportion of Non-charismatic clergy gave a high priority to the roles of counsellor and manager: the focus of their ministry is professional standards. Compared with the other groups, a greater proportion of Anti-charismatic clergy gave a high priority to the roles of minister of sacraments, preacher, pastor, teacher, visitor, theologian, apostle, prophet, spiritual director, pioneer and leader in the local community: the focus of their ministry is an open-minded, educated and worshipful congregation. It is an interesting sidelight on the role inventory used in this study that a greater proportion of Anti-charismatic curates give priority to the New Testament list of so-called charismatic ministries, apostle, prophet, pastor and teacher.

Observations on role priorities in the first three years of ministry

The lowest priorities for nearly all of the nine major churchmanship groups are the roles of fund-raiser, social worker and leader in the local community. Let us look at each of these three roles in turn, and then consider the comparatively low priority given to the role of visitor.

It may well be that the reason that fund-raiser is nearly always at the bottom of the list of role priorities for clergy is because today's generation of clergy believe that fund-raising and associated stewardship skills are priorities for laypeople rather than clerical members of the church. Certainly Davies, Watkins, Winter, Seymour and Short (1991, pp.75-76) found a similar low priority for fund-raising. In practice, many serving Anglican clergy talk about the growing demand upon their time of arranging or encouraging fund-raising events. Fletcher (1990, p.26) indeed sees 'pressure put upon you by the diocesan authorities to make sure the quota is paid' as one of the role ambiguities leading to clergy stress.

Much of the debate in the 1960s recorded in Chapter 1 was concerned with growing secularization in the nation as a challenge to the Anglican Church. There was a debate about the professionalization of the clergy consequent upon an increasingly differentiated and specialized 'secular' society (Dunstan, 1970, Golner, Terence and Ritti, 1973, Hinings and Foster, 1973, Jarvis, 1975, 1976). There were some who suggested that instead of being 'guardians of the sacred' (Martin, 1978) clergy would become social workers. That view seems to be decisively rejected by the role priorities that these clergy have revealed. However, in addition to rejecting the social worker role, they also are rejecting the role of leader in the local community which has been seen as an essential part of the established nature of the Church of England and its clergy. Admittedly Newby (1988) cautions against a 'rhetoric of community' which is in danger of nostalgic sanctifying of village life. Yet there has been a continuing debate in recent years about congregation-focused and parish-focused ministry which has sometimes centred round the sociologist's language of 'church' and 'sect' (Wilson, 1966, Martin, 1967). Russell concluded that 'the rural church in many areas has come to assume the character of a eucharistic sect as opposed to that of a community church' (Russell, 1986, p.248). Certainly concern has been expressed that the Church of England is moving to an associational rather than communal model for its ministry (Ecclestone, 1988). Davies, Watkins, Winter, Seymour and Short come to a different conclusion:

> 'Is the Church of England sectarian?' That was the question posed at the beginning of this chapter at least as far as more rural areas were concerned. Having now explored a variety of avenues and popular opinions the answer would not appear to be a resounding 'Yes'. In terms of the predominant clergy outlook the answer is a clear 'No'.
> (Davies et al., 1991, p.128)

If this is an accurate estimation of the attitude of clergy in general in the Church of England then it is important to remember the nature of the group being studied in this research. As curates in their first three years in ordained Anglican ministry these respondents have had less opportunity because of their transitional ministry than an incumbent to establish themselves as a leader in the local community.

The changing fortunes of the role of visitor during this longitudinal study are worthy of comment. All nine churchmanship groups follow the same pattern in their assessment of the priority they wish to give to this role: at the beginning of ministry a greater proportion give a high priority to visiting than did so at the beginning of training; this proportion declines in the second year and by the third year it is the smallest proportion of all the four times of measuring role prioritization. To give an example, 32 per cent of Central curates give it a high priority at the beginning of training, 54 per cent at the beginning of ministry, 49 per cent in the second year, and 24 per cent in the third year. Robbins and Francis (2000) found a decreasing emphasis on the role of visitor among women clergy between their first and their current appointment yet the Rural Church Project found that visiting made up the largest component of their respondents' pastoral work (Davies, Watkins, Winter, Seymour, and Short, 1990). Burgess (2000) suggests that Davies' clergy respond as they do because they are rural clergy. In an earlier study Burgess found that 'visiting occupied an average of 6 out of 58 hours weekly (10 per cent), but that 1.5 hours on average were in connection with rites of passage, mainly funerals; 3 hours for other kinds of visits with a specific purpose; and only 1.5 hours on general home visiting' (Burgess, 1998, p.165). Francis suggested that for Evangelical pastors 'the biggest discrepancies between what the pastors want for themselves and what the pastors perceive their congregations as wanting for them concern the roles of administrator and visitor' (Francis, 2000, p.25).

Conclusion

This research has considered the role prioritization shown by the clergy when they considered their own ministry. It is important to note, especially in the light of the last paragraph, two pieces of research by others about lay expectations of clergy role prioritization. Herbert (1988) in his study of stipendiary clergy refers to a Chester diocesan questionnaire for church members:

> One question asks, 'Which of the following do you believe should be priorities for the clergy in their ministry?' Of the ten answers provided, the two most clearly perceived priorities are the care of the lonely, sick and aged, and to pray.
> (Herbert, 1988, p.167)

Francis and Lankshear researched the attitudes of both Catholic and Evangelical lay people to the priorities of their clergy:

> There is also a clear consensus between evangelicals and catholics regarding the role of the clergy in today's church. The top priority ascribed to the clergy is neither as spiritual director, religious educator nor community leader, but as social carer. First and foremost churchgoers wish to see their clergy as exercising care over the aged, the lonely and the sick. The clergy are expected to combine the skills of social worker, health visitor and friendly neighbour.
> (Francis and Lankshear, 1992d, p.19)

It is of real concern and potential conflict that there should appear to be such discontinuity between clergy priorities and congregational priorities for clergy.

In the previous chapters we have seen that in general different forms of churchmanship do not attract different personality types, nor necessarily lead to greater or less happiness, greater proneness to burnout, or greater adoption of particularly masculine or feminine sex roles. This chapter has shown one area, that of role prioritization, where churchmanship does make a difference. When we look at clergy at different times in their ministry churchmanship makes a significant difference to their priorities in ministry.

Chapter 12

What training and support?

Introduction

The three dimensional churchmanship measure has revealed noticeable differences between the clergy as they assess their priorities in ministry. Changes in those priorities occurred both during ordination training and during the early years in ministry as they were under the supervision of a training incumbent. It is appropriate to look at those two areas of initial ministerial training and post-ordination ministry to see whether churchmanship makes a difference here too.

In a study of New Zealand Protestant ministers of religion, Dewe (1987) investigated sources of work stress and coping behaviours: the most important coping strategy Dewe discovered was systems of social support. In Oswald's study of those beginning ordained ministry in the USA he drew attention to the necessity for clergy to build such a support network for themselves (Oswald, 1980, p.20). For Anglican curates beginning their ordained ministry the natural source of primary support is their training incumbent. Burgess' (1998) small-scale qualitative study of curates revealed that such support was not always forthcoming:

> The curates were first asked how the relationship with their incumbents developed, and to indicate its good and bad features. To set this in perspective, the twenty interviews indicated that six curates believed their curacies were, or had been, good; four more felt they had been reasonably good, but with significant difficulties or shortcomings; and ten believed their curacies had been essentially unsatisfactory.
> (Burgess, 1998, p.74)

Dioceses would expect to provide support for curates through diocesan staff, bishops, archdeacons, Post Ordination Training (POT) officers and Rural or Area Deans. However Burgess' interviews suggested that such support is either patchy or too close to the management structure to be genuinely pastoral.

> 'Oh no ... I don't think I really could talk with my local archdeacon or my local bishop; I think the archdeacon was appointed ... because he was very good at chairing committees [and] it's very clear that that's his element. I don't really feel I could have sufficient confidence in my local bishop to feel free to talk with him. Amongst my colleagues, some like the bishop more than I do, but I don't think that gets translated into ... going and having a deep and meaningful conversation with him.'
> (verbatim statement from a curate, in Burgess, 1998, p.98)

The parish in which the curate works would seem to be a natural place from which to receive support. However there has been a wariness amongst clergy of building close friendships in the parish. As recently as 1986 Hodge could say, 'It is better not to have close friendships within the parish; it leads to jealousy. This can leave one's wife feeling rather isolated; but I'm afraid it is a price which must be accepted' (Hodge, 1986, p.201). It seems that Anglican curates have realized that they must provide their own support systems.

> 'You have to go and look for [help] ... as long as you appear to be coping, no one ever looks to see whether you are; as long as you give the appearance [of coping] that's fine ... [unless you have the confidence to ask] you could sink without trace – well, they'd probably notice the bubbles!'
> (verbatim statement from a curate, in Burgess, 1998, p.99)

In order to measure empirically clergy perceptions of the level of support they were receiving from a variety of different sources, Francis, Lankshear and Jones (1992) developed an inventory for the Church in Wales Clergy Survey. Respondents were asked 'how supportive did you find the following during your first curacy?' Responses were made on a seven-item numerical scale anchored by 1 'very little' to 7 'very much'. The 12 sources of support were: your training incumbent, rural dean, other local clergy, archdeacon, bishop, POT (post-ordination training) officer, congregation, churchwardens, PCC, community at large, family, personal friends. The same measure was used by Robbins (1996) in the *Women in Ministry Clergy Survey*.

Because the issue of support systems for clergy is so important, and because the previous empirical use of this measure provided an opportunity to compare results with other groups of clergy, it was decided to use the Francis/Lankshear/Jones measure alongside the churchmanship measure. It will reveal the differences that churchmanship makes to the curates' perceptions of their training institutions, both theological colleges and courses, and to the training and support they have received in their training parishes.

Churchmanship and theological training

It has long been recognized that certain theological colleges attract ordinands from particular churchmanship groups. Chapter 1 explains how many of the colleges were established in order to safeguard particular churchmanship positions. The three-dimensional measure provides an opportunity to discover the empirical truth about that and to compare the results in this study with earlier less selective measures of churchmanship. The Runcie (1970) classification for example continues to be used by the General Synod of the Church of England to assess the balance of churchmanship amongst those training for ordination in the Church of England at theological colleges which it labels as Evangelical, Tractarian, and Other. (Given its 1970 provenance the Runcie Report did not include theological courses as an option in theological training.)

In 1970 the classification showed that 34 per cent of ordinands were at Evangelical colleges, 27 per cent at Tractarian, and 40 per cent at Other colleges. Hodge (1988, p.11) used the same measure to report the 1985 figures as 49 per cent Evangelical, 25 per cent Tractarian, and 26 per cent Other, showing over those fifteen years a gradual rise in the number at Evangelical colleges, a stable number at Catholic colleges, and a steady decline in the Other category.

Using the same measure for 1994 (excluding the Welsh college at Llandaff and the non-residential courses) the comparable figures generated by this study are 56 per cent Evangelical, 22 per cent Tractarian and 22 per cent Other. The proportions show that over the twenty four years since Runcie the Tractarian colleges have continued to lose ground as the Evangelical colleges have moved into a majority position but that it is the Other colleges, the central colleges, which have seen the most obvious decline in ordinands. This measure of churchmanship shows that it is the centre ground of churchmanship that has continued to weaken since Hodge's (1988) report.

However, the weakness of the labelling approach to measuring churchmanship has been seen as its severe limitation in acknowledging the breadth and sophistication of most people's understanding of their own churchmanship position. By also using a measure that focuses solely on the Catholic/Evangelical dimension other elements of churchmanship are ignored. What is the composition of the churchmanship of the newly-ordained at each particular type of theological establishment? To give a full report on churchmanship and theological training in 1994 means including the Courses and the Welsh college as well.

Of those attending Evangelical colleges six per cent consider themselves as Catholic, eight per cent as Central and 86 per cent as Evangelical; 10 per cent as Liberal, 11 per cent as Middle-of-the-road and 79 per cent as Conservative; 79 per cent as Pro-charismatic, 17 per cent as Non-charismatic and four per cent as Anti-charismatic.

Of those attending Tractarian colleges 73 per cent consider themselves as Catholic, 22 per cent as Central and five per cent as Evangelical; 43 per cent as Liberal, 30 per cent as Middle-of-the-road and 27 per cent as Conservative; 20 per cent as Pro-charismatic, 23 per cent as Non-charismatic and 57 per cent as Anti-charismatic.

Of those attending Other colleges 55 per cent consider themselves as Catholic, 21 per cent as Central and 24 per cent as Evangelical; 63 per cent as Liberal, 11 per cent as Middle-of-the-road and 26 per cent as Conservative; 42 per cent as Pro-charismatic, 31 per cent as Non-charismatic and 27 per cent as Anti-charismatic.

Of those attending non-residential theological Courses 55 per cent consider themselves as Catholic, 15 per cent as Central and 30 per cent as Evangelical; 52 per cent as Liberal, 21 per cent as Middle-of-the-road and 27 per cent as Conservative; 53 per cent as Pro-charismatic, 26 per cent as Non-charismatic and 21 per cent as Anti-charismatic.

Because the numbers leaving Llandaff each year are comparatively small the following figures do not have the same reliability as the English figures. Of those attending the Welsh theological college 44 per cent consider themselves as

Catholic, 44 per cent as Central and 11 per cent as Evangelical; 55 per cent as Liberal, 22 per cent as Middle-of-the-road and 22 per cent as Conservative; 55 per cent as Pro-charismatic, 22 per cent as Non-charismatic and 22 per cent as Anti-charismatic.

Hodge reported that the rise in numbers of Evangelicals in training that he documented was leading to a difficulty for Evangelicals in finding parishes in which to serve their curacy: 'A larger proportion (59.4 per cent) of men trained at Evangelical colleges were ordained in dioceses other than their sponsoring diocese than was the case among those trained at Catholic (36.0 per cent) and Central (33.9 per cent) colleges' (Hodge, 1988, p.16). The situation was the same in this study analysing the responses of those who left colleges and courses for ordination in 1994: 53 per cent of Evangelicals were ordained in a different diocese to their sponsoring diocese, as against 37 per cent of Tractarians, and 42 per cent of those from Other colleges. Llandaff and the Courses for their different reasons expected to return their ordinands to their sponsoring dioceses and their figures for ordinands ordained in their sponsoring dioceses were 87 per cent for Llandaff and 79 per cent for the Courses. It is in the light of these results that we can reflect on earlier results showing significantly high correlations between the churchmanship of the curates and the perceived churchmanship of their training parishes and training incumbents.

Churchmanship and support in the parish

After their pre-ordination theological training the respondents in this study moved as all newly-ordained stipendiary Anglican clergy do into a training parish to continue their training in a setting which the Church of England calls 'ministry under supervision'. Crossing the threshold into a new job, a new role and a new home can be very intimidating: the experience of liminality is a valuable but sometimes traumatic one. 'Of all their career transitions this was the most traumatic and the most crucial' (Oswald, 1980, p.1). In such circumstances support is vital. Where do the newly-ordained find their support structures? From the past, from family and friends who have known them for some time? Or from the new situation and set of relationships in which they are finding themselves? From ordinary Christians or from other clergy within the diocesan structures? It is our intention to see whether or not the answers to these questions are influenced by the churchmanship of the curates.

In Table 12.1 the three groups on the Catholic/Evangelical dimension of churchmanship are shown and, underneath, the rank order of those giving the clergy a high level of support in year 1. Alongside each supporter is given the percentage of clergy in years 1, 2 and 3 who feel they have been given a high level of support from that source. So in year 1 the Evangelical clergy received most support from friends: 73 per cent felt they received a high level of support from friends. In year 2 65 per cent felt this, and 71 per cent in year 3.

Table 12.1 Levels of support in years 1, 2 and 3 according to Catholic / Evangelical churchmanship, by percentage

Catholic support group	years 1 2 3	Central support group	years 1 2 3	Evangelical support group	years 1 2 3
friends	75,73,67	family	81,73,81	friends	73,65,71
family	75,71,63	friends	75,72,81	family	71,68,75
vicar	71,36,31	vicar	68,48,62	vicar	71,52,42
wardens	62,45,50	congregation	59,48,52	congregation	67,57,61
congregation	62,59,57	wardens	51,54,43	wardens	59,48,41
PCC	48,26,25	PCC	39,36,34	PCC	34,28,28
community	30,36,29	community	34,45,43	other clergy	21,14, 9
other clergy	23,13,17	POT officer	34,21,29	rural dean	21,16,13
rural dean	22,15,15	other clergy	29,15,19	bishop	18,14,20
bishop	20,24,29	bishop	27,24,19	POT officer	17,16,22
POT officer	16,22,22	rural dean	24,27,15	community	17,14,22
archdeacon	15, 9,18	archdeacon	17,15,15	archdeacon	10, 7,10

As Table 12.1 shows, for each of these groups in each of the three years the greatest support came from family and friends. The importance of friends is echoed by the results of Robbins (1996) in her study of women in ministry. In the first year for all three groups the next four places are taken by the new Christian community the curate is joining, represented by vicar, wardens, PCC and congregation. There are differences though. The Central clergy give a significantly higher place to the POT officer than the other groups. The Evangelicals though receive significantly less support from the local community than the other two groups perhaps because of their more associational model of the church: for them the only place where they get less support is the archdeacon. In the second year, because there are a growing number of Catholics and Central clergy who are receiving less support from their incumbent, the vicar's positive support for his (remember that all of these training incumbents were male) Evangelical curate is significantly high. In the third year compared to the other groups the Catholics receive a significantly high level of support from their bishops, and a significantly low level of support from their training incumbents. With only 31 per cent of the Catholic curates receiving a high level of support from their vicars of all the nine churchmanship groups they are the least well supported by their incumbent.

In the first year, as Table 12.2 shows, the Liberal and Middle-of-the-road curates follow the pattern we have noted in Table 12.1 of receiving most support from friends and family: the Middle-of-the-road curates in particular receiving a great deal of support from their friends. The Conservatives though receive as much support from their training incumbent as from their friends. The Conservative clergy receive significantly less support from the local community than the other two groups. Like the Evangelicals with whom their results are often linked they too may be working with less of a 'parish church' model for ministry. The other significant finding for these groups is the higher level of support that the Middle-of-the-road clergy receive from their Rural Dean.

Table 12.2 Levels of support in years 1, 2 and 3 according to Liberal / Conservative churchmanship, by percentage

Liberal support group	years 1 2 3	Middle support group	years 1 2 3	Conservative support group	years 1 2 3
family	74,68,63	friends	83,61,66	family	73,74,78
friends	73,69,69	family	73,68,69	vicar	72,49,39
vicar	64,41,35	vicar	73,47,49	friends	72,70,72
congregation	58,54,56	congregation	68,56,60	congregation	66,60,60
wardens	53,44,46	wardens	61,58,60	wardens	61,49,39
PCC	40,27,27	PCC	46,34,32	PCC	36,27,27
community	27,32,31	other clergy	35, 5,14	other clergy	20,15,13
rural dean	24,19,16	community	31,34,32	bishop	20,22,22
bishop	19,16,28	rural dean	31,16,15	community	19,20,23
other clergy	17,16,14	POT officer	25,18,29	POT officer	18,20,18
POT officer	15,18,27	bishop	21,16,22	rural dean	17,15,13
archdeacon	13, 8,15	archdeacon	13, 3,20	archdeacon	11,12,11

In the second year the general pattern we have seen with the Catholic/Evangelical groups reasserts itself, with family and friends providing most support, the local church and community next and diocesan officers least. The poor archdeacon is not seen by any of the churchmanship groups as giving much in the way of support, but the three per cent figure expressed by the Middle-of-the-road group is the lowest of all the groups in any of the three years. By the third year the Conservatives have begun to be more aware of support from the local community but it is still significantly less than the other groups. The Middle-of-the-road clergy have a significantly high level of support from their churchwardens. All three groups show a noticeable decline in perceived support from the training incumbent.

As has been seen in other chapters, it is the Charismatic dimension which often discriminates least between groups, and that is true in terms of levels of positive support as well. Table 12.3 shows the Non-charismatics standing out from all the other churchmanship groups by giving a significant pride of place to their training incumbent though as with other groups this support declines over the three year period. They were also the group who found most support from their PCC in the first year.

Table 12.3 Levels of support in years 1, 2 and 3 according to Charismatic churchmanship, by percentage

Pro-charismatic support group	years 1 2 3	Non-charismatic support group	years 1 2 3	Anti-charismatic support group	years 1 2 3
family	74,68,76	vicar	83,46,39	friends	82,76,68
friends	72,60,72	friends	77,79,67	family	75,69,60
vicar	68,46,42	family	72,79,69	wardens	62,45,50
congregation	64,55,56	congregation	67,59,55	vicar	62,43,33
wardens	59,52,45	wardens	55,44,36	congregation	60,58,68
PCC	37,30,29	PCC	47,25,23	PCC	38,27,28
other clergy	21,15,13	community	32,31,17	community	30,37,35
community	20,21,27	rural dean	31,18, 9	other clergy	23,11,16
rural dean	20,17,16	POT officer	27,17,23	POT officer	17,21,19
bishop	20,19,23	other clergy	26,14,11	bishop	17,24,31
POT officer	17,19,25	bishop	23,16,20	rural dean	16,16,13
archdeacon	13, 8,13	archdeacon	16, 6,11	archdeacon	9,13,17

By the second year the Non-charismatics' incumbents are giving only as much support as the other groups' incumbents. In the third year a real difference between the groups is revealed by how they value the support of their families. On the one hand, for the Anti-charismatics the congregation has taken the place of the family in providing a high level of positive support. In this respect they compare favourably with Robbins' clergywomen (1996, p.154). On the other hand the Pro-charismatics are receiving significantly high levels of support from their families. Archdeacons continue to be the diocesan officer who is perceived as being the least likely to provide a high level of support.

Summary

There are differences between churchmanship groups in their assessment of the support they receive. In particular there are significant differences concerned with the issue of the perception of the place of the local community in giving support. In general though all the clergy in this study find that personal relationships from the past – friends and family – are the most important element in their support systems. Other clergy and diocesan staff are seen by all groups as providing the least support for these curates beginning in ministry. The churchmanship measure that is at the heart of this study does operate in such a way as to allow discrimination between levels of support, but the pattern of support is largely the same for all clergy whatever their churchmanship.

Chapter 13

What patterns of belief and behaviour?

Introduction

In the last two chapters we have seen that role prioritization is strongly affected by churchmanship but that perceptions of levels of support are not. In this chapter we ask, 'What difference does churchmanship make to patterns of belief and ministerial practice?' Writing in 1853 Coneybeare said that most of the differences between forms of churchmanship 'are much exaggerated by party-spirit. Most of them can be resolved into mere disputes about terms, which might be ended by stricter definition' (Coneybeare, 1853, p.339). It is the contention of this study that the differences are much stronger and deeper than 'mere disputes about terms' but are revealed by significant differences in doctrine and order.

Comparisons between the groups on each dimension of churchmanship reveal large areas where there is no significant disagreement between the groups over matters of belief or practice. For example, only three per cent of all the clergy of any churchmanship are not happy to conduct infant baptism at all. This is despite the growth in support for MORIB (the Movement for the Reform of Infant Baptism) during the period of the 1980s and 1990s (Owen, 1990). Again if we look at an issue where there is not such clear agreement, 54 per cent of the clergy said that they had experienced spiritual problems during the year. That percentage shows no significant variation across churchmanship groups. Again if we look at an issue which might be expected to divide Liberals from Conservatives, 56 per cent of the whole group of curates would be unhappy to conduct a marriage service in church for a same-sex couple, 14 per cent would not be unhappy and 30 per cent were unsure: those percentages were substantially the same across all nine churchmanship groups. However the presence of many similarities like these does not hide the fact that there are numerous significant differences between the groups both in matters of belief and of behaviour.

Tables are used to report both the differences between the churchmanship groups. In Tables 13.1, 13.2, 13.4, 13.5, 13.7 and 13.8 the numerical figure in the churchmanship column is the percentage of respondents from that churchmanship group who agree or agree strongly with the statement. Tables 13.3, 13.6 and 13.9 report the results of an inventory which comprises statements of routine behaviour. Since respondents were asked how often they did each of the items using a five point scale, 'always', 'nearly always', 'often', 'seldom' and 'never', in these tables of results the numerical figure in the churchmanship column is the percentage of respondents from that churchmanship group who always or nearly always do the action in the statement. In order to measure statistical significance each statement was dichotomized into either 'agree or agree strongly' and 'disagree or disagree strongly' for Tables 13.1, 13.2, 13.4, 13.5, 13.7 and 13.8, or 'always or nearly always' and 'seldom or never' for Tables 13.3, 13.6 and 13.9. Then a 2x3 contingency table was constructed with results from each of the three churchmanship groups on a particular dimension. The non-parametric chi-square test is then used to measure significant results with, in every case, two degrees of freedom (Walker, 1940). Only statistically significant results are reported.

Differences between Catholic, Central and Evangelical clergy

What is essential belief for a Christian today? The clergy were asked two questions about this. Was a belief in the Virgin Birth essential, and was a belief in the physical resurrection of Jesus essential? Thirty seven per cent of all the clergy agreed that a belief in the Virgin Birth was essential, but only 21 per cent of the Catholics agreed. A significantly high number of Evangelicals, 55 per cent, thought it essential. Amongst the clergy in general 65 per cent agreed that a belief in the physical resurrection of Jesus was essential, but a significantly high number of Evangelicals, 75 per cent, thought it essential.

Table 13.1 Differences in belief and practice (Catholic/Evangelical)

	Ca %	Ce %	Ev %
Happy to conduct baptisms for children from non-church families	79	81	45
Happy to conduct baptisms outside a main service	58	57	20
Prefer to offer a Thanksgiving for the birth of a child	6	19	54
A belief in the Virgin Birth is essential for a Christian	21	29	55
A belief in the physical resurrection of Jesus is essential ...	56	72	75
Happy to present Confirmation candidates under the age of 11	46	24	24
I am not happy with Confirmation at all	5	5	19
Holy Communion should be open to all who love the Lord Jesus	34	47	73
I believe that I should visit any parishioner who is in hospital	55	33	36
I am in favour of the ordination of women to the episcopate	65	86	50
It is important for clergy to say the Daily Office every day	71	48	24
I am unhappy with using female imagery for God	25	5	40

The Evangelicals were significantly unhappy with using female imagery for God whereas a majority of the clergy in general were happy with such imagery (Table 13.1). There was no difference though on the question of inclusive language where 90 per cent of the clergy were happy to use non-gender specific language of human beings in worship.

Perhaps surprisingly given the ferment in 1994 over the ordination of women to the priesthood there was no significant difference between the groups over the question of the ordination of women as priests. When the question of the ordination of women to the episcopate was raised it was the Central clergy who were significantly highly in favour, and the Evangelicals who had the most reservations.

Table 13.2 Differences in training and conviction (Catholic/Evangelical)

	Ca %	Ce %	Ev %
My vicar encourages my attendance at POT	71	84	78
I have thought about leaving the ministry this year	31	27	23
I feel I have to prove myself to my vicar	43	48	28
Training from my vicar and POT go hand in hand	6	36	22
I work harder than my vicar	15	12	7
My vicar is helping me to grow as a person	33	36	54
I intend to do further academic study	70	51	45
I see stipendiary ministry as a life long career	57	63	74
I enjoy going away on conferences	48	67	77
I have helped people become Christians this year	34	42	61
Seeing my spiritual director is a priority for me	73	74	34
A daily Eucharist is important for me	53	15	2

Table 13.3 Differences in patterns of behaviour (Catholic/Evangelical)

	Ca %	Ce %	Ev %
I have a weekly staff meeting with my vicar	65	75	77
I say the Daily Office together with my vicar	78	66	40
I make an annual retreat	50	45	27
I attend a daily Eucharist	38	9	3
I wear a clerical collar on duty	93	94	56
I wear robes/vestments for church services	97	91	64

It may come as no surprise to find the greatest number of differences between the groups on the Catholic/Evangelical dimension were over questions of liturgy and worship. The Central clergy are significantly more happy to conduct baptisms for children from non-church families and the Evangelicals least happy. A majority of the clergy are happy to conduct baptisms outside a 'main' service, with the Catholics significantly happy with such an arrangement and Evangelicals least happy with this practice. Evangelicals are significantly happier to offer a

Thanksgiving for the Birth of a Child to all families followed by baptism 'only to those who really mean it', whereas few of the other clergy would support this (Table 13.1).

When it comes to Confirmation a significant minority, 19 per cent, of the Evangelicals are not happy with Confirmation at all. The age at which candidates should be presented causes problems too: Catholics are significantly more happy to present candidates under the age of 11.

A significantly large number of Evangelicals believe that Holy Communion should be open to all who love the Lord Jesus. A daily Eucharist is attended by a significantly high number of Catholics, 38 per cent, but 53 per cent of Catholics say that a daily Eucharist is important for them. Twice as many of the clergy agree as disagree that it is important for every member of the clergy to say the Daily Office every day, but a significantly high number of Catholics believe this. In practice 59 per cent of the curates say the Office every day or nearly every day with their training incumbent, with a significantly high number of Catholics, 78 per cent, doing so (Table 13.3). Though a large majority of all clergy (81 per cent) always or nearly always wear robes or vestments for church services, it is no surprise that it is the Catholics who most do this: 13 per cent of the Evangelicals never or seldom do. However it is the Central clergy who are the ones who most wear a clerical collar when on duty always or nearly always. Table 13.3 shows that when it comes to personal discipline and spirituality, 39 per cent of the clergy always make an annual retreat: a significant 50 per cent of Catholics always or nearly always do.

For two thirds of the clergy seeing their spiritual director is a priority, but it is the Central clergy who record the highest percentage rating for this. Just under two thirds of the clergy enjoy going away on conferences, but it is the Evangelicals who are significantly keen on this (Table 13.2).

There are differences between the churchmanship groups too when it comes to pastoral practice in the parish. A quarter of the clergy do not believe that they should visit parishioners in hospital; this rises to 38 per cent of the Central clergy, but it is the Catholic group who significantly follow the practice of visiting parishioners in hospital. Just under half of all the clergy would say that they had helped people to become Christians in that year, but a significant 61 per cent of the Evangelicals would.

Randall (1997, pp.45-51) studied the diocesan handbooks concerned with the care and training of new ministers. These are issued to curates and their training incumbents and represent diocesan policy as well as good practice. Every handbook examined in that study expected there to be, at the least, a weekly staff meeting between curate and vicar plus another opportunity each month for a supervision meeting. In practice, as Table 13.3 shows, only 71 per cent of the clergy have a weekly staff meeting, reaching a significant low of 65 per cent among the Catholic clergy. This may be linked to the fact that a significant 15 per cent of the Catholic curates think that they work harder than their incumbent. Overall 42 per cent of the clergy felt that their vicar was helping them to grow as a person, but amongst the Evangelicals this figure rose to a significant 54 per cent. The Evangelicals too are least likely to feel that they have to prove themselves to their training incumbent, but the Central curates are significantly more likely to feel this.

The same diocesan handbooks make much of the training given by the diocese in POT and by the training incumbent in the parish working hand-in-hand (cf. Eastell, 1992). Only 17 per cent of all the clergy agreed with this: the Central curates were significantly more likely to agree with this and the Catholic curates least likely. Nevertheless three quarters of the training incumbents encouraged their curates to attend POT, with the incumbents of the Central curates taking a significant lead in this.

A significantly high number, 31 per cent, of the Catholic curates had thought about leaving the ministry that year, and it is the Catholic clergy who are least likely to see stipendiary ministry as lifelong.

Differences between Liberal, Middle-of-the-road and Conservative clergy

The ordination of women was an important issue in the year 1994, the first year when women training alongside men knew that they too would be ordained to the priesthood after a year as a deacon. Ten per cent of all the clergy are opposed to the ordination of women as priests, but the greatest support for their ordination comes from the Liberals. Fifteen per cent of all the clergy are opposed to the ordination of women as bishops, and again it is the Liberal clergy who are most in favour. Among all groups, however, there is a clear majority in favour of the ordination of women to both the priesthood and the episcopate.

Table 13.4 Differences in belief and practice (Liberal/Conservative)

	Li %	Mi %	Co %
Happy to conduct baptisms for children from non-church families	81	63	46
Happy to conduct baptisms outside a main service	56	48	21
Prefer to offer a Thanksgiving for the birth of a child	13	23	48
A belief in the Virgin Birth is essential for a Christian	11	54	58
A belief in the physical resurrection of Jesus is essential ...	48	83	76
Happy to present Confirmation candidates under the age of 11	39	52	21
Holy Communion should be open to all who love the Lord Jesus	45	46	64
I am happy to re-marry divorcees in church	55	26	20
I am in favour of the ordination of women to the priesthood	82	74	57
I am in favour of the ordination of women to the episcopate	80	66	40
It is important for clergy to say the Daily Office every day	59	72	26
I am happy to use inclusive language in worship and prayer	86	68	51
I am unhappy with using female imagery for God	17	32	42

On the two credal questions of whether belief in the virgin birth and the physical resurrection of Jesus are essential for a Christian, opinion is divided. A tiny majority of all the clergy do not believe that a belief in the virgin birth is essential: only a significantly low 11 per cent among the Liberal clergy believe that such a belief in the virgin birth is essential. Less than half of the Liberal clergy believe that a belief in the physical resurrection of Jesus is essential for a Christian.

A significant 42 per cent of Conservatives are unhappy using female imagery for God whereas a majority of the clergy in general are happy with such imagery. A majority of the clergy in all three groups are happy to use inclusive language in worship, but a significantly high number of Liberals are in favour of non-gender specific language.

Fifty two per cent of the curates believe that Holy Communion should be open to all who love the Lord Jesus, and this rises to a significant 64 per cent amongst Conservatives. The tables show that 40 per cent, a significantly high number, of Liberal clergy would say that a daily Eucharist is important for them, and a significant 28 per cent of them do in fact attend a daily Eucharist.

Just 29 per cent of the clergy prefer to offer a Thanksgiving for the birth of a child service to all families followed by baptism only for those who really mean it, but nearly half of the Conservatives wanted to do just that. It is the Liberal clergy who are most happy to conduct baptisms for children from non-church families. A small majority of clergy is happy to conduct baptisms outside a main public service, but only 21 per cent of Conservatives are happy to do this. Middle-of-the-road clergy are happier than others to present candidates for Confirmation under the age of 11.

A large number, 42 per cent, of the clergy are uncertain whether they would be happy to re-marry divorcees in church: 35 per cent would be happy to and 23 per cent would not be happy to. A significant majority of Liberals, however, are happy to conduct such a re-marriage.

Table 13.5 Differences in training and conviction (Liberal/Conservative)

	Li %	Mi %	Co %
I have thought about leaving the ministry this year	33	26	22
Deanery Synod is a priority for me	16	32	24
I feel I have to prove myself to my vicar	43	42	29
I took my full holiday entitlement this year	65	50	71
I enjoy going away on conferences	52	66	73
I have helped people become Christians this year	30	50	63
Seeing my spiritual director is a priority for me	70	58	40
A daily Eucharist is important for me	40	22	12

Conservative clergy are the ones who least agreed that it was important for every member of the clergy to say the Daily Office every day, with only 26 per cent agreeing as compared with 47 per cent of the clergy in general. It is Liberal curates who are significantly more likely to say the Daily Office most days with their incumbent.

Table 13.6 Differences in patterns of behaviour (Liberal/Conservative)

	Li %	Mi %	Co %
I say the Daily Office together with my vicar	70	64	47
I make an annual retreat	47	55	26
I attend a daily Eucharist	28	19	9
I read a Sunday newspaper every week	17	34	15
I wear a clerical collar on duty	91	81	61
I wear robes/vestments for church services	96	87	65
I work only two out of three sessions a day	12	11	3

More Liberals than any other group (70 per cent) see visiting their spiritual director as a priority in their lives. Conservative clergy are the least likely to make an annual retreat, but Middle-of-the-road clergy are significantly most likely to do so. Though 61 per cent of the Conservative clergy always or nearly always wear a clerical collar on duty, that is significantly less than the 91 per cent of Liberal clergy who do so. Though 81 per cent of all the clergy always wear robes or vestments to conduct services, only 65 per cent of Conservative clergy do.

One of the marks of Rutledge's (1993) 'new professional clergy' was their desire to be more disciplined about their use of time: they did not want to be seen as always on call. As part of that they spoke of clergy only working two out of the three sessions – morning, afternoon and evening – each day. Very few of the clergy in this study work only two out of three sessions each day, but the Conservatives are the least likely to do so. However they are also the group who made sure that they took their full entitlement of four weeks' holiday, unlike the Middle-of-the-road curates where only half received their full amount. The Middle-of-the-road clergy were, however, significantly more likely to make time every Sunday to read a Sunday paper.

Differences between Pro-charismatic, Non-charismatic and Anti-charismatic clergy

We have seen in previous chapters that the charismatic dimension is the one that produces the least number of significant differences between the churchmanship groups, and that is so here too.

Table 13.7 shows that Pro-charismatics are significantly in favour of offering a Thanksgiving for the birth of a child service first to everyone followed by baptism only for those who 'really mean it'. A slight majority of the clergy in general do not believe that a belief in the Virgin Birth is essential, but Pro-charismatics do believe it is essential. A majority in each of the three groups on this dimension agree that a belief in the physical resurrection of Jesus is essential, but again it is the Pro-charismatics who are most in support of this.

Table 13.7 Differences in belief and practice (Charismatic)

	P %	N %	A %
Prefer to offer a Thanksgiving for the birth of a child	42	20	9
A belief in the Virgin Birth is essential for a Christian	47	17	30
A belief in the physical resurrection of Jesus is essential ...	74	56	53
Holy Communion should be open to all who love the Lord Jesus	61	47	40
I am in favour of the ordination of women to the priesthood	76	64	62

Table 13.8 Differences in training and conviction (Charismatic)

	P %	N %	A %
I feel I have to prove myself to my vicar	34	31	48
My vicar feels threatened by me	28	38	47
I believe that I should keep the fees for funerals	8	4	17
I feel that POT is only a duty	32	27	48
Seeing my spiritual director is a priority for me	47	69	61
A daily Eucharist is important for me	13	28	49

A significant majority of Anti-charismatics agree that a daily Eucharist is important for them and 32 per cent of them are able to attend a daily Eucharist. It is the Pro-charismatics who are the greatest supporters of the idea that Holy Communion should be open to all who love the Lord Jesus. Of all the churchmanship groups on any of the three dimensions it is the Anti-charismatics who are the only ones where a significant number believe that they should keep the fees for the funerals and other services which they conduct rather than pay them into the Stipends Fund. It is the Non-charismatics who most wear robes for church services.

Seeing a spiritual director is less important for Pro-charismatics: 69 per cent of Non-charismatic clergy believe this is a priority for them, but only 47 per cent of Pro-charismatics. In two areas Anti-charismatics seem to have problems with their relations with their training incumbents: about half of them feel they have to prove themselves to him, and the same proportion think that he feels threatened by them. The same sort of number of Anti-charismatics feels that POT is only a duty.

A question was asked about participation in the National Lottery. It was expected given the Anglican Church's public stance on the Lottery and gambling in general that the numbers of clergy taking part in the Lottery would be small. So it proved. Amongst the curates 84 per cent had never bought a ticket, 10 per cent had seldom done so. As Table 13.9 shows, no Pro-charismatics buy a ticket every week. Of those who did buy lottery tickets, half bought them often, a sixth most weeks, and a third (two per cent of the population of curates) bought them every week. Of those who had ever bought tickets 78 per cent were Catholic, 16 per cent Central, and five per cent Evangelical; 61 per cent were Liberal, 22 per cent Middle-of-the-road, and 16 per cent Conservative; 22 per cent were Pro-charismatic, 35 per cent Non-charismatic, and 43 per cent Anti-charismatic.

Table 13.9 Differences in patterns of behaviour (Charismatic)

	P %	N %	A %
I attend Deanery Synod	55	60	74
I attend a daily Eucharist	9	25	32
I wear robes/vestments for church services	73	92	90
I take part in the National Lottery each week	0	6	6

Summary

Contrary to Coneybeare's (1853) contention that most of the differences between forms of churchmanship are mere disputes about terms, which could be ended by stricter definition, this chapter has shown that the churchmanship measure reveals divergences between the groups on each of the three axes of churchmanship in matters of doctrine, matters of ceremonial and liturgical practice and patterns of life. There is little difference between the churchmanship groups when we look at the personality of their adherents but there are large differences in theology, faith and order. Each of the nine major churchmanship groups has distinctive characteristics, and it is time to identify the idiosyncrasies of each group.

Chapter 14

Evangelicals and the rest

Introduction

This chapter draws together the results of this study by identifying the distinguishing characteristics of each of the nine churchmanship groups. In the sections on socio-biography the mean value for age, educational level and so on for the members of each churchmanship group is used. On each dimension we shall look at the groups in order of size; so, for example, on the Catholic/Evangelical dimension the Evangelicals will be considered first.

The Evangelical clergy

Socio-biography

The Evangelical clergy (N = 158) comprise nearly half (49.8 per cent) of the population studied. Their average age is 35.6 years – the youngest group on this dimension – and 81 per cent are male and 19 per cent female. Before they began training for the ministry their educational standard was as follows: seven per cent had reached the level of O-levels or GCSEs, nine per cent the level of A-levels, eight per cent had been in Higher Education below degree standard, 44 per cent had Bachelors degrees, 29 per cent had Masters degrees or other postgraduate qualifications, and three per cent had PhDs. The Evangelicals had more graduates entering theological training than the other groups on this dimension. Four fifths had been in work before ordination training, 75 per cent full-time and five per cent part-time. Of those in work 62 per cent were in professional and technical work, mostly teaching, 12 per cent in clerical work, and 10 per cent in sales.

Before beginning theological training this group had reached the following standard in public examinations in theology or religious education: 76 per cent had reached the level of O-levels or GCSEs, two per cent the level of A-levels, five per cent had been in Higher Education below degree standard, 13 per cent had Bachelors degrees in Theology or Religious Studies, and five per cent had Masters degrees or other postgraduate qualifications. The Evangelicals had the lowest number of theology graduates entering theological training amongst the groups on this churchmanship dimension. The most popular theological college for Evangelicals to study at was St John's Nottingham closely followed by Trinity College Bristol and Wycliffe Hall, Oxford. Half spent just two years at theological college. A large majority (91 per cent) trained for the ministry full-time, and just nine per cent on a non-residential Course.

In choosing a parish for their first curacy three per cent favoured city centre ministry, 39 per cent urban ministry, 33 per cent went to the suburbs, 18 per cent to a market town, and eight per cent into rural ministry. In addition to defining themselves as Evangelical, 13 per cent describe themselves as Liberal, nine per cent as Middle-of-the-road, and 79 per cent as Conservative; of their number 79 per cent are Pro-charismatic, 16 per cent Non-charismatic, and just five per cent Anti-charismatic. They perceive the churchmanship of the congregations in which they serve as follows: 25 per cent Catholic, 18 per cent Central, and 57 per cent Evangelical – so 43 per cent of the Evangelicals perceive themselves as serving in a congregation with a different churchmanship; 17 per cent Liberal, 18 per cent Middle-of-the-road, and 66 per cent Conservative; and 46 per cent Pro-charismatic, 30 per cent Non-charismatic, and 24 per cent Anti-charismatic.

They perceive the churchmanship of the incumbent who is training them as follows: 22 per cent Catholic, eight per cent Central, and 70 per cent Evangelical – so 30 per cent of them see themselves as serving alongside an incumbent with a different churchmanship; 18 per cent Liberal, 12 per cent Middle-of-the-road, and 70 per cent Conservative; and 53 per cent Pro-charismatic, 19 per cent Non-charismatic, and 28 per cent Anti-charismatic. Their training incumbents went to a variety of theological colleges but the most popular was St John's Nottingham. In the parishes in which they serve their curacies there are, in addition to the training incumbent, other members of staff: 35 per cent have a stipendiary priest colleague, 24 per cent a Non Stipendiary Minister (NSM) as colleague, 34 per cent have retired clergy on the team, and 77 per cent are in parishes with Readers. This supports the Rural Church Project's finding, reported in Chapter 2, that the more evangelical the clergyman, the greater the number of staff he is likely to have around him.

During their time in the parish 77 per cent of Evangelical clergy prefer to use the New International Version of the Bible for Bible study. For personal devotion as well 64 per cent prefer the NIV. Forty eight per cent serve in churches where there are NIV bibles in the pews and 27 per cent in churches where there are Good News Bibles in the pews.

When they began training for the ministry 28 per cent of the Evangelical curates were single, 71 per cent married, one per cent widowed, and one per cent divorced. By the end of the first year in ministry nearly 39 per cent of the single clergy had married meaning that 81 per cent of the group were now married – a remarkable by-product for Evangelicals of theological training. Of those who are married four per cent are married to a member of the clergy.

Those who are married saw their partner's relationship to the church and parish in which they worked as follows: two per cent were rather antagonistic, one per cent were disinterested, 26 per cent were individuals who were free to participate or not as a member of the church, 33 per cent were involved as a supporter in the background, 29 per cent were very involved as a team-worker, and eight per cent were very involved as a co-minister. The spouses of Evangelical clergy have significantly stronger expectations of being involved more visibly in the work of the church than other churchmanship groups.

By their third year in ministry 65 per cent were in the same parish with the same training incumbent, 21 per cent were in the same parish but had seen their vicar change, and 14 per cent had left their training parish. When the Evangelical clergy were asked if their curacy had been happy or unhappy 56 per cent said 'happy', 33 per cent said 'middling' and 11 per cent said 'unhappy'. When they were asked if their curacy had been effective or ineffective in preparing them for future ministry 47 per cent said it had been 'effective' – the lowest on this dimension, 46 per cent said 'middling' and seven per cent said 'ineffective'.

As they looked towards their next post most expected to stay in parish ministry with 34 per cent expecting to be incumbents, 34 per cent to be team vicars, and 16 per cent to serve another curacy. The most highly-favoured sector ministry post was as a college or university chaplain which six per cent would like to do. Twenty seven per cent would like to stay in the same diocese, 14 per cent would not.

Personality and disposition

The whole group of clergy in this study display a different personality profile from the general population: they are more stable and more tender-minded, with the male clergy more extraverted and the female clergy more introverted than people in general. The Evangelical clergy score significantly low on Neuroticism, and so accord with Rutledge's results (1999). In addition they score highest on Extraversion though not at a significant level. That personality disposition of stable extraversion is usually correlated with happiness (Francis and Robbins, 2000), but the Evangelicals did not score particularly highly on the Oxford Happiness Inventory. Why are Evangelicals not as happy as they could be? Why too do they score significantly highly on the Depersonalization subscale of the MBI? Tomlinson (1995) coined the term 'post-evangelical' for those who drop out of the Evangelical movement because they feel stifled by its culture. It may be that the strengths of Evangelicalism largely reflect its weaknesses. The stress on personal faith in Jesus can lead to excessive individualism rather than to joyful celebration. The message of redemption from sin can be so spiritualized as to encourage withdrawal from the world and suspicion of worldly things and worldly people. Confidence in the Bible as the word of God can lead to a sense of certainty bordering on arrogance instead of a blessed assurance.

Though none of the scores on the BSRI produced significant results, Evangelical men and Evangelical women scored highest on Masculinity and lowest on Femininity. In this way they seem to conform to the classic stereotype which sees Evangelicals being more concerned with muscular Christianity (Podles, 1999). They scored low on two of Francis and Thomas' subscales (1996a, 1996b, 1997), Traditional and Mystical experience.

Role priorities

For the Evangelicals the role of preacher is the highest priority and remains so from the beginning of their time in theological training to their third year in ministry. Bunting (1990) found that this was the role above all others for which the Low Church colleges – as he called them – were training ordinands. Francis (2000), in his major study of Evangelical Alliance church ministers, found that first and foremost Evangelical ministers from a variety of denominations wanted to be preachers.

As they began training the Evangelical curates gave a significantly higher priority to the roles of teacher, fellowship-builder, evangelist and manager. However, by the time they are ordained and have begun to work in the parish, the other churchmanship groups have changed their own priorities in such a way that the only role which Evangelicals significantly value is that of manager.

Their ordination as a priest is not so significant for Evangelicals that the role of minister of sacraments takes any priority: only 27 per cent of them give it a high priority. They do however give a significantly high priority to the role of evangelist. In the third year sacramental ministry is only a priority for 24 per cent. Preaching remains the highest priority, and the role of fellowship-builder is significantly more important for this group than for the others on this dimension.

Support

Throughout the three years of the curacy the Evangelical curates saw themselves receiving significantly less support from the local community than the other groups. Elsewhere in this study there have been indications that Evangelical curates are working more with an associational than a communal model of the church, and significant results like this contribute to that impression. In most other respects their pattern of support is the same as the other groups. However in the second year they see their vicar as giving significantly more support and help.

Belief and behaviour

The Evangelical curates show their concern for doctrine by their significantly high judgement that a belief in the Virgin Birth and physical resurrection of Jesus is essential for a Christian. A significantly high 61 per cent of them had helped people to become Christians that year. Though they eschew traditional patterns of ministerial support (they are significantly least likely to say the Daily Office, see a spiritual director or attend an annual retreat), they do like to attend conferences and they are the most likely to see stipendiary ministry as a lifelong career.

The Evangelicals have the most reservations about liturgical matters. More than half of them would prefer to offer a Thanksgiving service with baptism only for those who 'really mean it'. They are least happy to conduct baptisms for children from non-church families, and least happy to conduct baptisms outside normal worship. Francis and Lankshear noted that 'Evangelical churches are less actively involved in the baptism of infants and children than is the case throughout the Church of England as a whole' (Francis and Lankshear, 1995c, p.10). They are least happy with Confirmation, despite Francis and Lankshear's finding that 'Evangelical churches are considerably more actively involved in presenting teenagers over the age of thirteen for confirmation than is the case throughout the Church of England as a whole' (Francis and Lankshear, 1995c, p.12). Nearly three quarters believe that entry to Holy Communion should be open to all who love the Lord Jesus. A significantly low 64 per cent wear robes or vestments for church services, and only 56 per cent wear a clerical collar when on duty. They are the most unhappy with the use of female imagery for God. Only half of them are in favour of women bishops which is a significantly low proportion.

Their relationship with their training incumbent seems the most positive of the three groups on this dimension. They are the most likely to have a weekly staff meeting, and the most likely to believe that their vicar is helping them to grow as a person. They are the least likely to feel that they have to prove themselves to their vicar, and the least likely to believe that they work harder than their vicar. They are also the least likely to have had thoughts about leaving the ministry.

The Catholic clergy

Socio-biography

The Catholic clergy (N = 111) comprise 34.4 per cent of the population studied. Their average age is 36.5 years, and 76 per cent are male and 24 per cent female. Before they began training for the ministry their educational standard was as follows: 11 per cent had reached the level of O-levels or GCSEs, six per cent the level of A-levels, 19 per cent had been in Higher Education below degree standard, 32 per cent had Bachelors degrees, 22 per cent had Masters degrees or other postgraduate qualifications, and 10 per cent had PhDs. The Catholics had the highest proportion of PhDs from the churchmanship groups on this dimension entering theological training. Nearly three quarters had been in work, 62 per cent full-time and 11 per cent part-time. Of those in work 44 per cent were in professional and technical work, mostly teaching, and 10 per cent in clerical work.

Before beginning theological training they had reached the following standard in public examinations in theology or religious education: 60 per cent had reached the level of O-levels or GCSEs, four per cent the level of A-levels, 13 per cent had been in Higher Education below degree standard, 10 per cent had Bachelors degrees in Theology or Religious Studies, nine per cent had Masters degrees or other postgraduate qualifications, and four per cent had PhDs. The most popular theological college for Catholics to study at was Ripon College, Cuddesdon closely followed by Chichester and Lincoln. More than half (52 per cent) spent just two years at theological college. About four in five (79 per cent) trained for the ministry full-time, and a significantly high 21 per cent of Catholics trained on a non-residential Course.

In choosing a parish for their first curacy seven per cent favoured city centre ministry, 32 per cent urban ministry, 35 per cent went to the suburbs, 19 per cent to a market town, and seven per cent into rural ministry. In addition to defining themselves as Catholic, 65 per cent describe themselves as Liberal, 16 per cent as Middle-of-the-road, and 18 per cent as Conservative; of their number 28 per cent are Pro-charismatic, 28 per cent Non-charismatic, and 44 per cent Anti-charismatic. They perceive the churchmanship of the congregations in which they serve as follows: 68 per cent Catholic, 22 per cent Central, and 10 per cent Evangelical – so 32 per cent of the Catholics perceive themselves as serving in a congregation with a different churchmanship; 28 per cent Liberal, 20 per cent Middle-of-the-road, and 53 per cent Conservative; and 16 per cent Pro-charismatic, 39 per cent Non-charismatic, and 43 per cent Anti-charismatic.

They perceive the churchmanship of the incumbent who is training them as follows: 73 per cent Catholic, 16 per cent Central, and 12 per cent Evangelical – so 27 per cent of them see themselves as serving alongside an incumbent with a different churchmanship; 50 per cent Liberal, 15 per cent Middle-of-the-road, and 35 per cent Conservative; and 13 per cent Pro-charismatic, 35 per cent Non-charismatic, and 51 per cent Anti-charismatic. Their training incumbents went to a variety of theological colleges but the most popular was King's College London. In the parishes in which they serve their curacies there are, in addition to the training incumbent, other members of staff: 28 per cent have a stipendiary priest colleague, 22 per cent an NSM colleague, 39 per cent have retired clergy on the team, and 64 per cent are in parishes with Readers.

During their time in the parish 45 per cent of the Catholic clergy prefer to use the New Revised Standard Version of the Bible for Bible study. A significant number also use the Revised Standard Version or the Revised English Bible. For personal devotion as well 29 per cent prefer the NRSV although a significant number also use the RSV, the REB or the New Jerusalem Bible. Sixty eight per cent serve in churches where there are no bibles in the pews. If they do have bibles in the pews the most likely version is the RSV.

When they began training for the ministry 34 per cent of the Catholic curates were single, 58 per cent married, two per cent widowed, and three per cent divorced. Four-fifths of all the divorced clergy, and all of those who admitted to being in a same-sex relationship, were Catholic in churchmanship. By the end of the first year in ministry nearly 12 per cent of the single clergy had married meaning that 62 per cent of the group were now married. Of those who are married 15 per cent are married to a member of the clergy – this is the highest proportion on this churchmanship dimension.

Those who are married saw their partner's relationship to the church and parish in which they worked as follows: three per cent were rather antagonistic, 14 per cent were disinterested, 42 per cent were individuals who were free to participate or not as a member of the church, 32 per cent were involved as a supporter in the background, seven per cent were very involved as a team-worker, and just two per cent were very involved as a co-minister.

By their third year in ministry 60 per cent were in the same parish with the same training incumbent, 20 per cent were in the same parish but had seen their vicar change, and 20 per cent had left their training parish. When the Catholic clergy were asked if their curacy had been happy or unhappy 45 per cent said 'happy' – the lowest on this dimension, 45 per cent said 'middling' and 10 per cent said 'unhappy'. When they were asked if their curacy had been effective or ineffective in preparing them for future ministry 51 per cent said it had been 'effective', 43 per cent said 'middling' and five per cent said 'ineffective'.

As they looked towards their next post most expected to stay in parish ministry with 34 per cent expecting to be incumbents, 27 per cent to be team vicars, and 14 per cent to serve another curacy. The most highly-favoured sector ministry post was as a college or university chaplain which eight per cent would like to do. Thirty per cent would like to stay in the same diocese, 23 per cent would not.

Personality and disposition

The whole group of clergy in this study display a different personality profile from the general population: they are more stable and more tender-minded, with the male clergy more extraverted and the female clergy more introverted than people in general. Catholic clergy scored lowest on Extraversion and highest on Psychoticism, but not at a significant level: this concurs with Francis and Thomas' (1996a) research which found no significant differences between Catholic clergy and other clergy on the Eysenck personality dimensions. The results differ from Rutledge's (1999) who found higher N scores for Catholic clergy. In that Rutledge's study was of a standardized sample of all serving male clergy, the difference between the results of this study and the results of his study may be accounted for by the nature of the sample. Those who are Catholic in orientation and who were ordained to stipendiary ministry in 1994 are likely to be more robust in their identity because they will have had to come to terms with training alongside women who were also training for the priesthood: the greater anxiety, marked by a high N score, would then be a likely characteristic of serving clergy to whom female clergy would be more of an unknown.

The Catholic clergy score low on all three burnout subscales, and significantly low on the Depersonalization subscale. They are the least prone to burnout. In this respect they differ from Rutledge's serving Catholic clergy whose Depersonalization scores were not significantly different from other churchmanship groups. However the Catholic curates did not differ significantly from the other curates on Personal Accomplishment unlike Rutledge's serving Catholic clergy who are 'less likely to feel they are accomplishing as much in their ministry as the Evangelical clergy ($p < 0.05$)' (Rutledge, 1999, p.236). Given the upheavals for the Catholic movement in the Anglican Church leading up to 1994, these results suggest that the Catholic clergy are more optimistic and more positive in their contact with parishioners.

In a similar way the results for the Catholic curates on the Oxford Happiness Inventory, particularly after subjecting those results to multivariate analysis, show that as a group they are happier than Evangelicals of the same sex and the same personality disposition. Since there are no other published studies of the use of the Oxford Happiness Inventory with clergy it is not possible to discover whether this is generally true of Catholic clergy.

The correlation matrix for the Bem Sex Role Inventory showed Catholic churchmanship correlated with higher scores on the Femininity subscale. Though this result could not be replicated when male and female curates were assessed separately, nevertheless it points towards Catholic curates showing more 'sympathy and concern' (Argyle, 1994, p.128) in their roles. They scored highest on Francis and Thomas' Traditional religious experience subscale (Francis and Thomas, 1996a, 1996b, 1997).

Role priorities

At the beginning of training Catholic curates give the highest priority, and a significantly higher priority than Central or Evangelical curates, to the role of minister of the sacraments. This accords with Robbins and Francis' (2000) results for female Catholic stipendiary clergy at the same stage. As with Robbins and Francis these Catholic curates give a significantly higher priority to the role of spiritual director. Unlike Robbins and Francis' group these curates give a significantly higher priority to the role of visitor than the other two churchmanship groups on this dimension.

When the curates leave training and move into the parish, being a person of prayer becomes their top priority. They still rate the roles of minister of sacraments, visitor and spiritual director significantly more highly than the other groups. In addition at this stage they rate the role of apostle significantly more highly too. At the beginning of their second year the majority of the curates have been ordained priest. For the Catholic curates their highest role priority is now that of minister of sacraments, and they hold that significantly more highly than the other groups.

In their third year that highest priority for the role of minister of sacraments continues. In fact the order of their role priorities is almost identical to the order in the previous year. In addition to the sacramental role they give a significantly higher priority to four other roles: visitor, apostle, spiritual director and social worker. In general the priorities they carry into posts as incumbents and team vicars are the ones that they had as they entered into theological training.

Support

Over the three years of their curacy the Catholic curates showed a pattern of perceived support in their ministry which is not very different from that of the other groups: friends and family are the main source for support and encouragement. However there are significant differences in two areas by the third year of ministry. The Catholics receive a significantly high level of support from their bishops. The Catholics receive a significantly low level of support from their training incumbents: only 31 per cent of them perceive their vicar as giving them a high level of support.

Belief and behaviour

This low level of incumbent support is borne out by other responses of the Catholic curates. A significantly high 78 per cent say the Daily Office daily with their vicar – something which a significantly high 71 per cent feel clergy should do – but they are the least likely to have a weekly staff meeting with their vicar, to feel their vicar is helping them grow personally, and to have their vicar's encouragement to attend POT. In fact only six per cent of them feel that their vicar's training runs in parallel with the diocesan provision in POT. Nearly one in six of the Catholic curates feel that they work harder than their vicar, a significantly higher proportion compared to the other groups. Nearly a third have thought about leaving the ministry. They are the most keen to do further academic study with a significantly high 70 per cent wanting this.

They are the most likely to make an annual retreat but the least likely to attend conferences. The priority that they give to the role of visitor may explain their significantly high intention to visit any parishioner who is in hospital. Equally their high priority for the sacraments shows through in their practice: a daily Eucharist is most important for them, though only 38 per cent – still significantly higher than the other groups – are able to attend one. A significantly high 97 per cent of them wear robes or vestments for services in church. They are the most willing to conduct baptisms at other times than in the main Sunday services. Francis and Lankshear (1995b) showed that the Catholic churches are more actively involved in baptisms than other parts of the Church of England. They are also the most willing to present children under the age of 11 for Confirmation: 'Catholic parishes are considerably more active in preparing young people for confirmation under the age of 14' (Francis and Lankshear, 1995b, p.11).

When it comes to doctrine the Catholic curates are least concerned to make certain beliefs essential for Christians: just 56 per cent think that a belief in the physical resurrection of Jesus is essential, and 21 per cent that a belief in the Virgin Birth is essential.

The Central clergy

Socio-biography

The Central clergy (N = 50) comprise 15.8 per cent of the population studied. Their average age is 37.2 years – the oldest of the three groups on this dimension – and 71 per cent are male and 29 per cent female. Before they began training for the ministry their educational standard was as follows: five per cent had reached the level of O-levels or GCSEs, 12 per cent the level of A-levels, 12 per cent had been in Higher Education below degree standard, 39 per cent had Bachelors degrees, 27 per cent had Masters degrees or other postgraduate qualifications, and five per cent had PhDs. Nearly three quarters had been in work, 63 per cent full-time and 10 per cent part-time. Of those in work 57 per cent were in professional and technical work, mostly teaching, 14 per cent in clerical work, and nine per cent had just left the armed forces.

Before beginning theological training they had reached the following standard in public examinations in theology or religious education: 68 per cent had reached the level of O-levels or GCSEs, two per cent the level of A-levels, 12 per cent had been in Higher Education below degree standard, 17 per cent had Bachelors degrees in Theology or Religious Studies, two per cent had Masters degrees or other postgraduate qualifications, and two per cent had PhDs. The most popular theological college for Central curates to study at was Ripon College, Cuddesdon closely followed by Westcott House, Cambridge and Trinity College Bristol. Just under half (49 per cent) spent just two years at theological college. A large majority (85 per cent) trained for the ministry full-time, and 15 per cent of Central curates trained on a non-residential Course.

In choosing a parish for their first curacy three per cent favoured city centre ministry, 43 per cent urban ministry, 23 per cent went to the suburbs, 23 per cent to a market town, and 10 per cent into rural ministry. In addition to defining themselves as Central, 31 per cent describe themselves as Liberal, 38 per cent as Middle-of-the-road, and 33 per cent as Conservative; of their number 48 per cent are Pro-charismatic, 27 per cent Non-charismatic, and 24 per cent Anti-charismatic. They perceive the churchmanship of the congregations in which they serve as follows: 39 per cent Catholic, 44 per cent Central, and 18 per cent Evangelical – so 56 per cent of the Central curates perceive themselves as serving in a congregation with a different churchmanship; 22 per cent Liberal, 37 per cent Middle-of-the-road, and 42 per cent Conservative; and 20 per cent Pro-charismatic, 55 per cent Non-charismatic, and 26 per cent Anti-charismatic.

They perceive the churchmanship of the incumbent who is training them as follows: 53 per cent Catholic, 23 per cent Central, and 24 per cent Evangelical – so 77 per cent of them see themselves as serving alongside an incumbent with a different churchmanship; 33 per cent Liberal, 31 per cent Middle-of-the-road, and 37 per cent Conservative; and 31 per cent Pro-charismatic, 35 per cent Non-charismatic, and 36 per cent Anti-charismatic. Their training incumbents went to a variety of theological colleges but the most popular was King's College London, closely followed by Westcott House, Cambridge or Lincoln. In the parishes in which they serve their curacies there are in addition to the training incumbent other members of staff: 34 per cent have a stipendiary priest colleague, 22 per cent an NSM colleague, 44 per cent have retired clergy on the team, and 63 per cent are in parishes with Readers.

During their time in the parish 48 per cent of Central clergy prefer to use the New Revised Standard Version of the Bible for Bible study. For personal devotion as many use the NRSV as use the New International Version: 30 per cent in each case. Forty five per cent serve in churches where there are no bibles in the pews: if there are pew bibles they are likely to be NIV.

When they began training for the ministry 44 per cent of the Central curates were single, 49 per cent married, two per cent widowed, and five per cent divorced. By the end of the first year in ministry nearly seven per cent of the single clergy had married meaning that 51 per cent of the group were now married. Of those who are married five per cent are married to a member of the clergy.

Those who are married saw their partner's relationship to the church and parish in which they worked as follows: six per cent were rather antagonistic, 35 per cent were individuals who were free to participate or not as a member of the church, 35 per cent were involved as a supporter in the background, 12 per cent were very involved as a team-worker, and 12 per cent were very involved as a co-minister.

By their third year in ministry every one of them was still in the same parish, 81 per cent with the same training incumbent: 19 per cent of them had seen their vicar change. When the Central clergy were asked if their curacy had been happy or unhappy 62 per cent said happy, 34 per cent said 'middling' and five per cent said unhappy. When they were asked if their curacy had been effective or ineffective in preparing them for future ministry 62 per cent said it had been effective, 34 per cent said 'middling' and five per cent said ineffective.

As they looked towards their next post most expected to stay in parish ministry with 25 per cent expecting to be incumbents, 31 per cent to be team vicars, and 17 per cent to serve another curacy. The most highly-favoured sector ministry post was as a college or university chaplain which 10 per cent would like to do. Nineteen per cent would like to stay in the same diocese, 10 per cent would not.

Personality and disposition

The whole group of clergy in this study display a different personality profile from the general population: they are more stable and more tender-minded, with the male clergy more extraverted and the female clergy more introverted than people in general. Because such research as there has been in the past has focused on the polarity between Catholics and Evangelicals, there has been almost no acknowledgement of those who follow a middle way. As was said in Chapter 2 this has as much to do with ecclesiology (believing that Catholics and Evangelicals formed minority parties on the wings of a Broad Anglican church) as with empirical research. When looking at the three groups on this dimension, though, with the help of Eysenck's personality dimensions, it is the Central clergy who produce the only significantly high reading: they score highest on Neuroticism. It is they, not the Catholic clergy, who 'demonstrate less stability than their Evangelical colleagues, suffering greater degrees of anxiety' (Rutledge, 1999, p.182). Equally the high N score may indicate that they 'may exhibit more feminine characteristics of emotional care with a greater degree of empathy for their parishioners' (Rutledge, ibid.). They also score lowest on Psychoticism which also points towards a tender-minded attitude.

The Central curates score highest on the Personal Accomplishment and Emotional Exhaustion subscales of the MBI, but not at a significant level. However, taken alongside the EPQ scores, these may be pointers to a level of tension amongst the Central curates which would make them more prone to burnout. Equally when scores on the Oxford Happiness Inventory were examined the Central clergy are the least happy of all the nine churchmanship groups. The male Central clergy score lowest on BSRI Masculinity and highest on Femininity, and the female Central clergy score highest on Femininity: overall this churchmanship group, both male and female, have a softer approach. They score highly on Francis and Thomas' Mystical and Charismatic religious experience subscales (Francis and Thomas, 1996a, 1996b, 1997).

Role priorities

At the beginning of training Central curates gave highest priority to the role of person of prayer, but they gave no role a significantly higher place than the Catholics or the Evangelicals. The same is true for them at ordination, with the place of prayer securely at the top of their agenda. After ordination as priests, though, leader of public worship becomes their highest priority. Three roles become significantly more important for them than for the other groups: counsellor, apostle and spiritual director.

As they begin their third year in a curacy the Central curates still regard leading public worship as their highest priority. In two other areas they give a significantly higher priority than the other two groups, those of the counsellor and the leader in the local community. This last role was one that Robbins and Francis (2000) found correlated with Catholic rather than Central churchmanship among women clergy.

Support

The Central clergy follow the pattern of all the curates in finding the greatest support in ministry from their family and friends and the least support from diocesan staff. In one particular, though, they differ. For them in the first year of ministry the diocesan POT officer is perceived as giving a significantly higher level of support, with more than a third of the curates rating his or her support highly. This support is not perceived as continuing in years 2 and 3.

Belief and behaviour

The mention of POT in the last paragraph leads to two distinctive standpoints of the Central curates: they see their vicars giving significantly more encouragement to them to attend POT; and they are the ones who see their vicar's training and POT having most in common. However a significantly high 48 per cent believe that they have to prove themselves to their vicar. They are also the ones who give highest priority to seeing a spiritual director.

In the parish their public ministry is important: they give a significantly higher priority to wearing a clerical collar when 'on duty'. In addition they are the most happy at conducting baptisms for children from non-church families. Yet they are least happy at the prospect of visiting parishioners in hospital. They are the most advanced of these groups of clergy in the area of inclusivity: they are most in favour of the use of female imagery for God, and most in favour of the ordination of women to the episcopate.

The Conservative clergy

Socio-biography

The Conservative clergy (N = 163) comprise the majority (51.4 per cent) of the population studied on the Liberal/Conservative dimension. Their average age is 38.9 years, and 82 per cent are male and 18 per cent female. Before they began training for the ministry their educational standard was as follows: six per cent had reached the level of O-levels or GCSEs, eight per cent the level of A-levels, 10 per cent had been in Higher Education below degree standard, 44 per cent had Bachelors degrees, 28 per cent had Masters degrees or other postgraduate qualifications, and four per cent had PhDs. Just over three quarters had been in work, 72 per cent full-time and five per cent part-time. Of those in work 61 per cent were in professional and technical work, mostly teaching, and 14 per cent in clerical work.

Before beginning theological training they had reached the following standard in public examinations in theology or religious education: 76 per cent had reached the level of O-levels or GCSEs, two per cent the level of A-levels, six per cent had been in Higher Education below degree standard, 10 per cent had Bachelors degrees in Theology or Religious Studies, five per cent had Masters degrees or other postgraduate qualifications, and two per cent had PhDs. The Conservatives had the lowest proportion of theology graduates entering theological training on this dimension. The most popular theological colleges for Conservatives were St John's Nottingham and Trinity College Bristol. Just under half (49 per cent) spent two years at theological college. The great majority of this group (92 per cent) trained for the ministry full-time, and only eight per cent on a non-residential Course.

In choosing a parish for their first curacy three per cent favoured city centre ministry, 34 per cent urban ministry, 35 per cent went to the suburbs, 21 per cent to a market town, and seven per cent into rural ministry. In addition to defining themselves as Conservative, 12 per cent describe themselves as Catholic, 10 per cent as Central, and 77 per cent as Evangelical; of their number 71 per cent are Pro-charismatic, 18 per cent Non-charismatic, and 11 per cent Anti-charismatic. They perceive the churchmanship of the congregations in which they serve as follows: 28 per cent Catholic, 20 per cent Central, and 52 per cent Evangelical; 14 per cent Liberal, 17 per cent Middle-of-the-road, and 69 per cent Conservative – so 31 per cent of the Conservatives see themselves as serving in a congregation with a different churchmanship; and 45 per cent Pro-charismatic, 31 per cent Non-charismatic, and 25 per cent Anti-charismatic.

They perceive the churchmanship of the incumbent who is training them as follows: 28 per cent Catholic, 11 per cent Central, and 62 per cent Evangelical; 13 per cent Liberal, 11 per cent Middle-of-the-road, and 76 per cent Conservative –

so 24 per cent see themselves as serving alongside an incumbent with a different churchmanship; and 53 per cent Pro-charismatic, 18 per cent Non-charismatic, and 28 per cent Anti-charismatic. Their training incumbents went to a variety of theological colleges but the most common was St John's Nottingham. In the parishes in which they serve their curacies there are in addition to the training incumbent other members of staff: 32 per cent have a stipendiary priest colleague, 23 per cent an NSM colleague, 35 per cent have retired clergy on the team, and 76 per cent are in parishes with Readers. These results are different to those of the Rural Church Project which found that Conservative parishes generally had more staff. This study has found that, with the exception of Readers, there are more staff in Liberal parishes.

During their time in the parish 70 per cent of the Conservative clergy prefer to use the New International Version of the Bible for Bible study. For personal devotion as well they prefer the NIV: 62 per cent of them use this version. In addition 46 per cent serve in churches where there are NIV bibles in the pews.

When they began training for the ministry 28 per cent of the Conservative curates were single, 69 per cent married, one per cent widowed, and two per cent divorced. By the end of the first year in ministry about 32 per cent of the single clergy had married meaning that 78 per cent of the group were now married. Of those who are married five per cent are married to a member of the clergy.

Those who are married saw their partner's relationship to the church and parish in which they worked as follows: four per cent were rather antagonistic, 24 per cent were individuals who were free to participate or not as a member of the church, 32 per cent were involved as a supporter in the background, 32 per cent were very involved as a team-worker, and nine per cent were very involved as a co-minister.

By their third year in ministry 61 per cent were in the same parish with the same training incumbent, 23 per cent were in the same parish but had seen their vicar change, and 16 per cent had left their training parish. When the Conservative clergy were asked if their curacy had been happy or unhappy 49 per cent said happy – the lowest on this dimension, 41 per cent said middling and nine per cent said unhappy. When they were asked if their curacy had been effective or ineffective in preparing them for future ministry 42 per cent said it had been effective – the lowest on this dimension, 51 per cent said middling and six per cent said ineffective.

As they looked towards their next post most expected to stay in parish ministry with 35 per cent expecting to be incumbents, 33 per cent to be team vicars, and 18 per cent to serve another curacy. The most highly-favoured sector ministry post was as a college or university chaplain which six per cent would like to do. Thirty per cent would like to stay in the same diocese, 15 per cent would not.

Personality and disposition

The whole group of clergy in this study display a different personality profile from the general population: they are more stable and more tender-minded, with the male clergy more extraverted and the female clergy more introverted than people in general. When looking at the three churchmanship groups on this Liberal/Conservative dimension, the Conservative curates score highest on Extraversion and lowest on Neuroticism in a similar way to the Evangelical curates with whose scores they are often correlated. Unlike the Evangelicals though these results are not statistically significant. In the same way their scores on the Emotional Exhaustion and Depersonalization subscales of the MBI are the highest of the three groups. On the Oxford Happiness Inventory their scores are the lowest for the three groups: they are not as happy as the Liberal and Middle-of-the-road clergy. The male Conservative clergy fit the traditional masculine model with high scores on BSRI Masculinity and low scores on Femininity. They show low scores on Francis and Thomas' Traditional and Mystical religious experience subscales (Francis and Thomas, 1996a, 1996b, 1997).

Role priorities

For the Conservatives the role of preacher is the highest priority and remains highest from the beginning of their time in theological training to their third year in ministry. At the beginning of training they also give a significantly higher priority to the roles of teacher and evangelist. In their first year of ministry there are no roles to which they give a significantly higher priority. In their second year of ministry they again give a significantly higher priority to the role of evangelist, but by the third year again there are no roles to which they give a significantly higher priority.

Support

In their first year the Conservative curates assess the support they receive in a slightly different way to many other groups. For them family give the most support, but their training incumbent comes next on their list, giving at least as much support as friends. Apart from this singularity they follow generally the same pattern as other curates; like the Evangelicals, though, with whom they have links, in each of the three years they perceive themselves as receiving significantly less support from the local community. They also may see the congregation rather than the parish as their prime concern.

Belief and behaviour

The Conservative clergy show their concern for doctrine by their significantly high judgement that a belief in the Virgin Birth is essential for Christians, though the Middle-of-the-road curates have a stronger hold on the necessity of belief in the physical resurrection of Jesus. A significantly high 63 per cent of them had helped people to become Christians. Though they eschew traditional patterns of ministerial support (they are significantly least likely to say the Daily Office, attend Holy Communion daily, see a spiritual director or attend an annual retreat), 73 per cent of them do like to attend conferences.

The Conservatives have the most reservations about liturgical matters. About half of them would prefer to offer a Thanksgiving service with baptism only for those who 'really mean it'. They are least happy to conduct baptisms for children from non-church families, least happy to conduct baptisms outside normal worship, and least happy to present under 11s as Confirmation candidates. Nearly two thirds believe that entry to Holy Communion should be open to all who love the Lord Jesus. A significantly low 65 per cent wear robes or vestments for church services, and only 61 per cent wear a clerical collar when on duty. They are the least likely to be willing to conduct a second marriage in church after a divorce. They are the most unhappy with the use of female imagery for God and the use of inclusive language in worship. Only 57 per cent of them are in favour of women priests, and only two in five in favour of women bishops.

They are the least likely to feel that they have to prove themselves to their vicar, and, though they are the least likely to work only two sessions in a three session day, they are also the most likely to take their full holiday entitlement. They are the least likely to have had thoughts about leaving the ministry. Only 15 per cent of them can make time to read a Sunday newspaper.

The Liberal clergy

Socio-biography

The Liberal clergy (N = 107) comprise a third (33.2 per cent) of the population studied. Their average age is 36.7 years – the youngest group on this dimension – and 77 per cent are male and 23 per cent female. Before they began training for the ministry their educational standard was as follows: five per cent had reached the level of O-levels or GCSEs, four per cent the level of A-levels, 14 per cent had been in Higher Education below degree standard, 39 per cent had Bachelors degrees, 28 per cent had Masters degrees or other postgraduate qualifications, and 11 per cent had PhDs. They had the highest proportion of graduates and the highest proportion of PhDs entering theological training on this dimension. Three quarters had been in work, 63 per cent full-time and 12 per cent part-time. Of those in work 59 per cent were in professional and technical work, mostly teaching, and nine per cent in sales.

Before beginning theological training they had reached the following standard in public examinations in theology or religious studies: 60 per cent had reached the level of O-levels or GCSEs, five per cent the level of A-levels, 11 per cent had been in Higher Education below degree standard, 18 per cent had Bachelors degrees in Theology or Religious Studies, three per cent had Masters degrees or other postgraduate qualifications, and four per cent had PhDs. The most popular theological college for Liberals to study at were the Oxbridge colleges of Westcott House, Cambridge and Ripon College, Cuddesdon. About half (49 per cent) spent just two years at theological college. About four in five (79 per cent) trained for the ministry full-time, and 21 per cent on a non-residential Course.

In choosing a parish for their first curacy five per cent favoured city centre ministry, 34 per cent urban ministry, 33 per cent went to the suburbs, 20 per cent to a market town, and nine per cent into rural ministry. In addition to defining themselves as Liberal, 67 per cent describe themselves as Catholic, 14 per cent as Central, and 19 per cent as Evangelical; of their number 43 per cent are Pro-charismatic, 24 per cent Non-charismatic, and 32 per cent Anti-charismatic. They perceive the churchmanship of the congregations in which they serve as follows: 57 per cent Catholic, 28 per cent Central, and 16 per cent Evangelical; 36 per cent Liberal, 23 per cent Middle-of-the-road, and 41 per cent Conservative – so 64 per cent of them perceive themselves as serving in a congregation of a different churchmanship; and 23 per cent Pro-charismatic, 40 per cent Non-charismatic, and 38 per cent Anti-charismatic.

They perceive the churchmanship of the incumbent who is training them as follows: 65 per cent Catholic, 14 per cent Central, and 21 per cent Evangelical; 63 per cent Liberal, 15 per cent Middle-of-the-road, and 22 per cent Conservative – so 37 per cent of them see themselves as serving alongside an incumbent with a different churchmanship; and 19 per cent Pro-charismatic, 34 per cent Non-charismatic, and 49 per cent Anti-charismatic. Their training incumbents went to a variety of theological colleges but the most popular were Cuddesdon and King's College London. In the parishes in which they serve their curacies there are in addition to the training incumbent other members of staff: 33 per cent have a stipendiary priest colleague, 29 per cent an NSM colleague, 38 per cent have retired clergy on the team, and 64 per cent are in parishes with Readers.

During their time in the parish 53 per cent of the Liberal clergy prefer to use the New Revised Standard Version of the Bible for bible study. A significant number also use the Revised English Bible. For personal devotion as well they prefer the NRSV: 29 per cent of them use this version. A significant number though are as likely to use the REB, the Revised Standard Version or the New Jerusalem Bible. Fifty seven per cent serve in churches where there are no bibles in the pews. If there are bibles they are likely to be Good News Bibles.

When they began training for the ministry 34 per cent of the Liberal curates were single, 64 per cent married, and two per cent divorced. By the end of the first year in ministry nearly 18 per cent of the single clergy had married meaning that 68 per cent of the group were now married. Of those who are married a significantly high 12 per cent are married to a member of the clergy. Seventy per cent of all the divorced clergy, and all of those who said they were in a same-sex relationship were Liberal in churchmanship.

Those who are married saw their partner's relationship to the church and parish in which they worked as follows: two per cent were rather antagonistic, 15 per cent were disinterested, 47 per cent were individuals who were free to participate or not as a member of the church, 32 per cent were involved as a supporter in the background, and five per cent were very involved as a team-worker. None saw themselves as a co-minister.

By their third year in ministry 68 per cent were in the same parish with the same training incumbent, 17 per cent were in the same parish but had seen their vicar change, and 15 per cent had left their training parish. When the Liberal clergy were asked if their curacy had been happy or unhappy 50 per cent said happy, 39 per cent said middling and 12 per cent said unhappy. When they were asked if their curacy had been effective or ineffective in preparing them for future ministry 53 per cent said it had been effective, 40 per cent said middling and six per cent said ineffective.

As they looked towards their next post most expected to stay in parish ministry with 32 per cent expecting to be incumbents, 28 per cent to be team vicars, and 12 per cent to serve another curacy. The most highly-favoured sector ministry post was as a college or university chaplain which nine per cent would like to do. About a quarter (26 per cent) would like to stay in the same diocese, 21 per cent would not.

Personality and disposition

The whole group of clergy in this study display a different personality profile from the general population: they are more stable and more tender-minded, with the male clergy more extraverted and the female clergy more introverted than people in general. On none of the scales of the EPQ were the Liberal clergy significantly different from the other groups on this dimension though they are tougher-minded. This tougher attitude is backed up by their low scores on each of the three subscales of the MBI, showing them least prone to burnout. They had the highest happiness scores on the Oxford Happiness Inventory. The correlation matrix for the Bem Sex Role Inventory showed Liberal churchmanship correlated with higher scores on the Femininity subscale, though this result could not be replicated when male and female curates were assessed separately. They scored highest on Francis and Thomas' Mystical religious experience subscale (Francis and Thomas, 1996a, 1996b, 1997).

Role priorities

As they began their theological training Liberal curates gave the highest priority to the role of person of prayer: 80 per cent of them believe this is most important. In addition they give significantly higher priority to the roles of minister of sacraments, spiritual director and leader of the local community. This foremost priority for prayer continues as they begin parish ministry. In the first year in ministry they also give significantly higher priority to the roles of visitor and spiritual director. Robbins and Francis (2000) drew attention to 'the prominence of the ministry of visiting for the newly ordained curate' in their study of women in ministry. This finding may raise an important question for those responsible for shaping the experience of training parishes. Perhaps not knowing how best to deploy their new curates, training incumbents may be inclined to send them out on a round of visiting, which projects this aspect of ministry into a higher priority than anticipated during training or subsequently experienced in active ministry (Robbins and Francis, 2000, p.22). Certainly this role does not reappear for the Liberal curates as statistically significant again.

After ordination to the priesthood the role of leader of public worship becomes the highest priority for the Liberal clergy and continues so in their third year. The two roles for which they give significantly higher priority in the second year of ministry are those of minister of sacraments and spiritual director. In the third year Liberal curates have effectively settled their pattern of role priorities since their list virtually repeats that of the second year. They give statistically significant priority to four roles: minister of sacraments, prophet, counsellor, and spiritual director. At each of the four occasions when role priorities have been assessed the Liberal curates have given a significantly higher priority than the two other churchmanship groups on this dimension to the role of spiritual director. The finding earlier in this study of a correlation of Liberal churchmanship with the Mystical subscale on Francis and Thomas' (1996b) measure of religious experience may find support in the fact that Liberal clergy seem drawn to the role of spiritual director (Leech, 1977).

Support

The pattern of support for the Liberal clergy in general in each of the three years as a rule matches that for all the curates. Family and friends are the prime supporters, then the local church, and lastly diocesan staff. In none of the three years are they significantly different from the other groups.

Belief and behaviour

It would be expected that Liberal curates would not regard the espousal of particular doctrines as important, and so it proves. Only a statistically significant 11 per cent think that belief in the Virgin Birth is essential for a Christian, and less than half think that belief in the physical resurrection of Christ is essential. A significantly high number of Liberal clergy would be happy to re-marry divorcees in church. They are the most happy at the idea of both women priests and women bishops. They are most happy at the use of inclusive language in worship, and at the use of female imagery for God.

In the area of baptism policy they are the most happy to conduct baptisms for the children of non-church families, and to conduct baptisms outside the time of normal worship. They are the least likely group to feel that they have helped people to become Christians. Daily Holy Communion is a priority, and a statistically significant 70 per cent say the Daily Office with their vicar. Nearly all of them wear robes or vestments for services (96 per cent) and wear a clerical collar when on duty (91 per cent). Perhaps unsurprisingly, given their approval of the role of spiritual director, they are the group on this dimension who give the highest priority to seeing their spiritual director. Just under half, though, feel that they have to prove themselves to their vicar.

The Liberal curates are also the group who feel least commitment to Deanery Synod or, in Wales, the Ruri-decanal Conference, and the least happy at going away on conferences. They are the most likely to work only two sessions in a three session working day. They are also the group who are significantly more likely to have thought about leaving the ministry.

The Middle-of-the-road clergy

Socio-biography

The Middle-of-the-road clergy (N = 48) comprise 15.4 per cent of the population studied. Their average age is 39.6 years – the oldest group on this dimension – and they have a greater proportion of female clergy (32 per cent) to male clergy (68 per cent) than any other churchmanship group. Before they began training for the ministry their educational standard was as follows: 15 per cent had reached the level of O-levels or GCSEs, 20 per cent the level of A-levels, 16 per cent had been in Higher Education below degree standard, 28 per cent had Bachelors degrees, 21 per cent had Masters degrees or other postgraduate qualifications, and three per cent had PhDs. They had the lowest proportion of graduates entering theological training on this dimension. Four fifths had been in work, 72 per cent full-time and eight per cent part-time. Of those in work 45 per cent were in professional and technical work, mostly teaching, 15 per cent in clerical work, 10 per cent worked as higher level administrators and another 10 per cent in the armed forces.

Before beginning theological training they had reached the following standard in public examinations in theology or religious education: 65 per cent had reached the level of O-levels or GCSEs, three per cent the level of A-levels, eight per cent had been in Higher Education below degree standard, 13 per cent had Bachelors degrees in Theology or Religious Studies, and 13 per cent had Masters degrees or other postgraduate qualifications. The most popular theological colleges for Middle-of-the-road curates were Ripon College, Cuddesdon and Chichester. More than half (55 per cent) spent just two years at theological college. Over four-fifths (83 per cent) trained for the ministry full-time, and 17 per cent on a non-residential Course.

In choosing a parish for their first curacy eight per cent favoured city centre ministry, the majority (54 per cent) urban ministry, 21 per cent went to the suburbs, 10 per cent to a market town, and eight per cent into rural ministry. In addition to defining themselves as Middle-of-the-road, 35 per cent describe themselves as Catholic, 38 per cent as Central, and 28 per cent as Evangelical; of their number 43 per cent are Pro-charismatic, 28 per cent Non-charismatic, and 31 per cent Anti-charismatic. They perceive the churchmanship of the congregations in which they serve as follows: 55 per cent Catholic, 25 per cent Central, and 21 per cent Evangelical; 23 per cent Liberal, 35 per cent Middle-of-the-road, and 42 per cent Conservative – so 65 per cent see themselves as serving in a congregation with a different churchmanship; and 16 per cent Pro-charismatic, 48 per cent Non-charismatic, and 38 per cent Anti-charismatic.

They perceive the churchmanship of the incumbent who is training them as follows: 54 per cent Catholic, 18 per cent Central, and 28 per cent Evangelical; 31 per cent Liberal, 31 per cent Middle-of-the-road, and 38 per cent Conservative –

so 69 per cent see themselves as serving alongside an incumbent with a different churchmanship; and 11 per cent Pro-charismatic, 42 per cent Non-charismatic, and 47 per cent Anti-charismatic. Their training incumbents went to a variety of theological colleges but the most popular were King's College London and Westcott House, Cambridge. In the parishes in which they serve their curacies there are, in addition to the training incumbent, other members of staff: 32 per cent have a stipendiary priest colleague, 15 per cent an NSM colleague, 42 per cent have retired clergy on the team, and 62 per cent are in parishes with Readers.

During their time in the parish 34 percent of the Middle-of-the-road clergy prefer to use the New International Version of the Bible for Bible study. For personal devotion though they prefer the New Revised Standard Version or the Revised Standard Version. Fifty eight per cent serve in churches where there are no bibles in the pews. If there are any they are likely to be NIV bibles.

When they began training for the ministry 48 per cent of the Middle-of-the-road curates were single, 50 per cent married, and two per cent widowed. Middle-of-the-road was the most common churchmanship of the widowed curates. By the end of the first year in ministry about 11 per cent of the single clergy had married meaning that 55 per cent of the group were now married. Of those who are married eight per cent are married to a member of the clergy.

Those who are married saw their partner's relationship to the church and parish in which they worked as follows: five per cent were rather antagonistic, 29 per cent were individuals who were free to participate or not as a member of the church, 43 per cent were involved as a supporter in the background, 10 per cent were very involved as a team-worker, and a large proportion (14 per cent) were very involved as a co-minister.

By their third year in ministry 63 per cent were in the same parish with the same training incumbent, 23 per cent were in the same parish but had seen their vicar change, and 14 per cent had left their training parish. When the Middle-of-the-road clergy were asked if their curacy had been happy or unhappy 63 per cent said happy, 32 per cent said middling and six per cent said unhappy. When they were asked if their curacy had been effective or ineffective in preparing them for future ministry 63 per cent said it had been effective, 35 per cent said middling and eight per cent said ineffective. Middle-of-the-road clergy were significantly more happy with their curacy than the other groups and perceived it as significantly more effective.

As they looked towards their next post most expected to stay in parish ministry with 33 per cent expecting to be team vicars, 30 per cent to be incumbents, and 16 per cent to serve another curacy. The most highly-favoured sector ministry post was as a hospital chaplain which six per cent would like to do. Twenty six per cent would like to stay in the same diocese, 15 per cent would not.

Personality and disposition

The whole group of clergy in this study display a different personality profile from the general population: they are more stable and more tender-minded, with the male clergy more extraverted and the female clergy more introverted than people in general. On the EPQ scales the Middle-of-the-road curates scored lowest on E, highest on N and lowest on P showing them tending towards tender-minded neurotic introversion. They were also the most prone to a reduced sense of Personal Accomplishment. Both the male and female Middle-of-the-road curates scored lowest on BSRI masculinity and highest on BSRI femininity, but not at a significant level; as a mixed-sex group they scored significantly low on masculinity. They scored highly on Francis and Thomas' Traditional and Catholic religious experience subscales (Francis and Thomas, 1996a, 1996b, 1997).

Role priorities

Just like the Liberal curates, the Middle-of-the-road curates make person of prayer their highest priority at the beginning of training and after ordination, and leader of public worship their highest priority after priesting and in the third year of ministry. At the beginning of training a statistically significant 46 per cent of them give high priority to the role of visitor, and in the first year in the parish a statistically significant 63 per cent of them give a high priority to the role of minister of sacraments. In no other ways though during their first three years in ministry do they depart from the norms for the role priorities of curates in general.

Support

The Middle-of-the-road curates follow the recognized pattern of receiving most support from their friends and family, but in their first year in ministry they see themselves receiving a significantly high level of support from their Rural Dean. In the second year most notable from their pattern of support is their awareness that they receive least support from their archdeacon, and at a lower level than any of the other churchmanship groups in any of the three years. In their third year 60 per cent of the Middle-of-the-road curates perceive their churchwardens as giving them a significantly high level of support.

Belief and behaviour

That support from the Rural Dean referred to in the previous paragraph may well be linked to the fact that Middle-of-the-road curates are significantly more likely to make attendance at Ruri-decanal Conference or Deanery Synod a priority. They are also most likely to regard the Daily Office as a priority for all clergy, and to make an annual retreat themselves. They are the most likely to read a Sunday newspaper each week. Though this might indicate a willingness to manage their time in such a way as to include the important things, they are also the least likely to have taken their full holiday entitlement. In matters of doctrine it is the Middle-of-the-road curates, not the Conservative curates, who in significantly great numbers hold that a belief in the physical resurrection of Christ is essential. In the area of baptism and Confirmation policy they are the most willing to present candidates under the age of 11 for the bishop to confirm.

The Pro-charismatic clergy

Socio-biography

The Pro-charismatic clergy (N = 181) comprise a majority (56.9 per cent) of the population studied. Their average age is 37 years – the oldest on this dimension, and 75 per cent are male and 25 per cent female. Before they began training for the ministry their educational standard was as follows: nine per cent had reached the level of O-levels or GCSEs, nine per cent the level of A-levels, 11 per cent had been in Higher Education below degree standard, 39 per cent had Bachelors degrees, 26 per cent had Masters degrees or other postgraduate qualifications, and six per cent had PhDs. Nearly four fifths had been in work, 70 per cent full-time and nine per cent part-time. Of those in work 59 per cent were in professional and technical work, mostly teaching, and 13 per cent in clerical work.

Before beginning theological training they had reached the following standard in public examinations in theology or religious education: 74 per cent had reached the level of O-levels or GCSEs in Theology or Religious Studies, two per cent the level of A-levels, six per cent had been in Higher Education below degree standard, 12 per cent had Bachelors degrees in Theology or Religious Studies, four per cent had Masters degrees or other postgraduate qualifications, and one per cent had a PhD. This group has the lowest proportion of theology graduates entering theological training on this dimension. The most popular theological colleges for Pro-charismatics were St John's Nottingham and Trinity College Bristol. More than half (51 per cent) spent just two years at theological college. The great majority (87 per cent) trained for the ministry full-time, and just 13 per cent on a non-residential Course.

In choosing a parish for their first curacy only two per cent favoured city centre ministry, 39 per cent urban ministry, 33 per cent went to the suburbs, 17 per cent to a market town, and eight per cent into rural ministry. In addition to defining themselves as Pro-charismatic, 17 per cent describe themselves as Catholic, 14 per cent as Central, and 69 per cent as Evangelical; of their number 25 per cent are Liberal, 12 per cent Middle-of-the-road, and 63 per cent Conservative. They perceive the churchmanship of the congregations in which they serve as follows: 36 per cent Catholic, 22 per cent Central, and 43 per cent Evangelical; 19 per cent Liberal, 22 per cent Middle-of-the-road, and 58 per cent Conservative; and 44 per cent Pro-charismatic, 33 per cent Non-charismatic, and 23 per cent Anti-charismatic – so 56 per cent of them see themselves as serving in a congregation with a different churchmanship.

They perceive the churchmanship of the incumbent who is training them as follows: 34 per cent Catholic, 12 per cent Central, and 52 per cent Evangelical; 28 per cent Liberal, 16 per cent Middle-of-the-road, and 56 per cent Conservative; and 50 per cent Pro-charismatic, 22 per cent Non-charismatic, and 28 per cent Anti-charismatic – so 50 per cent of them see themselves as serving alongside an incumbent with a different churchmanship. Their training incumbents went to a variety of theological colleges but the most popular was St John's Nottingham. In the parishes in which they serve their curacies there are, in addition to the training incumbent, other members of staff: 34 per cent have a stipendiary priest colleague, 24 per cent an NSM colleague, 33 per cent have retired clergy on the team, and 76 per cent are in parishes with Readers.

During their time in the parish 62 per cent of the Pro-charismatic clergy prefer to use the New International Version of the Bible for Bible study. For personal devotion as well 53 per cent of them prefer the NIV. Thirty eight per cent serve in churches where there are NIV bibles in the pews but 29 per cent are in churches where there are no bibles in the pews: this is significantly different from the Evangelicals and the Conservatives with whom the Pro-charismatics are often linked and shows the discriminatory power of this churchmanship measure. It is interesting that in Steven's (2002) book *Worship in the Spirit: charismatic worship in the Church of England* neither 'bible' nor 'pew' appears in the index.

When they began training for the ministry 28 per cent of the Pro-charismatic curates were single, 68 per cent married, three per cent widowed, and two per cent divorced. By the end of the first year in ministry about 32 per cent of the single clergy had married meaning that 75 per cent of the group were now married. Of those who are married seven per cent are married to a member of the clergy.

Those who are married saw their partner's relationship to the church and parish in which they worked as follows: four per cent were rather antagonistic, three per cent were disinterested, 32 per cent were individuals who were free to participate or not as a member of the church, 30 per cent were involved as a supporter in the background, 22 per cent were very involved as a team-worker, and nine per cent were very involved as a co-minister.

By their third year in ministry 70 per cent were in the same parish with the same training incumbent, 18 per cent were in the same parish but had seen their vicar change, and 12 per cent had left their training parish. When the Pro-charismatic clergy were asked if their curacy had been happy or unhappy 57 per cent said happy – the highest proportion on this dimension, 34 per cent said middling and nine per cent said unhappy. When they were asked if their curacy had been effective or ineffective in preparing them for future ministry 50 per cent said it had been effective, 45 per cent said middling and four per cent said ineffective.

As they looked towards their next post most expected to stay in parish ministry with 35 per cent expecting to be incumbents, 32 per cent to be team vicars, and 13 per cent to serve another curacy. The most highly-favoured sector ministry post was as a college or university chaplain which eight per cent would like to do. Twenty six per cent would like to stay in the same diocese, 13 per cent would not.

Personality and disposition

The whole group of clergy in this study display a different personality profile from the general population: they are more stable and more tender-minded, with the male clergy more extraverted and the female clergy more introverted than people in general. The Pro-charismatic clergy score highest of the groups on this dimension on Extraversion, and lowest on Neuroticism and Psychoticism: they are stable tender-minded extraverts. In this respect these Pro-charismatics are similar to Francis and Thomas' (1997) charismatic ministers and Francis and Jones (1997) charismatic Christian adults who showed a significant correlation with stable extraversion. This personality style is least prone to burnout as their low scores on the Emotional Exhaustion and Personal Accomplishment subscales show. In the same way they were happiest of the three groups on the Oxford Happiness Inventory. When we looked at the BSRI, the male Pro-charismatic clergy scored lowest on Masculinity and the female Pro-charismatic clergy scored highest on Masculinity. Further research is under way into the forms of religious experience which are most common to high Masculinity scorers. It is interesting that these Pro-charismatic clergy scored highly on Francis and Thomas' Mystical religious experience subscale (Francis and Thomas, 1996a, 1996b, 1997).

Role priorities

All three groups on this dimension agreed at the beginning of training that their highest priority in ministry was to be a person of prayer. The Pro-charismatic curates also gave a significantly higher priority at the beginning of training to the roles of fellowship-builder, evangelist and counsellor. After ordination as deacons, though, the highest priority for the Pro-charismatics is preaching, and this continues to be true after ordination as priests. In this second year in ministry the Pro-charismatics also give significantly higher priority to the roles of fellowship-builder, evangelist and manager. By the third year in ministry the role of person of prayer has returned as the highest priority for this group: they are the only one of the nine churchmanship groups to have this as their highest priority as the curacy draws to an end and they move on to other parishes or sectors. Also they continue to give significantly higher priority to the roles of fellowship-builder and evangelist.

Support

The pattern of support for Pro-charismatic curates across the three years very much follows the pattern of curates in general, but there is one significant difference, and one absence that deserves comment. The significant difference is that in the third year the Pro-charismatics see themselves as receiving a statistically significant higher level of support from their families: over three quarters of the curates receive the highest levels of support from their family. What is absent is any correlation between Pro-charismatic churchmanship and perceived lack of support from the local community: the Pro-charismatics see themselves as receiving no more and no less support from the local community than the other groups on this dimension. It will be remembered from Chapter 12 that both the Evangelical curates and the Conservative curates, with whom the Pro-charismatics show a measure of correlation, perceive this lack of support. A value of this three-dimensional churchmanship measure is the way in which it enables the researcher to discriminate between the axes which map the semantic differential which is 'churchmanship'. Thus we can see that the presence or absence of charismatic influence is not the element in clergy self-designation which interacts with their involvement with and support from the local community. Some writers would claim that Pro-charismatics often have a more developed social theology than their Evangelical and Conservative colleagues (cf. Felton, 1978, Morgan, 1978, Scotland, 1995, pp.264-267).

Belief and behaviour

The Pro-charismatic clergy are the greatest supporters of the idea that Holy Communion should be open to 'all who love the Lord Jesus', and that a Thanksgiving for the birth of a child service should be offered to all families, followed by baptism 'only for those who really mean it'. This supports Francis, Lankshear and Jones' (2000) study showing lower numbers of infant baptisms in churches which have been influenced by the charismatic movement. In general though the charismatic dimension is not one which differentiates between groups on liturgical matters, though the Pro-charismatics are significantly less likely to wear robes for worship.

As a group they are significantly more of the opinion that the doctrines of the Virgin Birth and the physical resurrection of Jesus are essential beliefs for a Christian. A statistically significant 76 per cent of them are in favour of women priests. They are the least likely to think that their vicar feels threatened by them. None of them take part weekly in the National Lottery.

The Non-charismatic clergy

Socio-biography

The Non-charismatic clergy (N = 71) comprise 22.3 per cent of the population studied. Their average age is 35.9 years, and 75 per cent are male and 25 per cent female. Before they began training for the ministry their educational standard was as follows: seven per cent had reached the level of O-levels or GCSEs, seven per cent the level of A-levels, nine per cent had been in Higher Education below degree standard, 49 per cent had Bachelors degrees, 25 per cent had Masters degrees or other postgraduate qualifications, and four per cent had PhDs. This is the highest proportion of graduates entering theological training on this dimension. Seventy per cent were in work, 63 per cent full-time and seven per cent part-time: this group also had the largest proportion registered as unemployed at nine per cent. Of those in work 67 per cent were in professional and technical work, mostly teaching, and eight per cent were in either clerical work or sales.

Before beginning theological training they had reached the following standard in public examinations in theology or religious studies: 68 per cent had reached the level of O-levels or GCSEs, two per cent the level of A-levels, six per cent had been in Higher Education below degree standard, 14 per cent had Bachelors degrees in Theology or Religious Studies, seven per cent had Masters degrees or other postgraduate qualifications, and four per cent had PhDs – all of the Non-charismatic clergy who had PhDs had them in Theology. The most popular theological colleges for Non-charismatics were Wycliffe Hall, Oxford and Lincoln. Under half (44 per cent) spent two years at theological college; the majority spent three years or more. Just over four in five (82 per cent) trained for the ministry full-time, and 18 per cent on a non-residential Course.

In choosing a parish for their first curacy four per cent favoured city centre ministry, 42 per cent urban ministry, 27 per cent went to the suburbs, 16 per cent to a market town, and 11 per cent into rural ministry – the highest proportion on this dimension. In addition to defining themselves as Non-charismatic, 44 per cent describe themselves as Catholic, 19 per cent as Central, and 37 per cent as Evangelical; of their number 36 per cent are Liberal, 20 per cent Middle-of-the-road, and 44 per cent Conservative. They perceive the churchmanship of the congregations in which they serve as follows: 48 per cent Catholic, 18 per cent Central, and 34 per cent Evangelical; 22 per cent Liberal, 20 per cent Middle-of-the-road, and 59 per cent Conservative; and 18 per cent Pro-charismatic, 68 per cent Non-charismatic, and 14 per cent Anti-charismatic, so 32 per cent of them see themselves as serving in a congregation with a different churchmanship.

They perceive the churchmanship of the incumbent who is training them as follows: 51 per cent Catholic, 14 per cent Central, and 36 per cent Evangelical; 36 per cent Liberal, 14 per cent Middle-of-the-road, and 50 per cent Conservative; and 20 per cent Pro-charismatic, 47 per cent Non-charismatic, and 33 per cent Anti-charismatic, so 53 per cent of them see themselves as serving alongside an incumbent with a different churchmanship. Their training incumbents went to a variety of theological colleges but the most popular was Westcott House, Cambridge. In the parishes in which they serve their curacies there are, in addition to the training incumbent, other members of staff: 28 per cent have a stipendiary priest colleague, 19 per cent an NSM colleague, 33 per cent have retired clergy on the team, and 61 per cent are in parishes with Readers.

During their time in the parish 40 per cent of Non-charismatic clergy prefer to use the New Revised Standard Version of the Bible for Bible study. For personal devotion as well 27 per cent of them prefer the NRSV, followed closely by the New International Version. Forty four per cent serve in churches where there are no bibles in the pews. If there are pew bibles they are likely to be the NIV.

When they began training for the ministry 38 per cent of the Non-charismatic curates were single, 59 per cent married, and four per cent divorced. By the end of the first year in ministry another five per cent of the single clergy had married meaning that 61 per cent of the group were now married. Of those who are married six per cent are married to a member of the clergy.

Those who are married saw their partner's relationship to the church and parish in which they worked as follows: three per cent were rather antagonistic, nine per cent were disinterested, 27 per cent were individuals who were free to participate or not as a member of the church, 39 per cent were involved as a supporter in the background, 18 per cent were very involved as a team-worker, and three per cent were very involved as a co-minister.

By their third year in ministry 69 per cent were in the same parish with the same training incumbent, 23 per cent were in the same parish but had seen their vicar change, and eight per cent had left their training parish. When the Non-charismatic clergy were asked if their curacy had been happy or unhappy 53 per cent said happy, 42 per cent said middling and six per cent said unhappy. When they were asked if their curacy had been effective or ineffective in preparing them for future ministry 58 per cent said it had been effective – the highest on this dimension, 39 per cent said middling and three per cent said ineffective.

As they looked towards their next post most expected to stay in parish ministry with 33 per cent expecting to be team vicars, a significantly low 25 per cent to be incumbents, and 14 per cent to serve another curacy. The most highly-favoured sector ministry post was as a hospital chaplain which nine per cent would like to do. Thirty nine per cent would like to stay in the same diocese, six per cent would not.

Personality and disposition

The whole group of clergy in this study display a different personality profile from the general population: they are more stable and more tender-minded, with the male clergy more extraverted and the female clergy more introverted than people in general. The Non-charismatics score lowest on Extraversion and highest on Psychoticism: they are tough-minded introverts. They score highest on two of the MBI subscales, those for a reduced sense of Personal Accomplishment and Depersonalization: as such there must be concern about their proneness to burnout. They are the least happy group on the Oxford Happiness Inventory, significantly less happy than the Pro-charismatics. Female Non-charismatics score lowest on BSRI Masculinity and highest on Femininity: they most represent a traditional female personality. Male Non-charismatic clergy score significantly high on BSRI femininity: of all the clergy in this study they are the only male clergy with a significantly more feminine profile. It is hard to focus clearly though on what religious experiences are important to them since they recorded low scores on all six of Francis and Thomas' religious experience subscales – Catholic, Traditional, Born Again, Evangelical, Mystical and Charismatic (Francis and Thomas, 1996a, 1996b, 1997).

Role priorities

This is the group of all the nine churchmanship groups which has the least distinct pattern of role prioritization. At none of the four points do they have a priority in any role which is statistically significant. Their highest priority at the beginning of training and at the beginning of public ministry is to be a person of prayer. Their highest priority after ordination to the priesthood is to be a preacher, and their highest priority in the third year is to be a leader of public worship.

Support

In their first year in ministry the Non-charismatic curates show two significantly different emphases in their perception of support compared to other curates. Their greatest support comes from their training incumbent whom a statistically significant 83 per cent see as giving them the highest levels of support. In addition they receive a significantly higher level of support from their PCCs. In the second year though the vicar is only giving high support to 46 per cent of them, and to only 39 per cent of them in the third year. The pattern of support in years 1 and 2 shows no significant differences from other clergy. Do they have higher expectations of their relationship with their training incumbent than reality reveals?

Belief and behaviour

That appreciation of a training incumbent's support may well be reflected in the fact that Non-charismatics are the least likely to feel that they have to prove themselves to their vicar. There are only three other matters in this section where the Non-charismatic clergy are significantly different. They are least likely to regard a belief in the Virgin Birth as essential (just 17 per cent do). They are the most likely to wear robes or vestments for church services. They are most likely to make seeing a spiritual director a priority.

The Anti-charismatic clergy

Socio-biography

The Anti-charismatic clergy (N = 66) comprise 20.8 per cent of the population studied. Their average age is 35 years – the youngest of the three groups on this dimension – and 84 per cent are male and 16 per cent female. Before they began training for the ministry their educational standard was as follows: seven per cent had reached the level of O-levels or GCSEs, nine per cent the level of A-levels, 20 per cent had been in Higher Education below degree standard, 29 per cent had Bachelors degrees, 28 per cent had Masters degrees or other postgraduate qualifications, and seven per cent had PhDs. This group has the lowest proportion of graduates entering theological training. Just over three-quarters had been in work, 67 per cent full-time and nine per cent part-time: a marked proportion (16 per cent) were attending full-time education before ordination training. Of those in work 46 per cent were in professional and technical work, mostly teaching, and 15 per cent in clerical work.

Before beginning theological training they had reached the following standard in public examinations in theology or religious education: 56 per cent had reached the level of O-levels or GCSEs, seven per cent the level of A-levels, 12 per cent had been in Higher Education below degree standard, 11 per cent had Bachelors degrees in Theology or Religious Studies, 11 per cent had Masters degrees or other postgraduate qualifications, and two per cent had PhDs. The most

212   *Evangelicals Etcetera*

popular theological colleges for Anti-charismatics were Ripon College, Cuddesdon and Chichester. More than half (55 per cent) spent just two years at theological college. The great majority (87 per cent) trained for the ministry full-time, and 13 per cent on a non-residential Course.

In choosing a parish for their first curacy a notable 11 per cent favoured city centre ministry, 28 per cent urban ministry, 30 per cent went to the suburbs, 26 per cent to a market town, and four per cent into rural ministry. In addition to defining themselves as Anti-charismatic, 71 per cent describe themselves as Catholic, 18 per cent as Central, and 11 per cent as Evangelical; in addition 51 per cent are Liberal, 23 per cent Middle-of-the-road, and 26 per cent Conservative. They perceive the churchmanship of the congregations in which they serve as follows: 54 per cent Catholic, 33 per cent Central, and 14 per cent Evangelical; 26 per cent Liberal, 22 per cent Middle-of-the-road, and 52 per cent Conservative; and 14 per cent Pro-charismatic, 15 per cent Non-charismatic, and 71 per cent Anti-charismatic – so only 29 per cent see themselves as serving in a congregation with a different churchmanship.

They perceive the churchmanship of the incumbent who is training them as follows: 61 per cent Catholic, 15 per cent Central, and 24 per cent Evangelical; 38 per cent Liberal, 16 per cent Middle-of-the-road, and 46 per cent Conservative; and 17 per cent Pro-charismatic, 16 per cent Non-charismatic, and 67 per cent Anti-charismatic – so 33 per cent of them perceive themselves as serving alongside an incumbent with a different churchmanship. Their training incumbents went to a variety of theological colleges but the most popular was King's College London. In the parishes in which they serve their curacies there are, in addition to the training incumbent, other members of staff: 31 per cent have a stipendiary priest colleague, 24 per cent an NSM colleague, 51 per cent have retired clergy on the team, and 64 per cent are in parishes with Readers.

During their time in the parish 43 per cent of the Anti-charismatic clergy prefer to use the New Revised Standard Version of the Bible for Bible study. A significant number though will use the Revised Standard Version. For personal devotion as well they prefer the NRSV but a significant number will also use the RSV or the New Jerusalem Bible. Sixty seven per cent serve in churches where there are no bibles in the pews. If there are they are likely to be the New International Version.

When they began training for the ministry 44 per cent were single, 52 per cent married, and four per cent divorced. By the end of the first year in ministry a remarkable number of over 27 per cent of the single clergy had married meaning that 62 per cent of the group were now married. Of those who are married 11 per cent are married to a member of the clergy.

Those who are married saw their partner's relationship to the church and parish in which they worked as follows: eight per cent were disinterested, 42 per cent were individuals who were free to participate or not as a member of the church, 36 per cent were involved as a supporter in the background, 11 per cent were very involved as a team-worker, and three per cent were very involved as a co-minister.

By their third year in ministry only 50 per cent were in the same parish with the same training incumbent, 22 per cent were in the same parish but had seen their vicar change, and a high proportion of 28 per cent had left their training parish. When the Anti-charismatic clergy were asked if their curacy had been happy or unhappy 39 per cent said happy, 46 per cent said middling and 15 per cent said unhappy. When they were asked if their curacy had been effective or ineffective in preparing them for future ministry 45 per cent said it had been effective, 45 per cent said middling and 10 per cent said ineffective. The Anti-charismatics see themselves as having had a significantly less happy and less effective curacy than other curates.

As they looked towards their next post most expected to stay in parish ministry with 34 per cent expecting to be incumbents, 24 per cent to be team vicars, and 21 per cent to serve another curacy. The most highly-favoured sector ministry post was as a college or university chaplain which six per cent would like to do. Twenty five per cent would like to stay in the same diocese, a significantly high 25 per cent would not.

Personality and disposition

The whole group of clergy in this study display a different personality profile from the general population: they are more stable and more tender-minded, with the male clergy more extraverted and the female clergy more introverted than people in general. The Anti-charismatic curates score highest on EPQ Neuroticism: this can lead to a more empathetic approach to parishioners. However it could be linked to their high scores on Emotional Exhaustion and low scores on Depersonalization: they do not treat their 'clients' as objects but become drained in dealing with them. Female Anti-charismatic clergy score lowest on BSRI Femininity. Male Anti-charismatic curates score highest on Masculinity and lowest on Femininity: theirs is a traditional male profile. This study has shown pointers to a positive link between BSRI Femininity and the charismatic dimension of churchmanship, and a negative link between Masculinity and the charismatic but further research into this is to be encouraged. They scored highly on Francis and Thomas' Traditional and Catholic religious experience subscales (Francis and Thomas, 1996a, 1996b, 1997).

Role priorities

At the beginning of training the Anti-charismatic curates place the highest priority on being a person of prayer. Their second highest priority is minister of sacraments which is statistically significant. After ordination, prayer is still their top priority, and they give a significantly higher place to the sacraments than the other groups. After ordination as priests their highest priority is the leadership of public worship, and they continue to give a significantly higher priority to the sacraments. In their third year minister of sacraments is the highest priority role for them.

Support

In each of the three years of the curacy the Anti-charismatic curates' pattern of support did not differ significantly from that of curates in general. The only departure from the usual pattern of friends and family at the top, people in the parish and community in the middle, and diocesan staff at the bottom comes in the third year. Two-thirds (68 per cent) of the Anti-charismatic curates in the third year rate their congregation as giving them the most support, the same as the proportion who rate friends as highest, and far more than the rating for family. Though this did not reach the standard of statistical significance required for this study, nevertheless it stands out as a departure from the normal pattern.

Belief and behaviour

The Anti-charismatic clergy are most regular at a daily Eucharist. They are also the most assiduous in attending Deanery Synod or the Ruri-decanal conference in Wales: 74 per cent always or nearly always go.

Earlier it was seen that they were the least happy in their curacy and had a low regard for their curacy's effectiveness. Their relationship with their training incumbent seems to be reflected in the fact that nearly half, a significantly high proportion, feel that they have to prove themselves to their vicar, and a similar percentage think that their vicar feels threatened by them. Again, nearly half (48 per cent) feel that POT is only a duty. Finally a statistically significant proportion think that they should be allowed to keep the fees for the funerals and weddings that they take instead of passing them on to a Stipends fund.

Summary

This chapter and the previous three chapters have presented the evidence for the range of differences that churchmanship makes. There are clear differences in role prioritization. There are smaller but quite perceptible differences between churchmanship groups in their assessment of the support they receive. There are major and easily discernible divergences between the groups in matters of doctrine, matters of ceremonial, liturgical practice and patterns of life. In this chapter the collation of research evidence from this study has shown that each of the nine churchmanship groups has its distinctive pattern of beliefs and behaviour. We know much of what it means to be a Liberal or a Non-charismatic. The churchmanship measure has discriminated between churchmanship groups.

Chapter 15

Conclusion

Six questions gave shape and direction to this study.
- Can churchmanship be measured empirically?
- Is churchmanship a function of personality?
- Are some churchmanship groups more or less likely to burn out under the pressure of ministerial work?
- Are some churchmanship groups happier than others?
- Are some churchmanship groups more masculine or more feminine?
- Does churchmanship foster different patterns of belief or behaviour amongst Anglican clergy?

Each of these questions has been addressed and answered in this study. Taken together they draw us closer to an answer to the question, 'What is churchmanship?'

Throughout the empirical study we have used nine terms (Evangelical *et cetera*) recognizing that many complexities and variations of belief are gathered under each umbrella term. The notion that the nine terms represent areas of subjective self-identification has been assumed but so has been the recognition that clergy in particular use these terms to identify one another. We have established Daniel's conviction that the factor which most explains clergy choices is 'that particular religious ideology ... that nexus of beliefs and interpretations which in the Church of England is called churchmanship' (1968, p.117). Bryman, Ranson and Hinings defined churchmanship as 'that theological stance, or framework of religious belief, which defines a person's relation to God in specific forms of devotional and ritualistic activities, and defines for that person how to interpret his or her faith in the secular world' (1974, p.469). This study has affirmed that definition by revealing that churchmanship is generally not a function of personality, but a theological stance and a framework of religious beliefs. It is about intrinsic religious orientation, but that orientation is clothed in specific and identifiable beliefs and behaviours.

In Chapter 1 we were able to see historically how and where these characteristic theological stances developed. In Chapter 2 we had an overview of research into the empirical measurement of churchmanship. The deficiencies of previous measures were outlined, and the rationale for a new churchmanship measure expounded. The concept of a semantic differential grid with three quantifiable dimensions (Catholic/Evangelical, Liberal/Conservative, Positively/Negatively influenced by the charismatic movement) was developed, and the measure produced. From Chapter 3 onwards the results of the empirical study at the heart of this research have been presented. The three-dimensional churchmanship measure has been seen working effectively in delineating the nine distinctive churchmanship groups, three on each churchmanship axis. Though there are correlations between the three dimensions, both in the curates' own self-designations and in their perceptions of the churchmanship of their training incumbents and training parishes, nevertheless there are seen to be almost as many combinations of the self-designations as it is possible for there to be. The breadth and subtlety of the churchmanship choices of clergy has been indicated by the churchmanship measure. The links between the churchmanship measure and the Francis and Thomas (1996a, 1996b, 1997) scale of religious experience began to unpack the content of terms like 'Catholic' a little more clearly. The answer to the question, 'Can churchmanship be measured empirically?' has been shown to be, 'Yes'.

Chapters 5 to 10 outlined the development and testing of a set of measures of personality, burnout, happiness and sex role. In particular any correlation between these measures and religiosity, or any use of the measures with the clergy was considered. It was then shown that there is hardly any correlation between churchmanship and personality as measured by the EPQ and EPQR-S, or between churchmanship and burnout as measured by the Maslach Burnout Inventory, or between churchmanship and happiness as measured by the Oxford Happiness Inventory, or between churchmanship and sex role as measured by the Bem Sex Role Inventory. The answer to the question, 'Is churchmanship a function of personality so that particular types of people are drawn to particular forms of churchmanship?' has usually been shown to be, 'No'. Typically, as we have seen, different forms of churchmanship do not attract different personality types, and generally do not lead to greater or less happiness, greater proneness to burnout, or greater adoption of particularly masculine or feminine sex roles.

The final four chapters have answered the question, 'Does churchmanship foster different patterns of belief or behaviour amongst Anglican clergy?' The positive answer to this has been provided by a range of evidences for the difference that churchmanship makes. There are seen to be clear differences in role prioritization. There are smaller but perceptible differences between churchmanship groups in their assessment of the support they receive. There are major and easily discernible divergences between the groups in matters of doctrine, matters of ceremonial, liturgical practice and patterns of life. Each of the nine churchmanship groups is seen to have its distinctive pattern of beliefs and behaviour. These distinctive patterns of belief and behaviour are brought together in chapter fourteen which has identified the distinguishing characteristics of each of the nine churchmanship groups. In this way the effectiveness of the newly-developed churchmanship measure is revealed in outlining what is represented by each segment of churchmanship amongst Anglican stipendiary parochial clergy at the beginning of the twenty first century. It is to be hoped that as a result of this empirical research each of the churchmanship groups can see each of the other churchmanship groups as 'gifts of diversity' to the Church.

Bibliography

Abrams, M. (1973), 'Subjective Social Indicators', *Social Trends*, Vol. 4, pp.35-50.
Absalom, F. (1971), 'The Anglo-Catholic Priest: Aspects of Role Conflict', in M. Hill (ed.), *A Sociological Yearbook of Religion in Britain 4*, SCM, London, pp.46-61.
ACORA (1990), *Faith in the Countryside*, Churchman, London.
Andrews, F.M. and Withey, S.B. (1976), *Social Indicators of Well-Being*, Plenum Press, New York.
Archer, J. (1989), 'The Relationship Between Gender Role Measures: a Review', *British Journal of Social Psychology*, vol. 28, pp.173-184.
Archer, J. and Rhodes, C. (1989), 'The Relationship Between Gender-related Traits and Attitudes', *British Journal of Social Psychology*, vol. 28, pp.149-157.
Argyle, M. (1987), *The Psychology of Happiness*, Routledge, London.
Argyle, M. (1988), *Bodily Communication*, Methuen, London.
Argyle, M. (1991), *Cooperation*, Routledge, London.
Argyle, M. (1994) (5th ed.), *The Psychology of Interpersonal Behaviour*, Penguin, London.
Argyle, M. and Beit-Hallahmi, B. (1975), *The Social Psychology of Religion*, Routledge and Kegan Paul, London.
Argyle, M. and Crossland, J. (1987), 'Dimensions of Positive Emotions', *British Journal of Social Psychology*, vol. 26, pp.127-137.
Argyle, M. and Henderson, M. (1985), *The Anatomy of Relationships*, Heinemann, London.
Argyle, M. and Lu, L. (1990a), 'The Happiness of Extraverts', *Personality and Individual Differences*, vol. 11, pp.1011-1017.
Argyle, M. and Lu, L. (1990b), 'Happiness and Social Skills', *Personality and Individual Differences*, vol. 11, pp.1255-1261.
Argyle, M., Martin, M. and Crossland, J. (1989), 'Happiness as a Function of Personality and Social Encounters', in J.P. Forgas and J.M. Innes (eds), *Recent Advances in Social Psychology: an international perspective*, Elsevier Science Publishers BV, North-Holland pp.189-203.
Argyle, M., Martin, M. and Lu, L. (1995), 'Testing for Stress and Happiness: the Role of Social and Cognitive Factors', in C.D. Spielberger and I.G. Sarason (eds), *Stress and Emotion: anxiety, anger and curiosity*, Taylor and Francis, New York pp.173-187.
Arnold, J. and Bye, H. (1989), 'Sex and Sex-role Self-concepts as Correlates of Career Decision Making Self Efficacy', *British Journal of Guidance and Counselling*, vol. 17, pp.201-206.
Avis, P. (1989), *Anglicanism and the Christian Church: theological resources in historical perspective*, T. and T. Clark, Edinburgh.
Azzi, C. and Ehrenberg, R. (1975), 'Household Allocation of Time and Church Attendance', *Journal of Political Economy*, vol. 83, pp.27-56.
Back, P. (1989), *Where are They Now*, MARC, London.
Badham, P. (1998), *The Contemporary Challenge of Modernist Theology*, University of Wales Press, Cardiff.
Ballard-Reisch, D. and Elton, M. (1992), 'Gender Orientation and the Bem Sex Role Inventory: a Psychological Construct Revisited', *Sex Roles*, vol. 27, pp.291-306.
Bartlemann, F. (1980), *Azusa Street*, Bridge Publishing, London.

Batson, C.D., Schoenrade, P. and Ventis, W.K. (1993), *Religion and the Individual: a social-psychological perspective*, Oxford University Press, Oxford.
Bax, J. (1986), *The Good Wine: spiritual renewal in the Church of England*, Church House Publishing, London.
Baxter, C. (ed.) (1987), *Stepping Stones*, Hodder and Stoughton, London.
Bebbington, D. (1989), *Evangelicalism in Modern Britain: a history from the 1730s to 1980s*, Unwin, London.
Beck, T., Ward, C.H., Mendelson, M., Hock, J. and Erbaugh, J. (1961), 'An Inventory for Measuring Depression', *Archives of General Psychiatry*, vol. 7, pp.158-216.
Belcastro, P.A. and Gold, R.S. (1983), 'Teacher Stress and Burnout', *Journal of School Health*, vol. 53, pp.404-407.
Belcastro, P.A., Gold, R.S. and Grant, J. (1982), 'Stress and Burnout: Physiologic Effects on Correctional Teachers', *Criminal Justice and Behaviour*, vol. 9, pp.387-395.
Bell, P.M.H. (1969), *Disestablishment in Ireland and Wales*, SPCK, London.
Bem, S.L. (1974), 'The Measurement of Psychological Androgyny', *Journal of Consulting and Clinical Psychology*, vol. 42, pp.155-162.
Bem, S.L. (1975), 'Sex Role Adaptability: One Consequence of Psychological Androgyny', *Journal of Personality and Social Psychology*, vol. 31, pp.634-643.
Bem, S.L. (1977), 'On the Utility of Alternative Procedures for Assessing Psychological Androgyny', *Journal of Consulting and Clinical Psychology*, vol. 45, pp.196-200.
Bem, S.L. (1981a), *Bem Sex Role Inventory: professional manual*, Consulting Psychologists Press, Palo Alto, CA.
Bem, S.L. (1981b), 'Gender Schema Theory: a Cognitive Account of Sex Typing', *Psychological Review*, vol. 88, pp.354-364.
Bem, S.L. (1982), 'Gender Schema Theory and Self-schema Theory Compared: a Comment on Markus, Crane, Bernstein and Siladi's "Self-Schemas and Gender"', *Journal of Personality and Social Psychology*, vol. 43, pp.1192-1199.
Bem, S.L. (1993), *The Lenses of Gender: Transforming the Debate on Sexual Inequality*, Yale University Press, New Haven, CT.
Best, G. (1967), 'Popular Protestantism in Victorian Britain', in R. Robson (ed.), *Ideas and Institutions of Victorian Britain: essays in honour of George Kitson Clark*, G. Bell, London, pp.115-142.
Bishop, D.V.M. (1977), 'The P scale and Psychosis', *Journal of Abnormal Psychology*, vol. 86, pp.127-134.
Blazer, D. and Palmore, E. (1976), 'Religion and Aging in a Longitudinal Panel', *The Gerontologist*, vol. 16, pp.82-85.
Blizzard, S.W. (1955), 'The Roles of the Rural Parish Minister, the Protestant Seminaries and the Science of Social Behaviour', *Religious Education*, vol. 50, pp.383-392.
Blizzard, S.W. (1956), 'The Minister's Dilemma', *The Christian Century*, vol. 73, pp.505-9.
Blizzard, S.W. (1958a), 'The Parish Minister's Self-image of his Master Role', *Pastoral Psychology*, vol. 89, pp.25-32.
Blizzard, S.W. (1958b), 'The Protestant Parish Minister's Integrating Roles', *Religious Education*, vol. 53, pp.374-380.
Block, J. (1977), 'P Scale and Psychosis: Continued Concerns', *Journal of Abnormal Psychology*, vol. 85, pp.431-434.
Board of Education (1988), *Children in the Way: new directions for the Church's children*, National Society/Church House Publishing, London.
Bosher, R.S. (1951), *The Making of the Restoration Settlement: the influence of the Laudians 1649-1662*, Dacre Press, Westminster.
Boyd, I.R. (1995), 'What are the Clergy for? Clerical Role Uncertainty and the State of Theology', *Theology*, vol. 783, pp.187-196.

Bradburn, N.M. (1969), *The Structure of Psychological Well-Being*, Aldine, Chicago.
Brebner, J., Donaldson, J., Kirby, N. and Ward, L. (1995), 'Relationships between Happiness and Personality', *Personality and Individual Differences*, vol. 19, pp. 251-8.
Brebner, J. and Martin, M. (1995), 'Testing for Stress and Happiness: the Role of Personality Factors', in C.D. Spielberger and I.G. Sarason (eds), *Stress and Emotion: anxiety, anger and curiosity*, Taylor and Francis, New York, pp.139-172.
Breckler, S.J. (1984), 'Empirical Validation of Affect Behaviour and Cognition as Distinct Components of Attitude', *Journal of Personal and Social Psychology*, vol. 47, pp.1191-1205.
Brickman, P., Coates, D. and Janoff-Bulman, R. (1978), 'Lottery Winners and Accident Victims: is Happiness Relative?', *Journal of Personality and Social Psychology*, vol. 36, pp.917-927.
Brierley, P. (1991), *'Christian' England; what the 1989 English Church Census reveals*, Marc Europe, London.
Brierley, P., Myers, B. and Marshall, L. (1991), *Leaders under Pressure*, Marc Europe, London.
Brockman, N. (1978), 'Burnout in Superiors', *Review for Religious*, vol. 37, pp.75-89.
Brownmillar, S. (1975), *Against our Will: men, women and rape*, Simon and Schuster, New York.
Brunstein, J.C. (1993), 'Personal Goals and Subjective Well-being', *Journal of Personality and Social Psychology*, vol. 65, pp.1061-1070.
Bryman, A. (1989), 'The Value of Re-studies in Sociology: the Case of Clergy and Ministers, 1971 to 1985', *Sociology*, vol. 23, pp.31-53.
Bryman, A., Ranson, S. and Hinings, C.R. (1974), 'Churchmanship and Ecumenism', *Journal of Ecumenical Studies*, vol. 11, pp.467-475.
Buchanan, C.O. (1984), 'Anglican Evangelicalism: the State of the 'Party', *Anvil*, vol. 1, pp.7-18.
Buchanan, C.O. (1994), 'Evangelicalism: the Latest State of the Party', *Anvil*, vol. 11, pp.103-110.
Buchanan, C.O. (1998), *Is the Church of England Biblical?*, Darton, Longman and Todd, London.
Bunting, I.D. (1990), *The Places to Train*, Marc Europe, London.
Burgess, N. (1998), *Into Deep Water: the experience of curates in the Church of England*, Kevin Mayhew, Bury St Edmunds.
Burgess, N. (2000), 'A home-going parson ...', *Theology*, vol. 811, pp.37-45.
Burgess, S.M. and McGee, G.B. (eds) (1989), *Dictionary of Pentecostal and Charismatic Movements*, Zondervan, Grand Rapids, MI.
Burke, R.J. and Greenglass, E.R. (1989a), 'Psychological Burnout among Men and Women in Teaching: an Examination of the Cherniss Model', *Human Relations*, vol. 42, pp.261-273.
Burke, R.J. and Greenglass, E.R. (1989b), 'Sex Differences in Psychological Burnout in Teachers', *Psychological Reports*, vol. 65, pp.55-63.
Burns, A. (1999), *The Diocesan Revival in the Church of England c1800-1870*, OUP, Oxford.
Byrne, B.M. (1991), 'Burnout: Investigating the Impact of Background Variables for Elementary, Intermediate, Secondary and University Educators', *Teaching and Teacher Education*, vol. 7, pp.197-209.
Caird, D. (1987), 'Religiosity and Personality: are Mystics Introverted, Neurotic or Psychotic?' *British Journal of Social Psychology*, vol. 26, pp.345-346.
Campbell, A., Converse, P.E. and Rodgers, W.L. (1976), *The Quality of American Life*. Sage, New York.

Cann, A. and Siegfried, W. (1990), 'Gender Stereotypes and Dimensions of Effective Leader Behaviour', *Sex Roles*, vol. 23, pp.413-419.
Capel, S.A. (1991), 'A longitudinal Study of Burnout in Teachers', *British Journal of Educational Psychology*, vol. 61, pp.36-45.
Carey, G. (1988), 'Parties in the Church of England', *Theology*, vol. 91, pp.266-273.
Carr, W. (1989), *The Pastor as Theologian: the integration of pastoral ministry, theology and discipleship*, SPCK, London.
Carter, M., Kay, W.K. and Francis, L.J. (1996), 'Personality and Attitude toward Christianity among Committed Adult Christians', *Personality and Individual Differences*, vol. 20, pp.265-266.
Cartledge, M.J. (1999), 'Empirical Theology: Inter- or Intra-disciplinary?' *Journal of Beliefs and Values*, vol. 20, pp.98-104.
Carver, C.S. and Scheier, M.F. (1990), 'Origins and Functions of Positive and Negative Affect: a Control-process View', *Psychological Review*, vol. 97, pp.19-35.
Central Board of Finance (1991), *We Believe in the Holy Spirit*, Church House Publishing, London.
Chadwick, O. (ed.) (1960), *The Mind of the Oxford Movement*, A. and C. Black, London.
Chadwick, O. (1966), *The Victorian Church*, A. and C. Black, London.
Chadwick, O. (1990), *The Spirit of the Oxford Movement*, CUP, Cambridge.
Chadwick, O. (1992), *The Christian Church in the Cold War*, Penguin, London.
Chandler, A. (1994), 'Munich and Morality: the Bishops of the Church of England and Appeasement', *Twentieth Century British History*, vol. 5, pp.77-99.
Child, R. (1970), *In his own Parish: pastoral care through parochial visiting*, SPCK, London.
Clegg, H. (1966a), 'Evangelicals and Tractarians'. *The Historical Magazine of the Protestant Episcopal Church*, vol. 35, pp.111-153.
Clegg, H. (1966b), 'Evangelicals and Tractarians', *The Historical Magazine of the Protestant Episcopal Church*, vol. 35, pp.237-294.
Clegg, H. (1967), 'Evangelicals and Tractarians', *The Historical Magazine of the Protestant Episcopal Church*, vol. 36, pp.127-178.
Coan, R.W. (1977), *Hero, Artist, Sage or Saint?*, Columbia University Press, New York.
Coate, M.A. (1989), *Clergy Stress*, SPCK, London.
Coates, C.H. and Kistler, R.C. (1965), 'Role Dilemmas of Protestant Clergymen in a Metropolitan Community', *Review of Religious Research*, vol. 6, pp.147-152.
Cocksworth, C. (1993), *Evangelical Eucharistic Thought in the Church of England*, CUP, Cambridge.
Collins, W., Friedman, E. and Pivot, A. (1978), *The Directory of Social Change*, Wildwood House/Savoy, Manchester.
Collinson, P. (1967) *The Elizabethan Puritan Movement*, Clarendon Press, Oxford.
Collinson, P. (1982), *The Religion of Protestants: the church in English society 1559-1625*, Clarendon Press, Oxford.
Coneybeare, W.J. (1853), 'Church Parties', *Edinburgh Review*, vol. 98, pp.273-342.
Constantinople, A. (1973), 'Masculinity-femininity: an Exception to a Famous Dictum?', *Psychological Bulletin*, vol. 80, pp.389-407.
Cordes, C.L. and Dougherty, T.W. (1993), 'A Review and an Integration of Research on Job Burnout', *Academy of Management Review*, vol. 18, pp.621-656.
Cortina, J.M. (1993), 'What is Coefficient Alpha: an Examination of Theory and Applications', *Journal of Applied Psychology*, vol. 78, pp.98-104.
Costa, P.T. and McCrae, R.R. (1980), 'Influence of Extraversion and Neuroticism on Subjective Well-being: Happy and Unhappy people', *Journal of Personality and Social Psychology*, vol. 38, pp.668-678.

Costa, P.T. and McCrae, R.R. (1984), 'Personality as a Lifelong Determinant of Wellbeing', in C.Matatesta and C.Izard (eds), *Affective Processes in Adult Development and Aging,*. Sage, Beverley Hills, CA, pp.141-156.

Costa, P.T., McCrae, R.R. and Zonderman, A.B. (1987), 'Environmental and Dispositional Influences on Well-being: Longitudinal Follow-up of an American National Sample', *British Journal of Psychology*, vol. 78, pp.299-306.

Coward, B. (1980), *The Stuart Age: England 1603-1714*, Longman, London.

Cowles, M., Darling, M. and Skanes, A. (1992), 'Some Characteristics of the Simulated Self', *Personality and Individual Differences*, vol. 13, pp.501-510.

Cragg, G.R. (1950), *From Puritanism to the Age of Reason*, CUP, Cambridge.

Craston, C. (ed.) (1981), *The Charismatic Movement in the Church of England*, Church Information Office, London.

Crockford's *Clerical Directory* (1995) (94th edn), Church House Publishing, London.

Cronbach, L.J. (1951), 'Coefficient Alpha and the Internal Structure of Tests', *Psychometrika*, vol. 16, pp.297-344.

Crumbaugh, J. (1968), 'Cross-validation of a Purpose-in-life Test based on Frankl's Concepts', *Journal of Individual Psychology*, vol. 24, pp.74-81.

Cupitt, D. (1984), *The Sea of Faith*, BBC, London.

Curry, G. (1997), 'Evangelicals in the Church of England', *Churchman*, vol. 111, pp.315-326.

Cuthbert, N. (1994), *Charismatics in Crisis*, Kingsway, Eastbourne.

Daniel, M.G. (1967), *London Clergymen: the ways in which their attitudes to themselves and their work have changed in the first ten years of their ministry*, Unpublished MPhil dissertation, London School of Economics, University of London.

Daniel, M.G. (1968), 'Catholic, Evangelical and Liberal in the Anglican Priesthood', in D. Martin (ed.), *A Sociological Yearbook of Religion*, SCM, London, pp.115-123.

Daniel, S. and Rogers, M.L. (1981), 'Burnout and the Pastorate: a Critical Review with Implications for Pastors', *Journal of Psychology and Theology*, vol. 9, pp.232-249.

Davie, G. (1994), *Religion in Britain since 1945: believing without belonging*, Blackwell, Oxford.

Davies, D. (1993), 'Spirituality, Churchmanship, and English Anglican Priests', *Journal of Empirical Theology*, vol. 6, pp.5-18.

Davies, D., Watkins, C., Winter, M., Pack, C., Seymour, S. and Short, C. (1991), *Church and Religion in Rural England*, T. and T. Clark, Edinburgh.

Davies, D., Watkins, C., Winter, M., Seymour, S. and Short, C. (1990), *The Rural Church Project Report vol. 1 Rural Church: Staff and Buildings, vol. 2 The Clergy Life, vol. 3 Parish Life and Rural Religion, vol. 4 The Views of Rural Parishioners*, The Royal Agricultural College/The University of Nottingham, Cirencester.

Davies, G. (1937), *The Early Stuarts 1603-1660*, OUP, Oxford.

Davies, G. (1983), 'Squires in the East End?' *Theology*, vol. 86, pp.249-259.

de Vaus, D. (1984), 'Workforce Participation and Sex Differences in Church Attendance', *Review of Religious Research*, vol. 25, pp.247-256.

de Vaus, D. and McAllister, I. (1987), 'Gender Differences in Religion: a Test of the Structural Location Theory' *American Sociological Review*, vol. 51, pp.472-481.

Dewe, P.J. (1987), 'New Zealand Ministers of Religion: Identifying Sources of Stress and Coping Processes', *Work and Stress*, vol. 1, pp.351-364.

Diener, E. (1984), 'Subjective Well-being', *Psychological Bulletin*, vol. 95, pp.542-575.

Diener, E. and Diener, C. (1996), 'Most People are Happy', *Psychological Science*, vol. 7, pp.181-185.

Diener, E. and Emmons, R.A. (1985), 'The Independence of Positive and Negative Affect', *Journal of Personality and Social Psychology*, vol. 47, pp.1105-1117.

Diener, E., Emmons, R.A., Larsen, R.J. and Griffen, S. (1985), 'The Satisfaction with Life Scale', *Journal of Personality Assessment*, vol. 49, pp.71-75.

Diener, E., Larsen, R.J., Levine, S. and Emmons, R.A. (1985), 'Intensity and Frequency: Dimensions underlying Positive and Negative Affect', *Journal of Personality and Social Psychology*, vol. 48, pp.1253-1265.

Diener, E. and Lucas, R.A. (1998), 'Personality and Subjective Well-being', in D. Kahneman, E. Diener and N. Schwarz (eds), *Hedonic Psychology: scientific perspectives on enjoyment, suffering and well-being*, Russell Sage, New York pp.97-124.

Diener, E. and Lucas, R.A. (1999), 'The Experience of Emotional Well-being', in M. Lewis and J.M. Haviland (eds), *Handbook of Emotions (2nd edition)*, Guilford, New York pp.405-415.

Diener, E., Sandvik, E. and Larsen, R.J. (1985), 'Age and Sex Effects for Emotional Intensity', *Developmental Psychology*, vol. 2, pp.542-546.

Diener, E., Sandvik, E., Seidlitz, L. and Diener, M. (1992), 'The Relationship between Income and Subjective Well-being: Relative or Absolute?', *Social Indicators Research*, vol. 28, pp.253-281.

Diener, E., Wolsic, B. and Fujita, F. (1995), 'Physical Attractiveness and Subjective Well-being', *Journal of Personality and Social Psychology*, vol. 68, pp.653-663.

Dixon, P. (1994), *Signs and Revival*, Kingsway, Eastbourne.

Dobbins, G., Long, W., Dedrick, E. and Clemons, T. (1990), 'The Role of Self-monitoring and Gender on Leader Emergence: a Laboratory and Field Study', *Journal of Management*, vol. 16, pp.609-618.

Dowell, S. and Williams, J. (1994), *Bread, Wine and Women: the ordination debate in the Church of England*, Virago Press, London.

Dudley-Smith, T. (2001), *John Stott: a global ministry*, IVP, Leicester.

Dunn, J. (1982), 'The Authority of Scripture according to Scripture', *Churchman*, vol. 96, pp.17-26.

Dunne, M.P., Martin, N.G., Pangan, T. and Heath, A.C. (1997), 'Personality and Change in the Frequency of Religious Observance', *Personality and Individual Differences*, vol. 23, pp.527-530.

Dunstan, G.R. (1970), 'The Sacred Ministry as a Learned Profession', in G.R. Dunstan (ed.), *The Sacred Ministry*, SPCK, London, pp.1-10.

Eagly, A.H. (1987), *Sex Differences in Social Behaviour: a social-role interpretation*, Erbaum, Hillsdale, NJ.

Eagly, A.H. and Johnson, B. (1990), 'Gender and Leadership Style: a Meta-analysis', *Psychological Bulletin*, vol. 108, pp.233-256.

Eagly, A.H. and Karau, S. (1991), 'Gender and the Emergence of Leaders: a Meta-analysis', *Journal of Personality and Social Psychology*, vol. 60, pp.685-710.

Eagly, A.H., Makhijani, M. and Klonsky, B. (1992), 'Gender and the Evaluation of Leaders: a Meta-analysis', *Psychological Bulletin*, vol. 111, pp.3-22.

Eagly, A.H. and Wood, W. (1991), 'Explaining Sex Differences in Social Behaviour: a Meta-analytical Perspective', *Personality and Social Psychology Bulletin*, vol. 17, pp.306-315.

Eastburg, M.C., Williamson, M., Gorsuch, R. and Ridley, C. (1994), 'Social Support, Personality and Burnout in Nurses', *Journal of Applied Social Psychology*, vol. 24, pp.1233-1250.

Eastell, J.K. (1992), *The Continuing Religious Education of the Clergy within the Church of England with Specific Reference to the Diocese of London*, Unpublished PhD dissertation, Institute of Education, University of London.

Ecclestone, G. (ed.)(1988), *The Parish Church?* Mowbray, Oxford.

Eddison, J. (ed.) (1983), *'Bash': a study in spiritual power*, Marshall Pickering, Basingstoke.
Edwards, D.L. (ed.) (1963), *The Honest to God Debate*, SCM Press, London.
Edwards, D.L. (1982), *Christian England: its story to the Reformation*, Fount, London.
Edwards, D.L. and Stott, J. (1988), *Essentials: a Liberal-Evangelical dialogue*, Hodder and Stoughton, London.
Ekhardt, B.N. and Goldsmith, W.M. (1984), 'Personality Factors of Men and Women Pastoral Candidates: Part 1, Motivational Profile', *Journal of Psychology and Theology*, vol. 12, pp.109-118.
Ellis, L.J. and Bentler, P.M. (1973), 'Traditional Sex-determined Role Standards and Sex Stereotypes', *Journal of Personality and Social Psychology*, vol. 25, pp.28-34.
Ellison, C.G., Gay, D. and Glass, T. (1989), 'Does Religious Commitment Contribute to Individual Life Satisfaction?' *Social Forces*, vol. 68, pp.100-123.
Emmons, R.A. (1986), 'Personal Strivings: an Approach to Personality and Subjective Well-being', *Journal of Personality and Social Psychology*, vol. 51, pp.1058-1068.
Emmons, R.A. and Diener, E. (1985), 'Personality Correlates of Subjective Well-being', *Personality and Social Psychology Bulletin*, vol. 11, pp.89-97.
Emmons, R.A. and King, L.A. (1988), 'Conflict among Personal Strivings: Immediate and Long-term Implications for Psychological and Physical Well-being', *Journal of Personality and Social Psychology*, vol. 54, pp.1040-1048.
Ensor, R.C.K. (1936), *England 1870-1914*, OUP, Oxford.
Evans, W. (1986), 'Personality and Stress', *Personality and Individual Differences*, vol. 7, pp.251-253.
Every, G. (1956), *The High Church Party 1688-1714*, SPCK, London.
Eysenck, H.J. (1947), *Dimensions of Personality*, Routledge, London.
Eysenck, H.J. (1952), *The Scientific Study of Personality*, Routledge and Kegan Paul, London.
Eysenck, H.J. (1953), *The Structure of Human Personality*, Methuen, London.
Eysenck, H.J. (1954), *The Psychology of Politics*, Routledge and Kegan Paul, London.
Eysenck, H.J. (1959), *Manual of the Maudsley Personality Inventory*, University of London Press, London.
Eysenck, H.J. (1961), 'Personality and Social Attitudes', *Journal of Social Psychology*, vol. 53, pp.243-248.
Eysenck, H.J. (1967) *The Biological Basis of Personality*, C.C. Thomas, Springfield, IL.
Eysenck, H.J. (1977), *Crime and Personality*, Paladin, St Albans.
Eysenck, H.J. (1991), 'Dimensions of Personality: 16, 5 or 3? – Criteria for a Taxonomic Paradigm', *Personality and Individual Differences*, vol. 12, pp.773-790.
Eysenck, H.J. (1992), 'Four Ways Five Factors are not Basic', *Personality and Individual Differences*, vol. 13, pp.667-673.
Eysenck, H.J. and Eysenck, M. (1985), *Personality and Individual Differences: a natural science approach*, Plenum Press, New York.
Eysenck, H.J. and Eysenck, S.B.G. (1964), *Manual of the Eysenck Personality Inventory*, Hodder and Stoughton, London.
Eysenck, H.J. and Eysenck, S.B.G. (1975), *Manual of the Eysenck Personality Questionnaire*, Hodder and Stoughton, London.
Eysenck, H.J. and Eysenck, S.B.G. (1976), *Psychoticism as a Dimension of Personality*, Hodder and Stoughton, London.
Eysenck, S.B.G., Eysenck, H.J. and Barrett, P. (1985), 'A Revised Version of the Psychoticism Scale', *Personality and Individual Differences*, vol. 6, pp.21-29.
Feltey, K.M. and Poloma, M.M. (1991), 'From Sex Differences to Gender Role Beliefs: Exploring Effects on Six Dimensions of Religiosity', *Sex Roles*, vol. 25, pp.181-193.

Felton, P. (1978), 'Towards a Charismatic Social Theology', *Theological Renewal*, vol. 8, pp.22-29.
Fichter, J.H. (1984), 'The myth of Clergy Burnout', *Sociological Analysis*, vol. 45, pp.373-382.
Field, B. (1989), *Fit for this Office*, Collins Dove, Melbourne.
Field, C.D. (1993), 'Adam and Eve: Gender in English Free Church Constituency', *Journal of Ecclesiastical History*, vol. 44, pp.63-79.
Field-Bibb, J. (1991) *Women Towards Priesthood: ministerial politics and feminist praxis*, CUP, Cambridge.
Fimian, M.J. (1984), 'Organisational Variables related to Stress and Burnout in Community-based Programmes', *Education and Training of the Mentally Retarded*, vol. 19, pp.201-209.
Firestone, S. (1971), *The Dialectic of Sex: the case for feminist revolution*, Jonathan Cape, London.
Fishbein, M. and Azjen, I. (1974), 'Attitudes towards Objects as Predictors of Single and Multiple Behaviour Criteria', *Psychological Review*, vol. 81, pp.59-74.
Fletcher, B.C. (1990), *Clergy under Stress: a study of homosexual and heterosexual clergy in the Church of England*, Mowbray, London.
Francis, L.J. (1976) *An Enquiry into the Concept 'Readiness for religion'*, Unpublished PhD dissertation, University of Cambridge.
Francis, L.J. (1979), 'The Child's Attitude towards Religion: a Review of Research', *Educational Research*, vol. 21, pp.103-108.
Francis, L.J. (1991a), 'The Personality Characteristics of Anglican Ordinands: Feminine Men and Masculine Women?' *Personality and Individual Differences*, vol. 12, pp.1133-1140.
Francis, L.J. (1991b), 'Personality and Attitude towards Religion among Adult Churchgoers in England', *Psychological Reports*, vol. 69, pp.791-794.
Francis, L.J. (1992a), 'Neuroticism and Intensity of Religious Attitudes among Clergy in England', *Journal of Social Psychology*, vol. 132, pp.577-580.
Francis, L.J. (1992b), 'Is Psychoticism really a Dimension of Personality Fundamental to Religiosity?' *Personality and Individual Differences*, vol. 13, pp.645-652.
Francis, L.J. (1992c), 'Male and Female clergy in England', *Journal of Empirical Theology*, vol. 5, pp.31-38.
Francis, L.J. (1993a), 'Personality and Religion among College Students in the UK', *Personality and Individual Differences*, vol. 14, pp.619-622.
Francis, L.J. (1993b), 'The Dual Nature of the Eysenckian Neuroticism Scales: a Question of Sex Differences?' *Personality and Individual Differences*, vol. 15, pp.43-59.
Francis, L.J. (1997), 'The Psychology of Gender Differences in Religion: a Review of Empirical Research', *Religion*, vol. 27, pp.81-96.
Francis, L.J. (1998), 'Happiness is a Thing called Stable Extraversion: a Further Examination of the Relationship between the Oxford Happiness Inventory and Eysenck's Dimensional Model of Personality and Gender', *Personality and Individual Differences*, vol. 26, pp.5-11.
Francis, L.J. (2000), *Pastoral Care Today: practice, problems and priorities in churches today*, CWR, Farnham.
Francis, L.J. (2002), 'Personality Theory and Empirical Theology', *Journal of Empirical Theology*, vol. 15, pp.37-53.
Francis, L.J. (2004), 'The Francis Psychological Type Scales (FPTS): Internal Consistency, Reliability and Relationship with the MBTI', In press.
Francis, L.J. and Astley, J. (1996), 'Personality and Prayer among Adult Churchgoers: a Replication', *Social Behaviour and Personality*, vol. 24, pp.405-408.

Francis, L.J. and Bolger, J. (1997), 'Personality, Prayer and Church Attendance in Later Life,' *Social Behaviour and Personality*, vol. 25, pp.335-338.

Francis, L.J., Brown, L.B., Lester, D. and Philipchalk, R. (1998), 'Happiness as Stable Extraversion: a Cross-cultural Examination of the Reliability and Validity of the Oxford Happiness Inventory among Students in the UK, USA, Australia and Canada', *Personality and Individual Differences*, vol. 24, pp.167-171.

Francis, L.J. and Daniel, E.D. (1997), 'Personality and Prayer among Churchgoing Methodists in England', *Journal of Beliefs and Values*, vol. 18, pp.235-237.

Francis, L.J. and Jones, S.H. (1997), 'Personality and Charismatic Experience among Adult Christians', *Pastoral Psychology*, vol. 45, pp.421-428.

Francis, L.J., Jones, S.H. and Martineau. J. (1996), 'Personality and Religion: Who goes to Church for Fun?' *Irish Journal of Psychology*, vol. 17, pp.71-74.

Francis, L.J., Jones, S.H. and Wilcox, C. (1997), 'Religiosity and Dimensions of Psychological Well-being among 16-19 year olds', *Journal of Christian Education*, vol. 40, pp.15-20.

Francis, L.J., Jones, S.H. and Wilcox, C. (2000), 'Religiosity and Happiness: during Adolescence, Young Adulthood and Later Life', *Journal of Psychology and Christianity*, vol. 19, pp.245-257.

Francis, L.J., Kaldor, P., Shevlin, M. and Lewis, C.A. (2004), 'Assessing Emotional Exhaustion among the Australian Clergy: Internal Reliability and Construct Validity of the Scale of Emotional Exhaustion in Ministry (SEEM)', *Review of Religious Research*, vol. 45, pp.269-277.

Francis, L.J. and Katz, Y.J. (1992), 'The Relationship between Personality and Religiosity in an Israeli Sample', *Journal for the Scientific Study of Religion*, vol. 31, pp.153-162.

Francis, L.J. and Kay, W.K. (1995), 'The Personality Characteristics of Pentecostal Ministry Candidates', *Personality and Individual Differences*, vol. 18, pp.581-594.

Francis, L.J. and Lankshear, D.W. (1990), 'The Impact of Church Schools on Village Church Life', *Educational Studies*, vol. 16, pp.117-129.

Francis, L.J. and Lankshear, D.W. (1991a), *Continuing in the Way: children, young people and the Church*, National Society, London.

Francis, L.J. and Lankshear, D.W. (1991c), 'Do Small Churches hold a Future for Children and Young People?' *Modern Churchman*, vol. 33, pp.15-19.

Francis, L.J. and Lankshear, D.W. (1992d), 'The Catholic Evangelical Consensus: a Study on the Attitudes of the Laity', *Contact*, vol. 108, pp.17-22.

Francis, L.J. and Lankshear, D.W. (1995b), *In the Catholic Way: children, young people and the Church in catholic parishes of the Church of England*, National Society/The Church Union, London.

Francis, L.J. and Lankshear, D.W. (1995c), *In the Evangelical Way: children, young people and the Church in evangelical parishes of the Church of England*, National Society, London.

Francis, L.J. and Lankshear, D.W. (1996), 'The Comparative Strength of Evangelical and Catholic Anglican churches in England', *Journal of Empirical Theology*, vol. 9, pp.5-22.

Francis, L.J., Lankshear, D.W. and Jones, S.H. (1992), *The Church in Wales Clergy Survey*, Trinity College Carmarthen, Carmarthen.

Francis, L.J., Lankshear, D.W. and Jones, S.H. (1998), 'Evangelical Identity among Young People: a Comparative Study in Empirical Theology', *Anvil*, vol. 15, pp.255-269.

Francis, L.J., Lankshear, D.W. and Jones, S.H. (2000), 'The Influence of the Charismatic Movement on Local Church Life: a Comparative Study among Anglican Rural, Urban and Suburban Churches', *Journal of Contemporary Religion*, vol. 15, pp.121-130.

Francis, L.J., Lankshear, D.W. and Pearson, P.R. (1989), 'The Relationship between Religiosity and the Short Form JEPQ (JEPQ-S) Indices of E, N, L and P among Eleven Year Olds', *Personality and Individual Differences*, vol. 10, pp.763-769.

Francis, L.J. and Lester, D. (1997), 'Religion, Personality and Happiness', *Journal of Contemporary Religion*, vol. 12, pp.81-85.

Francis, L.J., Lewis, J.M., Brown, L.B., Philipchalk, R. and Lester, D. (1995), 'Personality and Religion among Undergraduate Students in the United Kingdom, United States, Australia and Canada', *Journal of Psychology and Christianity*, vol. 14, pp.250-262.

Francis, L.J. and Pearson, P.R. (1985a), 'Extraversion and Religiosity', *Journal of Social Psychology*, vol. 125, pp.269-270.

Francis, L.J. and Pearson, P.R. (1985b), 'Psychoticism and Religiosity among 15-year olds', *Personality and Individual Differences*, vol. 6, pp.397-398.

Francis, L.J. and Pearson, P.R. (1988), 'Religiosity and the Short Scale EPQ-R Indices of E, N and L compared with the JEPI, JEPQ and EPQ', *Personality and Individual Differences*, vol. 9, pp.653-657.

Francis, L.J. and Pearson, P.R. (1990), 'Personality Characteristics of Mid-career Anglican Clergy', *Social Behaviour and Personality*, vol. 18, pp.347-350.

Francis, L.J. and Pearson, P.R. (1993), 'The Personality Characteristics of Student Churchgoers', *Personality and Individual Differences*, vol. 15, pp.373-380.

Francis, L.J., Pearson, P.R., Carter, M. and Kay, W.K. (1981), 'Are Introverts more Religious?' *British Journal of Social Psychology*, vol. 20, pp.101-104.

Francis, L.J., Pearson, P.R. and Kay, W.K. (1982), 'Eysenck's Personality Quadrants and Religiosity', *Social Behaviour and Personality*, vol. 21, pp.262-264.

Francis, L.J., Pearson, P.R. and Kay, W.K. (1983b), 'Neuroticism and Religiosity among English School Children', *Journal of Social Psychology*, vol. 114, pp.99-102.

Francis, L.J. and Robbins, M. (1996a), 'A Woman's Voice in a Man's World: Listening to Women Clergy in the Church in Wales before the Vote', *Contemporary Wales*, vol. 9, pp.74-90.

Francis, L.J. and Robbins, M. (1996b), 'Differences in the Personality Profile of Stipendiary and Non-stipendiary Female Anglican Parochial Clergy in Britain and Ireland', *Contact*, vol. 119, pp.26-32.

Francis, L.J. and Robbins, M. (1999), *The Long Diaconate: 1987-1994*, Gracewing, Leominster.

Francis, L.J. and Robbins, M. (2000), 'Religion and Happiness: a Study in Empirical Theology', *Transpersonal Psychology Review*, vol. 4(2), pp.17-21.

Francis, L.J. and Robbins, M. (2004), *Personality and the Practice of Ministry: a study in empirical theology*, Grove Books, Cambridge.

Francis, L.J. and Rodger, R. (1994), 'The Influence of Personality on Clergy Role Prioritisation, Role Influences, Conflict and Dissatisfaction with Ministry', *Personality and Individual Differences*, vol. 16, pp.947-957.

Francis, L.J. and Stubbs, M.T. (1987), 'Measuring Attitudes towards Christianity: from Childhood to Adulthood', *Personality and Individual Differences*, vol. 8, pp.741-743.

Francis, L.J. and Thomas, T.H. (1992), 'Personality Profile of Conference-going Clergy in England', *Psychological Reports*, vol. 70, p.682.

Francis, L.J. and Thomas, T.H. (1996a), 'Are Anglo Catholic Priests more Feminine: a Study among Male Anglican Clergy', *Pastoral Sciences*, vol. 15, pp.15-22.

Francis, L.J. and Thomas, T.H. (1996b), 'Mystical Orientation and Personality among Anglican Clergy', *Pastoral Psychology*, vol. 45, pp.99-105.

Francis, L.J. and Thomas, T.H. (1997), 'Are Charismatic Ministers more Stable? A Study among Male Anglican Clergy', *Review of Religious Research*, vol. 39, pp.61-69.

Francis, L.J. and Wilcox, C. (1993), 'Personality, Prayer and Church Attendance among 16- to 18-year old Girls in England', *Journal of Social Psychology*, vol. 134, pp.243-246.

Francis, L.J. and Wilcox, C. (1996), 'Religion and Gender Orientation', *Personality and Individual Differences*, vol. 20, pp.119-121.

Francis, L.J. and Wilcox, C. (1998a), 'The Relationship between Eysenck's Personality Dimensions and Bem's Masculinity and Femininity Scales Revisited', *Personality and Individual Differences*, vol. 25, pp.683-687.

Francis, L.J. and Wilcox, C. (1998b), 'Religiosity and Femininity: do Women really Hold a More Positive Attitude toward Christianity?' *Journal for the Scientific Study of Religion*, vol. 37, pp.462-469.

Freud, S. (1950), *Totem and Taboo*, Routledge and Kegan Paul, London.

Freudenberger, H.J. (1974), 'Staff Burn-out', *Journal of Social Issues*, vol. 30, pp.159-165.

Freudenberger, H.J. (1975), 'The Staff Burn-out Syndrome in Alternative Institutions', *Psychotherapy: Theory, Research and Practice*, vol. 12, pp.73-82.

Fuller, R.H. (1986), 'The Classical High Church Reaction to the Tractarians', in G. Rowell (ed.), *Tradition Renewed: the Oxford Movement Conference papers*, Darton, Longman and Todd, London, pp.51-63.

Furlong, M. (ed.) (1984), *Feminine in the Church*, SPCK, London.

Furlong, M. (1991), *A Dangerous Delight: women and power in the church*, SPCK, London.

Furnham, A. (1981), 'Personality and Activity Preference', *British Journal of Social Psychology*, vol. 20, pp.57-68.

Furnham, A. (1996), *All in the Mind: the essence of psychology*, Whurr Publishers, London.

Furnham, A. and Brewin, C.R. (1990), 'Personality and Happiness', *Personality and Individual Differences*, vol. 11, pp.1093-1096.

Garden, A-M, (1989), 'Burnout: the Effect of Psychological Type on Research Findings', *Journal of Occupational Psychology*, vol. 62, pp.223-234.

Garnham, N. (2001), 'Both Praying and Playing: "Muscular Christianity" and the YMCA in north-east County Durham', *Journal of Social History*, vol. 35, pp.397-407.

Ghiselli, E.E. (1955), *The Measurement of Occupational Aptitude*, University of California Press, Berkeley, CA.

Gibson, H.M. (1994), 'Adolescents' Images of God', *Panorama*, vol. 6, pp.105-114.

Gibson, P. (1979), 'A Partisan Appeal for a Liberal Mission', *Theology*, vol. 72, pp.163-169.

Gibson, W. (1994), *Church, State and Society 1760-1850*, Macmillan, London.

Gill, J.J. (1980), 'Burnout – a Growing Threat in Ministry', *Human Development*, vol. 1, pp.65-71.

Gillings, V. and Joseph, S. (1996), 'Religiosity and Social Desirability: Impression Management and Self-deceptive Positivity', *Personality and Individual Differences*, vol. 21, pp.1047-1050.

Glock, C.Y., Ringer, B.B. and Babbie, E.R. (1967), *To Comfort and to Challenge*, University of California Press, Berkeley, CA.

Glowinkowski, S.P. and Cooper, C.L. (1985), 'Current Issues in Organizational Stress Research', *Bulletin of the British Psychological Society*, vol. 39, pp.205-210.

Goktepe, J. and Schneier, C. (1988), 'Sex and Gender Effects in Evaluating Emergent Leaders in Small Groups', *Sex Roles*, vol. 19, pp.29-36.

Goktepe, J. and Schneier, C. (1989), 'Role of Sex, Gender Roles and Attraction in Predicting Emergent Leaders', *Journal of Applied Psychology*, vol. 74, pp.165-167.

Gold, Y. (1984), 'The Factorial Validity of the Maslach Burnout Inventory in a Sample of California Elementary and Junior High School Classroom Teachers', *Educational and Psychological Measurement*, vol. 44, pp.1009-1016.

Gold, Y. (1985), 'The Relationship of Six Personal and Life History Variables to Standing on Three Dimensions of the Maslach Burnout Inventory in a Sample of Elementary and Junior High School Teachers', *Educational and Psychological Measurement*, vol. 45, pp.377-387.
Goldie, M. (1996), 'The Search for Religious Liberty 1640-1690', in J. Morrill (ed.), *The Oxford Illustrated History of Tudor and Stuart Britain*, OUP, Oxford, pp.293-309.
Goldingay, J. (1996), 'Charismatic Spirituality: some Theological Reflections', *Theology*, vol. 99, pp.178-187.
Goldsmith, M. (1994), *Knowing me, Knowing God*, Triangle, London.
Goldsmith, W.M. and Ekhardt, B.N. (1984), 'Personality Factors of Men and Women Pastoral Candidates: Part 2, Sex Role Preferences', *Journal of Psychology and Theology*, vol. 12, pp.211-221.
Golembiewski, R.T., Munzenrider, R. and Carter, D. (1983), 'Phases of Progressive Burnout and their Work Site Covariants: Critical Issues in OD Research and Praxis', *Journal of Applied Behavioural Science*, vol. 19, pp.461-481.
Golner, F.H., Terence, T. and Ritti, R. (1973), 'Priests and Laity: a Profession in Transition', *Sociological Review Monographs*, vol. 20, pp.119-137.
Goodhew, D. (2003), 'The Rise of the Cambridge Inter-Collegiate Christian Union, 1910-1971', *Journal of Ecclesiastical History*, vol. 54, pp.62-88.
Gorsuch, R.L. (1988), 'Psychology of Religion', *Annual Review of Psychology*, vol. 39, pp.201-221.
Gray, J.A. (1972), 'The Psychophysiological Basis of Introversion-extraversion: a Modification of Eysenck's Theory', in V.D. Nebylitsyn and J.A. Gray (eds), *The Biological Basis of Individual Behaviour*, The Academic Press, New York, pp.185-205.
Greeley, A. (1992), 'Religion in Britain, Ireland and the USA', in R. Jowell, L. Brook, G. Prior and B. Taylor (eds), *British Social Attitudes: the 9th report*, Dartmouth Publishers, Aldershot.
Green, D.E. and Walkey, F.H. (1988), 'A Confirmation of the Three-factor Structure of the Maslach Burnout Inventory', *Educational and Psychological Measurement*, vol. 41, pp.579-585.
Green, D.E., Walkey, F.H. and Taylor, A.J.W. (1991), 'The Three-factor Structure of the Maslach Burnout Inventory: a Multicultural, Multinational Confirmatory Study', *Journal of Social Behaviour and Personality*, vol. 6, pp.453-472.
Greene, G. (1961), *A Burnt-Out Case*, Penguin, London.
Greenglass, E.R., Burke, R.J. and Ondrack, M. (1990), 'A Gender-role Perspective of Coping and Burnout', *Applied Psychology: An International Review*, vol. 39, pp.5-27.
Gross, P.R. (1989), 'Stress and Burnout in Ministry: a Multivariate Approach', *Lutheran Theological Journal*, vol. 23, pp.27-31.
Gryskiewicz, N. and Buttner, E.H. (1992), 'Testing the Robustness of the Progressive Phase Burnout Model for a Sample of Entrepreneurs', *Educational and Psychological Measurement*, vol. 52, pp.747-751.
Gunstone, J. (1968), 'Catholics in the Church of England', in J. Wilkinson (ed.), *Catholic Anglicans Today*, Darton, Longman and Todd, London, pp.183-204.
Gunstone, J. (1982), *Pentecostal Anglicans*, Hodder and Stoughton, London.
Gurin, G., Veroff, J. and Feld, S. (1960), *Americans View their Mental Health*, Basic Books, New York.
Hadaway, C. and Roof, W. (1978), 'Religious Commitment and the Quality of Life in American Society', *Review of Religious Research*, vol. 19, pp. 295-307.
Haig, A. (1984), *The Victorian Clergy*, Croom Helm, London.
Hannaford, R. (2000), 'The Legacy of Liberal Anglican Theology', *Theology*, vol. 103, pp.89-96.

Happold, F.C. (1963), *Mysticism: a study and an anthology*, Pelican, Harmondsworth.
Harding, S.D. (1982), 'Psychological Well-being in Great Britain: an Evaluation of the Bradburn Affect Balance Scale', *Personality and Individual Differences*, vol. 3, pp.167-175.
Harel, I. and Papert, S. (eds) (1991), *Constructionism*, Ablex, Norwood, NJ.
Harper, M. (1965), *As at the Beginning*, Hodder and Stoughton, London.
Harris, T. (1995), *Popular Culture in England 1500-1850*, Macmillan, London.
Harrison, J. (1983), *Attitudes to Bible, God, Church*, Bible Society, London.
Hastings, A. (1986), *A History of English Christianity 1920-1985*, Collins, London.
Headey, B., Glowacki, T., Holmstrom, E. and Wearing, A. (1985), 'Modelling Change in Perceived Quality of Life', *Social Indicators Research*, vol. 17, pp.276-298.
Heaven, P.C.L. (1990), 'Religious Values and Personality Dimensions', *Personality and Individual Differences*, vol. 11, pp.953-956.
Hebert, A.G. (1957), *Fundamentalism and the Church of God*, SCM, London.
Heeney, B. (1976), *A Different Kind of Gentleman: parish clergy as professional men in early and mid-Victorian England*, Archon Books, Connecticut.
Heerboth, J.R. and Ramanaiah, N.V. (1985), 'Evaluation of the BSRI Masculine and Feminine Items using Desirability and Stereotype Ratings', *Journal of Personality Assessment*, vol. 49, pp.264-270.
Heise, D.R. (1984), 'The Semantic Differential and Attitude Research', in G.F. Summers (ed.), *Attitude Measurement*, Rand McNally, Chicago, pp.235-253.
Herbert, T.D. (1988), *The nature and purpose of the stipendiary ministry in the Church of England*, Unpublished MPhil dissertation, University of Manchester.
Hick, J. (ed.) (1977), *The Myth of God Incarnate*, SCM, London.
Hickin, L. (1968), 'Liberal Evangelicals in the Church of England', *Church Quarterly Review*, vol. 169, pp.43-54.
Hilliard, D. (1982), 'UnEnglish and Unmanly: Anglo-Catholicism and Homosexuality', *Victorian Studies*, vol. 25, pp.181-210.
Hills, P. and Argyle, M. (1998a), 'Positive Moods derived from Leisure and their Relationship to Happiness and Personality', *Personality and Individual Differences*, vol. 25, pp.523-535.
Hills, P. and Argyle, M. (1998b), 'Musical and Religious Experiences and their Relationship to Happiness', *Personality and Individual Differences*, vol. 25, pp.91-102.
Hinings, C.R. and Foster, B.D. (1973), 'The Organization Structure of Churches: a Preliminary Model', *Sociology*, vol. 7, pp.93-106.
Hocken, P. (1975), 'Charismatics and Mystics', *Theological Renewal*, vol. 1, pp.11-17.
Hodge, F.V. (1986), *A Handbook for the Newly Ordained and Other Clergy*, Mowbray, Oxford.
Hodge, M. (1988), *Patterns of Ministerial Training*, ACCM, London.
Hollenweger, W. (1992), 'The Critical Tradition of Pentecostalism', *Journal of Pentecostal Theology*, vol. 1, pp.10-25.
Holloway, D. (1993), *The Background to, and Need for Reform*, Privately published paper for Reform.
Holme, I., Helgeland, A., Hjerman, I., Leren, P. and Lund-Larsen, P.G. (1977), 'Coronary Risk Factors in Various Occupational Groups: the Oslo Study', *British Journal of Preventative and Social Medicine*, vol. 31, pp.96-100.
Hopkins, B. (ed.) (1992), *Planting New Churches*, Eagle, Guildford.
Hopkins, H.E. (1977), *Charles Simeon of Cambridge*, Hodder and Stoughton, London.
Hopkinson, W.H. (1983), *Changing emphasis in self-identity amongst Evangelicals in the Church of England*, Unpublished MPhil dissertation, University of Nottingham.

Hough, J.C. and Cobb, J.B. (1985), *Christian Identity and Theological Education*, Scholars Press, Chico, CA.
Hughes, A. (1961), *The Rivers of the Flood*, Faith Press, London.
Hummel, C. (1993), *Fire in the Fireplace*, IVP, London.
Hylson-Smith, K. (1989), *Evangelicals in the Church of England 1734-1984*, T. and T. Clark, Edinburgh.
Hylson-Smith, K. (1993), *High Churchmanship in the Church of England*, T. and T. Clark, Edinburgh.
Iannaccone, L.R. (1990), 'Religious Practice: a Human Capital Approach', *Journal for the Scientific Study of Religion*, vol. 29, pp.297-314.
Iwanicki, E.F. and Schwab, R.L. (1981), 'A Cross Validation Study of the Maslach Burnout Inventory', *Educational and Psychological Measurement*, vol. 41, pp.1167-1174.
Jackson, D.N. (1974), *Personality Research Form Manual*, Research Psychologists, Goshen, NY.
Jagger, P.J. (1978), *A History of the Parish and People Movement*, Faith Press, Leighton Buzzard.
Jarvis, P. (1975), 'The Parish Ministry as a Semi-profession', *Sociological Review*, vol. 23, pp.911-922.
Jarvis, P. (1976), 'A Profession in Process: a Theoretical Model for the Ministry', *Sociological Review*, vol. 24, pp.351-364.
Jay, E. (ed.) (1983), *The Evangelical and Oxford Movements*, CUP, Cambridge.
Jenkins, G.H. (1987), *The Foundations of Modern Wales 1642-1780*, OUP, Oxford.
John, J. (1995), *What is Affirming Catholicism?* Darton, Longman and Todd, London.
Jones, D.L. and Francis, L.J. (1992), 'Personality Profile of Methodist Ministers in England', *Psychological Reports*, vol. 70, p.538.
Jones, J.R. (1972), *The Revolution of 1688 in England*, Weidenfeld and Nicolson, London.
Jones, S.H. and Francis, L.J. (1997), 'The Fate of the Welsh Clergy: an Attitude Survey among Male Clerics in the Church in Wales', *Contemporary Wales*, vol. 10, pp.182-199.
Jud, G.J., Mills, E.W. and Burch, G.W. (1970), *Ex-pastors: why men leave the parish ministry*, Pilgrim Press, Philadelphia.
Kafai, Y.B. and Resnick, M. (eds) (1996), *Constructionism in Practice: designing, thinking and learning in a digital world*, Lawrence Erlbaum, Mahwah, NJ.
Kammer, A. (1978), 'Burn-out – a Dilemma for the Jesuit Social Activist', *Studies in the Spirituality of Jesuits*, vol. 10(1).
Katz, D. and Braly, K.W. (1933), 'Racial Prejudice and Racial Stereotypes', *Journal of Abnormal and Social Psychology*, vol. 30, pp.175-193.
Kay, W.K. (1981), 'Psychoticism and Attitude to Religion', *Personality and Individual Differences*, vol. 2, pp.249-252.
Kay, W.K. (2000), *Pentecostals in Britain*, Paternoster, Carlisle.
Killick, F. and Peirce, J. (1997), 'Working towards Gender Equality: Exploring an Appropriate Methodology', *British Journal of Theological Education*, vol. 9, pp.9-16.
Kimlicka, T.A., Sheppard, J.M., Sheppard, P.L. and Wakefield, J.A. (1988), 'The Relationship between Eysenck's Personality Dimensions and Bem's Masculinity and Femininity Scales', *Personality and Individual Differences*, vol. 9, pp.833-835.
King, H. and Bailar, J.C. (1969), 'The Health of the Clergy: a Review of Demographic Literature', *Demography*, vol. 6, pp.27-43.
King, J. (1969), *The Evangelicals*, Hodder and Stoughton, London.
Kings, G. (2003), 'Canal, River and Rapids: contemporary Evangelicalism in the Church of England', *Anvil*, vol. 20, pp.167-179.
Kirkcaldy, B., Thome, E. and Thomas, W. (1989), 'Job Satisfaction among Psychosocial Workers', *Personality and Individual Differences*, vol. 10, pp.191-196.

Kirkpatrick, L.A. and Hood, R.W. (1990), 'Intrinsic-extrinsic Religious Orientation: the Boon or Bane of Contemporary Psychology of Religion', *Journal for the Scientific Study of Religion*, vol. 29, pp.442-462.

Kline, P. (1993), *Personality: the psychometric view*, Routledge, London.

Knight, F. (1995), *The Nineteenth Century Church and English Society*, CUP, Cambridge.

Knight, F. (1996), 'The Influence of the Oxford Movement in the Parish 1833-1860: a Reassessment', in P. Vaiss (ed.), *From Oxford to the People: reconsidering Newman and the Oxford Movement*, Gracewing, Leominster, pp.127-140.

Komarovsky, M. (1950), 'Functional Analysis of Sex Roles', *American Sociological Review*, vol. 15, pp.508-516.

Ladd, T. and Mathisen, J.A. (2002), *Muscular Christianity: Evangelical Protestants and the development of American Sports*, Baker Books, Grand Rapids, MI.

Larsen, R.J. and Diener, E. (1987), 'Affect Intensity as an Individual Difference Characteristic: a Review', *Journal of Research in Personality*, vol. 21, pp.1-39.

Lauer, R.H. (1973), 'Organisational Punishment: Punitive Relations in a Voluntary Association: a Minister in a Protestant Church', *Human Relations*, vol. 26, pp.189-202.

Lee, R.T. and Ashforth, B.E. (1990), 'On the Meaning of Maslach's Three Dimensions of Burnout', *Journal of Applied Psychology*, vol. 75, pp.743-747.

Leech, K. (1977), *Soul Friend*, Sheldon Press, London.

Lenski, G.E. (1953), 'Social Correlates of Religious Interest', *American Sociological Review*, vol. 18, pp.533-544.

Levin, J.S. (1994), 'Religion and Health: is there an Association, is it Valid, and is it Causal?' *Social Science and Medicine*, vol. 38, pp.1475-1482.

Lewis, C.A. (1998), 'Towards a Clarification of the Association between Religiosity and Life Satisfaction', *Journal of Beliefs and Values*, vol. 19, pp.119-122.

Lewis, C.A., Joseph, S. and Noble, K.E. (1996), 'Is Religiosity associated with Life Satisfaction?' *Psychological Reports*, vol. 79, pp.429-430.

Lewis, C.A., Lanigan, C., Joseph, S. and de Fockert, J. (1997). 'Religiosity and Happiness: No Evidence for an Association among Undergraduates', *Personality and Individual Differences*, vol. 22, pp.119-121.

Lewis, C.A. and Maltby, J. (1995), 'Religiosity and Personality among USA Adults', *Personality and Individual Differences*, vol. 18, pp.293-295.

Lewis, C.A. and Maltby, J. (1996), 'Personality, Prayer and Church Attendance in a Sample of College Students in the USA', *Psychological Reports*, vol. 78, pp.1-3.

Liller, K.D. and McDermott, R.J. (1990), 'An Exploratory Study of Occupational Burnout among Selected Health Educators', *Health Education*, vol. 21, pp.36-40.

Lippa, R.A. (1995), 'Gender-related Individual Differences and Psychological Adjustment in terms of the Big Five and Circumplex Models', *Journal of Personal and Social Psychology*, vol. 69, pp.1184-1202.

Lithgow, J. (1983), *Modernists and Radicals*, Unpublished MA dissertation, University of Wales Lampeter.

Lloyd, R. (1966), *The Church of England 1900-1965*, SCM Press, London.

Lodhi, P.H. and Thomas, G. (1991), 'Effects of Experimentally Induced Response in Assessing Eysenckian Dimensions of Personality', *Personality and Individual Differences*, vol. 12, pp.811-817.

Louden, S.H. (1998), *The Greying of the Clergy: an assessment of role, stress, burnout and personality among Roman Catholic parish clergy in England and Wales*, Unpublished PhD dissertation, University of Wales, Trinity College Carmarthen.

Louden, S.H. and Francis, L.J. (1999), 'The Personality Profile of Roman Catholic Parochial Secular Priests in England and Wales', *Review of Religious Research*, vol. 41, pp.65-79.

Louden, S.H. and Francis, L.J. (2003), *The Naked Parish Priest: what priests really think they're doing*, Continuum, London.
Lu, L. (1999), 'Personal or Environmental Causes of Happiness: a Longitudinal Analysis', *Journal of Social Psychology*, vol. 139, pp.79-90.
Lu, L. and Argyle, M. (1991), 'Happiness and Cooperation', *Personality and Individual Differences*, vol. 12, pp.1019-1030.
Lu, L. and Argyle, M. (1992), 'Receiving and Giving Support: Effects on Relationships and Well-being', *Counselling Psychology Quarterly*, vol. 5, pp.123-133.
Lu, L. and Argyle, M. (1993), 'TV Watching, Soap Opera and Happiness', *Kaohsiung Journal of Medical Sciences*, vol. 9, pp.501-507.
Lu, L. and Argyle, M. (1994), 'Leisure Satisfaction and Happiness: a Function of Leisure Activity', *Kaohsiung Journal of Medical Sciences*, vol. 10, pp.89-96.
Lu, L. and Shih, J.B. (1997), 'Sources of Happiness: a Qualitative Approach', *Journal of Social Psychology*, vol. 137, pp.181-187.
Lucas, R.E., Diener, E. and Suh, E. (1996), 'Discriminant Validity of Well-being Measures', *Journal of Personality and Social Psychology*, vol. 71, pp.616-628.
Luckman, T. (1967), *The Invisible Religion*, Macmillan, New York.
McCarthy, P. (1985), 'Burnout in Psychiatric Nursing', *Journal of Advanced Nursing*, vol. 10, pp.305-310.
Maccoby, E. and Jacklin, C. (1974), *The Psychology of Sex Differences*, Stanford University Press, Stanford, CA.
McCrae, R.R. and Costa, P.T. (1988), 'Psychological Resilience among Widowed Men and Women: a 10-year Follow-up of a National Sample', *Journal of Social Issues*, vol. 44, pp.129-142.
McGrath, A.E. (1993), *The Renewal of Anglicanism*, SPCK, London.
McGreal, R. and Joseph, S. (1993), 'The Depression-Happiness Scale', *Psychological Reports*, vol. 73, pp.1279-1282.
McIntosh, D.N., Silver, R.C. and Westman, C.B. (1993), 'Religion's Role in Adjustment to a Negative Life Event: Coping with Loss of a Child', *Journal of Personality and Social Psychology*, vol. 65, pp.812-821.
McKennell, A.C. and Andrews, F.M. (1980), 'Models of Cognition and Affect in Perception of Well-being', *Social Indicators Research*, vol. 8, pp.257-298.
Machlowitz, M. (1980), *Workaholics: living with them, working with them*, Addison-Wesley, Reading.
Magnus, K.B., Diener, E., Fujita, F. and Pavot, W. (1993), 'Extraversion and Neuroticism as Predictors of Objective Life Events: a Longitudinal Analysis', *Journal of Personality and Social Psychology*, vol. 65, pp.316-330.
Major, H.D.A. (1927), *English Modernism: its origin, methods, aims*, Harvard University Press, Cambridge, MA.
Malony, H.N. and Hunt, R.A. (1991), *The Psychology of Clergy*, Morehouse Publishing, Harrisburg, PA.
Maltby, J. (1995), 'Personality, Prayer and Church Attendance among US Female Adults', *Journal of Social Psychology*, vol. 135, pp.529-531.
Maltby, J. (1997), 'Personality Correlates of Religiosity among Adults in the Republic of Ireland', *Psychological Reports*, vol. 81, pp.827-831.
Maltby, J. and Lewis, C.A. (1996), 'Measuring Intrinsic and Extrinsic Orientation towards Religion: Amendments for its Use among Religious and Non-religious Samples', *Personality and Individual Differences*, vol. 21, pp.937-946.
Maltby, J., Talley, M., Cooper, C. and Leslie, J. (1995), 'Personality Effects in Personal and Public Orientations toward Religion', *Personality and Individual Differences*, vol. 19, pp.157-163.

Manlove, E.E. (1993), 'Multiple Correlates of Burnout in Child Care Workers', *Early Childhood Research Quarterly*, vol. 8, pp.499-518.
Manwaring, R. (1985), *From Controversy to Co-existence: Evangelicals in the Church of England 1914-1980*, CUP, Cambridge.
Marshall, J. (1980), 'Pansies, Perverts and Macho Men: Changing Conceptions of Male Homosexuality', in K. Plummer (ed.), *The Making of the Modern Homosexual*, Hutchinson, London, pp.133-154.
Martin, D.W. (1967), *A Sociology of English Religion*, SCM, London.
Martin, D.W. (1978), *A General Theory of Secularisation*, Basil Blackwell, Oxford.
Martin, D.W. and Mullen, P. (eds) (1981), *No Alternative: the Prayer Book controversy*, Basil Blackwell, Oxford.
Martin, D.W. and Mullen, P. (eds) (1984), *Strange Gifts: a guide to charismatic renewal*, Blackwell, Oxford.
Martin, M. and Clark, D.M. (1985), 'Cognitive Mediation of Depressed Mood and Neuroticism', *IRCS Medical Science*, vol. 13, pp.252-253.
Maslach, C. (1973), 'Detached Concern in Health and Social Service Professions', Paper presented at the annual meeting of the American Psychological Association, Montreal.
Maslach, C. (1976), 'Burned-out', *Human Behaviour*, vol. 5, pp.16-22.
Maslach, C. (1978a), 'Job Burn-out: how People Cope', *Public Welfare*, vol. 36, pp.56-58.
Maslach, C. and Jackson, S.E. (1981), *Maslach Burnout Inventory*, Consulting Psychologists Press, Palo Alto, CA.
Maslach, C. and Jackson, S.E. (1985), 'The Role of Sex and Family Variables in Burnout', *Sex Roles*, vol. 12, pp.837-851.
Maslach, C. and Jackson, S.E. (1986), *Maslach Burnout Inventory (second edition)*, Consulting Psychologists Press, Palo Alto, CA.
Maslach, C. and Pines, A. (1977), 'The Burn-out Syndrome in the Day Care Setting', *Child Care Quarterly*, vol. 6, pp.100-113.
Maton, K.I. (1989), 'The Stress-buffering Role of Spiritual Support: Cross-cultural and Prospective Investigations', *Journal for the Scientific Study of Religion*, vol. 28, pp.310-323.
Matthews, D.B. (1990), 'A Comparison of Burnout in Selected Occupational Fields', *Career Development Quarterly*, vol. 38, pp.230-239.
Matthews, G and Deary, I.J. (1998), *Personality Traits*, CUP, Cambridge.
Mayfield, G. (1965), *Like Nothing on Earth*, Darton, Longman and Todd, London.
Meier, S.T. (1984), 'The Construct Validity of Burnout', *Journal of Occupational Psychology*, vol. 57, pp.211-219.
Melinsky, M.A.H. (1992), *The Shape of the Ministry*, The Canterbury Press, Norwich.
Miller, J. (1973), *Popery and Politics in England 1660-1688*, CUP, Cambridge.
Mischel, W. (1993), *Introduction to Personality*, Harcourt Brace Jovanovich, Orlando, FL.
Moberg, D.O. (1962), *The Church as a Social Institution*, Prentice-Hall, Englewood Cliffs, NJ.
Mol, H. (1985), *The Faith of Australians*, George Allen and Unwin, Sydney.
Moore, P. (ed.) (1978), *Man, Woman and Priesthood*, SPCK, London.
Morgan, C. (1978), 'To Renew the Human Face of the Earth', *Theological Renewal*, vol. 10, pp.14-23.
Morris, J.(1991), *Women in Early Christian Priesthood*, Christian Women's Resource Centre/St Joan's International Alliance.
Morrison, T., Greene, L. and Tischler, N. (1985), 'Manifestations of Splitting in the Large Group', *Journal of Social Psychology*, vol. 125, pp.601-611.
Moses, J. (1995), *A Broad and Living Way: Church and State a continuing Establishment*, The Canterbury Press, London.

Myers, I.B. and McCaulley, M.H. (1985), *Manual: a guide to the development and use of the Myers-Briggs Type Indicator*, Consulting Psychologists Press, Palo Alto, CA.

Myers, D.G. and Diener, E. (1995), 'Who is Happy?' *Psychological Science*, vol. 6, pp.10-19.

Myers, I.B. (1980), *Gifts Differing*, Consulting Psychologists Press, Palo Alto, CA.

Nagoshi, C.T., Pitts, S.C. and Nakata, T. (1993), 'Intercorrelation of Attitudes, Personality and Sex Role Orientation in a College Sample', *Personality and Individual Differences*, vol. 14, pp.603-604.

Nauss, A.H. (1973), 'The Ministerial Personality: Myth or Reality?' *Journal of Religion and Health*, vol. 12, pp.77-96.

Neill, S. (1958), *Anglicanism*, Penguin Books, Harmondsworth.

Nelsen, H.M., Cheek, N.H. and Au, P. (1985), 'Gender Differences in Images of God', *Journal for the Scientific Study of Religion*, vol. 24, pp.396-402.

Nelsen, H.M. and Nelsen, A.K. (1975), *Black Church in the Sixties*, University Press of Kentucky, Lexington, KY.

Nelsen, H.M. and Potvin, R.H. (1981), 'Gender and Regional Differences in the Religiosity of Protestant Adolescents', *Review of Religious Research*, vol. 22, pp.268-285.

Newbigin, L. (1952), *The Household of God*, SCM Press, London.

Newby, H. (1988), *The Countryside in Question*, Hutchinson, London.

Niebuhr, H.R. (1959), *The Kingdom of God in America*, Harper Torchbooks, New York.

Nockles, P. (1994), *The Oxford Movement in Context: Anglican High Churchmanship 1760-1857*, CUP, Cambridge.

Noor, N.M. (1993), *Work and Family Roles in relation to Women's Well-being*, Unpublished DPhil dissertation, University of Oxford.

Nye, J., and Forsyth, D. (1991), 'The Effects of Prototype-based Biases on Leadership Appraisals: a Test of Leadership Categorisation Theory', *Small Group Research*, vol. 22, pp.360-379.

Okun, M.A. and George, L.K. (1984), 'Physician- and Self-ratings of Health, Neuroticism and Subjective Well-being among Men and Women', *Personality and Individual Differences*, vol. 5, pp.533-539.

O'Reilly, C.T. (1957), 'Religious Practice and Personal Adjustment of Older People', *Sociology and Social Research*, vol. 42, pp.119-121.

Orchard, A. and Francis, L.J. (1998), 'Neuroticism and Strength of Religious Attitudes among Churchgoers in England', *Journal of Beliefs and Values*, vol. 19, pp.231-236.

Osgood, C.E. (1952), 'The Nature and Measurement of Meaning', *Psychological Bulletin*, vol. 49, pp.197-237.

Osgood, C.E., Suci, G. and Tannenbaum, P. (1957), *The Measurement of Meaning*, University of Illinois Press, Urbana, IL.

Oswald, R.M. (1980), *Crossing the Boundary between Seminary and Parish*, Alban Institute, Washington, DC.

Otranto, G. (1991), 'Notes on the Female Priesthood in Antiquity', *Journal of Feminist Studies in Religion*, vol. 7, pp.78-93.

Owen, C. (ed.) (1990), *Reforming Infant Baptism*, Hodder and Stoughton, Dunton Green.

Packer, J.I. (1959), *'Fundamentalism' and the Word of God*, IVF, London.

Packer, J.I. (1978), *The Evangelical Anglican Identity Problem*, Latimer House, Oxford.

Page, R.J. (1965), *New Directions in Anglican Theology*, Mowbray, London.

Park, C., Cohen, L.H. and Herb, L. (1990), 'Intrinsic Religiousness and Religious Coping as Life Stress Moderators for Catholics versus Protestants', *Journal of Personality and Social Psychology*, vol. 59, pp.562-574.

Patterson, W.B. (1997), *King James VI and I and the Reunion of Christendom*, CUP, Cambridge.

Paul, L. (1964), *The Deployment and Payment of the Clergy*, CIO, London.
Paul, L. (1973), *A Church by Daylight*, Hodder and Stoughton, London.
Pavot, W. and Diener, E. (1993), 'Review of the Satisfaction With Life Scale', *Psychological Assessment*, vol. 5, pp.164-172.
Penhale, F. (1986), *The Anglican Church Today: Catholics in crisis*, Mowbray, London.
Penn, R., Rose, M. and Rubery, J (eds)(1994), *Skill and Occupational Change*, OUP, Oxford.
Percy, M.W. (1993), *Signs, Wonders and Church Growth: the theme of power in contemporary Christian fundamentalism with special reference to the works of John Wimber*, Unpublished PhD dissertation, University of London.
Percy, M.W. (1998), *Power and the Church: ecclesiology in an age of transition*, Cassell, London.
Perham, M. (1978), *The Eucharist: Alcuin Club manual 1*, SPCK, London.
Peterson, L. and Roy, A. (1985), 'Religious Anxiety, Meaning and Purpose: Religion's Consequences for Psychological Well-being', *Review of Religious Research*, vol. 27, pp.49-62.
Petre, J. (1994), *By Sex Divided: the Church of England and women priests*, Harper Collins, London.
Pickering, W.S.F. (1989), *Anglo-Catholicism: a study in religious ambiguity*, Routledge, London.
Piedmont, R.L. (1993), 'A Longitudinal Analysis of Burnout in the Health Care Setting: the Role of Personal Dispositions', *Journal of Personality Assessment*, vol. 61, pp.457-473.
Pierce, C.M.B. and Molloy, G.N. (1989), 'The Construct Validity of the Maslach Burnout Inventory: some Data from Down Under', *Psychological Reports*, vol. 65, pp.1340-42.
Podles, L.J. (1999), *The Church Impotent: the femininisation of Christianity*, Spence Publishing Company, Dallas, TX.
Poloma, M.M. and Gallup, G.H. (1991), *Varieties of Prayer: a survey report*, Trinity Press International, Philadelphia.
Powers, S. and Gose, K.F. (1986), 'Reliability and Construct Validity of the Maslach Burnout Inventory in a Sample of University Students', *Educational and Psychological Measurement*, vol. 46, pp.251-255.
Putney, C. (2001), *Muscular Christianity: manhood and sports in Protestant America, 1880-1920*, Harvard University Press, Cambridge, MA.
Quebedeaux, R. (1975), *Charismatic Renewal: the origins, development and significance of neo-Pentecostalism as a religious movement in the United States and Great Britain 1901-1974*, Unpublished DPhil dissertation, University of Oxford.
Rafferty, J.P., Lemkau, J.P., Purdy, R.R. and Rudisill, J.R. (1986), 'Validity of the Maslach Burnout Inventory for Family Practice Physicians', *Journal of Clinical Psychology*, vol. 42, pp.488-492.
Ragins, B. (1991), 'Gender Effects in Subordinate Evaluations of Leaders: Real or Artefact', *Journal of Organizational Behaviour*, vol. 12, pp.259-268.
Ramsey, A.M. (1960), *From Gore to Temple: the development of Anglican theology between 1889 and 1939*, Longman, London.
Ramsey, A.M. (1972), *The Christian Priest Today*, SPCK, London.
Ramsey, A.M., Terwilliger, R.E. and Allchin, A.M. (1974), *The Charismatic Christ*, Darton, Longman and Todd, London.
Randall, K.J. (1997), *The First Year of Ministry: the education, expectation and training of stipendiary curates in the Church of England and the Church in Wales*, Unpublished MPhil dissertation, University of Wales.
Randall, K.J. (2004), 'Burnout as a Predictor of Leaving Anglican Parish Ministry', *Review of Religious Research*, vol. 46, pp.20-26.

Randall, K.J. and Francis, L.J. (1996), 'Clergy Response Rates to Surveys: are they really a Function of Age?' *Psychological Reports*, vol. 79, pp.701-702.
Ranson, S., Bryman, A. and Hinings, B. (1977), *Clergy, Ministers and Priests*, Routledge and Kegan Paul, London.
Rayburn, C.A., Richmond, L.J. and Rogers, L. (1982), 'Women, Men and Religion: Stress within Sanctuary Walls', *Journal of Pastoral Counselling*, vol. 17, pp.75-83.
Rayburn, C.A., Richmond, L.J. and Rogers, L. (1986), 'Men, Women and Religion: Stress within Leadership Roles', *Journal of Clinical Psychology*, vol. 42, pp.540-546.
Reardon, B.M.G. (1971), *From Coleridge to Gore: a century of religious thought in Britain*, Longmans, London.
Reeves, M. (ed.) (1999), *Christian Thinking and Social Order: conviction politics from the 1930s to the present day*, Cassell, London.
Richards, A. (1997), *The Toronto Experience: an exploration of the issues*, Church House Publishing, London
Rim, Y. (1993a), 'Happiness and Coping Styles', *Personality and Individual Differences*, vol. 14, pp.617-618.
Rim, Y. (1993b), 'Values, Happiness and Family Structure Variables', *Personality and Individual Differences*, vol. 15, pp.595-598.
Rizzo, J.R., House, R.J. and Lirtzman, S.I. (1970), 'Role Conflict and Ambiguity in Complex Organizations', *Administrative Science Quarterly*, vol. 15, pp.150-163.
Robbins, M. (1996), *Women in the Church of England: a comparison of stipendiary and non-stipendiary ministry*, Unpublished MPhil dissertation, University of Wales.
Robbins, M. and Francis, L.J. (1996), 'Are Religious People Happier? A Study among Undergraduates', in L.J. Francis, W.K. Kay and W.S. Campbell (eds), *Research in Religious Education*, Gracewing, Leominster, p.207-218.
Robbins, M. and Francis, L.J. (2000), 'Role Prioritization among Clergywomen: the Influence of Personality and Church Tradition among Female Stipendiary Anglican Clerics in the UK', *British Journal of Theological Education*, vol. 11, pp.7-23.
Robbins, M., Francis, L.J. and Rutledge, C. (1997), 'The Personality Characteristics of Anglican Stipendiary Parochial Clergy: Gender Differences Revisited', *Personality and Individual Differences*, vol. 23, pp.199-204.
Robbins, M., Hair, J. and Francis, L.J. (1999), 'Personality and Attraction to the Charismatic Movement: a Study among Anglican Clergy', *Journal of Beliefs and Values*, vol. 20, pp.239-246.
Roberts, D. (1994), *The Toronto Blessing*, Kingsway, Eastbourne.
Robinson, J.A.T. (1963), *Honest to God*, SCM, London.
Robinson, T.N. (1990), 'Eysenck Personality Measures and Religious Orientation', *Personality and Individual Differences*, vol. 11, pp.915-921.
Rose, M. (1999), *Forecasting Job Satisfaction in Britain: what occupational profiling tells us*, Department of Social and Policy Sciences, University of Bath.
Rose, S.D. (1987), 'Women Warriors: the Negotiation of Gender in a Charismatic Community', *Sociological Analysis*, vol. 48, pp.245-258.
Rosenkrantz, P.S., Vogel, S.R., Bee, H., Broverman, I.K. and Broverman, D.M. (1968), 'Sex Role Stereotypes and Self-concepts in College Students', *Journal of Consulting and Clinical Psychology*, vol. 32, pp.287-295.
Rowell, G. (1983), *The Vision Glorious: themes and personalities of the Catholic Revival in Anglicanism*, OUP, Oxford.
Rowell, G. (ed.) (1986), *Tradition Renewed: the Oxford Movement Conference Papers*, Darton, Longman and Todd, London.
Roxborough, J. (1979), 'As at the Beginning in Britain: Michael Harper, Edward Irving and the Catholic Apostolic Church', *Theological Renewal*, vol. 11, pp.17-23.

Runcie, R. (chair) (1970), *A Report of the Commission Appointed by the Archbishops of Canterbury and York to Prepare a Re-organization Scheme for the Theological Colleges*, Church House, London.
Russell, A.J. (1970), *A Sociological Analysis of a Clergyman's Role with special reference to its Development in the Early Nineteenth Century*, Unpublished DPhil dissertation, University of Oxford.
Russell, A.J. (1980), *The Clerical Profession*, SPCK, London.
Russell, A.J. (1986), *The Country Parish*, SPCK, London.
Russell, C. (1990), *The Causes of the English Civil War*, OUP, Oxford.
Russell, C. (1996), 'The Reformation and the Creation of the Church of England', in J. Morrill (ed.), *The Oxford Illustrated History of Tudor and Stuart Britain*, OUP, Oxford, pp.258-292.
Rutledge, C.J.F. (1993), *Parochial Clergy Today: a study of role, personality and burnout among clergy in the Church of England*, Unpublished MPhil dissertation, University of Wales.
Rutledge, C.J.F. (1999), *Exploring Burnout among Male Anglican Parochial Clergy: a function of role and personality?* Unpublished PhD dissertation, University of Wales.
Rutledge, C.J.F. and Francis, L.J. (2004), 'Burnout among Male Anglican Parochial Clergy in England: a Modified Form of the Maslach Burnout Inventory', *Research in the Social Scientific Study of Religion*, Forthcoming.
Ryff, C.D. (1989), 'Happiness is Everything, or is it? Explorations on the Meaning of Psychological Well-being', *Journal of Personality and Social Psychology*, vol. 57, pp.1069-1081.
Ryff, C.D. and Keyes, C.L.M. (1995), 'The Structure of Psychological Well-being Revisited', *Journal of Personality and Social Psychology*, vol. 69, pp.719-727.
Saklofske, D.H. and Eysenck, S.B.G. (1978), 'Cross Cultural Comparison of Personality: New Zealand Children and English Children', *Psychological Reports*, vol. 42, pp.1111-1116.
Sarup, M. (1996), *Identity, Culture and the Postmodern World*, University of Georgia Press, Athens, GA.
Saward, M. (1987), *The Anglican Church Today: Evangelicals on the move*, Mowbray, London.
Schein, V.E. (1973), 'The Relationship between Sex Role Stereotypes and Requisite Management Characteristics', *Journal of Applied Psychology*, vol. 57, pp.95-100.
Schein, V.E. (1975), 'Relationships between Sex Role Stereotypes and Requisite Management Characteristics among Female Managers', *Journal of Applied Psychology*, vol. 60, pp.340-344.
Schimmack, U. and Diener, E. (1997), 'Affect Intensity: separating Intensity and Frequency in Repeatedly Measured Affect', *Journal of Personality and Social Psychology*, vol. 57, pp.1069-1081.
Schmidt, T.E. (1995), *Straight and Narrow?* IVP, Leicester.
Schwab, R.L. and Iwanicki, E.F. (19820, 'Who are our Burned out Teachers?' *Educational Research Quarterly*, vol. 7, pp.5-16.
Scotland, N. (1995), *Charismatics and the Next Millennium: do they have a future?* Hodder and Stoughton, London.
Scotland, N. (1997), 'Evangelicals, Anglicans and Ritualism in Victorian England', *Churchman*, vol. 111, pp.249-265.
Sedgwick, J. (1993), *Why Women Priests: the ordination of women and the apostolic ministry*, Darton, Longman and Todd, London.
Selye, H. (1956), *The Stress of Life*, McGraw-Hill, New York.

Shin, D.C. and Johnson, D.M. (1978), 'Avowed Happiness as an Overall Assessment of the Quality of Life', *Social Indicators Research*, vol. 5, pp.475-492.
Siann, G. (1994), *Gender, Sex and Sexuality*, Taylor and Francis, London.
Smail, T. (1983), 'Envoi', *Theological Renewal*, vol. 25, p.1.
Smail, T., Wright, N. and Walker, A. (1993), *Charismatic Renewal: the search for a theology*, SPCK, London.
Smith, D.L. (1998), *A History of the Modern British Isles 1603-1707*, Blackwell, Oxford.
Spence, J.T., Helmreich, R. and Stapp, J. (1975), 'Ratings of Self and Peers on Sex Role Attributes and their relation to Self-esteem and Conceptions of Masculinity and Femininity', *Journal of Personality and Social Psychology*, vol. 32, pp.29-39.
Springer, K. (ed.) (1987), *Riding the Third Wave: what comes after renewal?* Marshall Pickering, Basingstoke.
SPSS, Inc. (1988), *SPSS User's Guide*, McGraw-Hill, New York.
Stake, J.E., Zand, D. and Smalley, R. (1996), 'The Relation of Instrumentality and Expressiveness to Self-concept and Adjustment: a Social Context Perspective', *Journal of Social and Clinical Psychology*, vol. 15, pp.167-190.
Stambaugh, J.E. and Balch, D.L. (1986), *The New Testament in its Social Environment*, Westminster Press, Philadelphia.
Steele, C.M. (1997), 'A Threat in the Air: how Stereotypes Shape Intellectual Identity and Performance', *American Psychologist*, vol. 52, pp.613-629.
Stephenson, A.M.G. (1984), *The Rise and Decline of English Modernism*, SPCK, London.
Steven, J.H.S. (2002), *Worship in the Spirit: charismatic worship in the Church of England*, Paternoster, Carlisle.
Stevens, G.B. and O'Neill, P. (1983), 'Expectation and Burnout in the Developmental Disabilities Field', *American Journal of Community Psychology*, vol. 11, pp.615-627.
Stibbe, M.W.G. (1993), 'The Theology of Renewal and the Renewal of Theology', *Journal of Pentecostal Theology*, vol. 3, pp.71-90.
Strachan, G. (1975), 'Theological and Cultural Origins of the Nineteenth Century Pentecostal Movement', *Theological Renewal*, vol. 1, pp.17-25.
Strack, F., Argyle, M. and Schwarz, N. (eds) (1991), *Subjective Well-being*, Pergamon Press, Oxford.
Stronstad, R. (1984), *The Charismatic Theology of St Luke*, Hendrickson, Peabody, MA.
Swenson, W.M. (1961), 'Attitudes towards Death in an Aged Population', *Journal of Gerontology*, vol. 16, pp.49-52.
Sykes, S.W. (1982), 'Anglicanism and Protestantism', in S.W. Sykes (ed.), *England and Germany: studies in theological diplomacy*, P. Long, Frankfurt, pp.123-139.
Sykes, S.W. and Gilley, S.W. (1986), 'No Bishop, No Church! the Tractarian Impact on Anglicanism', in G. Rowell (ed.), *Tradition Renewed: the Oxford Movement Conference Papers*, Darton, Longman and Todd, London, pp.120-139.
Symonds, P.M. (1924), 'On the Loss of Reliability in Ratings due to Coarseness of the Scale', *Journal of Experimental Psychology*, vol. 7, pp.456-461.
Tamayo, A. and Dugas, A. (1977), 'Conceptual Representation of Mother, Father and God according to Sex and Field of Study', *Journal of Psychology*, vol. 97, pp.79-84.
Terman, L.M. and Miles, C.C. (1936), *Sex and Personality: studies in masculinity and femininity*, Russell and Russell, New York.
Thomas, R. (1962), 'Comprehension and Indulgence', in G.F. Nuttall and O. Chadwick, (eds), *From Uniformity to Unity*, SPCK, London, pp.189-254.
Thompson, E.H. (1991), 'Beneath the Status Characteristic: Gender Variations in Religiousness', *Journal for the Scientific Study of Religion*, vol. 30, pp.381-394.
Thompson, K. (1970), *Bureaucracy and Church Reform: the organization and response of the Church of England to social change 1800-1965*, Clarendon Press, Oxford.

Thorne, A. (1987), 'The Press of Personality: a Study of Conversation between Introverts and Extroverts', *Journal of Personality and Social Psychology*, vol. 53, pp.718-726.
Thorold, A. (1928), *Readings from Friedrich von Hügel*, J.M. Dent and Sons, London.
Tidball, D.J. (1994), *Who are the Evangelicals: tracing the roots of today's movements*, Marshall Pickering, London.
Tiller, J. (1983), *A Strategy for the Church's Ministry*, CIO Publishing, London.
Tomlinson, D. (1995), *The Post-Evangelical*, Triangle, London.
Torgessen, K. (1993), *When Women were Priests: women's leadership in the early church and the scandal of their subordination in the rise of Christianity*, Harper and Row, San Francisco, CA.
Towler, R. and Coxon, A.P.M. (1979), *The Fate of the Anglican Clergy*, Macmillan, London.
Trevor-Roper, H. (1987), *Catholics, Anglicans and Puritans*, Secker and Warburg, London.
Tyacke, N. (1990), *Anti-Calvinists: the rise of English Arminianism, c.1590-1640*, Clarendon Press, Oxford.
van der Ploeg, H.M., van Leeuwen, J.J. and Kwee, M.G.T. (1990), 'Burnout among Dutch Psychotherapists', *Psychological Reports*, vol. 67, pp.107-112.
van der Ven, J.A. (1993), *Practical Theology: an empirical approach*, Kok Pharos, Kampen.
van der Ven, J.A. (1998), *Education for Reflective Ministry*, Peeters, Louvain.
van Horn, J.E., Schaufeli, W.B. and Enzmann, D. (1999), 'Teacher Burnout and Lack of Reciprocity', *Journal of Applied Social Psychology*, vol. 29, pp.91-108.
Vasey, M. (1995), *Strangers and Friends: a new explanation of homosexuality and the Bible*, Hodder and Stoughton, London.
Veenhoven, R. (1994), 'Is Happiness a Trait: Tests of the Theory that a Better Society does not make People any Happier', *Social Indicators Research*, vol. 32, pp.101-160.
Vergote, A. and Aubert, C. (1973), 'Parental Images and Representations of God', *Social Compass*, vol. 19, pp.431-444.
Vergote, A. and Tamayo, A. (1981), *The Parental Figure and the Representation of God*, Mouton, The Hague.
Vergote, A., Tamayo, A., Pasquali, L., Bonami, M., Pattyn, M-R. and Custers, A. (1969), 'Concept of God and Parental Images', *Journal for the Scientific Study of Religion*, vol. 8, pp.79-87.
Vidler, A.R. (1957), *Essays in Liberality*, SCM Press, London.
Vidler, A.R. (ed.) (1962), *Soundings: essays concerning Christian understanding*, CUP, Cambridge.
Vidler, A.R. (1974), *The Church in an Age of Revolution*, Penguin, Harmondsworth.
Vine, I. (1978), 'Facts and Values in the Psychology of Religion', *Bulletin of the British Psychological Society*, vol. 31, pp.414-417.
von Glaserfeld, E. (1996), *Radical Constructivism*, Falmer Press, New York.
Walker, A. (1985), *Restoring the Kingdom*, Hodder and Stoughton, London.
Walker, D. (1976), *A History of the Church in Wales*, Church in Wales Publications, Penarth.
Walker, H. (1940), 'Degrees of Freedom', *Journal of Educational Psychology*, vol. 31, pp.253-269.
Walker, M. and Baker, M. (1993), 'The Relationship between Sex-role Orientation and Vocational Undecidedness: an Exploratory Study', *British Journal of Guidance and Counselling*, vol. 21, pp.290-299.
Walker, P.K. (1988), *The Anglican Church Today: rediscovering the Middle Way*, Mowbray, London.

Walsh, J., Haydon, C. and Taylor, S. (eds) (1993), *The Church of England c.1689-c.1833: from Toleration to Tractarianism*, CUP, Cambridge.
Ward, G. (1997), *The Postmodern God*, Blackwell, Oxford.
Warner, J. and Carter, J.D. (1984), 'Loneliness, Marital Adjustment and Burnout in Pastoral and Lay Persons', *Journal of Psychology and Theology*, vol. 12, pp.125-131.
Warr, P., Barter, J. and Brownbridge, G. (1983), 'On the Independence of Positive and Negative Affect', *Journal of Personality and Social Psychology*, vol. 44, pp.644-651.
Warren, Y. (2002), *The Cracked Pot: the state of today's Anglican parish clergy*, Kevin Mayhew, Stowmarket.
Watson, D., Clark, L.A. and Tellegen, A. (1988), 'Development and Validation of Brief Measures of Positive and Negative Affect: the PANAS Scales', *Journal of Personality and Social Psychology*, vol. 54, pp.1063-1070.
Watson, D. and Walker, L.M. (1996), 'The Long-term Stability and Predictive Validity of Trait Measures of Affect', *Journal of Personality and Social Psychology*, vol. 70, pp.567-577.
Watson, P.J., Morris, R.J., Foster, J.E. and Hood, R.W. (1986), 'Religiosity and Social Desirability', *Journal for the Scientific Study of Religion*, vol. 25, pp.215-232.
Webster, A. (1983), 'Inge, W.R.', in G.S. Wakefield (ed.), *A Dictionary of Christian Spirituality*, SCM Press, London.
Welsby, P.A. (1984), *A History of the Church of England 1945-1980*, OUP, Oxford.
Westwood, G. (1960), *A Minority: a report on the life of the male homosexual in Great Britain*, Longmans, London.
White, J., Joseph, S and Neil, A. (1995), 'Religiosity, Psychoticism and Schizotypal Traits', *Personality and Individual Differences*, vol. 19, pp.847-851.
Whiteman, A. (1962), 'The Church of England Restored', in G.F. Nuttall and O. Chadwick, (eds), *From Uniformity to Unity*, SPCK, London.
Whitley, B.E. (1984), 'Sex-role and Psychological Well-being', *Journal of Sex Roles*, vol. 12, pp.207-221.
Whittaker, C. (1983), *Seven Pentecostal Pioneers*, Marshall Pickering, Basingstoke.
Wilcox, C. and Francis, L.J. (1997a), 'Beyond Gender Stereotyping: Examining the Validity of the Bem Sex-Role Inventory among 16- to 19-year old Females in England', *Personality and Individual Differences*, vol. 23, pp.9-13.
Wilcox, C. and Francis, L.J. (1997b), 'The Relationship between Neuroticism and the Perceived Social Desirability of Feminine Characteristics among 16-19 year old Females', *Social Behaviour and Personality*, vol. 25, pp.291-293.
Wilkinson, A. (1978a), *The Church of England and the First World War*, SPCK, London.
Wilkinson, A. (1978b), 'Requiem for Anglican Catholicism?' *Theology*, vol. 81, pp.40-45.
Wilkinson, A. (1986), *Dissent or Conform: war, peace and the English churches 1900-1945*, SPCK, London.
Williams, C.G. (1981), *Tongues of the Spirit: a study of Pentecostal glossolalia and related phenomena*, University of Wales Press, Cardiff.
Williams, D.G. (1982), 'Relationships between the Bem Sex Role Inventory and the Eysenck Personality Questionnaire', *Personality and Individual Differences*, vol. 3, pp.223-224.
Williams, D.R., Larson, D.B. and Buckler, R.E. (1991), 'Religion and Psychological Distress in a Community Sample', *Social Science and Medicine*, vol. 32, pp.1257-1262.
Williams, J.E. and Bennett, S.M. (1975), 'The Definition of Sex Stereotypes via the Adjective Check List', *Sex Roles*, vol. 1, pp.327-337.
Williams, P. (1984), 'Why Anvil?' *Anvil*, vol. 1, pp.1-5.
Williams, R. (2003), 'Hooker the Theologian', *Journal of Anglican Studies*, vol. 1, pp.104-116.

Wilson, B.R. (1966), 'Religion in Secular Society', in R. Robertson (ed.)(1969), *Sociology of Religion*, Penguin Books, Harmondsworth, pp.152-162.

Wilson, E. (1978), *Sociobiology: the new synthesis*, Belknap, Cambridge.

Wilson, W.R. (1965), 'Relation of Sexual Behaviours, Values and Conflicts to Avowed Happiness', *Psychological Reports*, vol. 17, pp.371-378.

Wilson, W.R. (1967), 'Correlates of Avowed Happiness', *Psychological Bulletin*, vol. 67, pp.294-306.

Winton, M. and Cameron, J. (1986), 'Stress and Burnout in the Ministry', *Contact*, vol. 90, pp.2-10.

Witherington, B. (1989), *Women in the Earliest Churches*, CUP, Cambridge.

Wood, W., Rhodes, N. and Whelan, M. (1989), 'Sex Differences in Positive Well-being: a Consideration of Emotional Style and Marital Status', *Psychological Bulletin*, vol. 106, pp.249-264.

Worrall, B.G. (1988), *The Making of the Modern Church: Christianity in England since 1800*, SPCK, London.

Wright, N. (1986), *The Radical Kingdom: restoration in theory and practice*, Kingsway Publications, Eastbourne.

Wright, N.T. (1980), *Evangelical Anglican Identity*, Latimer House, Oxford.

Yinger, J.M. (1970), *The Scientific Study of Religion*, Macmillan, New York.

Zevon, M.A. and Tellegen, A. (1982), 'The Structure of Mood Change: an Idiographic/Nomothetic Analysis', *Journal of Personality and Social Psychology*, vol. 38, pp.668-678.

Index of authors

Abrams, M. 122
Absalom, F. 22, 33
ACORA 52
Allchin, A.M. 28
Andrews, F.M. 119, 121, 122
Archer, J. 140
Argyle, M. 67, 89, 119–25, 130, 140–142, 189
Arnold, J. 141
Ashforth, B.E. 104
Astley, J. 81, 89
Au, P. 143
Avis, P. 3
Azjen, I. 58
Azzi, C. 143

Babbie, E.R. 142, 143
Back, P. 31
Badham, P. 19, 30, 42, 71
Bailar, J.C. 108
Baker, M. 141
Balch, D.L. 156
Ballard-Reisch, D. 140, 141
Bartlemann, F. 17
Barrett, P. 67, 79, 94, 95, 125
Barter, J. 120, 121
Batson, C.D. 126, 143
Bax, J. 30, 71
Baxter, C. 32
Bebbington, D. 9, 18
Beck, T. 123
Beit-Hallahmi, B. 89, 142
Belcastro, P.A. 104, 106
Bell, P.M.H. 12
Bem, S.L. 12, 67, 137, 139, 141, 145, 148
Bentler, P.M. 137
Best, G. 12, 133
Bishop, D.V.M. 79
Blazer, D. 126
Blizzard, S.W. 154, 156, 158
Block, J. 79, 94
Board of Education 53
Bolger, J. 96

Bosher, R.S. 6
Boyd, I.R. 156
Bradburn, N.M. 118, 120, 127
Braly, K.W. 137
Brebner, J. 130
Breckler, S.J. 58
Brewin, C.R. 122, 124, 125, 130
Brickman, P. 119
Brierley, P. 32, 51, 53, 107
Brockman, N. 107
Brown, L.B. 125, 128, 130, 144
Brownbridge, G. 120, 121
Brownmillar, S. 134
Brunstein, J.C. 122
Bryman, A. 49, 50, 53, 154, 155, 158, 160, 212
Buchanan, C.O. 16, 18, 21, 22, 26, 30, 32, 34, 35, 39, 131
Bunting, I.D. 51, 155, 156, 158, 185
Burch, G.W. 154
Burgess, N. 165–8
Burgess, S.M. 25
Burke, R.J. 105, 106, 116
Burns, A. 8
Buttner, E.H. 105, 115
Bye, H. 141
Byrne, B.M. 105, 114

Caird, D. 80, 89
Cameron, J. 107, 154
Campbell, A. 122, 126
Cann, A. 146
Capel, S.A. 105, 116
Carey, G. 33, 35
Carr, W. 160
Carter, D. 105, 115
Carter, J.D. 109
Carter, M. 89, 96
Cartledge, M.J. 65
Carver, C.S. 122
Central Board of Finance 30
Chadwick, O. 6, 9, 10, 25
Chandler, A. 20
Cheek, N.H. 143

Index of authors

Child, R. 160
Clark, D.M. 124
Clark, L.A. 120, 121, 124
Clegg, H. 10
Clemons, T. 145
Coan, R.W. 118
Coate, M.A. 107, 154
Coates, C.H. 154
Coates, D. 119
Cobb, J.B. 155
Cocksworth, C. 18, 42
Cohen, L.H. 106
Collins, W. 144
Collinson, P. 3
Coneybeare, W.J. 9, 44, 45, 53, 174, 182
Constantinople, A. 137
Converse, P.E. 122, 126
Cooper, C.L. 96, 101
Cordes, C.L. 102
Cortina, J.M. 75
Costa, P.T. 105, 120, 124
Coward, B. 4
Cowles, M. 88
Coxon, A.P.M. 46, 53, 81, 85, 89, 147, 155
Cragg, G.R. 5
Craston, C. 30, 59
Crockford's *Clerical Directory* 69
Cronbach, L.J. 75, 123, 140
Crossland, J. 67, 119, 123, 124
Crumbaugh, J. 127
Cupitt, D. 32
Curry, G. 27
Cuthbert, N. 43

Daniel, E.D. 81, 89, 96
Daniel, M.G. 47–9, 53, 58, 158, 212
Daniel, S. 107
Darling, M. 88
Davie, G. 43
Davies, D. 52, 53, 58, 164, 165
Davies, G. 4, 33
Deary, I.J. 79
Dedrick, E. 145
Dewe, P.J. 167
Diener, C. 124
Diener, E. 118–22, 124, 127
Diener, M. 119
Dixon, P. 35
Dobbins, G. 145

Donaldson, J. 130
Dougherty, T.W. 102
Dowell, S. 36, 37
Dudley-Smith, T. 38
Dugas, A. 143
Dunn, J. 34
Dunne, M.P. 89, 96
Dunstan, G.R. 165

Eagly, A.H. 135, 140, 145, 146
Eastburg, M.C. 106, 116
Eastell, J.K. 177
Ecclestone, G. 165
Eddison, J. 21
Edwards, D.L. 24, 32
Ehrenberg, R. 143
Ekhardt, B.N. 146
Ellis, L.J. 137
Ellison, C.G. 126
Elton, M. 140, 141
Emmons, R.A. 120–122, 124, 127
Ensor, R.C.K. 15
Enzmann, D. 104
Erbaugh, J. 123
Evans, W. 106, 116
Every, G. 7
Eysenck, H.J. 66, 67, 78–80, 82, 88, 89, 94, 95, 120, 125, 144, 147
Eysenck, M. 120
Eysenck, S.B.G. 66, 67, 79, 80, 82, 88, 89, 94, 95, 120, 125, 147

Feld, S. 119
Feltey, K.M. 144
Felton, P. 207
Fichter, J.H. 101, 108
Field, B. 37
Field, C.D. 142
Field-Bibb, J. 36
Fimian, M.J. 107
Firestone, S. 134
Fishbein, M. 58
Fletcher, B.C. 108, 146, 164
Fockert, J. de 127
Forsyth, D. 145
Foster, B.D. 165
Francis, L.J. 12, 33, 34, 37, 38, 40, 54–56, 58, 59, 62, 65–67, 69, 73, 75, 80–86, 88–92, 95–9, 108, 110, 125–8, 130, 142–8, 152, 153, 155, 158–60, 165, 166,

168, 171, 185, 186, 189, 191,
  193, 213
Friedman, E. 144
Freud, S. 143
Freudenberger, H.J. 101
Fujita, F. 119, 121
Fuller, R.H. 10
Furlong, M. 36
Furnham, A. 122, 124, 125, 130, 134

Gallup, G.H. 142
Garden, A-M. 116
Garnham, N. 64, 133
Gay, D. 126
George, L.K. 119
Ghiselli, E.E. 60
Gibson, H.M. 143
Gibson, P. 29
Gibson, W. 13
Gill, J.J. 107, 108
Gilley, S.W. 12
Gillings, V. 81, 96
Glaserfeld, E. von 136
Glass, T. 126
Glock, C.Y. 142, 143
Glowacki, T. 121
Glowinkowski, S.P. 101
Goktepe, J. 145, 146
Gold, R.S. 104, 106
Gold, Y. 104, 114
Goldie, M. 7
Goldingay, J. 31, 118
Goldsmith, M. 100
Goldsmith, W.M. 146
Golembiewski, R.T. 105, 115
Golner, F.H. 165
Goodhew, D. 21
Gorsuch, R.L. 57, 106, 116
Gose, K.F. 104
Grant, J. 106
Gray, J.A. 124
Greeley, A. 142
Green, D.E. 104
Greene, G. 101
Greene, L. 146
Greenglass, E.R. 105, 106, 116
Griffen, S. 121, 122, 127
Gross, P.R. 107, 154
Gryskiewicz, N. 105, 115
Gunstone, J. 22, 25
Gurin, G. 119

Hadaway, C. 126
Haig, A. 13, 14
Hair, J. 82, 90, 97
Hannaford, R. 33
Happold, F.C. 76
Harding, S.D. 120
Harel, I. 136
Harper, M. 25
Harris, T. 2, 3
Harrison, J. 142
Hastings, A. 18, 24, 26, 27
Haydon, C. 7
Headey, B. 121
Heath, A.C. 89, 96
Heaven, P.C.L. 89, 95
Hebert, A.G. 22
Heeney, B. 13
Heerboth, J.R. 139
Heise, D.R. 58
Helgeland, A. 108
Helmreich, R. 137, 139
Henderson, M. 120
Herb, L. 106
Herbert, T.D. 166
Hick, J. 29
Hickin, L. 19
Hilliard, D. 12, 133, 146
Hills, P. 124
Hinings, C.R. 49, 50, 53, 155, 158, 160,
  165, 212
Hjerman, I. 108
Hock, J. 123
Hocken, P. 25, 77
Hodge, F.V. 168
Hodge, M. 50, 51, 156, 169, 170
Hollenweger, W. 36
Holloway, D. 39
Holme, I. 108
Holmstrom, E. 121
Hood, R.W. 57, 80
Hopkins, B. 30
Hopkins, H. E. 8
Hopkinson, W.H. 27
Horn, J.E. van 104
Hough, J.C. 155
House, R.J. 101
Hughes, A. 22
Hummel, C. 31
Hunt, R.A. 107, 154
Hylson-Smith, K. 3, 4, 9, 11, 16, 18, 21–
  22, 30, 42

Index of authors

Iannaccone, L.R. 143
Iwanicki, E.F. 103, 104, 114

Jacklin, C. 137
Jackson, D.N. 146
Jackson, S.E. 66, 102, 110, 114
Jagger, P.J. 23, 34
Janoff-Bulman, R. 119
Jarvis, P. 165
Jay, E. 10
Jenkins, G.H. 7, 8
John, J. 38
Johnson, B. 140, 145
Johnson, D.M. 118
Jones, D.L. 82
Jones, J.R. 6
Jones, S.H. 55, 56, 58, 59, 62, 81, 82, 85, 89, 90, 126, 127, 168
Joseph, S. 81, 96, 126, 127
Jud, G.J. 154

Kafai, Y.B. 136
Kaldor, P. 67
Kammer, A. 107
Karau, S. 145
Katz, D. 137
Katz, Y.J. 96
Kay, W.K. 82, 89, 90, 95–7, 144
Keyes, C.L.M. 119
Killick, F. 36
Kimlicka, T.A. 142
King, H. 108
King, J. 21, 26, 131
King, L.A. 122
Kings, G. 42
Kirby, N. 130
Kirkcaldy, B. 105, 106, 116
Kirkpatrick, L.A. 57
Kistler, R.C. 154
Kline, P. 83
Klonsky, B. 146
Knight, F. 2, 13
Komarovsky, M. 137
Kwee, M.G.T. 105

Ladd, T. 64, 133
Lanigan, C. 127
Lankshear, D.W. 33, 34, 54–6, 58, 59, 62, 81, 89, 166, 168, 186, 191
Larsen, R.J. 121, 122, 127
Lauer, R.H. 154

Lee, R.T. 104
Leech, K. 200
Leeuwen, J.J. van 105
Lemkau, J.P. 104
Lenski, G.E. 143
Leren, P. 108
Leslie, J. 96
Lester, D. 125, 127, 128, 130, 144
Levin, J.S. 127
Levine, S. 121
Lewis, C.A. 57, 67, 96, 126, 127
Lewis, J.M. 144
Liller, K.D. 107
Lippa, R.A. 148
Lirtzman, S.I. 101
Lithgow, J. 25
Lloyd, R. 15, 20, 24, 27
Lodhi, P.H. 88
Long, W. 145
Louden, S.H. 65, 147, 158
Lu, L. 123–5, 130
Lucas, R.E. 121, 122
Luckman, T. 143
Lund-Larsen, P.G. 108

McAllister, I. 142
McCarthy, P. 104
McCaulley, M.H. 62
Maccoby, E. 137
McCrae, R.R. 105, 120, 124
McDermott, R.J. 107
McGee, G.B. 25
McGrath, A.E. 42
McGreal, R. 127
McIntosh, D.N. 107
McKennell, A.C. 122
Machlowitz, M. 108
Magnus, K.B. 121
Major, H.D.A.
Makhijani, M. 146
Malony, H.N. 107, 154
Maltby, J. 57, 81, 96
Manlove, E.E. 116
Manwaring, R. 27
Marshall, J. 146
Marshall, L. 107
Martin, D.W. 30, 59, 142, 143, 165
Martin, M. 67, 123–5
Martin, N.G. 89, 96
Martineau. J. 81, 85
Maslach, C. 66, 102, 104, 105, 110, 114

Mathisen, J.A. 64, 133
Maton, K.I. 106
Matthews, D.B. 106, 116
Matthews, G. 79
Mayfield, G. 35
Meier, S.T. 104
Melinsky, M.A.H. 20, 27
Mendelson, M. 123
Miller, J. 6
Mills, E.W. 154
Mischel, W. 78
Moberg, D.O. 142, 143
Mol, H. 136
Molloy, G.N. 104
Moore, P. 37
Morgan, C. 207
Morris, J. 37
Morrison, T. 146
Moses, J. 35
Mullen, P. 30, 59
Munzenrider, R. 105, 115
Myers, B. 107
Myers, D.G. 119
Myers, I.B. 62, 63

Nagoshi, C.T. 142
Nakata, T. 142
Nauss, A.H. 146
Neill, S. 4, 7–9, 12, 23
Nelsen, A.K. 142
Nelsen, H.M. 142, 143
Newbigin, L. 23
Newby, H. 165
Niebuhr, H.R. 20
Noble, K.E. 126
Nockles, P. 10
Noor, N.M. 123
Nye, J. 145

Okun, M.A. 119
O'Neill, P. 105
O'Reilly, C.T. 126
Ondrack, M. 106, 116
Orchard, A. 91
Osgood, C.E. 57, 58, 60, 71, 77
Oswald, R.M. 167, 170
Otranto, G. 37
Owen, C. 174

Packer, J.I. 22, 27
Page, R.J. 21

Palmore, E. 126
Pangan, T. 89, 96
Papert, S. 136
Park, C. 106
Patterson, W.B. 4
Paul, L. 154
Pavot, W. 121
Pearson, P.R. 80, 89, 95, 96, 144
Penhale, F. 33
Penn, R. 109
Percy, M.W. 29, 31
Perham, M. 27
Peterson, L. 126
Petre, J. 39
Philipchalk, R. 125, 128, 130, 144
Pickering, W.S.F. 24, 34
Piedmont, R.L. 105, 106, 111
Pierce, C.M.B. 104
Peirce, J. 36
Pines, A. 104, 114
Pitts, S.C. 142
Pivot, A. 144
Ploeg, H.M. van der 105
Podles, L.J. 185
Poloma, M.M. 142, 144
Potvin, R.H. 142
Powers, S. 104
Purdy, R.R. 104
Putney, C. 64, 133

Quebedeaux, R. 16

Rafferty, J.P. 104
Ragins, B. 145
Ramanaiah, N.V. 139
Ramsey, A.M. 13, 28, 155
Randall, K.J. 69, 110, 156, 157, 177
Ranson, S. 49, 50, 53, 155, 158, 160, 212
Rayburn, C.A. 107
Reardon, B.M.G. 11
Reeves, M. 20
Resnick, M. 126
Rhodes, C. 140
Richards, A. 36
Richmond, L.J. 107
Ridley, C. 106, 116
Rim, Y. 123, 125
Ringer, B.B. 142, 143
Ritti, R. 165
Rizzo, J.R. 101

Index of authors

Robbins, M. 37, 38, 40, 56, 81–5, 90, 91, 96, 97, 126–8, 147, 155, 158–60, 165, 168, 171, 185, 193
Roberts, D. 34
Robinson, J.A.T. 24
Robinson, T.N. 89
Rodger, R. 97, 155, 159
Rodgers, W.L. 122, 126
Rogers, L. 107
Rogers, M.L. 107
Roof, W. 126
Rose, M. 109
Rose, S.D. 146
Rosenkrantz, P.S. 137
Rowell, G. 18, 33
Roxborough, J. 16
Roy, A. 109
Rubery, J. 109
Rudisill, J.R. 104
Runcie, R. 49, 50, 70, 168
Russell, A.J. 13, 165
Russell, C. 3, 5
Rutledge, C.J.F. 56, 65, 66, 71, 82–6, 90, 91, 92, 96, 99, 106, 109–14, 128, 155, 160, 180, 185, 189
Ryff, C.D. 119

Saklofske, D.H. 89
Sandvik, E. 119
Sarup, M. 136
Saward, M. 33, 131
Schaufeli, W.B. 104
Scheier, M.F. 122
Schein, V.E. 145
Schimmack, U. 121
Schmidt, T.E. 36
Schneier, C. 145, 146
Schoenrade, P. 126, 143
Schwab, R.L. 103, 104, 114
Schwarz, N. 120
Scotland, N. 11, 28, 30, 31, 36, 43, 207
Sedgwick, J. 38
Seidlitz, L. 119
Selye, H. 101
Seymour, S. 53, 164, 165
Shevlin, M. 67
Shih, J.B. 123
Shin, D.C. 118
Short, C. 53, 164, 165
Siann, G. 136
Siegfried, W. 146

Silver, R.C. 107
Skanes, A. 88
Smail, T. 35
Smalley, R. 140
Smith, D.L. 4, 6
Spence, J.T. 137, 139
Springer, K. 16, 25, 31
SPSS, Inc. 69
Stake, J.E. 140
Stambaugh, J.E. 156
Stapp, J. 137, 139
Steele, C.M. 136
Stephenson, A.M.G. 16, 21, 25
Steven, J.H.S. 205
Stevens, G.B. 105
Stibbe, M.W.G. 36
Stott, J. 32
Strachan, G. 16
Strack, F. 120
Stronstad, R. 36
Stubbs, M.T. 126
Suci, G. 57, 58, 60, 71, 77
Suh, E. 122
Swenson, W.M. 107
Sykes, S.W. 12, 60
Symonds, P.M. 60

Talley, M. 96
Tamayo, A. 143
Tannenbaum, P. 57, 58, 60, 71, 77
Taylor, A.J.W. 104
Taylor, S. 7
Tellegen, A. 120, 121, 124
Terence, T. 165
Terman, L.M. 137
Terwilliger, R.E. 28
Thomas, G. 88
Thomas, R. 6
Thomas, T.H. 12, 75, 76, 81, 82, 86, 89, 90, 92, 97–9, 148, 153, 189, 213
Thomas, W. 105, 106, 116
Thome, E. 105, 106, 116
Thompson, E.H. 144, 148
Thompson, K. 15
Thorne, A. 124
Thorold, A. 17
Tidball, D.J. 22
Tiller, J. 155
Tischler, N. 146
Tomlinson, D. 185
Torgessen, K. 37

Towler, R. 46, 53, 81, 85, 89, 147, 155, 158
Trevor-Roper, H. 5
Tyacke, N. 5

Vasey, M. 36
Vaus, D. de 142, 143
Veenhoven, R. 125
Ven, J.A. van der 65
Ventis, W.K. 126, 143
Vergote, A. 143
Veroff, J. 119
Vidler, A.R. 16, 24, 60
Vine, I. 89

Walker, A. 28, 35, 156
Walker, D. 12
Walker, H. 175
Walker, M. 141
Walker, P.K. 33–5, 60
Walkey, F.H. 104
Walsh, J. 7
Ward, C.H. 123
Ward, G. 32
Ward, L. 130
Warner, J. 109
Warr, P. 120, 121
Warren, Y. 154
Watkins, C. 53, 164, 165
Watson, D. 120, 121, 124
Watson, P.J. 80
Wearing, A. 121
Webster, A. 17
Welsby, P.A. 23
Westman, C.B. 106

Westwood, G. 146
White, J. 96
Whiteman, A. 5
Whitley, B.E. 137
Whittaker, C. 17
Wilcox, C. 96, 125–7, 142, 144, 145, 148, 152
Wilkinson, A. 20, 22, 24, 25, 29, 33
Williams, C.G. 25, 32
Williams, D.G. 142
Williams, D.R. 106
Williams, J. 36, 37
Williams, J.E. 137
Williams, P. 34
Williams, R. 3
Williamson, M. 106, 116
Wilson, B.R. 165
Wilson, E. 134
Wilson, W.R. 119
Winter, M. 53, 164, 165
Winton, M. 107, 154
Witherington, B. 37
Withey, S.B. 119, 121, 122
Wolsic, B. 119
Wood, W. 125, 135
Worrall, B.G. 16
Wright, N. 28, 35, 42, 156
Wright, N.T. 27

Yinger, J.M. 143

Zand, D. 140
Zevon, M.A. 120
Zonderman, A.B. 105, 124

Index of themes

administrator 49, 97, 154, 157–61, 163, 164, 166
analysis of variance 85, 92, 98, 115, 129, 130, 149, 151, 152
Anglo-Catholics 11, 16, 18, 22–5, 27, 29, 32–4, 37, 38, 46, 47, 50, 51, 61, 82, 86, 92, 97, 146, 148, 152
Anti-charismatic 60, 61, 72, 73, 75, 93, 115, 130, 152, 160–162, 164, 169, 170, 173, 180, 182, 184, 188, 192, 195, 196, 199, 202, 203, 205, 209, 211–4
apostle 156–8, 160–164, 190, 194
archdeacons 97, 167, 168, 171, 172, 204
Arminians 4, 8, 28, 42

Bem Sex Role Inventory 67, 133–153, 185, 190, 194, 197, 200, 204, 207, 210, 213, *see also* masculinity, femininity
Bible 1–3, 13, 17, 22, 43, 47, 53, 142, 184, 185, 188, 192, 196, 199, 203, 206, 209, 212
bishops 5, 7, 14, 18, 20, 27, 33, 36, 38, 39, 41, 43, 45, 75, 97, 108, 167, 168, 171, 178, 190
Born Again 75, 76, 210
Broad Church 12, 13, 34, 42, 44, 45, 49, 50
burnout 65, 101–17, 153, 189, 193, 200, 207, 210

Calvinists 3, 4, 8, 42
Catholic 11, 12, 14, 20, 22, 27, 29, 33, 37, 42, 45, 47, 49, 51–4, 56, 58–61, 71, 72, 75, 76, 83, 85, 92, 98, 112, 114, 129, 130, 147–51, 156, 158–63, 166, 169–71, 175–8, 182, 184, 187–95, 199, 202, 204, 205, 209, 210, 212, 213
Central 34, 46, 47, 49–53, 56, 61, 71, 86, 92, 98, 114, 129, 150–152, 158, 160–163, 165, 169–71, 175–8, 182, 184, 188, 191–5, 199, 202, 205, 209, 212
charismatic Evangelicals 27, 51
charismatic movement 25–7, 30, 31, 35, 36, 42, 50, 55, 56, 59, 60, 72, 73, 86, 118, 157, 208
chi-square 175
Church in Wales 7, 12, 36, 39, 40, 67, 148, 168, 169
churchmanship groups, nine empirically derived *see* Evangelical, Central, Catholic, Liberal, Middle-of-the-road, Conservative, Pro-charismatic, Non-charismatic, Anti-charismatic
clerical collar 177, 180, 187, 194, 198, 201
coefficient alpha 75, 76, 103, 110, 123, 128, 140, 148
confirmation 54–56, 177, 187, 191
Conservative 49, 53, 55, 56, 58–61, 71–73, 83, 86, 92, 98, 129, 130, 149–52, 160–163, 169–71, 178–80, 182, 184, 188, 192, 195–9, 202, 205, 209, 212
Conservative Evangelical 42, 46, 50, 52, 53, 55, 57, 58
correlations 58, 73, 74, 80–83, 85, 87–90, 93, 95–7, 99, 103, 106, 111–3, 116, 120, 121, 123–8, 130, 141, 142, 149, 151, 153, 185, 190, 194, 200, 201, 207
counsellor 49, 93, 155–64, 194, 201, 207

Daily Office 177, 179, 186, 191, 197, 201, 204
Depersonalization 102–4, 110, 112–6, 185, 189, 197, 210, 213
diaconate 33, 36, 39, 40, 56, 66, 67, 110, 147

Emotional Exhaustion 67, 102–5, 109, 110, 112–4, 193, 197, 207, 213

empirical research 15, 33, 36, 40, 44, 47, 48, 50, 53, 56, 58, 59, 61, 64, 66, 71, 72, 77, 80, 85, 88, 92, 102, 109, 121, 137–9, 142, 143, 145, 148, 154, 155, 158, 168, 193, 215
empirical theology 64–5
EPQ 66, 79, 81, 83, 90, 94, 95, 97, 114, 120, 124, 125, 142, 147, 148, 193, 200, 204, 213; *see also* extraversion, neuroticism, psychoticism
EPQR-S 67, 79, 81–4, 90, 91, 95, 97, 98, 147
Eucharist 18, 20, 26, 177, 179, 181, 191, 214
Evangelical 7–10, 14, 15, 17–19, 21, 22, 24–7, 31–4, 37–9, 42, 44, 45, 47, 49, 51–6, 58–62, 69–73, 75, 76, 83, 85, 92, 93, 98, 107, 112, 114, 115, 118, 129–31, 144, 146, 148–52, 156, 158–63, 166, 168–171, 175–7, 182–9, 192, 193, 195, 199, 202, 205, 209, 210, 212
Evangelical Alliance 9, 59, 73, 158, 186
Evangelicalism 18, 21, 22, 31, 34, 42, 50, 55, 62, 131, 133, 185
evangelist 21, 51, 155, 156, 159–64, 186, 197, 207
extraversion 79–87, 94, 111–3, 120, 124–6, 128, 130, 131, 142, 147, 152, 185, 189, 197, 206, 210

factor analysis 79, 94, 102–4
fellowship-builder 157, 160–4, 186, 207
femininity 12, 66, 133, 134, 137–42, 144, 146–52, 185, 190, 194, 197, 200, 204, 210, 213
Francis Scale of Attitude to Christianity 95, 126, 127, 145
fundamentalism 22, 31, 42, 73
fund-raiser 157, 163, 164

happiness 118–32, 153, 185, 189, 193, 197, 200, 207, 210
High Church 6, 7, 10–12, 14, 17, 19, 44, 45, 47, 50, 158
Holy Communion *see* Eucharist
Holy Spirit 8, 25, 27, 28, 30, 31, 36, 41

homosexuality 34, 36, 41, 70, 146, 174, 188, 199

infant baptism 54, 55, 174, 176, 208

Latitudinarians 5–10, 12, 17, 44, 46
leader in the local community 159, 160, 163–165, 194
leader of public worship 155, 157, 159–164, 194, 201, 204, 210
Liberal 11, 12, 19, 28–30, 32, 38, 47, 49, 51–3, 55–61, 71–3, 75, 76, 83, 86, 92, 98, 116, 129, 130, 149–151, 160–163, 169–71, 178–80, 182, 184, 188, 192, 195, 198–202, 205, 209, 212
Liberal Evangelical 18, 46, 50, 55, 73
liturgy 1, 5, 9, 12, 16, 18, 23, 26, 27, 29, 30, 42, 43, 52, 176, 182, 186, 198, 208, 214
Low Church 6, 7, 10, 44, 45, 47, 51, 159, 186

manager 155, 157, 160–164, 186, 207
marital status 66, 68, 70, 119, 122, 184, 188, 192, 193, 196, 199, 203, 206, 209, 212
masculinity 66, 133, 137–42, 144, 146–152, 185, 194, 197, 204, 207, 210, 213
Maslach Burnout Inventory 67, 101–117, 185, 193, 197, 200, 210; *see also* Depersonalization, Emotional Exhaustion, Personal Accomplishment
Methodists 7, 8, 14, 17, 26, 50, 81, 82, 89, 96
Middle Way 33–5, 42, 54, 61
Middle-of-the-road 61, 71, 86, 92, 98, 150–152, 160–163, 169–72, 178–80, 182, 184, 188, 192, 195, 199, 202–5, 209, 212
minister of the sacraments 157, 160–164, 186, 190, 200, 201, 204, 213
Modern Catholic 52, 53, 58
Modernists 16, 19–21, 24, 28, 44, 46, 47, 49, 50, 58, 73, 158
multiple regression 54, 124, 126, 130, 145
multivariate analysis 144, 189

Mystical 17, 75, 76, 185, 194, 197, 200, 201, 207, 210

neuroticism 79, 86, 88–93, 99, 106, 111–114, 120, 121, 124–6, 128, 130, 131, 142, 147, 185, 193, 197, 206, 213
Non-charismatic 60, 61, 72, 99, 115, 129, 152, 160, 164, 169, 170, 172, 173, 180–182, 184, 188, 192, 195, 196, 199, 202, 203, 205, 208–12

Open Evangelical 52, 53
ordination of women 7, 35–7, 39, 41, 42, 62, 71, 72, 133, 146, 147, 175, 178, 195
Oxford Happiness Inventory 67, 122–32, 185, 189, 193, 197, 200, 207, 210

pastor 34, 49, 93, 154–64, 167
Pentecostalism 16, 17, 23, 25, 31, 35, 36, 54, 59, 82, 90, 97
person of prayer 155, 157, 158, 160–164, 190, 194, 200, 204, 207, 210, 213
Personal Accomplishment 102–5, 110–112, 114–6, 189, 193, 204, 207, 210
personality 12, 64–6, 75, 78–101, 105–7, 111–4, 116, 120, 121, 124, 126–128, 130, 133, 140–142, 144, 146–9, 153, 154, 185, 189, 193, 196, 200, 203, 206, 210, 213, 215
pietism 25, 33, 131
pioneer 155, 157, 160, 161, 163, 164
post ordination training 167, 168, 171, 178, 181, 191, 194, 214
Prayer Book Catholic 46, 50
preacher 34, 49, 51, 132, 154, 157–64, 186, 197, 207, 210
priesthood 22, 33, 34, 36–41, 51, 56, 66, 67, 69, 107, 108, 154, 155, 158, 178, 184, 186, 189, 190, 192, 194, 201, 210, 213
principal component analysis 79, 160
Pro-charismatic 52, 60, 61, 72, 73, 75, 77, 85, 86, 90, 115, 118, 129, 152, 160, 162, 164, 169, 170, 173, 180, 182, 184, 188, 192, 195, 196, 199, 202, 203, 205–9, 212
prophet 155, 156, 158, 160, 162–4, 201
Protestants 2, 3, 6, 7, 13, 22, 23, 29, 33, 46, 86, 99, 131, 132, 146, 167
psychoticism 79, 94, 95, 97–9, 106, 111, 113, 114, 124–7, 130, 131, 142, 144, 147, 189, 193, 206, 210
Puritans 3–6, 33, 45, 46, 131, 132

qualitative research 52, 167
quantitative research 44, 52, 53, 57, 58, 64, 66

Radical 47, 51, 52
religious experience 67, 75–8, 124, 190, 194, 197, 200, 201, 204, 207, 210, 213
resurrection 13, 19, 156, 175, 179, 181, 186, 191, 197, 201, 204, 208
robes 12, 18, 131, 177, 180, 181, 187, 191, 198, 201, 208, 211
role priorities 13, 15, 42, 49, 51, 66, 67, 97, 101, 107, 113, 154–66, 186, 190, 194, 197, 200, 204, 207, 210, 213, 214
roles of parish clergy *see* administrator, apostle, counsellor, evangelist, fellowship-builder, fund-raiser, leader in the local community, leader of public worship, manager, minister of the sacraments, pastor, person of prayer, pioneer, preacher, prophet, social worker, spiritual director, teacher, theologian, visitor
Roman Catholic Church 9, 11, 12, 17, 23, 25, 26, 34, 39, 41, 50, 101, 107, 147, 158
Rural or Area Deans 168, 172, 204
rural environment 33, 54–6, 165, 166, 184, 188, 192, 195, 199, 202, 205, 209, 212

semantic differential grid 57–60, 72, 77, 207, 215
sex role 125, 133–153
social worker 157, 160, 163–6, 190

spiritual director 17, 155, 157–64, 177, 180, 181, 186, 190, 194, 197, 200, 201, 211
statistical tests *see* analysis of variance, chi-square, coefficient alpha, factor analysis, multiple regression, multivariate analysis, principal component analysis, Student's t-test
stress 101, 102, 105–8, 113, 116, 146, 154, 164, 167
Student's t-test 85, 92, 116, 129, 151, 152
subjective well-being 118–20, 123, 124, 126, 127
suburban environment 33, 54, 55, 56

teacher 154, 156, 158–64, 186, 197
theologian 51, 65, 155, 157, 160, 163, 164
theological colleges 13, 14, 27, 45, 47, 49, 51, 57, 67, 69, 70, 72, 81, 147, 155, 157, 158, 168, 184, 188, 192, 195, 196, 199, 202, 203, 205, 209, 211, 212

theological courses 51, 67, 69, 70, 147, 157, 159, 168–170
Tractarians 10, 11, 13, 25, 44, 45, 49, 51, 69, 70, 133, 168, 169, 170
Traditional 75, 76, 185, 190, 197, 204, 210, 213
Traditional Catholic 52, 53
training incumbents 66, 67, 71, 74, 75, 85, 161, 163, 167–73, 177, 178, 181, 184, 185, 187, 188, 190, 192, 193, 196, 197, 199, 200, 203, 205, 206, 209, 211, 212, 214

urban environment 33, 54–6, 184, 187, 192, 195, 199, 202, 205, 209, 212

vestments *see* robes
Virgin Birth 13, 19, 175, 180, 186, 191, 197, 201, 208
visitor 155–7, 159–66, 177, 180, 190, 191, 194, 200, 204

women bishops 178, 187, 198, 201

Ex Libris
Alun J. Brookfield